# THE THIRD REVOLUTION

D0223174

The third revolution in human history is the revolution of the professionals. The first was the Neolithic Revolution, when settled agriculture allowed craftsmen, priests, warriors, and rulers to found cities and civilizations. The second was the Industrial Revolution, which released a majority for work in mass production, transport, and urban services. The third has, through phenomenal productivity in agriculture and industry, created a professional society.

Highly skilled workers in services from government and management to medicine, education, leisure, and entertainment enjoy living standards, comforts, and enjoyment beyond all previous expectations. But with these achievements is a concurrent danger for society arising from the self-destructive greed and corruption among professional elites.

In *The Third Revolution* Harold Perkin concludes a 'trilogy' of books. Widening his arguments to a contemporary and global scale, the author examines the professional societies of both free market and command economies – the United States, Britain, France, the two Germanies, the Soviet Union, and Japan – and traces the rise of a global professional society since the Second World War.

**Harold Perkin** is Professor of History and Higher Education at Northwestern University. Among his books are *The Origins of Modern English Society, 1780–1880* (1969) and *The Rise of Professional Society* (1989).

# THE THIRD REVOLUTION

Professional elites in the modern world

*Harold Perkin*

London and New York

First published 1996
by Routledge
11 New Fetter Lane, London EC4P 4EE

Simultaneously published in the USA and Canada
by Routledge
29 West 35th Street, New York, NY 10001

Routledge is an International Thomson Publishing company

© 1996 Harold Perkin

Typeset in Palatino by
Datix International Limited, Bungay, Suffolk
Printed and bound in Great Britain by
Clays Ltd, St Ives PLC

All rights reserved. No part of this book may be reprinted or
reproduced or utilized in any form or by any electronic,
mechanical, or other means, now known or hereafter
invented, including photocopying and recording, or in any
information storage or retrieval system, without permission in
writing from the publishers.

*British Library Cataloguing in Publication Data*
A catalogue record for this book is available from the British Library

*Library of Congress Cataloguing in Publication Data*
Perkin, Harold James.
The Third Revolution: professional elites in the modern world / Harold Perkin.
Includes bibliographical references and index.
1. Professions – History. 2. Professions – Sociological aspects.
I. Title.
HT687.P49   1996
305.5′53–dc20      95–44146

ISBN  0–415–14337–3 (hbk)
ISBN  0–415–14338–1 (pbk)

Governments, the economy, schools, everything in society, are not for the benefit of the privileged minorities. We can look after ourselves. It is for the benefit of the ordinary run of people, who are not particularly clever or interesting (unless, of course, we fall in love with one of them), not highly educated, not successful or destined for success, in fact, nothing very special. It is for the people who, throughout history, have entered history outside their neighbourhoods as individuals only in the records of their births, marriages, and deaths. Any society worth living in is one designed for them, not for the rich, the clever, the exceptional, although any society worth living in must provide room and scope for such minorities. But the world is not made for our personal benefit. A world that claims that this is its purpose is not a good world, and ought not to be a lasting one.

(Eric Hobsbawm, in a lecture given at the new
Central European University, Budapest, reprinted in the
*New York Review of Books*, 16 December 1993, p. 64.)

# CONTENTS

List of tables                                               ix
Preface                                                       xi

1  THE THIRD SOCIAL REVOLUTION                                1
   *The Neolithic Revolution*                                 2
   *The Industrial Revolution*                                3
   *The post-Industrial Revolution*                           6
   *The major trends of professional society*                 8
   *The great arch*                                          20

2  THE UNITED STATES: A FREE MARKET FOR
   CORPORATIONS                                              28
   *Freedom for whom?*                                       28
   *The corporate–federal complex*                           31
   *The dangers of inequality*                                34
   *Structural change and the export of jobs*                36
   *The threat of decline*                                    40
   *Corporate neo-feudalism*                                  42
   *The irresponsible elite*                                  47

3  BRITAIN: KEYSTONE OF THE ARCH                             49
   *The myopia of cliometrics*                                50
   *Lost leadership in the Third Revolution*                  51
   *The debate about economic decline*                        58
   *The social causes of economic decline*                    62
   *The perils of minority government*                         65

4  FRANCE: A PLANNED MERITOCRACY                             77
   *A skewed meritocracy*                                      78
   *L'état, c'est nous*                                        84
   *The service revolution*                                    88
   *The second sex*                                            90
   *The incorporation of big business*                         92
   *Over-regulation and corruption*                            95

5 GERMANY: TWO VERSIONS OF PROFESSIONAL
  SOCIETY                                                        100
  *The burden of the past*                                       100
  *Towards professional meritocracies*                           104
  *The survival of patriarchy*                                   108
  *The legacy of the German state*                               109
  *Higher education and social mobility*                         112
  *German industry: voluntary versus compulsory cooperation*     114
  *A comparison of elites*                                       119

6 SOVIET RUSSIA: GULLIVER'S GIANT                                123
  *A qualitative change in the meritocracy*                      124
  *The reasons for* perestroika                                  128
  *The privileged Marxist elite*                                 131
  *Self-destruction by corruption*                               134
  *The final collapse*                                           143

7 JAPAN: A FLOATING WORLD                                        147
  *The changing role of the bureaucracy*                         149
  *Managed capitalism and the economic miracle*                  156
  *Individualism in the arms of collectivism*                    160
  *Japan in the global economy*                                  165
  *The price of success: the quality of life*                    166
  *The outsiders: fringe workers, women, and the minorities*     167
  *'Money politics' and the nemesis of corruption*               170
  *An ideal professional society?*                               174

8 TOWARDS A GLOBAL PROFESSIONAL SOCIETY                          177
  *Diversity among professional societies*                       177
  *Global professional society*                                  184
  *The contradictions of free-market theory*                     187
  *The origins of Anglo–American individualism*                  190
  *Widening Anglo–American inequality*                           192
  *Does it matter?*                                              195
  *A global ray of hope*                                         196

  EPILOGUE: WHAT IS TO BE DONE?                                  202
  *The continental European answer*                              205
  *The East Asian answer*                                        207
  *Anglo-Saxon attitudes*                                        209
  *A new structure of rewards*                                   212

  *Notes*                                                        219
  *Select bibliography*                                          234
  *Index*                                                        246

# TABLES

1.1    Real national income per capita lin 1982–84 US dollars          9
1.2    Percentage distribution of employment                          10
1.3    Social origins of politicians by party                         12
1.4    Social origins of civil servants and parliamentarians by
       father's occupation                                            12
1.5    Social origins of top business men by father's occupation      13
1.6    Percentage of women in the labour force                        13
1.7    (a) Women students in higher education                         14
       (b) Women teachers in higher education                         14
1.8    Growth of government expenditure                               14
1.9    Public employment as a percentage of the total workforce       15
1.10   Government provision of primary incomes: wages, salaries,
       and transfer payments                                          15
1.11   Public expenditure on social security, social services, health,
       and education as a percentage of GDP                           16
1.12   Social security transfers as a percentage of GDP               16
1.13   Age participation ratio of students in higher education        17
1.14   Adult population with a post-secondary degree                  17

# PREFACE

This book is the third volume of an unintended trilogy. It could not have been conceived when the first volume was written, because the most important developments it deals with had not yet happened. The first book, *The Origins of Modern English Society, 1780–1880*, was an attempt to show how the second great revolution in human history, the Industrial Revolution, which began in Britain in the eighteenth century and spread around the world by the mid-twentieth, was a social revolution with social causes, social processes, and profound social effects. It was, I argued:

> a revolution in human productivity, in the capacity of men to wring a living from nature, and therefore in both the number of human beings who could be supported on a given area of land and the abundance of their means and enjoyment of life.

It enabled a minority of a much larger population to grow the food for all the rest, releasing the majority for other kinds of work, including modern industry, mechanized transport, large-scale government, mass warfare, and the professions. It created the modern city in which the majority of the population came to live. In time it also created large-scale organizations, from assembly-line factories and multi-disciplinary universities to large-scale government bureaucracies and business corporations. It also had profound cultural and moral effects, enabling art, literature and music, science, and religious discourse to reach millions by technological communications hitherto unknown, and expanding the responsibility for one's neighbour from the parish of the old poor law to the whole nation in the welfare state. Despite the costs in long and heavy labour for many workers, it was, in short, a rise to a new plane of social, economic, political, and cultural existence.

It was the long-range sequel, I further argued, to the first great social revolution in history, or rather in pre-history since it necessarily occurred before history could begin. That first great transition was the Neolithic Revolution, which by replacing hunter-gathering with settled agriculture enabled a small minority of the population to live for the first time in cities and produce goods and services in exchange for their food. The services included the arts and crafts, government, military protection, religious ritual, and medical and legal services, on a scale and permanency previously impossible. Among them was the invention of writing and thus of history, the recording of events until then preserved only in myth and legend. That revolution, too, enabled more people to live on the same area of land and even to build up great empires over greater spaces than most modern nations. It also facilitated the production and dissemination of arts and sciences, music and literature, religion and philosophy. It raised mankind to a new plane of existence, but since most still lived by the sweat of their brows, more for the few who ruled and fought, thought and prayed, than for the many who laboured in the fields and workshops.

The third revolution, the subject of this book, is a third turn of the same screw. The transition we are currently living through is enlarging the population still further, enabling most people to live in cities or in direct contact with city services, and raising the standard of living for nearly everyone to heights undreamed of even by the rich in former times. It depends on technology to the extent that automation, electronics, 'lean production', biochemistry, and biotechnology have enabled a shrinking minority to produce the consumer goods as well as the food for the majority, who are now released for other work, chiefly in services, from a vast range of new professions like business management or information technology to catering, retailing, entertainment, and transport. But to call it a technological revolution is to put the cart before the horse. Technology does not invent and install itself. It is human ingenuity in the form of specialized expertise that does that, and it requires sophisticated organization to make it work on the necessary scale. It is professional expertise that creates the technology and bureaucratic management that organizes it, not the other way round. It is in effect Adam Smith's division of labour, raised to a higher power of applied intelligence and expertise. That is why I call the third revolution the rise of professional society.

Pre-industrial society created by the first revolution was dominated by those who controlled the scarce resource of land, the landlords, who reigned over most organized societies for three or four millennia. Industrial society was dominated by those who controlled the scarce resource of material capital in machinery, factories and banks, the industrial capitalists, whose hegemony lasted a mere two hundred years, if that. Post-industrial society is dominated by those who control the scarce resource of brainpower and expertise, that is, human capital, the invested value of their training and education. Unlike land and material capital, human capital is as expandable as human ability and training can make it, and therefore extends much further down the social scale than earlier forms of capital. It is also as diverse as there are forms of trained expertise, which is why it can be extensive and still scarce in any particular form. But the forms in which it has the power to dominate tend to be those which control the flows of income: government bureaucracy and corporate management.

This third revolution in one country I tried to explain in the second volume of the trilogy, *The Rise of Professional Society: England since 1880*. There I showed how the professionals, the 'forgotten middle class' of Victorian England – forgotten because they left themselves out of their tripartite models of society – gradually took over the business of government and the government of business by replacing the placemen of the old aristocratic system with a meritocratic civil service, and the owner-managers of family firms with corporate managers. They also professionalized local government, replacing corrupt officials and bumbling beadles with skilled administrators and public health officers; the universities, replacing bachelor dons with career lecturers and researchers; the hospitals, replacing part-time doctors with specialized consultants; the courts, replacing the circumlocution offices with a reformed prosecution and legal aid service; and the army, replacing purchase of commissions with a college-trained officer corps.

By the mid-twentieth century the professionals had captured all the major institutions of Britain's government and economy and were poised to take over the running of society. They set up the main divisions of the welfare state, the National Health Service, the nationalized industries, the great business corporations, and ran them with unprecedented success for over a quarter of a century.

In the post-war world, however, for reasons connected mainly with the survival of old industrial class attitudes, they were unable to keep up with the rates of economic growth in rival countries, and a running quarrel broke out between the two wings of professionalism, the public sector professionals, who wished to see an expansion of their services for everyone, and the private sector professionals, chiefly the managers of big business and their friends, who wanted less public spending and lower taxes. This led to a revival of neo-classical economics, the free market ideology of the early nineteenth century, and a backlash against the welfare state and the mixed economy. Dressed in old-fashioned class language, the 'Victorian values' of the entrepreneurial business class versus the 'dependency culture' of the 'nanny state', it was in reality a struggle between two professional groups: the managers of big business and their supporters in the right-wing media and think tanks who preached the free market but did not practise it, and the 'one-nation' professionals in all three political parties who believed in social justice and social cohesion as the best means of invoking the willing cooperation on which economic growth depended.

The triumph of the Thatcherites in Britain, like that of the Reaganites and Gingrich Republicans in the United States, was the victory of the private sector professionals over the rest of society. It represents a dangerous aspect of professional society, indeed of all societies: the tendency of all dominant elites who control the flows of income to steer more and more of it to themselves. It is dangerous not merely because it is unfair and generates feelings of resentment which culminate in social pathologies like crime, drug taking, homelessness, mental illness, riots, and rebellion. The main danger is that it will lead to what Marx called the 'contradictions of capitalism', which are really the contradictions of every society that distributes its resources so unequally that morale collapses and with it economic success. In other words, over-exploitation by the ruling elite is self-destructive, not merely for the society but for members of the elite themselves.

This book sets out to extend this analysis in international perspective, through a study of the seven leading post-industrial societies across the globe since the Second World War: the United States, Britain, France, the two Germanies, the old Soviet Union, and Japan. Though at different stages of evolution, they are, or were, all increasingly dominated by professional elites, either corporate managerial or state bureaucratic or both. What they have in common are ten interconnected trends: dramatically higher living standards than the third and intermediate worlds; the occupational dominance of services; a subtle change in social structure from horizontal class to vertical professional hierarchies; recruitment (increasingly but by no means perfectly) by merit; the incorporation of women into the professional workforce; the enormous growth of government; the rise of the welfare state; the expansion of higher education; the concentration of industry in a few large-scale corporations, either private or state-owned; and the globalization of the world economy.

Despite these convergencies, they are seven very different societies with different histories, political structures, and social values. They have adopted and adapted to professional society in very different ways. They lie, as it were, on a great arch, from the most free-market oriented society, the United States, to the most state-centralized command economies, the old Soviet Union and the defunct German Democratic Republic. In between there are different forms of mixed economy, ranging from Britain, once the keystone of the arch with a balance of private and state industries and a pioneering welfare state, to France on the state-planning, *dirigiste* side of the arch, and West Germany, with its free but highly modified 'social market economy', on the other. Japan, perhaps the most successful of all post-industrial societies, has managed to span both ends of the arch, with a symbiosis of government bureaucracy and corporate management which has paid off in amazing economic growth and competitive achievement.

They have all benefited from the enormous gains that professional society offers: longer and healthier life; more comfort and enjoyment than any previous age; solutions to many of the problems and diseases – even genetic ones – faced for centuries by humanity; incomparable mobility at unprecedented speeds; instant communication with friends and relations around the globe; push-button access to worldwide entertainment, sport, music, opera, and theatre; and electronic recovery of information from global data banks and libraries. At the same time they have all paid the costs of these achievements: the widening of the distribution of income and prestige as the best jobs go to the able and highly educated, skilled manufacturing jobs are exported to low-cost areas and countries, and the uneducated are relegated to low-wage 'in-person' services or to unemployment; the consequent decline in morale and the concomitant rise in crime, drugs, public disorder, and mental illness already mentioned; and the congestion, pollution, and stresses of life in overcrowded cities. Balancing the benefits against the costs calls for a moral calculus of a high order.

The calculus is different for each country. That is why this book is structured, after a comparative introduction dealing with the common trends and their differential impact on the divergent societies, to treat each country separately but in a rolling comparison. The major theme in each is the provenance and character of the professional elites, their success in establishing their dominance, and the temptations they are under to exploit their society to excess, thus risking their own and their society's decline or even destruction. As Lord Acton so memorably said, 'Power tends to corrupt, and absolute power corrupts absolutely.' This has been amply proved in the case of the Soviet Union and East Germany, where the *nomenklatura*, the Russian term for the Communist Party elite, exploited the peasants and workers to the point of exhaustion. Its collapse had little to do with ideology, since no one in authority believed any longer in communism. It was simply due to the greed and corruption of the ruling elite, who in effect operated a mafia-type protection racket and gave little in return. As Soviet workers proverbially said, 'They pretend to pay us, so we pretend to work.' The result was economic failure followed by political collapse.

The West triumphalized over the end of the Cold War and the collapse of communism. But that does not mean that the democratic countries are immune from the same disease. Exploitation by state bureaucracies and even more by corporate managements has reached astonishing proportions in the last twenty or thirty years, to levels which would have to be labelled corrupt if they had not been made legal in many cases by the same self-serving elites. Illegal corruption itself has been increasingly investigated and exposed in all five Western countries (and many others) among both politicians and big business men. The most important kind, however, is not individual peculation but what Chalmers Johnson, in the case of Japan, has called 'structural corruption', the built-in rewards that the system offers to politicians, bureaucrats, and corporate managers, who receive lucrative appointments and 'compensation for loss of office' for cooperating with the elite to perpetuate the exploitation and the inequitable distribution of income. This is endemic everywhere, but Britain and the United States are now the worst offenders, and those two countries are becoming, after the collapse of the Eastern bloc, the slowest growing of post-industrial societies and the most vulnerable to the threat of decline.

A concluding chapter deals with the globalization of professional society, and the extension of exploitation by the elites to the international plane, particularly through the transnational corporations (TNCs) which now dominate the world economy. A global ray of hope remains, however, as the more intelligent TNCs realize that good behaviour can be good business and therefore construct codes of responsible conduct towards their workers, customers, and host nations. Enlightened self-interest, they recognize, is more profitable than narrowly selfish greed. Some of their home societies have learned this lesson better than others, notably the continental Europeans with their adoption of the German 'social market economy', now being extended by the European Union to all its members except 'opt-out' Britain; and the East Asians with their Confucian tradition of group solidarity, 'individualism in the arms of collectivism', by which politicians and bureaucrats, managers and workers, collaborate for the benefit of all. Only the British and Americans, with their narrow view of the ownership of industry by the shareholders rather than the 'stakeholder capitalism' elsewhere, resist this enlightened approach, and are already paying for it in relative economic decline and social pathology.

The Epilogue, finally, moves beyond history to ask: What is to be done? The short answer is to raise the performance of all to the level of the best. This requires a new structure of rewards which pays people to cooperate willingly to the end of long-term profitability, growth, and security, rather than for short-term profit-taking by the few. Professional society is the most creative system the world has ever seen, bringing material, cultural, intellectual, and moral benefits on a scale not dreamed of by earlier generations, even among the rich and powerful. How can we enjoy the enormous benefits of professional society without allowing the professional elites to abuse their power and exploit their societies to the point of exhaustion and collapse? That is the most important question the world has to face in the twenty-first century.

A work of this scope is necessarily based on the researches and writings of hundreds of other scholars, in many different disciplines. The notes at the end of the book are meant only to support the text and cannot document every source on which it is based. I have tried to list in the Select Bibliography the most important works I have consulted, some of them briefly, but in the interests of space I have had to leave out many more that I have used over thirty years of teaching international comparative social history. I am indebted to them all and thank them sincerely.

There are many other scholars who have helped me, sometimes unwittingly, in this project, and I cannot mention them all. I particularly wish to thank those foreign scholars in the countries concerned who helped me on my visits there with inside knowledge and shrewd observations on their rapidly changing societies. They include: in France, Jean-Pierre Jallade, Olivier Bertrand, and Ladislav Cerych of the Institut Européen d'Education et de Politique Sociale in Paris; in Germany, Ulrich Teichler of the Wissenschaftliche Zentrum für Berufs-und Hochschulforschung at the Gesamthochschule Kassel, Hartmut Kaelble of the Freie Universität Berlin, and Lutz Reuter of the Bundeswehr Universität, Hamburg; in Japan, Akira Arimoto and Yoshihito Yasuhara of Hiroshima University, Mitsuhiko Iyoda of St Andrews University, Osaka, Kazuyuki Kitamura and Ikuo Amano of Tokyo University, and Takekazu Ehara of Kyoto University; and in Russia, Tatyana Zaslavskaya, Director of the Institute for Public Opinion, Moscow, Leonid Volkov, Deputy of the Russian Parliament, of the Institute of History of the USSR, and Olga Meshcheriakova, of Moscow, my interpreter in both language and mores.

In Britain my debts are too many to count, but I wish to thank particularly Jaroslav Krejci, Emeritus Professor of Lancaster University, for his invaluable insights into divided Germany and much else, Geoffrey Hosking and Olga Crisp of the Centre for Soviet and East European Studies, London University, for help with the USSR and Russian contacts, Heather McCallum of Routledge, for her enthusiasm and expertise, and David Marquand of Sheffield University for his infallible intellectual and moral support.

Likewise in the United States, I have many debts: to my specialist colleagues at Northwestern University who read and commented, much too kindly, on the relevant chapters: John Bushnell on Russia, Peter Hayes on Germany, Bill Heyck on Britain, Laura Hein on Japan, and Tessie Liu on France. Other readers, to whom I am deeply grateful, include James Cronin of Boston College, Massachusetts, Sally Chappell and her husband Walter Kitt of Chicago, and the students on my graduate course on post-industrial societies in 1994, Greg Barton, James Brennan, Peggy Klein, Maria Kolby, Karen Morrissey, and Marc Rodriguez, who read and discussed every chapter with remarkable patience and constructive insight.

I owe an especial debt to the John Simon Guggenheim Foundation for a year's fellowship and funding for research in Britain, France, Germany, Russia, and Japan, and to Northwestern University for topping up my salary and benefits for that year. My colleagues at Northwestern have been a source of lively intellectual discourse throughout my eleven years there, and made a temporary immigrant and, I hope, friendly critic feel at home and one of them.

My family deserve all the thanks I can give, for endless discussions and exemplification of professionalism: my wife Joan, whose books on Victorian women are now read across the world, my daughter Deborah, whose television documentaries on women's liberation in this century have been shown in Paris and Chicago, and my son Julian, whose electronic innovations for the *Financial Times* are tying together the financial publishing centres of the planet.

Finally, I must also thank my old friend Eric Hobsbawm, whose politics are quite different from mine, for producing, in the *New York Review of Books* in December 1993, the perfect epigraph for this book: to paraphrase him, The world is not for the privileged minorities, but for the ordinary run of people – who, I would add, still do most of the world's work and are entitled to enjoy it.

# 1

# THE THIRD SOCIAL REVOLUTION

The modern world is the world of the professional expert. Just as pre-industrial society was dominated by landlords and industrial society by capitalists, so post-industrial society is dominated by professionals. Their power, prestige, influence, and incomes stem from their possession of specialized knowledge, based on education, competitive merit, and experience on the job – in a word, on their human capital. Just as pre-industrial society was dominated by landlords who controlled the scarce resource of land for agriculture, and industrial society by capitalists who controlled the scarce resource of physical investment in factories and machines, so post-industrial society is dominated by those who control the scarce resource of expertise in its manifold forms.

In the modern world of professional expertise the concept must be taken in its widest sense, to include not only the traditional professions, from lawyers and doctors to engineers and accountants, but also professional bureaucrats in government and professional managers in business corporations. The professionals have created this world with its fantastic range of sophisticated products and services, and their leading lights have received and are receiving high rewards, prestige, status, and in some cases permanent wealth for their efforts.

So much is well-known to historians and social scientists from the work of John Kenneth Galbraith, Daniel Bell, Alvin Gouldner, Ralf Dahrendorf, and Robert B. Reich,[1] who see the benefits of this transition, but what is less recognized are the dangers that arise from professional domination of society. While they have enormously increased the wealth and power of their communities and solved many of the ills that have plagued mankind for millennia, at the same time they represent a threat to the well-being of themselves and their neighbours. They are capable for the first time in human history – unwittingly, for they have the best of intentions – of destroying humanity and perhaps all life on the planet. Even before that should happen they may, simply by pursuing their own self-interest, come to exploit their societies more effectively than the landlords and capitalists before them. All power is power for exploitation

1

and destruction as well as for creation and distributive justice, and the top professionals have amassed more power than any previous generation of elites. Indeed, it is not too much to say that the collapse of communism in the Soviet Union and Eastern Europe, and the current relative economic decline of some of the leading countries of the West, have less to do with ideology than with the short-sighted selfishness of their respective professional elites.

To understand this we have to see the post-industrial revolution which is now transforming the world in long historical perspective. The world we know is the product of three great social revolutions which encompass the whole of human history: the Neolithic Revolution, the Industrial Revolution, and the as yet incomplete post-Industrial Revolution or, as I prefer to call it, the rise of professional society.

## THE NEOLITHIC REVOLUTION

The Neolithic Revolution was the result of the development of settled agriculture around 6,000 BC, which enabled human beings for the first time to make nature grow what they wanted instead of living on what she grudgingly provided.[2] The food surplus thus garnered supported a larger population – five or more times as large as from hunting and gathering – and allowed a small minority of them to specialize in other kinds of work, as craftsmen (especially of the new, highly finished stone tools which gave the modern name to the period), artists, warriors, priests, and rulers, and to build the first towns and cities. The city (*civis*) gave its name to civilization, which produced the culture, the arts and crafts, the temples and palaces, and – it must be said – the weapons and fortifications, that have characterized history ever since. Above all, it created history itself: writing, invented for the purposes of administration and ritual, had as by-product the preservation, more reliable than oral tradition, of a record of events, and so access to the past beyond human memory.

The immense rise in the scale of organization stemming from this first revolution and the consequent growth in collective wealth and power created the first kingdoms and empires, and enabled them to grow, chiefly by conquest, to ecumenical size. Over the next several millennia political entities as large as Sumeria, Egypt, China, Persia, and Rome – and, by an independent and later development, the Inca and Aztec empires in the Western hemisphere – governed stretches of the earth's surface larger than most modern nation states. It was a mega-revolution in human society.

Although it brought wealth and power to the few, it had deleterious as well as beneficial effects for the many. After the casual, carefree, improvident life of hunting and gathering in humanity's Eden, it represented for most a decline into heavy and continuous labour: 'In the sweat of thy brow shalt thou eat bread.' It also meant yielding part of the surplus food to the organizers and defenders of the community: to emend Marx, 'All history is the history of the struggle for income.' The dominant elite, whether slave owners, tribute takers, or feudal lords, controlled the scarce resource, the land, and so were able to extract 'surplus value' from the food producers and use it to 'live like lords' and expand their span of command. The struggle for survival and conquest made warfare the normal state of relations between neighbouring communities. But there were benefits, in the internal peace which reigned for long periods within the borders, and the high culture, the arts of painting, sculpture, poetry, drama, music, and dance which could delight some of the people some of the time. Compared with pre-history, it was a life on a higher plane of existence.

There were even professionals, officials, priests, doctors, and lawyers, but they were for the most part subservient to the rich and powerful, servants rather than masters (except perhaps in the very few theocracies known to history). They were nevertheless key players in the process. They invented, or set on a more permanent basis than oral tradition, all the arts and sciences: bureaucracy, organized religion, philosophy, mathematics, astronomy, medicine, law. Above all, the priests and bureaucrats invented writing, and so made history itself possible. That is why history begins with the cities of the Neolithic Revolution and not before.

One other service was provided by the European clergy, which made medieval Europe different from other civilizations and paved the way for a further round of worldwide social change. Because of the separation of church and state and the consequent equality of the Gelasian 'two swords', political control was never unified in Europe. A space was left between Empire and Papacy through which independent thought, protest, and innovation could creep in and prevent the built-in stasis of most empires and theocracies. The Renaissance, the Reformation, the Scientific Revolution, and the Enlightenment, all found nourishing soil in which to grow, and independent thinkers, innovators and inventors could pursue unregulated paths. Thus Europe, rather than some other area, became the birthplace of the next great social revolution.

## THE INDUSTRIAL REVOLUTION

The second great transition, the Industrial Revolution which began in Britain in the eighteenth century and spread to Europe, North America and other parts of the world during the nineteenth and twentieth centuries, was a similar rise in the scale of organization, the means of life, and the standard of living.[3] It is fashionable now to question the revolutionary character of the Industrial Revolution on the grounds that it took longer than analogous political revolutions, but in the longer time scale of human history two hundred years is short indeed. The critics can hardly deny its introduction of dramatically higher living standards, the exponential growth of population and urbanization, and the profound transformation of society – or their own benefits from it in the means of scholarship, research, and communication. Their argument is based on the slow growth of the aggregate economic statistics, which hide the rapid change in the industrializing sector of the dual economy and reduce its dynamism to the mean of the whole. It is rather like denying that a baby is a new living entity because it changes the weight of the mother too slowly to notice in the early stages of gestation. The difference is in the qualitative outcome, not the quantifiable rate of average growth.

Since a further agricultural revolution was integral to industrialism, a larger food surplus enabled a majority of a much bigger population to do other work, and to congregate in much greater towns and cities. The population grew exponentially, again to five or more times the previous size, and concentrated in urban centres which grew together into great conurbations. Factories sprang up to replace domestic and other small workshops. Cities were joined by new roads, canals and railroads, telegraph and telephone. Domestic comforts unknown to pre-industrial aristocracies appeared and filtered down the social scale: piped water, indoor plumbing, gas and electricity, cooking stoves, household gadgetry, and central heating. Mass production supplied huge quantities of consumer goods, more varied and complex than ever before. By the mid-twentieth century even manual workers could command amenities – radio, gramophones, public telephones, cinema, medical drugs, vitamins, false teeth, detergents, bicycles and private cars, cheap long-distance holidays – beyond the dreams of the pre-industrial rich. It was the second rise to a higher plane of human existence.

There were, of course, costs as well as benefits. Wage labour could be even more back-breaking and tedious, working hours for a time became longer and more wearisome, conditions of work in factories and mines were dangerous to health, life and limb, living conditions in the industrial towns were marred by crime, dirt, and pollution, the diseases of overcrowding and insanitary surroundings increased for a time, the business cycle intermittently threw thousands into unemployment, and the degree of exploitation, measured by the widening gap between rich and poor, undoubtedly increased for several generations.

In the long run, however, the ingenuity which had created the problems was, under the pressures of humanitarianism and democratic protest, brought to bear upon them, and living and working conditions for all except the very poorest improved, while progressive taxation and welfare measures reduced the distance between rich and poor – though not without resistance by those who saw themselves as paying for them. Exploitation could now be exported to the Third World, where poor peasants, plantation labourers, and miners supplied the food, fuel, and raw materials demanded by the developed countries at terms of trade favourable to the buyers.

To supply the sophisticated needs of this new and more complex civilization, specialization proliferated, and numberless new occupations arose or grew much larger: engineers of many kinds, civil, mechanical, chemical, electrical, electronic, and so on, accountants and company secretaries, authors and journalists, medical specialists and dentists, research scientists and statisticians, university professors and school teachers, architects and quantity surveyors, social workers and counsellors, and all the many professional services we call upon today. The university was transformed from seminary for priests and finishing school for gentlemen into a professional school for every expert occupation, from politics and engineering to economics and business management. The new science of statistics played the role that writing had done in the first revolution, and made not only history but the social sciences the handmaidens of state policy and economic growth.

While owner-managing capitalists undoubtedly predominated, often joining forces with the older landlords in a new plutocracy, the expanding and increasingly salaried professional class quietly infiltrated all the upper ranges of the political, economic, and social institutions. Government became dependent on the bureaucracy of civil servants who themselves were more specialized and indispensable than the politicians. Business began to concentrate in great corporations, mainly private in most countries but state-owned in others, where control was increasingly exercised by professional managers. Private not-for-profit organizations, from universities and research foundations to charities for every conceivable cause, were run by professionals who exercised increasing influence and power over philanthropy, education, and research.

As the scale of organization rose still higher, with the massive growth of government and the corporations in the twentieth century, the professionals running them came to think of themselves less as servants and more as the indispensable masters of the enterprise. Like the capitalists in pre-industrial, aristocratic society, they grew in power and influence until they were in a position to take over, not by confrontation or violent revolution but by seduction and infiltration – as, indeed, the capitalists had taken over from the landowners before them. They, rather than the new electronics and information technology which were only the means, created the third great social revolution, the post-industrial revolution of our time.

5

## THE POST-INDUSTRIAL REVOLUTION

The third great transition is, then, the seductive revolution of the professionals. Whether we call it post-industrial – a useful but negative term which describes it by what it is not – or the revolution of information technology, automation, 'lean production', or, as I prefer, the rise of professional society, it is, like its predecessors, a revolution in human organization.[4] At the heart of it is a further rise in manufacturing productivity parallel to the rise in agricultural productivity in the Industrial Revolution. Just as efficient agriculture enabled a minority of the workforce to produce enough food to release the majority for industrial and other work, so high-tech manufacturing, but much more skilled management, 'just-in-time' organization, and 'lean production' techniques, enable a minority to produce enough consumer goods to release the majority for other work. What happened to agriculture in the second revolution, the production of food by a shrinking minority of the workforce, is now happening to the production of manufactured goods: a shrinking minority of workers are able to produce the consumer goods for other workers.

Other work means services of many kinds, from flipping hamburgers or driving buses to open-heart surgery or space research. Yet 'service revolution' is as inadequate a term for it as post-industrialism. Only the sophisticated services which have transformed human life, from biotechnical discoveries and electronic communications to televised entertainment and advanced education, are relevant to the transformation, and only what Robert Reich has called the 'symbolic analysts', the manipulators of symbolic knowledge, are its protagonists. Such knowledge-based services are the province of professional experts, without whom they would not exist. And professional knowledge is based on human capital, created by advanced education and experience on the job, and is itself the scarce resource that enables the professionals to command high 'rents' and rewards in kind.

Technology does not invent, install, or maintain itself, but needs human beings to bring it into production. It is thus not the technology that matters but the human skill and social organization which lie behind it. In other words, it is the professional experts who have constructed the system, which in turn has created them. And among the professionals most responsible, the key players are the professional managers of the great corporations and their counterparts in government, the state bureaucrats. They stand at the apex of the new society, controlling its economy and administering its policies and, increasingly, distributing the income and arranging its social relations.

Professionals, it is true, differ from older elites in that expertise is not a resource like land or capital that depends on its overall, as distinct from

6

its particular, scarcity. There can be as many professionals as there are experts to supply specialized services and, in theory at least, the professional elites can stretch as far down the social scale as higher and technological education can create knowledge-based jobs. As long as the particular expertise is scarce – science or medicine, administrative know-how or legal skill, computational dexterity or electronic engineering – the expert can command a rent as surely as the landlord or owner of industrial capital.

But some professions – different ones at different times – have always been more equal than others, and as the clergy rose to the top – below the aristocracy – from the Middle Ages to the seventeenth century, the lawyers in the eighteenth and nineteenth century, and the scientists and engineers in the twentieth,[5] so the dominant professions in the new society are, surprisingly perhaps, not the high priests of the new technology but those who employ and set them to work, the corporate managers and state bureaucrats. They are the elites who will make or break modern post-industrial society, who will lead it to its full potential of service to the community or pitch it down into the abyss of corruption, violent conflict, and self-destruction. Which road professional society will take depends not merely on the intelligence, enlightenment and integrity of the elite professions but on the unique cultural inheritance, social structure, and political ingenuity of each advanced country. That is why only a comparative study of the new society in its international perspective can reveal what the future is likely to hold for us in this third and most crucial phase in the history of humanity.

This book, therefore, deals with six – seven if we count both Germanies from 1945 to 1989 – of the most advanced professional societies since the Second World War: Britain, France, the two Germanies, the United States, the Soviet Union, and Japan. These seven not only demonstrate what professional societies have in common but how differently countries with disparate histories, cultural traditions, social structures, and political systems approach the new society and are transformed by it. They range from the most capitalist or free-market oriented to the most state-controlled command economy. At one end stands the United States, the archetype of the free-enterprise society; at the other stood, until 1991, the prototype of the command economy, the Soviet Union.

These are ideal types, of course, and no society represents a 'pure' example of the extremes: the 'military–industrial complex' in the United States has more involvement by the state than most Americans admit, and the Soviet Union depended more for its food and consumer goods on peasants' private plots and the so-called 'mafia', bridging officialdom and the black market, than communist theory allowed, but the contrast is stark enough to warrant the distinction. In between are various mixes of public–private enterprise, from the 'social market economy' of West Germany through the now declining 'mixed economies' of Britain and France, and the state–corporation alliance of Japan, to the most prosperous and successful of the command economies, East Germany. All had in common that they were increasingly organized and controlled by professionals, principally by corporate managers and/or state bureaucrats who, to quote Tom Lehrer, 'did well by doing good'. At the same time, the societies they headed evolved their own idiosyncratic structures and values, and had very varying degrees of political and economic success.

## THE MAJOR TRENDS OF PROFESSIONAL SOCIETY

What they have in common are ten major trends. Unlike James Burnham's managerial revolution, Max Weber's bureaucratization, or Vilfredo Pareto's circulation of elites,[6] the rise of professional society is more than a change at the top, the replacement of one elite by another. It transforms society from top to bottom. It raises living standards not just for the few but for every member of society. It puts most of its man- and woman-power into services rather than agriculture and manufacturing. It substitutes professional hierarchy for class as the primary matrix of the social structure. It recruits to those hierarchies by means of meritocracy, entailing an increase in social mobility from below. It extends this to women, thus ensuring their (admittedly limited) emancipation. It entails the massive growth of government, including the universal benefits of the welfare state, which enlarges and moralizes the concept of citizenship. It expands the provision of higher education in order to create human capital. It concentrates production of both goods and services in large business corporations whether private or state-owned, in a new structure of corporate neo-feudalism. And, paradoxically perhaps, it threatens to erode the nation state by internationalizing corporate neo-feudalism and creating a global economy.

### High living standards for all

First, the post-industrial societies as a whole (not just the seven dealt with here) become very rich compared with the rest of the world and are characterized by high and steeply rising living standards. That is why they are envied by the rest and imitated by those which are able to follow them. Table 1.1 shows the growth of the seven major ones in GNP per capita, compared with the stagnating or declining low and middle income countries, in real terms at 1982–84 US dollars. All such measures are somewhat misleading, in that rich countries pay for many goods and services which people in poor countries provide for themselves without

Table 1.1 Real national income per capita in 1982–84 US dollars

| | USA | Britain | France | W. Gmny | E. Gmny | Japan | USSR |
|---|---|---|---|---|---|---|---|
| 1950 | 8,216 | 5,000 | 4,147 | 3,600 | | 1,486 | |
| 1966 | 12,104 | 5,975 | 6,807 | 6,345 | 8,932* | 3,203 | 8,316* |
| 1980 | 14,580 | 9,871 | 14,442 | 16,208 | 8,724 | 11,992 | 5,528 |
| 1991 (ER) | 16,298 | 12,839 | 15,385 | 18,241 | na | 19,822 | na |
| 1991 (PPP) | 16,298 | 11,463 | 13,323 | 14,450 | | 13,914 | |

| | Low-income states | Lower mid-income states | Upper mid-income states |
|---|---|---|---|
| 1980 | 340 | 1,021 | 3,025 |
| 1991 | 257 | 1,167 | 1,820** |

Sources: 1950: A. Maddison, 'Growth and Slowdown in Advanced Capitalist Economies', Journal of Economic Literature, vol. 25, p. 683; 1966–80: World Bank, World Development Reports, 1970, 1989, 1993; 1991: OECD, Economic Surveys, 1994; calculated by Table 746: 'Purchasing power of the dollar, 1950–93', Statistical Abstract of US 1994, p. 489
Notes: ER = exchange rate valuations; PPP = purchasing power parities; na = not available; *artificial figures, due to inflated official rates of exchange of the Ostmark and rouble to the US dollar; **fall due to the falling revenues of oil-producing states

entering the market and are therefore not included in the measured GNP. No one could live at all in a rich country on an average Third World money income. But the differentials are gigantic enough to show the enormous advantages of development.

## The rise of service industries

Second, professional society is characterized by the swing from agriculture and manufacturing industry to services. Just as the second revolution saw a swing from agriculture to industry, so the third brings about a transition from both to non-material production. Table 1.2 shows how the labour force in all seven countries, once predominantly in the production of goods, has moved overwhelmingly into the production of services. As late as 1960 industry and agriculture together occupied between a half and three quarters of the workforce in six of the seven countries. Only in the United States, the acknowledged leader in the third revolution, did services employ more than half the occupied population. By 1991 services employed some three fifths or more of the workforce in the West and by 1980 some two fifths or more even in East Germany and the late Soviet Union.

## Class into hierarchy

Third, the shift to services reinforces a profound change in the social structure. Industrial society was characterized by class divisions as the old struggle for income between land, capital, and labour expressed itself

Table 1.2 Percentage distribution of employment

|  | USA | Britain | France | W. Gmny | E. Gmny | Japan | USSR |
|---|---|---|---|---|---|---|---|
| **1960** | | | | | | | |
| Agriculture | 8.3 | 4.3 | 22.4 | 14.2 | 17.2 | 32.5 | 38.8 |
| Industry | 33.7 | 48.5 | 39.1 | 48.2 | 48.3 | 28.3 | 32.4 |
| Services | 58.0 | 47.2 | 38.4 | 37.8 | 34.5 | 39.3 | 28.8 |
| **1980** | | | | | | | |
| Agriculture | 3.6 | 2.6 | 8.7 | 5.6 | 11.4 | 10.4 | 20.0 |
| Industry | 30.5 | 37.8 | 36.0 | 44.2 | 49.5 | 35.3 | 39.0 |
| Services | 65.9 | 59.6 | 55.3 | 50.3 | 39.1 | 54.2 | 41.0 |
| **1991** | | | | | | *(1987)* | |
| Agriculture | 2.9 | 2.6 | 5.8 | 3.7 | na | 6.7 | 19.0 |
| Industry | 25.3 | 27.2 | 29.5 | 39.3 | na | 34.4 | 38.0 |
| Services | 71.8 | 70.0 | 64.8 | 57.4 | na | 58.9 | 43.0 |

Sources: OECD, *Labour Force Statistics* (Paris, 1968, 1981, 1994); Council for Mutual Assistance, *Statistical Yearbook* (London, 1978)
Note: na = not available

through class institutions – trade unions, employers' associations, land-owners' pressure groups, and the like – uniting large sectors of the population. Since service industries are more fragmented and more difficult to organize and also generate career ladders rather than sharp divisions between 'us' and 'them', the new society creates professional hierarchies which cut across and overlie the old vertical structures of class and compete with each other for society's resources.

Public competition is obvious in the case of the public sector professions – defence, law and order, social welfare, health, education, and so on – which compete in the annual budget for a greater share of government spending. Competition is the ideology of the private sector, where the managers of the corporations compete with each other for market share and in takeover battles, but they also compete for government contracts, favourable legislation, subsidies, and tax breaks, as well as for influence and control over government.

The master conflict of professional society, at least in the West, is the competition between the public and private sectors over taxation and government spending, the former wanting more public spending, at least on their own particular service, the latter wanting lower taxes and less state intervention – though it must be added that the corporations also want more spending on their own particular products and services, for example in the defence, construction, or pharmaceutical industries. Both compete for domination of the central government, and the leading echelons among the more successful, typically the bureaucrats or the corporate executives, emerge as the ruling elite.

This vertical fault line accounts for the main ideological struggle in professional society, most markedly in the United States and Britain, where the critical divide in politics is between the devotees of free-market individualism and those who believe in a more collective approach to society's problems, between those who oppose any government intervention beyond the most minimal and those who see the state as protector of the common interest against the depredations of the rich and powerful. Both claim to offer the best means to a prosperous society and the fairest possible distribution of income, and both have had their opportunity to try to implement it, one in the period of Keynesian consensus for a generation after the Second World War, and the other in the triumph of Thatcherism and Reaganomics in the 1980s and 1990s. Which ideology has been more effective in achieving its promises it is one of the aims of this book to explore. Suffice it for the moment to say that both can be used to cover exploitation by the ruling elite, and the central theme will be the extent to which the different elites have abused their power at the expense of their societies.

## Meritocracy

Professionalism requires, fourth, a means of recruiting specialized experts, particularly those who occupy the top elite positions and control the political and economic power and the flows of income. Recruitment by merit is the most efficient means of meeting the need for expertise, and so meritocracy of some sort characterizes all professional societies, though in all of them it is skewed in favour of some candidates over others. It operates differently in different societies, in both the breadth and depth of its reach. France and Japan have the most explicit meritocracies and recruit to most of their elite positions from a handful of higher education institutions. West Germany has a broader road, at least for the middle class, but its tripartite school system cuts it off from most of the working class. The United States prides itself on the American dream that anyone can rise to wealth and power by his/her own efforts, though in practice some find it much easier than others. The old Soviet Union and East Germany proclaimed an ideology of equality, and recruited from much lower levels than the rest, though increasingly they rewarded political correctness and loyalty above non-political talent. Britain, with its backlog of public (i.e. private, fee-paying) schools for about 5 or 6 per cent of the age group, was the least meritocratic, but even there the expansion of higher education enabled larger numbers of working-class children than on the continent to acquire the means of rising through the professional hierarchies.

Social mobility is notoriously difficult to measure, but what studies there are confirm that the late twentieth century has seen a great expansion of

11

educational opportunity which has benefited some of the less favoured groups in society. This can be seen in Tables 1.3 to 1.5, which show the social background of politicians, civil servants, and business men in some of the countries. Unsurprisingly, most of them still come from the higher ranges of society, except in East Germany and the USSR, although with small but significant numbers beginning to come from the lower middle, manual working and peasant classes. In each Western country, the left of centre party draws more of its leaders from the lower ranges of society, but less than might be expected. This is because political representatives usually have higher education, which is skewed in favour of the higher classes, and politics of all shades attracts people from those classes.

Here again higher education is an essential qualification for bureaucrats and a useful one for entry into political assemblies, and so gives an advantage to the managerial and professional classes. American business is clearly more self-recruiting than the rest, but except in France very few business leaders come from the working class.

*Table* 1.3 Social origins of politicians by party

| | | | | | | *Percentage (1970s)* | | | | | |
| | USA | | Britain | | France | | W. Gmny | | E. Gmny | Japan | USSR |
|---|---|---|---|---|---|---|---|---|---|---|---|
| | Dem | Rep | Lab | Con | Left | Cen/Rt | SPD | CDU | SUP | LDP | CP |
| Upper | 86 | 75 | 54 | 96 | 80 | 97 | 48 | 70 | 92* | 96 | 44** |
| Lower | 14 | 25 | 46 | 4 | 20 | 3 | 52 | 30 | 8 | 4 | 56 |

*Sources*: Joel D. Aberbach *et al.*, *Bureaucrats and Politicians in Western Democracies* (Harvard University Press, 1981), p. 60; Jaroslav Krejci, *Social Structure in Divided Germany* (Croom Helm, 1976), p. 105; Basile Kerblay, *Modern Soviet Society* (Methuen, 1977), p. 249
*Notes*: Upper = upper and upper middle-class, except in East Germany and USSR; lower = lower middle-class (white-collar), manual workers and peasants; *officials and professionals; **white-collar workers, including officials (1981)

*Table* 1.4 Social origins of civil servants and parliamentarians by father's occupation

| | | | | | (1970s) | | | | |
| | USA | | | Britain | | France | | Germany | |
|---|---|---|---|---|---|---|---|---|---|
| | CS | P Ex | Congress | CS | MP | CS | MP | CS | MP |
| UM + P | 39 | 49 | 32 | 51 | 55 | 66 | 54 | 46 | 36 |
| LM + P | 29 | 27 | 30 | 17 | 9 | 30 | 22 | 21 | 15 |
| WCol | 18 | 18 | 22 | 20 | 12 | 3 | 18 | 21 | 20 |
| ManW | 14 | 6 | 16 | 12 | 24 | 1 | 6 | 12 | 29 |

*Source*: Joel D. Aberbach *et al.*, *Bureaucrats and Politicians in Western Democracies* (Harvard University Press, 1981), p. 55
*Notes*: CS = civil servants; P Ex = political executives in US administration; MP = member of parliament or equivalent; UM + P = upper managerial and professional; LM + P = lower managerial and professional; WCol = white-collar; ManW = manual workers

Table 1.5 Social origins of top business men by father's occupation

|  | USA | Percentage (1960s, 1970s) Britain | France | W. Germany |
|---|---|---|---|---|
| Business | 69 | 46 | 45 | 44 |
| CS + professional | | 33 | 33 | 12 |
| White collar | 31 | 18 | 18 | 13 |
| Manual worker | | 3 | 4 | 18 |

Source: Hartmut Kaelble, *Social Mobility in the 19th and 20th Centuries* (Berg, 1985), pp. 100–10
Note: CS = civil servant; figures for W. Germany omit farmers, 8 and others, 5

## The incorporation of women

A fifth, related trend, one which marks the first major revolution in relations between the sexes since pre-feudal and perhaps pre-historic times, is the emancipation of women. Women have always worked, but mostly in the lowest paid and least prestigious jobs, but now they have increased their share of middle-class employment in all the advanced countries, partly because they have overtaken men in the service industries, though still at the lower levels. Table 1.6 shows the increasing proportion of women in employment in the five capitalist countries. This was in part due to the induction of women into professional and managerial jobs. Feudal and capitalist societies had always submerged women, since men owned most of the land and capital, and made the laws of property to ensure that they held on to it. Professional expertise, by contrast, cannot easily be monopolized by men, though many still try to keep women out of the main professions or restrict their promotion. Once women broke into higher education and proved beyond doubt that they were as capable as men of acquiring human capital, they could no longer be excluded from a share of the jobs. Table 1.7(a) shows the increase in the higher education share of women in the post-war period. Their growth in ability, qualification, and expertise rather than the women's movement as such – which had always existed but did not get very far under previous dispensations of property – helps to explain the simultaneous, if limited, emancipation of women in all post-industrial

Table 1.6 Percentage of women in the labour force

|  | USA | Britain | France | W. Gmny | Japan |
|---|---|---|---|---|---|
| 1960 | 32.5 | 32.7 | 33.3 | 37.3 | 40.7 |
| 1980 | 42.0 | 39.2 | 39.8 | 37.8 | 38.7 |
| 1987 | 44.3 | 41.4 | 42.5 | 39.3 | 39.9 |

Source: OECD, *Historical Statistics, 1960–87* (Paris, 1989), p. 33, Table 2.3

*Table 1.7(a)* Women students in higher education

| | USA | Britain | France | Percentage<br>W. Germany | Japan | E. Germany |
|---|---|---|---|---|---|---|
| 1950 | 30 | 24 | 34 | 16 | 11 | 34 |
| 1960 | 37 | 23 | 41 | 23 | 29 | 33 |
| 1980 | 51 | 37 | 48 (1975) | 41 | 33 | 58 |
| 1989/90 | 54 | 44 | 54 | 40 | 39 | 52 |

*Source*: 1950–60: Hartmut Kaelble, *Social Mobility in the 19th and 20th Centuries* (Berg, 1985) pp. 86–87; 1980–90: UNESCO, *Statistical Abstract 1993*, Table 3.11

*Table 1.7(b)* Women teachers in higher education

| | USA | Britain | France | Percentage<br>W. Germany | Japan | E. Germany |
|---|---|---|---|---|---|---|
| 1980 | 24 | 18 | na | 14 (1985) | 14 | 27 |
| 1989/90 | 31 | 19 | na | 24 | 16 | na |

*Source*: as for Table 1.7(a)

societies. Women seized an opportunity that had not been on offer before. That does not mean of course that women have become completely equal in contemporary society. Elites do not open themselves willingly to newcomers of any kind, by class, race or gender, even in higher education where women form a far smaller share of the teaching staff than of the students, as Table 1.7(b) shows. Women still have both biological and cultural disadvantages – the burden of childbearing and the customary responsibility for childrearing and domestic work – which unfairly restrict their appointment and promotion prospects in a male-dominated professional world. They now have a ticket to ride, but it often does not take them very far.

## The growth of government

A sixth, more structural trend is the enormous growth of the government in all advanced societies. Table 1.8 shows the growth of public

*Table 1.8* Growth of government expenditure

| | USA | Britain | Percentage of GNP<br>France | W. Germany | Japan |
|---|---|---|---|---|---|
| 1960 | 27.6 | 32.6 | 27.5 | 32.5 | 18.3 |
| 1982 | 37.6 | 47.4 | 50.7 | 49.4 | 34.2 |
| 1991 | 36.7 | 39.7 | 47.0 | 44.2 | 34.4* |

*Sources*: OECD, *Economic Studies*, Spring 1985; *Economic Surveys: UK, 1994*: Basic Statistics
*Note*: *Receipts, not disbursements

expenditure as a proportion of GNP in the five Western countries of this study, at least until the 1980s when it began to tail off and even retreat. No official figures are available for East Germany and Soviet Russia, though estimates for the German Democratic Republic suggest that under Ulbricht between 1971 and 1973 the share of private enterprise in national income decreased from 5.4 to 3.9 per cent and of mixed (semi-state) enterprise from 8.9 to 0.9 per cent.[7] In pre-industrial and industrial society, the proportion of GNP collected by the government in peacetime rarely exceeded 10 per cent; in Western Europe it has grown from about 20 per cent in 1950 to approaching 50 per cent by 1982, while even in free-enterprise America and corporate–paternalist Japan it has grown to about 37 and 34 per cent respectively.[8] In the Eastern bloc it could theoretically be 100 per cent but never reached that level: in Soviet Russia, for example, one third of the food in the cities was produced by peasants bringing in their baskets of produce.

Table 1.9 shows the growth in public employment as a proportion of the total labour force, which is less than the growth of expenditure because the latter includes transfer payments under the welfare state. Even in the East, public employment was not quite 100 per cent: in the USSR peasant plots provided as much as a third of the food, and in East Germany, even after Ulbricht's 'reforms', 7 per cent of the employment was still in private or semi-private enterprise.[9] About two fifths of the expenditure, then, consists of transfer payments, social security, family benefits, pensions, unemployment pay, and the like, and most of the rest of salaries to civil servants, teachers, the military, and private employees via government contracts, as shown in Table 1.10. That is why the state

*Table 1.9* Public employment as a percentage of the total workforce

|      | USA  | Britain | France | W. Germany |
|------|------|---------|--------|------------|
| 1951 | 17.0 | 26.6    | 17.5   | 14.4       |
| 1981 | 18.3 | 31.4    | 32.6   | 18.3       |

*Source*: Richard Rose, *Public Employment in Western Nations* (Cambridge University Press, 1985), p. 11

*Table 1.10* Government provision of primary incomes: wages, salaries, and transfer payments

|      | Percentage | | | |
|------|------|---------|--------|------------|
|      | USA  | Britain | France | W. Germany |
| 1951 | 23.2 | 33.9    | 37.3   | 23.2       |
| 1981 | 41.7 | 56.3    | 55.4   | 50.6       |

*Source*: Richard Rose, *Public Employment in Western Nations* (Cambridge University Press, 1985), p. 45

can take so much and still leave private citizens to spend most of the national income on private consumption. Private consumption in purchasing power parities in 1991 averaged about 60 per cent in the five leading Western countries.[10] But the channelling of so much income through the state increases the control of professional bureaucrats over the system.

## The welfare state

The growth of the welfare state is therefore the seventh major trend. Table 1.11 shows the rise in public expenditure on social security, social services, health, and education as a percentage of GNP. Of these expenditures, social security transfers alone amounted to a half or more, shown in Table 1.12, representing a considerable redistribution of income, though more from the same people when of working age, healthy, and employed than from the rich to the poor.

The welfare state represents an expansion of the concept of citizenship. While it is now fashionable to denounce welfare spending on other people, state benefits for oneself are hotly defended, even by the affluent, who resist cuts in pensions, health services, education (especially higher education), policing, road construction, and the like. Citizenship has expanded from legal equality, an initial claim to equality before the law, then to political equality, participation and eligibility in elections, and finally to social equality, a right to income support in the exigencies of life, to education at secondary and even for the qualified at university

*Table 1.11* Public expenditure on social security, social services, health, and education as a percentage of GDP

|        | USA | Britain | France | W. Germany | Japan |
|--------|-----|---------|--------|------------|-------|
| 1960   | 11  | 14      | 13     | 20         | na    |
| 1981   | 20  | 24      | 29     | 32         | na    |
| 1991*  | 11  | 22      | 30     | 23         | na    |

*Source*: OECD, *Social Expenditures, 1960–90*, p. 85; World Bank, *World Development Report, 1993*, Table 11
*Note*: *Central government only (most education by local governments)

*Table 1.12* Social security transfers as a percentage of GDP

|        | USA  | Britain     | France | W. Germany | Japan |
|--------|------|-------------|--------|------------|-------|
| 1960   | 5.0  | 6.8         | 13.5   | 12.0       | 3.8   |
| 1981   | 11.1 | 12.9        | 20.3   | 17.2       | 10.6  |
| 1987   | 10.8 | 14.0 (1986) | 21.9   | 16.0       | 11.8  |

*Source*: OECD, *Historical Statistics, 1960–87*, p. 63

level, to affordable medical treatment, decent housing and a clean environment, and progressive taxation to pay for all these.[11] The welfare state is
under attack from the right in Western countries, but this only underlines
the tenacity with which citizens cling to its benefits, which have survived
in large degree the onslaught of Reaganomics and Thatcherism. Its
survival is due not only to public demand, but to the welfare professionals who administer it, fighting for their jobs as well as for their belief that
the service be provided to meet the need.

## The centrality of higher education

Education is one of the more expensive items in the welfare state, for the
obvious reason that professional society needs a trained workforce and a
larger proportion of highly educated people than any previous era. The
eighth major trend, therefore, is the unprecedented expansion of higher
education in all developed or would-be developed societies. Since about
1960 virtually all countries have doubled or trebled the numbers of young
people attending universities and colleges, the leading post-industrial
societies most of all. Table 1.13 shows the expansion of student numbers
as a percentage of the 20–24-year-old age group in the seven countries.
The figures are for all students, full-time and part-time, and do not allow
for length of course, drop-out rates, etc. Consequently, they do not measure the output of graduates, which differs markedly between countries.

Table 1.14 shows the result in terms of the percentage of the adult
population with a university or college degree (much higher in the
younger than in the older age groups).

The explosion of higher education which accompanies the transition to
professional society is one of the most influential factors in the new social

Table 1.13 Age participation ratio of students in higher education

| | Percentage of 20–24 age groups | | | | | | |
| | USA | Britain | France | W. Gmny | E. Gmny | Japan | USSR |
|---|---|---|---|---|---|---|---|
| 1960 | 32.1 | 8.5 | 7.5 | 6.1 | 16.3 | 9.5 | 11.0 |
| 1988 | 59.6 | 22.8 | 34.8 | 31.8 | 33.1 | 30.1 | 23.6 |

Source: UNESCO, Statistical Yearbooks

Table 1.14 Adult population with a post-secondary degree

| | Percentage of persons 25–64 years old | | | |
| | USA | Britain | France | W. Germany |
|---|---|---|---|---|
| 1991 | 36 | 16 | 15 | 22 |

Source: Statistical Abstract of US, 1994, p. 860

structure and the social attitudes of the population. Some degree of meritocracy becomes unavoidable, and it is no longer possible for controlling elites to rely on the ignorance of the people to accept their propaganda, as the collapse of the Soviet Union and its satellites bears witness. The politics of the new society has to become far more sophisticated and directed to the rational self-interest of a more intelligent population, as Gorbachev realized when he promulgated *perestroika*.

## The rise of the giant corporation

The ninth major trend is the concentration of business in a declining number of giant corporations, whether private or state-owned. In Britain where the trend began, as in America and Germany, in the late nineteeth century, the largest 100 manufacturing companies in 1909 produced 15 per cent of the output; by 1930 they produced 26 per cent; by 1970 45 per cent. Today the largest 200 firms produce about 85 per cent of total manufacturing output. Much the same is true of services: six supermarket chains sell two thirds of the food sold over the counter; four high street banks account for most deposit banking; a dozen insurance firms dominate their market. The wave of mergers and takeovers since 1957 increased the stock market valuation of the 100 largest quoted companies from 60 per cent to over 90 per cent of the total.[12] The same wave is swallowing up companies in the United States and Western Europe, and has been given a further boost by the investment opportunities opened up in Eastern Europe. In Japan it is less rapid only because the *keiretsu*, the rings of companies owning each other's shares – Mitsubishi, for example, is a closed ring of about eighty companies – are already so concentrated and protect themselves from corporate raiders, and they use large numbers of tied suppliers who are technically independent.

The drive for concentration is powered by the ambition of corporate managers – and most companies are now headed by professional managers rather than traditional capitalists, even where the top managers bear capitalist family names like Ford or Du Pont, Siemens or Thyssen, Honda or Toyoda – to expand their market share and their span of control. It matters not whether the company is owned by shareholders or by the state. The only difference when a state corporation is privatized is that the CEO immediately receives a huge increase in salary, *viz.* Lord King of British Airways, Roland Smith of British Aerospace, Sir Iain Vallance of British Telecom, or Cedric Brown of British Gas. Managers are interchangeable between sectors, though they understandably prefer to be responsible to remote, anonymous, invisible shareholders rather than to potentially interventionist government ministers and bureaucrats. Chief executives have become feudal barons, increasingly difficult for national governments to reign in, especially where they operate globally, across national frontiers.

## The global economy

The tenth and final major trend is the globalization of the world economy. The drive for market share and access to supplies of raw materials, fuel, especially oil, and cheap labour, does not stop at national frontiers. Some multinationals own factories, mines, oil fields, banks, plantations, agribusinesses, and sales outlets in many countries, and have turnovers larger than the Gross National Product of most member states of the United Nations. In 1994 the United Nations Conference on Trade and Development identified some 37,500 transnational corporations with 200,000 foreign affiliates and $4.8 trillion in global sales, which employed some 73 million workers directly and 150 million all told, nearly a fifth of non-farm paid employment in the world.[13]

Amongst these the 100 largest (excluding those in banking and finance) held $3.4 trillion in global assets, accounted for $3.5 trillion in sales (about 72 per cent of the total), and employed some 12.4 million workers (about 17 per cent of the TNCs' workforce). Of the top 100, seventy-seven were based in the five Western countries of this study: twenty-nine in the United States, sixteen in Japan, twelve in France, eleven in Britain (including two, Unilever and Royal Dutch/Shell, jointly with the Netherlands), and nine in Germany (and all the rest were in European or English-speaking countries).[14] They manufacture, export, and import a huge share of the world's commodities; the international banks do most of the world's financial business. Some of them also export polluting operations and disposal of waste products overseas: American chemical companies to Mexico or India, Japanese nuclear waste to France or Britain, and so on. Though they lack means of military coercion save through their influence with powerful governments, decisions in their boardrooms can make or break the economies of whole cities, regions, even nation states. Twenty-five per cent of the United States' manufacturing is now done abroad, 15 per cent of Germany's and, surprisingly in view of its massive overseas investments, only 10 per cent of Japan's.[15] The huge American and British trade deficits accumulated under the Reagan–Bush and Thatcher–Major regimes owe less to European and Japanese competition than to the import of goods made by American and British companies overseas.

The ability of the multinationals to evade regulation and control is manifested by endless instances, from shipping lines that operate under flags of convenience to escape safety and labour laws and oil-spill prevention, to international banks that practise fraud and launder drug profits. Most foreign investment, over three quarters in the 1980s, is still in developed countries, but the current drive to invest in areas of low wages like Latin America, China, and Eastern Europe is a threat even to the most advanced national economies.[16] It could mean the import of Third World living standards to the First World. The multinational corporations are the 'overmighty subjects' of the modern age. Like the English barons under King John or the German princes under the Holy Roman Empire, they are extremely difficult to control. They represent a new form of international corporate neo-feudalism which is, potentially at least, more powerful than the nation state itself.

## THE GREAT ARCH

The seven countries illustrate these ten trends in very different ways. Britain resisted the transition and clings to an out-of-date class system that perpetuates industrial conflict and discourages economic growth. France, West Germany, and Japan, more natural meritocracies, have embraced it, though with social costs in inequality and frustration of the 'merit-poor' which may yet prove politically destabilizing if economic depression returns. The old Soviet Union and the late German Democratic Republic paid the price of a pathological version of professionalism, the rule of the overmighty state bureaucrat, in economic collapse and political disintegration. The United States has gone to the other extreme and glorified the overmighty corporate executive, culminating in outrageous rewards to chief executive officers both in failure and success, scandals on Wall Street, destabilization of the savings and loans industry plus multi-billion dollar government compensation to its depositor-victims, and a massive trade deficit due in part to the import of goods, parts, and raw materials produced by American multinationals overseas.

One way to conceptualize these differences is to see them as lying on a great arch, from the classic free-market economy – strictly, the corporate managerial – to the most extreme command economy – strictly, the state bureaucratic. This is necessarily an oversimplification, since there is no such thing as a completely free market without a framework of regulation to define property, contract, buyer and seller, and there is no command economy without a black market and, in practice, an economic mafia. The American free market overlies an industrial–military complex – or, rather, a corporate–governmental complex, since it is much wider than the defence establishment – supported by federal contracts, research projects, subsidies, and bailings-out. Before *perestroika* the Soviet command economy only worked because the black market provided the consumer goods that the official system could not, and because the economic mafia supplied raw materials and components to state factories and collective farms which they would otherwise have been unable to produce. The great arch is therefore narrower in reality than it is in abstract logic.

Britain is, or was, the keystone of the arch: a mixed economy with a pioneering welfare state and, until the Thatcher privatizations of the late 1980s, one of the largest nationalized sectors in the West. Industrial concentration has gone further than elsewhere and it was the nursery, along with the United States, of the multinational corporation. There too the contest between public and private sector professionals has been most intense, with the welfare professionals and the business managers quarrelling bitterly over taxation and welfare spending. This is because British politics, despite the emergence of a virtually one-party state, is balanced on a knife edge, and a tiny percentage of the popular vote could change the balance. Hence, questions of taxation and public expenditure loom even larger in Britain than in the United States, the home of the politics of the pocket book. The rivalry of the public and private sector professions also owes something to the remnants of class politics, since the two parties, while ostensibly representing capital and labour respectively, are increasingly led by politicians drawn from business management and its allies and from non-business professions such as education, local government, trade union officialdom, journalism, and similar occupations. Politics is often conducted, therefore, in the language of class warfare more appropriate to industrial than to post-industrial society. It is the language of the old class struggle for income, a zero sum game in which, instead of cooperating to increase the size of the cake, the two parties fight over their respective shares.[17] At the industrial level this is the main reason for Britain's economic decline. At the level of economic policy it discourages collaboration between the state bureaucrats and the corporate managers of the kind that has created economic miracles in France, West Germany, and Japan, and has made Britain the post-industrial country most vulnerable to the vicissitudes of the global economy.

France and West Germany have avoided this mistake. Both have a long history of collaboration between government and business, and both had meritocratic education systems and proto-welfare states long before the Second World War. The French invented bureaucracy, and the government has been interested in economic growth since Colbert under Louis XIV. Prussia, the parent of imperial Germany, drafted the Junkers into state service and deliberately fostered industrialization through technical education, railway building, state-encouraged banking, and military contracts, and took industry into partnership for the good of the fatherland. Their economic success was based on different principles, the French on indicative planning which required close communication between government planners and private business men, the Federal German Republic's on an ostensibly American-type free market but modified into a 'social market economy' that combines private enterprise with a generous welfare state, and the Democratic German Republic's economic leadership of the Eastern bloc on a particularly rigid version of the command economy.

The French elites were, and are, recruited from the *grandes écoles* and the civil service *grands corps*. Since the war their alumni have increasingly dominated both the expanding government bureaucracy and, by the process known as *pantouflages*, migration from the civil service to the mixed and private sectors, the nationalized industries, the banks, and the private corporations themselves. The top echelons in the government bureaucracy and the private corporations talk to each other in the same language because they were classmates in the same schools. Getting things done is as easy as picking up the telephone.[18]

The West German elites are not so narrowly recruited as the French, but they are just as elitist, being overwhelmingly middle-class graduates who traditionally served the state as civil servants and teachers and have since the Second World War extended their turf into private industry, where they occupy the top echelons. With their traditional self-discipline and what Dahrendorf calls 'the habit of obedience' they have brought the efficiency of the old Junker bureaucracy into the private corporations.[19] The now defunct German Democratic Republic was, in theory at least, much more meritocratic and drew its officials and managers from a wider swathe of society. Over three quarters of the People's Chamber, a fair sample of the party elite, came in 1970 from the ranks of the peasants and workers.[20] Since then, unsurprisingly, more of them have come from elite party families, whatever their parents' original class. Sadly, this meritocracy, selected for its political correctness and party loyalty rather than its competence, failed to save East Germany from political despotism, ultimate economic collapse, and absorption by its bigger and more prosperous brother.

The United States and the defunct Soviet Union form opposite pillars of the arch, the most triumphantly free-market and the most dogmatically state-centralized versions of professional society. Yet neither is (or was) quite as extreme as it claimed. Chester Barnard, the pioneer of American business education, thought of the United States as long ago as the 1930s as the American administrative state, modelled on his own company, American Telephone and Telegraph, the telecommunications giant. He lauded the corporate executive as the ideal citizen, morally superior to and more efficient than any government official but just as dedicated to planning and bureaucracy.[21] This is ironic, since if politicians are corrupt it is the rich and especially the corporations that corrupt them. Since his day the archetypal corruption of Tammany Hall has been overtaken by the archetypal corruption of Wall Street junk bond conmen and savings and loans embezzlers, and honours in chicanery have become more equal between the public and private sectors.

The American government is intertwined with the economy, with big business, the banks, the oil industry, the defence industries, subsidized agriculture, the health insurance companies, the universities, the research foundations, and most other private sector institutions. It monitors, regulates, subsidizes, bails out, and contracts with almost every industry and service. To a greater extent than in other free world countries, government service is a revolving door, and high executives move in and out of the public sector with every change of administration and some-times more often. The lobbies and special interests – highly skilled and specialized professions in themselves – spend millions of dollars influencing government decisions, which can make the difference between jackpot profits and disastrous losses for their clients. The 1993–94 attempt by President and Hillary Clinton to reform health care was defeated by the $400 million spent in advertising and lobbying by the insurance companies and private hospitals. In the clash between public and private sectors over taxation and public spending *both* appear to have won, with tax reductions unmatched by cuts in public expenditure. The result has been a record budget deficit which, allied to the record trade deficit related to it by the resultant consumer spending spree of the 1980s, has contributed to the relative economic decline of the United States chronicled by Paul Kennedy, at the very moment of its triumph in the Cold War.[22] To a large extent this is due to the success of the over-mighty neo-feudal corporation: both deficits stem from overspending on government contracts and overseas operations and from the export of jobs and capital by American multinationals.

The late Soviet Union was the prototype of the bureaucratic command economy and the all-powerful state official. It inherited a strong bureau-cratic state from the Tsarist regime and turned it into a ruthless meritoc-racy. In 1981 the 17.5 million members of the Soviet Communist Party came nearly equally from the blue-collar (43.4 per cent) and white-collar classes (43.8 per cent), and the rest from the peasantry (12.8 per cent) – though, increasingly, many of these were the children of party officials who originated in those classes. Less than half a million of them belonged to the *nomenklatura*, officials and candidates for office in the party and economic apparatus, and only one in ten of these belonged to the leadership group.[23] Whatever their origins, at all levels the party activists became professionalized, in the sense that their positions depended on their human capital, assisted by their political loyalty.

According to Alex Simirenko, the party was *the* profession at the head of all the professions, and had become a sort of church whose function was to extract the contributions of the faithful and give ideological comfort and economic guidance in return.[24] Unfortunately, like the pre-Reformation Papacy they yielded to the temptations of irresponsible power and abused their position to extract more than the society could afford, thus foolishly ensuring their own demise. It is ironical that Marx's warning about 'the contradictions of capitalism' – its extraction of so much surplus value that the producers of wealth cannot afford to buy their own products so that the system implodes into self-destructive depression – should have come to apply first to 'the contradictions of communism'. The extraction of surplus value by the *nomenklatura* squeezed the proletariat to the point of collapse.

Tatyana Zaslavskaya, 'the woman who invented *perestroika*', shows how the *nomenklatura* turned themselves from a social group into a new ruling class, with privileged access to state property and incomes in kind, including sumptuous apartments, *dachas* in the country, domestic servants, big cars, vouchers for scarce goods in the state shops, special stores for foreign imports, exclusive clinics for themselves and their families, privileged education for their children, private holiday resorts, and even – shades of the aristocratic *ancien régime* – special hunting areas.[25] To Arkady Vaksberg, a courageous Russian investigative journalist, the situation was more outrageous still: the Soviet mafia infiltrated government at all levels, up to and including Brezhnev's son-in-law, Churbanov, and perhaps to Brezhnev himself. The lifting of the veil by *glasnost* exposed corruption of the most naked kind, with bribes of thousands of roubles in unmarked envelopes and 'presents' of gold watches and jewellery, passing upwards for every kind of service and promotion, and brothels disguised as country clubs for the entertainment of officials in every region and republic.[26] Meanwhile, the Russian and colonial peoples who paid for all this were living at subsistence standards, gulled by the promise of prosperity and equality for their grandchildren. The nemesis of the *nomenklatura* was the revolution of 1989.

If *perestroika* was the come-uppance of a corrupt professional society, it was also the protest of honest professionals against the criminals who ran it. Gorbachev represented a new generation of educated bureaucrats who knew the system from the inside well enough to gain power, but could see it sliding into decline. While he did not wish to give up the control of the one-party state, he determined to reform it and root out the corruption.[27] He was brought down by his own naivety, his failure to see that the corrupt *nomenklatura* would fight like jackals for their privileges, and his inability to prevent their sabotaging of the reform process. Fortunately, their reactionary leaders were so incompetent that they could not even manage a successful coup in August 1991, and both he and they were replaced by Boris Yeltsin – though they still hang on grimly to the hope of defeating him. Even now the new Russian parliament, before its brutal defeat by Yeltsin, was more concerned with its members' perks and privileges than with regenerating the economy. And the old mafia has reemerged, converting the black market into a distorted free market and outperforming the American and Italian mafia in protection racketeering, gangsterism, and murder.

The irony, and possible tragedy, of a sophisticated professional society, however, is that it cannot operate without trained and experienced professionals. That is why most of the former officials and managers remain in place and why even the free-market enterprises in Russia and Eastern Europe – except in East Germany where West German managers have taken over – are run by ex-communists. The regimes may even, according to one well informed observer, John Lukacs, be reverting to one-party states.[28] Whether in the new Commonwealth of Independent States they will cooperate with the reformers or sabotage the reconstruction remains to be seen. The army, that huge bureaucracy, for example, is already said to be out of control, and less interested in defeating the Chechens than in preserving its own power and privileges. The current anarchy and gangsterism may well end in the imposition of a new despotism. Whatever happens, the power of the professionals will determine it.

Japan is the exception to every rule and appears to stand at both ends of the great arch of professional society. At one pillar it is ostensibly a classic free-market economy on the American model, with giant corporations almost monopolizing the domestic market and with their huge profits buying up investment properties overseas in the United States, Britain and Europe, the East Asian 'little tigers', Australia and New Zealand, now even in Eastern Europe. At the other pillar, alongside a weak and corrupt political system it has a powerful government bureaucracy that cooperates with the politicians and big business in steering 'Japan Incorporated' through ever-changing transitions to new sunrise industries.

Although one must avoid the myth of Japanese cultural exceptionalism, which both the Japanese themselves and their competitors assiduously foster, not everything in Japan is quite what it seems. The Japanese professional elite is more unified than any other in the non-communist world. The ostensibly independent *keiretsu*, the closed rings of companies owning each other's shares, are intimately linked with the factions in the (until 1993) permanently ruling Liberal Democratic Party and with officials in specific ministries. The politicians, bureaucrats, and corporate managers are all recruited from the same handful of highly competitive and meritocratic universities, notably Tokyo, Kyoto, Waseda, and Keio – the top echelons, indeed, from one school of one university, the Law School of Todai, the University of Tokyo. They are linked to their classmates through *jinmyaku*, literally 'veins in the rock' but in practice telephone networks which facilitate policy making in the interests of both government and the corporations. Many of them are in fact the same people at different stages of the life cycle: by the practice of *amakudari* ('descent from heaven') – parallel to the French *pantouflages* but later in their careers – high officials in the ministries parachute down to top positions in the corporations.[29] In this way, to paraphrase Charles Wilson of General Motors in the 1950s, what is good for the corporations is good for Japan and vice versa. Allowing for the weakness of the Japanese state, which enabled those irresponsible 'corporations', the army and the navy, to dictate policy in the 1930s and 1940s, it is easy to guess which is the wheel horse.

Given its cultural traditions of group loyalty and *wa* (social harmony), Japan would appear to be the most successful example of a professional society in the post-industrial world. It spans both ends of the great arch, the corporate free market and the paternalist state. Herman Kahn's forecast as long ago as 1970 that it would be the leading power of the twenty-first century may well be right.[30] While amply rewarding its guiding elite, often in hidden ways which defy analysis, it seems so far to have avoided the trap of over-exploitation, of extracting so much surplus value that the economy implodes or the people rebel – though the erosion of lifelong employment and the newly aroused discontent with 'money politics' and ubiquitous corruption are beginning to take effect. On the other hand, the rapid aging of the population may undermine the economic miracle. When the elderly begin to outnumber the active population, the key to success, the high savings rate, will fall, and Japan may decline to a more normal mass-consumer society.[31] Meanwhile, however, Japan, despite the recent recession – induced by the high value of the yen due to the very success of Japanese trade and the falling purchasing power of the West – would seem to be the very model of a successful professional society. Those who, despite complaining about the massive size of the Japanese trade balance, crow over the apparent slackening of Japanese economic growth and the declining threat of 'Japan as Number One', may be triumphing prematurely.

It is obvious by now that the form post-industrial society takes, however powerful the forces of professionalism, is influenced by its previous political system, social structure, moral values, and cultural traditions. These in turn are determined by its history, by the industrial and pre-industrial societies that preceded it and the ease or difficulty of the particular path by which it travelled. The aim of this book is not merely to illuminate the transition in seven typical cases but also to explore the way in which the historical experience predisposed the professional elites to act equitably in the interests of the whole society or greedily and self-destructively in their own corrupt interest.

Professional society has enormous potential for enhancing human life and ensuring social justice, but it also presents the professional elites with egregious opportunities for exploitation. At one end of the great arch lies the potential tyranny of Big Brother, the overmighty state bureaucracy, whose decaying remains are still fouling Russia and

Eastern Europe. At the other end lies the more subtle and insidious seductions of Big Sister, the overmighty corporations, which now dominate the global economy and are more powerful than most nation states. Both have the potential for producing the good life materially, intellectually, and culturally for all citizens but they are also capable of exploiting their societies for the benefit of the dominant professional elite. How to navigate between the two is the most important question for mankind in the twenty-first century.

# 2

# THE UNITED STATES
## A free market for corporations

The United States of America stands as the fixed pillar at one end of the great arch. It is the promised land of free enterprise. The free market is enshrined in the Constitution and the Bill of Rights. James Madison, 'the father of the Constitution', described himself as 'the friend to a very free system of commerce', and his sacred offspring expressly forbade Congress to make any law 'impairing the Obligation of Contracts'; 'nor shall private property be taken for public use without just compensation'. The Fifth Amendment states: 'No person shall be ... deprived of life, liberty, or property, without due process of law ...' The Constitution as amended in 1789 established the first great common market and with it the conditions for what Americans boast is the most successful system of free enterprise in the world.

That boast is made most proudly by the great corporations, like the oil company that celebrated the bicentennial of the Constitutional Convention by distributing a pamphlet, *The Second American Revolution*, to national newspapers, schools and universities, and an estimated audience of 51 million people.[1] The unconscious irony escaped its authors: that a multinational corporation, dedicated to limiting the supply side of the market by narrowing it to a few hundred giant corporations – the 'seven sisters' in its own industry – should praise the very system it exists to undermine.

### FREEDOM FOR WHOM?

Adam Smith, writing in the year the American colonists threw off the British yoke, warned against the propensity of producers to combine against the community:

> People of the same trade seldom meet together, even for merriment or diversion, but the conversation ends in a conspiracy against the public, or in some contrivance to raise prices. It is impossible to prevent such meetings, by any law which could either be executed, or would be consistent with liberty and justice.[2]

28

With unconscious irony, the apologists for American corporate capitalism have hijacked the first critic of the 'mercantile system' against which their forefathers rebelled, and placed his name on their mastheads. The reason is obvious: American free enterprise has become freedom for the great corporations and their professional managers.

The corporations have, of course, been the dynamic force behind the astonishing success of the American economy and, ultimately, behind the political and military strength that 'made America Number One'. Olivier Zunz in *Making America Corporate* has shown how corporations like Ford, Du Pont, International Harvester, Metropolitan Life Insurance, and the major railroad companies transformed American business in the late nineteenth and twentieth centuries.[3] They were instrumental in changing its matrix from the small-scale family firm to the large-scale company with its multiple factories, offices and depots, its huge bureaucracy of managers and clerks, its hordes of workers in plants, warehousing and transportation, and its swarms of travelling salesmen. Alfred D. Chandler, dean of American business history, has demonstrated how the giant corporation replaced the market with managerial control and coordination, internalized transactions between buyer and seller, substituted planning and negotiation between departments for bargaining between suppliers and purchasers, invented the multi-divisional structure in place of independent firms, and constructed the managerial career ladder with its regular salary scales, fixed promotion breaks, fringe benefits, perquisites, and pension rights. The key to mass production and distribution was no longer Adam Smith's 'invisible hand' but the 'visible hand' of the professional manager, planning every stage of manufacture, from the purchase of raw materials, fuel, and components, to the final sale of the product. The large-scale enterprises of the United States, Britain, and Germany, he says elsewhere, 'have provided a fundamental dynamic or force of change in capitalist economics since the 1880s'.[4] The result was a bottomless cornucopia of consumer goods and services at decreasing real prices and – until recently – secure, well-paid employment for the great majority of the American people.

But *free* enterprise in Adam Smith's sense it was not. As John D. Rockefeller, doyen of corporate capitalism, said at the end of his active career, 'The day of combination is here to stay. Individualism has gone for ever, never to return.'[5] Arthur J. Eddy in *The New Competition* (1912) put it more succinctly: 'Competition is war, and "War is Hell".'[6] Lord Bryce, following Albert Shaw's study of intervention by local state legislatures in 1887, found that the American belief in *laissez-faire* as the main principle of government was groundless: 'The new democracies of America are just as eager for state interference as the democracy of England.'[7]

What Americans discovered in the Progressive Era was that the burgeoning free market together with industrialism and the rise of an urban civilization threatened to reduce the old social order to chaos. As Robert Wiebe has shown, the federal government tried to impose order on this chaos by creating a regulatory state run by an increasingly professional bureaucracy of agencies, from the Interstate Commerce Commission to regulate the railways (1887) and the National Forest Service (1891) to the Federal Reserve Board for control of the banking system (1915) and the National Park Service for conservation of the surviving wilderness (1916).[8] This was the beginning of the 'American administrative state' praised by Chester Barnard, pioneer of American business education, modelled on his own corporation, American Telephone and Telegraph – in effect, a blueprint for the professionalization of government.[9] Barnard recognized that the corporations anticipated the state in the attempt to impose order on the chaos of the free market. Corporate capitalists came to understand that unregulated competition was wasteful, inefficient and, above all, insecure. Profitability depended upon controlling the vagaries of the market and ensuring that it operated in the most predictable and effective manner. The investment of vast capital in mass production and cheap products of high quality could only be justified if sales and profits could be guaranteed, which meant bringing them under the control of a large, single, bureaucratic enterprise.

Even Joseph Schumpeter, who saw 'large concerns' as responsible for the 'creative destruction' that was the driving force of economic progress, believed that they were undermining free competition and ultimately capitalism itself.[10] As with the traditional professions of law, medicine and the clergy, professional management was a device for controlling the market. This does not mean that they could single-handedly control the market, and certainly not the whole of it. But the limitation of even a small part of it resulted in significant price advantages and, more significantly, an increase in market share. Moreover, each corporation was surrounded by a penumbra of suppliers and contractors who were part of the market. It can best be thought of as a dense body, a supernova in the continuum of economic space, with greater gravitational pull and therefore able, as in Einstein's universe, to bend the market towards itself, without controlling the whole of space.

The price of mass production and unprecedented efficiency was loss of independence for the small business man, and loss of bargaining power for the consumer. As Charles Perrow pointed out in debate with Chandler, the profitability of the system stemmed not from reducing transaction costs and from managerial coordination:

Profits came from control of markets and competition, control of labor, and the ability to externalize many other costs that are social

30

in nature, that is to force communities to bear them and not to have them reflected in the price of the goods and services.[11]

Part of the cost was borne by the small traders squeezed out of the market and replaced by corporate middle managers and salesmen, part by the consumers who now faced a shrinking number of monopolistic suppliers, and part by the public and the taxpayers who paid in ill health or dollars for the pollution and support costs of industry's waste disposal and human casualties. The loss had compensations, it might be argued: independence for the small business man had meant insecurity, fluctuating profit and loss, fear of bankruptcy and ruin; free bargaining power for the consumer meant *caveat emptor*, a choice of variable and unreliable goods at fluctuating prices, and a lack of warranty and redress. But to pretend that the costs were not paid and that the old free market of pre-corporate, small-scale capitalism still exists is naive self-deception.

## THE CORPORATE–FEDERAL COMPLEX

A second illusion, alternately indulged and protested by the free enterprise lobby, is that American business and government are independent entities, as constitutionally separate as church and state. Big business likes to have it both ways: it constantly denounces state intervention and pleads to 'get government off our backs', but when it succeeds in reducing taxation and intervention it simultaneously regrets it and demands government help and support. As far back as the Progressive Era, the big business corporations, far from opposing government intervention, actively supported the Interstate Commerce Commission, the Federal Reserve Board, and the labour regulation acts, to outwit smaller competitors and defeat interventionist local state governments. C. E. Perkins, President of the Chicago, Burlington and Quincy Railroad, believed that a federal board of commerce was a better buffer between the railroads and the public than leaving it to local politicians who sided with their constituents.[12] Big business and big government have coexisted ever since, and *laissez-faire* has always been more trumpeted than followed. The deregulations of the 1980s which led, for example, to the airline bankruptcies and the savings and loans scandals were followed by Chapter 11 bankruptcies (which enable a company to carry on business while deferring its debts), at the expense of their creditors and their employees' pension rights, and by multi-billion dollar bail-outs paid out of taxation. The end of the Cold War and the 'peace dividend' have evoked cries for government help from defence-dependent communities unable to make the transition to civil production by themselves.

American business and government are intimately intertwined and

31

exist in quasi-biological symbiosis. What President Eisenhower in his departing speech in 1961 famously called the 'military–industrial complex' is only the tip of an iceberg that floats down throughout the economy. It is a corporate–federal complex rather than merely a military–industrial one. Government contracts, not only for defence procurements but for a vast range of goods and services, from office supplies and electronic machinery to water control, school furniture and books, pharmaceuticals and vehicles, scientific and sociological research, legal and financial advice, and dealings in government debt, fuel a large part of the economy. Planned subsidies to agriculture, lumbering, rail-roads and other ailing industries, and unplanned subsidies like the $400 billion to the savings and loan industry and similar doles or loans to failing companies like Chrysler and Lockheed (in the 1970s) added still more. And most of the spending on infrastructure, from roads and air-ports to police and rescue services, is a direct, though justifiable, subvention to private industry.

As in other advanced countries, government has grown exponentially since the Second World War. Public expenditure as a proportion of GNP rose from 27.6 per cent in 1960 to 36.7 per cent in 1991, and government employment from 17.0 per cent of the employed population in 1951 to 18.3 per cent in 1981, not counting those indirectly employed on government contracts.[13] Despite the much trumpeted tax cuts under President Reagan (which along with the doubling of the defence budget inaugurated the record deficit), taxes on income (including the social security and medicare levies which have risen to more than a third of the total) have increased to pay for the expansion. Much of it comes back, it is true, to the domestic economy in the shape of salaries of government employees and transfer payments to pensioners and welfare beneficiaries, which together provided in 1981 42 per cent of primary incomes.[14] Altogether, government involvement in the economy is as great, indirectly if not directly, as in any country west of the old Iron Curtain.

Government is more intertwined than elsewhere with business in the United States through the constant interchange of personnel. While the civil service in most advanced societies is a permanent corps – even though, as in France and Japan, some bureaucrats may 'parachute down' into permanent private employment – in the United States the higher ranks are political appointments which change with every new administration, and sometimes more often.[15] At the top, government service is a revolving door, with officials coming and going between Washington and the head offices of corporations and major law firms every few years. Examples on the Republican side include George Schultz and Caspar Weinberger of Bectel, Donald Regan of Merril Lynch, John Lehman, Assistant Secretary of the Navy who resigned to become a consultant to McDonnel Douglas, and his assistant, Melvyn Paisley of Boeing. Democratic administrations tend to employ fewer corporate executives and more lawyers, lobbyists, and academics, like Warren Christopher, President Clinton's Secretary of State, Ron Brown, Secretary of Commerce, or Donna Shelala, Secretary for Health and Human Services. In this respect, lawyers and lobbyists are a well-heeled and well-connected segment of the corporate system; for example, Ron Brown commanded an income of half a million dollars as a lobbyist, while in 1987 1,318 partners of the largest law firms earned on average $739,000, within sight of the CEOs of the 800 largest corporations ($1,280,000).[16]

Elected politicians, too, have direct connections with big business. Some, like George Bush, Nelson Rockefeller and Edward Kennedy, are big business men in their own right. Others, like Richard Nixon, friend of Bebe Rebozo and Howard Hughes, and Senators David Boren of Oklahoma and Lloyd Bentsen of Texas, ex-Secretary of the Treasury, friends of the oil companies, have big business behind them. The connection, however, is more subtle: since corporate executives prefer to leave politics to those who are less serious than themselves about money and power, they habitually back both sides in the race so as to be sure to earn the gratitude of the winner. This happy relationship is as old as the corporations. The Senate was cartooned in 1893 with nine or ten fat, top-hatted 'trusts' telling the legislators how to vote.[17] Standard Oil funded both Republican and Democratic Senators. As Rockefeller's most senior director, Henry H. Rogers, told Ida Tarbell in 1902,

> We put our hands in our pockets and give them some good sums of money for campaign purposes and then when a bill comes up that is against our interests we go to the manager and say, 'There's such and such a bill up. We don't like it and we want you to take care of our interests.' That's the way everybody does it.[18]

Little has changed since then. George Bush's presidential election campaign in 1992 was supported by 'Team 100', a club of multi-millionaires chaired by former Secretary of Commerce Bob Mosbacher, but many of them also reinsured by supporting Bill Clinton. The finance house Goldman Sachs, for example, cheerfully funded both sides, to 'support the political process', they said, and 'in the hope that when we come to Washington they will remember us'.[19] What would be considered political corruption in many other countries is perfectly legal in the United States. With the cost of elections running into millions, even for Congressional seats, 'money politics', though channelled through Political Action Committees and direct funding of media advertisements, is even more blatant in America than in Japan, and the corporations have the most money.

33

## THE DANGERS OF INEQUALITY

Given the power of money in American politics, it is amazing that American democracy works as well as it does. This is partly because of the puritan strain in American culture and the moral condemnation of corruption when it comes to light – though, as in early New England, the condemnation is stronger than the deterrence. It is also partly due to the enlightened self-interest of the more intelligent corporate executives, who see that taxation, though deplorable, supports lucrative government contracts and welfare services that help to maintain a fit and healthy workforce and stave off political discontent. Unfortunately, not all executives are so intelligent, and in the cult of greed unleashed in the 1980s some of them behaved outrageously, grabbing all they could and letting the devil take the consequences. Between 1983 and 1988 the average compensation of the CEOs surveyed by *Business Week* more than doubled, from $900,000 to $2,025,000.[20] Irresponsible ideologues and practitioners like Michael Milken, Ivan Boesky, Martin Siegal and Dennis Levine told them that 'greed is good', and that the best CEO was the highest paid, however badly his company was doing.[21] The market would balance out all interests and, as Bernard Mandeville, Adam Smith's predecessor and the real godfather of conscienceless free enterprise, put it, 'private vices, public benefits'.[22]

In the consequent spending spree of the 1980s, fuelled by military Keynesianism and rising debt both public and private, the economy boomed artificially. Property values and stock market prices soared, and the rich got richer. The number of millionaires nearly trebled, from 574,000 in 1980 to 1.5 million in 1988, and that of billionaires doubled, from twenty-six to fifty-two. Average incomes of the top 1 per cent increased by three quarters, from $174,498 in 1977 to $303,900 in 1987, while their tax burden fell, from 30.9 per cent in 1977 to 23.1 per cent in 1984. This enabled the concentration of accumulated wealth to intensify: by 1983 the top one half of 1 per cent owned 27 per cent of national assets, the top 10 per cent owned 68 per cent.[23] Leaving aside convicted criminals like Ivan Boesky the inside trader, Michael Milken the junk bond dealer, and Charles Keating the savings and loans swindler, even the honest rich made a killing.

Meanwhile, average family incomes scarcely moved or, rather, declined in the early 1980s before recovering again: in 1986 dollars, from $30,025 in 1977 (and $30,820 in 1973) to $27,591 in the recession of 1982 and $30,853 in 1987. Since, with more women working, it now took more breadwinners to earn the family wage, income per worker actually fell, in fixed dollars from $318 per week in 1980 (and $376 in 1972) to $312 in 1987. Even allowing for the decline in family size, from 3.6 persons in 1970 to 3.2 in 1987, this meant that the rich really were richer and the poor poorer. As Kevin Phillips has shown, the ratio between the top quintile (20 per cent) and the bottom quintile around 1980 was already larger in the United States than in other advanced countries: in round terms twelve-fold, compared with ten-fold in Canada, nine-fold in France, eight-fold in Britain, five-fold in West Germany, and four-fold in Japan. Since then the American gap has widened still further. Between 1977 and 1987, in fixed (1987) dollars, only the top quintile had gained and all the rest had lost. Within that quintile, the top 1 per cent gained 49.8 per cent in average income, the top 5 per cent 23.4 per cent, the top 10 per cent 16.5 per cent, and the second decile (10–20 per cent) only 1 per cent. All the rest had lost income, from 1.8 per cent in the third decile (between the seventieth and eightieth percentiles) to a loss of 14.8 per cent in the bottom decile.[24]

Since Phillips reported, inequality has increased still further. According to the Census Bureau, from 1989 to 1993 the typical American household lost $2,344 in real annual income, a fall of 7 per cent. Practically all the rise in national income went to the top one fifth (with 48.2 per cent of national income against the bottom one fifth's 3.6 per cent), while the earnings of college educated workers stagnated, and the number of households in poverty (with less than $14,763 per annum at 1993 prices) increased from 13.1 per cent to 15.1 per cent. In other words, the average American family paid for the windfall gains of the rich, while the poorest families paid most of all. The 'liberated' free market meant free handouts for the rich paid for by the poor. As Robert B. Reich, Secretary for Labor, remarked, 'America has the most unequal distribution of income of any industrialized nation in the world'.[25]

Social justice is rejected as a concept and ruled out of court by the followers of Friedrich von Hayek and Milton Friedman, and unfairness is the least of the problems arising from inequality. Most societies since history began have been unequal and have learned to live with it. Those that did not, from the Roman to the Romanov empires, were fatally weakened by too much greed and exploitation. The danger does not lie in unfairness as such but in the deeper consequences of inequality when it becomes too extreme. Karl Marx warned against 'the contradictions of capitalism': when the capitalists take too much 'surplus value' the workers are unable to buy the produce of their labour and the economic system breaks down. Ironically, he failed to warn against the 'contradictions of communism', and, a century after his death, too much exploitation in the Soviet Union and Eastern Europe led inexorably to system collapse.

Yet, *pace* the triumphalist right wing, the defeat of communism does not prove that capitalism, especially in its corporate form, is immune to the same disease. *Any* society in which inequality reaches the extremes of exploitation is vulnerable to self-destruction. At whatever level of production, if the ruling elites who control the flows of income either through the public or the private sectors or both, take more than a sustainable share of the society's resources, the system becomes increasingly unstable, and finally implodes. First of all, the very perception of unfairness has political consequences, through the politics of envy which produces rising discontent with authority, burgeoning crime, riots, looting, and local 'rebellions', whether or not these are recognized as such. It is no coincidence that the advanced country with the largest gap between rich and poor already has the highest crime rates, the most violence, and the biggest incidence of inner city riots. Much more important, however, are the economic consequences: rising unemployment of both labour and capital, a spate of bankruptcies and liquidations, record debt both public and private, a fall in the rate of economic growth compared with competing countries, and ultimately incurable depression and economic decline. We have already seen this happen in the Soviet Union and its ex-colonies. Could it happen in the United States?

It very nearly happened in the inter-war period. After the politics of greed of the 'roaring twenties' – so like the roaring eighties – the Crash of 1929 brought on the Great Depression in which by 1933 GNP was cut by a third and one in every four Americans was unemployed. The country was kept afloat by the New Deal and saved by rearmament for the anti-fascist free world and the Second World War. Since then, what John Kenneth Galbraith has called *The Culture of Contentment*, the appeasement of the middle class by rising prosperity, their share of the benefits of the welfare state (which in pensions, public education, and the like is far greater than the share of the so-called welfare dependants), and a sense of superiority to the underclass, has kept the middle class – i.e. the middle 60 per cent of the population, unlike in Europe where it means the 25–30 per cent just below the very rich – reasonably happy with the system, persuaded by cynical politicians to blame a discontented and racially skewed underclass for the high taxation the politicians themselves have caused.[26]

## STRUCTURAL CHANGE AND THE EXPORT OF JOBS

No doubt the culture of complacency could go on for ever, if the underlying economic structure could be maintained intact and middle-class incomes kept rising. What has happened in the last few years, however, is a fundamental change in the structure, exacerbated by the politics of greed unleashed in the 1980s, but principally due to the logic of the corporate structure of the expanding global economy. By this logic, national economies like the United States can be insidiously undermined by the profit-seeking operations of the corporations. The short-sighted pursuit of self-interest urged on by the free-marketeers of the

Reagan–Bush years has merely brought nemesis much nearer.[27] The threat lies in the structural shift in American business which is reducing manufacturing and moving its centre of gravity overseas. The consequent loss of well-paid jobs for American skilled workers is inadequately compensated by the growth of low-paid unskilled jobs in the service sector, and the expansion of no longer secure employment for the highly paid 'Yuppies' of the financial and professional service sector. Between 1970 and 1990 imports of manufactured goods went from 11.4 per cent of value added in manufacturing to about 40 per cent. This was only partly compensated for by an increase in manufactured exports, from 12.5 per cent of value added to 31 per cent. Yet the trend is undeniable: American employment in manufacturing shrank between 1970 and 1990 from 27.3 per cent of the occupied population to 17.4 per cent. Between a quarter and a third of this decline was due to the export of jobs overseas, the rest to 'downsizing', partly by labour-saving productivity but also by off-loading high-paid work to low-paid subcontractors.[28] Between 1960 and 1986 the proportion of manufactured imports to every $100 of domestic manufactures increased from $14 to $45. More than half the value was not in finished products but in parts, design, engineering, financial and other services, and most of this in turn was traded *within* corporations, including foreign multinationals, but in large part imports from American foreign affiliates operating overseas. According to one estimate, no less than 72 per cent of imports occurred within global corporations.[29] While American employment benefited from British, Japanese and other direct investment, and some downsizing of domestic operations was due to labour-saving technology, much of the loss of American jobs was due to the relocation of American production overseas.

Free market economists argue that the export of jobs is a myth and that most of the output of American overseas subsidiaries is sold abroad.[30] But this takes little account of the import of parts and materials within multinationals, and does not allow for the loss of American jobs in industries which might have supplied those exports. Whatever the cause, the result is a shift from well-paid skilled work to low-paid, low-grade service employment: 11.4 million of the 12 million jobs created between 1981 and 1987 were in services, more than half of these in 'poverty services' (retail trade, personal services, domestic service, and the like) and construction, trucking, and wholesale distribution.[31]

This structural shift, the well-known movement of the employed population with economic growth from agriculture and manufacturing to services, has gone further in the United States than in any other country: from 58 per cent in services in 1960 to 72 per cent in 1991.[32] Most services are not the high-grade, high-paid, professional occupations of sociological imagination but low-grade, low-paid, unskilled work such as fast-food and other retail selling, garbage collection, taxi driving and mass transit, and the like. The significant aspect of this restructuring has been analysed by Robert B. Reich, whose book entitled *The Work of Nations* demonstrates the emergence of three broad categories of work: *routine production*, which can be exported anywhere in the world where raw materials and parts can be obtained or assembled at whatever wages; *in-person services*, like transportation and retail distribution, which can only be provided on the spot, usually at low pay; and what he calls *symbolic–analytic services*, the highly-skilled, highly-paid work of applying, manipulating, and transmitting information in all its manifold forms, from medical, legal, and educational advice to technology, design, and finance, to corporate management and government administration.[33] This distribution was confirmed by a Labor Department survey in 1994, which showed that, while unemployment has continued in the 1980s and 1990s for the under-educated, managers and professionals have taken two thirds of the new jobs, and while average pay rose by 2.5 per cent between 1990 and 1994, managers' and supervisors' salaries rose at nearly twice that rate, leaving average pay for production and non-supervisory workers continuing to fall.[34]

The United States has always led the way in the globalization of the economy, beginning with the offshore factories of Ford and General Motors in Britain and elsewhere before the First World War. The trend was intensified after the Second World War, when Marshall Aid and the strong dollar enabled American corporations to invest heavily in most of the allied countries. American investment in physical assets overseas grew from $11.8 billion in 1950 to $75.5 billion in 1970. Since then it has soared, to $213.5 billion in 1980, and is still growing. In consequence, while the American share of world exports fell between 1957 and 1983 from 21 per cent to 14 per cent, the share of American affiliates abroad grew from 6 per cent to 10 per cent. A third of the revenues and profits of the 200 largest American corporations came from overseas operations, often as in the case of Ford and Chrysler offsetting domestic losses. In the development of the 'global factory' made possible by modern transport and telecommunications, the United States has gone furthest of all.[35]

Other countries are engaged in the same development, but with the exception of Britain have not used it to oppress labour. The American and British governments have conducted a relentless campaign against the trade unions, passing laws to reduce the rights of workers to strike or even to organize, deregulating industrial controls, downplaying health and safety inspection, and breaking strikes, like that of the air traffic controllers under Reagan and the coal miners under Thatcher, in the public sector. In part this is a consequence of the structure of American and British business, in which the corporation is owned exclusively by the shareholders and can ignore the other stakeholders, the workers and creditors and even, except through indirect market pressure, the customers. The aim of the game is not long-term growth and investment in future products but short-term profits, to reward shareholders and top managers, and to keep up the stock exchange value of the company shares so as to fight off takeover bids and corporate raids. Instead of continuous innovation for the benefit of all stakeholders, including workers and consumers, the management must look to the next balance sheet and even to the next day's share price. As the late Akio Morita of Sony pointed out, 'The United States looks ten minutes ahead while Japan looks ten years ahead';[36] that is, while Japanese companies have a time-horizon of ten years, during which they expect to introduce a series of new, improved, and cheaper products, American (and British) companies have a time-horizon of ten minutes, the time it takes to register a fall on the stock exchange computers. The result, both of the export of jobs and of falling investment, is what Morita called the 'hollowing of American industry', the shift from making goods at home to receiving profits made elsewhere: 'The US is abandoning its status as an industrial power.'[37]

Reich rightly sees this development as a threat to the blue-collar working class, the backbone of the old social and political structure, who are in danger of 'proletarianization' as they are replaced by low-paid workers overseas and robots at home and pushed down into the un-skilled underclass. This is the end of the 'American dream' which has sustained wave after wave of immigrants, from the Southern and Eastern Europeans of the late nineteenth century, to the Hispanics and Asians of the late twentieth, and has been the best hope for African-Americans of rising out of the ghetto.

The threat is not confined to manufacturing. Because of the speed-of-light telecommunications that are making information instantly available throughout the world, not all the symbolic–analytic work can be kept in the United States. Some information analysis and processing is already being exported overseas: software design to Britain, Ireland and even to Malaysia and the Philippines, credit card and airline ticket handling to India and the West Indies, banking services to Switzerland, Luxembourg, and the Cayman Islands, wherever there are English-speaking white-collar workers of sufficient education. As Sumil Tagore of Kessler Marketing Intelligence of Newport, Rhode Island, noted in 1989: 'Thousands of jobs will be lost. When you send data to Asia or South America you don't know how many people are being displaced in New York or Texas.'[38] No doubt the head office can remain at home, but there is no reason why high-grade symbolic–analytic services should remain in a country without a strong manufacturing and goods-exporting base, however fine its higher education, when the same work can be done more cheaply nearer the industry which it services. Reich points out that by 1990 only 20 per cent of the value of computers was in the hardware and 80 per cent in the software, but the users are likely to take their software from the company or its suppliers that make the machines.[39] Invisible exports have always ridden on the back of a strong visible exporting economy. Margaret Thatcher's belief that the City of London's financial services and invisible exports would compensate for the decline in Britain's manufacturing base has proven to be a tragic illusion: the net balance on invisible trade is no more than 1 per cent. The American economy is currently in danger of going the same way.

It may go faster if the free-marketeers have their way, and use the threat of exporting jobs and capital to put still more pressure on labour's share of the returns from industry. Unlike most West European countries (excluding Britain) and Japan, which have tried to beat the profit squeeze of the 1970s and 1980s by cooperating with labour to invest in productivity-raising technology, American corporations have chosen to make labour the scapegoat for the crisis and have used the recession and the weakness of the trades unions to reduce wages, speed up work flows, downsize the full-time workforce, and introduce contingent, part-time and subcontract workers doing the same work at lower wages. The 'casino society' has waged a 'one-sided class war' to increase profits by forcing down the cost of labour, a strategy which began with the blue-collar workers in the old mass-production industries but is now affecting the white-collar workers and middle managers of the traditional middle class. Instead of reducing costs by investing in labour-intensive technology to increase the total pie, big business chose, in the words of Arnold Weber, Assistant Secretary for Labor under President Nixon, to 'zap labor'.[40] As a strategy for short-term profitability this succeeded in the 1980s but in the long term it is self-destructive. Henry Ford in 1913 doubled his workers' wages to $5 a day, in the shrewd belief that they would then be able to buy his cars. His present-day successors in the big corporations are doing the reverse, cutting wages or firing workers without a thought for where tomorrow's customers will find the money to buy their products. Such a strategy is a formula for their own and their nation's decline.

## THE THREAT OF DECLINE

To what extent is the United States vulnerable to the threat of economic implosion that has already destroyed the communist regimes in Soviet Russia and Eastern Europe? Right-wing triumphalists like Francis Fukuyama, Joseph Nye and Henry Nau may believe that America is assured of permanent supremacy, and that it won the Cold War because the Reagan strategy of turning up the heat in the arms race forced the Soviets to spend themselves into bankruptcy and stretched the communist system to breaking point.[41] The reality is that the Soviet regime was already destroying itself long before Star Wars increased the strain, if indeed it did. (The Soviets almost certainly knew that the Star Wars evidence was faked, and that incoming missiles in the tests were designed to self-destruct.) The *nomenklatura* threw themselves into an orgy of corruption and self-indulgence at the expense of the mass of people living at Spartan levels of consumption. The result, as we shall see in Chapter 6, was a crisis of political legitimacy that Gorbachev was unable to solve by half-hearted reforms that failed to stop the corruption, even under his successors. The lesson is that greed is ultimately self-destructive and topples the elites that practise it.

Could the United States go the same way? That depends on how enlightened the self-interest of the managing corporate elites will be. Nothing in their behaviour in recent years suggests that they will halt their rake's progress towards heedless self-destruction. Their downsizing and export of jobs, both blue- and white-collar, thus hollowing out some States-side corporations to mere head-office shells, is only the start of the primrose path. James Champy, the business school guru who persuaded corporations in the 1980s to increase profits by firing labour, including middle managers, and outsourcing production to subcontractors and consultants on lower pay and conditions, has now admitted that it was all a mistake, and that those companies which took his advice have proved to be less profitable than those which did not.[42]

More symptomatic is the trend for top executives to pay themselves ludicrously gigantic rewards. Graef S. Crystal and Robert A. G. Monks, both former consultants on executive compensation, were so appalled by the greed and selfishness they were asked to endorse – if they did not do so they were fired – that they have started a movement for reform.[43] They found that CEOs commonly choose members of the board from among their friends, ply them with rewards and privileges from lavish fees to 'golden parachutes' (huge compensations for loss of office), and then ask them to fix the CEOs' remuneration packages. Says Monks, 'In 1989, the average CEO at the largest 200 American companies received $2.8 million in salary and bonuses, in addition to lucrative pension and insurance packages.'[44] Some, like Stephen Wolf of United Airlines, Robert Stempel of General Motors, and James Robinson III of American Express, took home millions more, not only in salary and benefits but in stock options which could give them huge gains if activated at the right time. Steven J. Ross of Time–Warner, for example, gained in all $64 million dollars from payouts of restricted stock over seventeen years, adding an average of $3.8 million a year to his already substantial remuneration.[45] And they did not have to earn these 'incentive rewards': in 1989 the CEOs of Manufacturers Hanover Trust, Borden, Phillips Petroleum, General Dynamics, Tenneco, Amoco, and Caterpillar all received fat increases despite a drop in their companies' profits. On average, CEOs' compensation more than trebled between 1977 and 1987, twice the rate of inflation, and their marginal tax rate fell from 50 per cent to 28 per cent, while profits stagnated (i.e. fell by a third in real terms), and hourly wages for their workers lagged behind inflation.[46] To quote a Japanese critic, 'Lee Iacocca, chairman of Chrysler Corporation and a cheer-leader of the Japan bashers ... typifies that irresponsible breed of American executives who have become fabulously wealthy on the backs of American workers.'[47] Whereas, according to Kevin Phillips, CEOs' compensation in 1979 averaged twenty-nine times that of the average manufacturing worker, by 1988 it averaged no less than ninety-three times.[48] A structure of rewards that overpays corporate executives to lose money while paying their workers and potential customers less is a recipe for industrial decline.

The greed and irresponsibility of the 1980s are now provoking a back-lash. Monks and Crystal and a large lobby of influential critics from business itself, including Anne Hansen of the Council of Institutional Investors, Ira Millstein, the corporate lawyer who helped topple Stempel of General Motors, and Ralph Whitworth of United Shareholders, are beginning to force corporations which lose money to fire incompetent executives and restructure their boards.[49] Their remedies include hiring genuinely independent non-executive directors who are not beholden to the CEO and can rein in his extravagances; more active institutional share-holders from the banks, mutual funds, insurance companies, and pension funds which own the bulk of the equity and can insist on putting dividends before executive compensation; the abolition of 'poison pills' by which the managers can activate 'rights plans' to defeat hostile takeover bids; and the restoration of shareholders' control over managerial pay, perquisites, pensions, 'golden parachutes', and the like. The proposed reforms fall far short of, say, the German system of 'co-determination', which gives some power to the other stakeholders, the employees, the bankers and long-term creditors, but they are meant to be a start towards ending the complete irresponsibility of CEOs and their cronies. It is doubtful, however, whether the institutional managers who control most of the equity in the big corporations see a long-term interest in fundamentally changing the system of executive pay.

## CORPORATE NEO-FEUDALISM

In keeping with the American principle of individual property rights, the reformers are attempting to put control back 'where it belongs', in the hands of the shareholders, to reunite ownership and control whose separation Berle and Means observed as early as 1932.[50] It is, unfortun-ately, a forlorn hope, since under corporate capitalism this is simply to transfer control from one layer of corporations to the next tier of financial institutions. They have an interest in enlarging company dividends at the expense of managerial rewards in the corporations they partly own, but their managers are just as deeply embedded in the culture of executive self-interest as those they theoretically control. To ask them to discipline the system is like asking mafia godfathers to rein in the underlings who produce their 'tribute'.

At the heart of the problem is the fragmentation of property under Anglo–American corporate capitalism. By a species of 'subinfeudation', similar to the feudal disintegration in the wake of the crumbling Roman empire, ownership has been split up into multiple layers of 'owners', who are in effect claimants on some part of the flow of income from the property. In the same way that ownership after the Norman Conquest was fragmented and fractionally delegated by the king to his barons, by them to their knights, and by the latter in turn to the actual tillers of the soil who supplied the food and services upon which all claimants lived, so under modern capitalism as it is practised in the most advanced countries of the West, above all in Britain and America, the corporate structure has fragmented the flow of income upwards and downwards to a host of claimants, each of whom gets a share in return for contingent services to those above and below them in the hierarchy. The investment institutions are the dukes and earls, the corporations the barons, the divisions and subsidiaries the knights, the subcontractors and franchisees the squires and yeomen, and the workers the peasants or peons of the system. In the same way, property at each level is contingent, not absolute, and the flow of income is dependent upon the service rendered by each participant.

There are endless examples of this sort of structure in almost every industry in the United States, and some, like the nineteen giant 'conglomerates' identified by Chandler, across several industries. Its construction began in the nineteenth century, with the famous oligopolies in the oil industry exposed by Henry Demarest Lloyd and Ida M. Tarbell and the 'muckrakers' of the Progressive Era, and the dozen or more trusts in sugar, beef, coal, iron, steel, tin, copper, and so on, accused of monopolizing their industries at the turn of the century.[51] The movement reached an early peak in the great merger wave of banks, oil pipelines, railroads, and steamship lines, which culminated in the Morgan–Rockefeller 'Money Trust' investigated by the Pujo Committee in 1913.[52] J. P. Morgan had helped to construct or reorganize many of the large corporations, including U. S. Steel (1901), International Harvester (1902), and A.T.& T. (1906), and the connections between the investing institutions were already well-established. Public utilities were natural monopolies within their regions, and Samuel Insull of Commonwealth Edison, for example, chairman of about seventy companies and director of seventy more, owned a personal fortune of $150 million but controlled capital, mainly in electric supply companies, of $3 billion.[53] E. I. Du Pont de Nemours bought out, took over or simply squeezed out of business hundreds of black powder firms and agencies, and then went on to develop banks and chemical, artificial leather, plastic, dyestuffs, and rayon divisions, finally taking over General Motors with Pierre Du Pont as CEO, before handing over to Alfred P. Sloane, who made General Motors the biggest company in the world.[54]

Long before the Second World War, most of the great corporations of today were already in existence and cooperating to carve up the market and dominate the American economy. They had become so large and powerful that governments could not allow them to fail, however badly managed. Lee Iacocca, chairman of the near-bankrupt Chrysler company, asking for a government loan of $1.2 billion, told a Congressional Committee in 1979 that they had a no-win choice: 'You can pay now or pay later.' Since the Labor Department estimated that a Chrysler failure would result in a loss of 300,000 jobs, an increase from 9 to 16 per cent in unemployment in the Detroit area, a $1.5 billion increase in welfare payments, and a fall of 1.5 per cent in national GNP, the government paid up.[55]

The law in Britain and America has not kept up with this transformation. Whereas in Germany, Japan, France, and elsewhere, some account has been taken by the law of the claims of employees and consumers as well as shareholders, in the United States and its common law parent Britain, where the theory of absolute property originated and still dominates people's minds, every object must have a single identifiable owner, and the corporation belongs to the shareholders and to no one else. In practice, of course, this means that ownership is like the Cheshire cat in *Alice in Wonderland*: it disappears as soon as you question it. It is this indeterminacy that gives the people in physical possession, the corporate executives, the power to do as they like with the other claimants' property. Transferring their freedom to make hay upwards to the next tier of institutional managers in the banks, insurance companies and pension funds is no remedy for the problem.

Corporate neo-feudalism is more complicated than that, however. There are two aspects to it, intra-national and international. Internally to each national economy, the corporation is like the trunk of a huge tree. Upwards from it radiates a topgrowth of investing institutions and individuals which it must nourish with profits and dividends, mostly whole branches in the shape of holding companies, financial bodies, insurance companies, mutual funds, pension funds, and the like, which in turn nourish thousands of leaves and twiglets, the individual investors, shareholders, and pensioners. Downwards it has roots that nourish it, its own divisions, subsidiaries, subcontractors, sales outlets and franchisees, whose workers produce the goods and services that instigate the income flow. If the roots and branches work together, the whole tree flourishes. But if any part of it demands more than its share of nourishment, the flows are distorted and the tree begins to shrivel up and die. In the American case some trunks have become greedy and bloated and in danger of cancerous decay. There are, of course, many trees, and they are interlinked like the canopy and root system of a tropical forest. In the life cycle of the forest, many trees fall and rot away and are replaced by new growth just as strong as the old. TWA and Pan-American Airlines decline, and Steve Jobs and Steve Wozniak create Apple Computers and Bill Gates Microsoft, even bigger giants. It is difficult to tell at any one time whether the forest as a whole is healthy and expanding or sickly and declining, still more how it is faring compared with others in competing regions. Its survival may depend on factors outside its influence, on the national and global climate as well as on its own creative or destructive efforts.

Globally, the forests of corporate neo-feudalism are spreading and becoming intertwined. Chandler identified some 401 multinational corporations, each with over 20,000 employees in 1973, which dominated the world economy. Of these, more than half, 211, were headquartered in the United States. In industry after industry – food, tobacco, textiles, apparel, lumber, paper, oil, rubber, chemicals, leather, machinery, transportation equipment, instruments – America led with half or nearly half the world's largest corporations. Twenty years later, according to the United Nations *World Investment Report, 1994*, twenty-nine of the 100 largest multinationals and 157 of the top 500 were headquartered in the United States. Increasingly, however, most of their employees work not in the United States but in plants and offices scattered around the world, from Europe to the Pacific Rim, from Latin America to South Asia, and now even in Russia and Eastern Europe.[56]

This, Chandler would argue, is no threat to the American people. The profits, larger because of cheap land, labour and materials overseas, come back to the United States and add to its GNP. Others point to the investment of British, European, Japanese, and other foreign capital in car plants, oil companies, hotels, and retail stores in the United States, to prove that the global economy works both ways, bringing in jobs as well as export them. This is true, but demonstrates another aspect of the global economy: because of the competition by governments, both local and national, to bring in foreign investment, offering free land, infrastructure, and tax breaks to the incomers, it now pays the corporations to invest anywhere but at home. They go wherever costs, especially wages and taxes, are low, including the more depressed and union-free areas of the United States. The aim is to get inside the domestic market in case it closes, and imported parts and exported profits ensure that the corporate headquarters get the gains, not the producing areas overseas. That the exchange for the American people as distinct from the corporations is increasingly unequal, however, can be seen from the balance of pay-ments, which runs steadily against the United States. Nevertheless, to adapt the cynical *bon mot* of Charles Wilson of General Motors in the 1950s, what is good for the multinationals is good for America, and vice versa, a proposition which some critics, like that unlikely pair of allies Ross Perrot and Ralph Nader, are beginning to deny.

If it were true, then the loss of skilled manufacturing jobs and the consequent unemployment and shift to low-paying, unskilled services would simply be the price the country would have to pay for progress and prosperity. In fact, however, the cost is much greater than that and may ultimately be suicidal. The current record trade deficit – 63 per cent of GNP in 1992 – has little to do with the Japanese, who import more American goods per head than Americans do Japanese goods, but is overwhelmingly due to the import of goods made by American com-panies overseas. The deficit is not in itself lethal, at least in the short run, but is a symptom of the erosion of the manufacturing base which, if not remedied, will in time undermine America's ability to pay its way. Although the American economy is still the largest and most productive in the world, the rate of economic growth has been falling ever since the immediate post-war years. From an annual average of 4.5 per cent in the 1940s and 4.0 per cent in the 1950s and 1960s, it has slid to 2.8 and 2.7 per cent in the 1970s and 1980s, and to less than 1 per cent in the early 1990s (and a fall of 0.5 per cent in 1991).[57] Growth rates have been falling all over the world since the oil crises of the 1970s, but until recently were still ahead of the American ones. The American economy in 1960–90 grew by 1.7 per cent a year, compared with 2.0 per cent for Britain, 2.4 per cent for France and (West) Germany, 3.0 per cent for Italy, and 4.1 per cent for Japan.[58] *The Economist* has pointed out that a persistent lag of 1 per cent per annum was enough to cause Britain's decline from a world superpower to a second-rate European state.[59] Hence, despite 'victory' in the Cold War, the fierce debate over the possibility of America's decline from superpower status.[60]

The result, more important for the ordinary American than playing world policeman, would be declining real incomes and falling pur-chasing power for all goods and services, whether produced at home or overseas. This would hit first – it is already hitting – the most vulnerable people, the poor and the minorities, leading to rising crime, drug use, political protest, inner city riots, and disillusion with the ability of govern-ment to cope with social problems like rising welfare costs and urban decay, but it would not stop there. Already the middle class feels threat-ened by its declining prosperity,[61] still more by the lack of jobs for its expensively educated children, who no longer believe that they will be as affluent as their parents. For the first time in two centuries, the American dream is felt to be beyond the reach of a majority of the population.

The irony is that, in the Congressional elections of 1994, some of them – although less than one in five of the adult population – appear to have turned to the very people, the Republican clients of big business, who have brought them to this pass.

## THE IRRESPONSIBLE ELITE

If the United States does decline – not absolutely but, as with Britain, relative to faster growing countries – then the fault will lie squarely with the managers of the great corporations and their allies in government. They are directly responsible in two ways. First, they have allowed their leadership to slip, like British companies before them, not so much in inventiveness in which they often still lead, but in innovation, the application of new technology to domestic production, and consequently in productivity. The only manufacturing industries in which the United States still leads in world exports are aircraft, armaments, chemicals and, it is now claimed, in the recovery in electronics connected with the 'superhighway'. Second, they have exported both the new technology and the capital and jobs to support it overseas to cheap-labour, low-tax countries, thus creating domestic depression, unemployment, bankruptcies of satellite firms, and adding to the trade deficit. Unfortunately, while causing the problems and difficulties of the threatening crisis, they are responsible only to themselves, which means that they are in the strictest sense irresponsible: with their oligopolistic control over the market and their hegemonic influence with government, they cannot be held to account for the consequences of their actions. Only when the United States economy finally declines will they pay the price of failure.

Paradoxically, the more successful the American multinationals, the more likely they are to undermine the American economy and, ultimately, American political and military power. The free marketeers argue that this does not matter: the market will supply American consumers with the best available goods at the cheapest world prices. But if the trend continues, the American consumer will no longer have the purchasing power to buy the goods, wherever they are made, and the weak dollar inexorably produced by the deficit (unless it is kept strong by high interest rates, which discourage investment) will ensure that those goods are beyond the reach of the average American. Then the professional managers of the great corporations will regret, too late, that they have destroyed the goose and lost its golden eggs.

The United States is the classic home of the professional society on the free market model. It is also the classic victim of the characteristic pathology of that model. The free market, as we have seen, means freedom principally for the professional executives of the great corporations.

Although many of them have behaved with admirable restraint, an increasing number in the last twenty years have been tempted into the besetting sin of power without responsibility: *carpe diem*, short-term acquisitiveness, unenlightened self-interest, and self-destructive greed. They have excuses for their behaviour: the reluctance of government to rein them in, partly out of belief in the naive version of the free-market ideology preached by the media and the politicians funded by big business, more out of fear of electors gulled by those politicians; the structure of corporate property which imputes ownership to anonymous and remote shareholders whose only interest lies in short-term dividends, thus leading corporate managers to pursue short-term investment policies; the absurd belief that American companies are burdened with higher taxes and larger welfare benefits than their competitors;[62] above all, the power and influence of the corporate lobbies, which preach a creed appropriate to the small business world of Adam Smith and the American founding fathers but utterly irrelevant to a world in which a few hundred multinationals dominate the global economy.

Such excuses are no substitute for remedial action. Americans can choose between freedom for corporate managers and freedom for themselves. Government should not do for its citizens what they can best do for themselves, but it must set the rules of the game and force the most powerful players to play by them. The corporations are the overmighty subjects of the neo-feudal system of post-industrial capitalism. That system has been enormously productive and beneficial for the majority of the people, nowhere more so than in the United States. It would be a tragedy if the new feudal lords, the top professional managers of the great corporations, should overwhelm the most creative and, until recently, the most successful of professional societies, and bring it and themselves to decline, if not to entropy.

# 3

# BRITAIN
## Keystone of the arch

Britain is, or was, the keystone of the great arch that stretches from the most free-market oriented to the most state-centralized of the post-industrial societies. It has, or had before the privatizations of the Thatcher era, the most balanced mixed economy, a pioneering welfare state and one of the most concentrated business sectors in the free world. In Europe, if indeed not in the world, it led the way in most of the major trends of professional society: in the rise of living standards until the mid-1960s, the swing to services, the rise of professional hierarchies in both public and private sectors, a modest degree of meritocracy with more upward mobility from the working class than in most countries west of the Iron Curtain, the legal emancipation of women, the growth of government and the welfare state, the opening of higher education to a wider section of the population, the concentration of business in large corporations, and a long-standing involvement in the global economy. Yet it is idiosyncratic in its professionalism, curiously backward in the rivalry between its public and private sectors, still class-conscious in its politics and industrial relations, the slowest growing of Western economies, and the least successful of the major democratic post-industrial societies.

This is all the more surprising since Britain was the undisputed pioneer of the second great social revolution, the Industrial Revolution of the eighteenth and nineteenth centuries, and was the model that rival nations followed closely in their bid for economic growth and political and military power. Many historians now question whether that great transition was revolutionary at all since it took more than a century to transform Britain and nearer two to migrate to the rest of the now developed world. They argue that it took too long to deserve the name of revolution, that it was part of a slow, gradual, and continuous evolution in which no dramatic spurt of economic growth can be discerned in the statistics, and that the Victorian economy still contained large elements of the traditional domestic and small workshop type, horsedrawn transport and sailing ships alongside the new factories, railways, and

49

steamships.[1] But this profoundly underestimates the enormous change in history introduced by the second social revolution, which transformed the whole scale and level of human existence. It is based on an econometric approach to social development which has inbuilt limitations.

## THE MYOPIA OF CLIOMETRICS

The econometric or 'cliometric' approach has its uses, in deconstructing the elements and processes of economic growth, but it has explanatory limits when applied to the way major developments have always emerged in human society. They first appear like embryos, then newborn babies, toddlers, children and adolescents, before growing into giants and replacing their parents. Statistics of economic growth, like all statistical averages, gravitate to the mean, and muffle new developments under a blanket of older productions, which disguise the new until it is too massive to be neglected. In later Industrial Revolutions, particularly in Germany, Russia and Japan, Gerschenkron's concept of the dual economy is invoked to compensate for this numerical myopia, and the growth of the modern sector is treated separately from the torpid evolution of the traditional economy.[2] That concept has not normally been applied to the British Industrial Revolution, where it is every bit as valid: the modern sector in textiles, pottery, brewing, and iron manufacture is swamped in the econometric statistics by the sluggish growth of agriculture and the traditional crafts. As Joel Mokyr has pointed out, while economic change was slow and gradual, 'the Industrial Revolution as a clustering of technological changes in a wide array of industries in a short period was as violent and sudden as Gibbens and Toynbee thought'.[3] Its effects on society were even more dramatic.

In the long perspective of history, the Industrial Revolution which began in Britain two centuries ago is still the second major turning point in the history of mankind. It was:

> a rise in human productivity, on such a scale that it raised, as it were the logarithmic index of society, that is, it increased by a multiple (rather than a fraction) both the number of human beings which a given area of land would support, and their standard of life, or consumption of goods and services ... Such a rise in scale required, involved and implied drastic changes in society itself: in the size and distribution of the population, in its social structure and organization, and in the political and administrative superstructure which they demanded and supported. It was in brief a social revolution: a revolution in social organization, with social causes as well as social effects.[4]

It would be perverse to argue that the revolution that transformed the whole world failed to do the same for the country where it began. During the nineteenth century British production of goods and services increased sixteen-fold, while the population increased nearly four-fold, thus raising the average standard of living more than four-fold. The urban population grew from about a fifth, mostly in tiny towns by modern standards, to four fifths, mostly in large towns and cities, and the old pre-industrial society of ranks and orders was replaced by a new class society in which nationwide groups competed for a share of the national income through organized industrial and political conflict. The conflict, violent at first, gradually came to be channelled through class institutions, trade unions, employers' associations, political parties, and pressure groups, to create a viable class society in which the competing groups recognized each other's right to bargain. However slow and gradual the statistical economic growth, the aggregate change was dramatic and empowering enough to persuade other countries, notably the United States, Germany, France, Russia, and Japan, to envy and emulate Britain. Since then the second social revolution has spread with accelerating speed around the whole world.

## LOST LEADERSHIP IN THE THIRD REVOLUTION

Given its head start, it is not surprising that Britain was one of the pioneers of the third great social revolution, in all ten major trends. What is surprising is that it lost its place among the leaders so quickly. As Sidney Pollard has remarked,

the only economic miracle was the British failure to take part in the progress of the rest of the world. Surely it must have required a powerful and sustained effort, or most unusual circumstances, to prevent the world boom from spilling over into Britain as well.[5]

At the end of the Second World War Britain seemed to be in the second best position, after the United States, to take the lead in world trade. With all other rivals devastated by the war, its pharmaceutical and modern high-tech industries such as cars and television all booming, its export trade surged to heights unseen since 1914, and its economic growth accelerated to rates never seen before, even at the height of the Industrial Revolution, 3 to 4 per cent a year in the first decade or so. Despite the post-war austerity, living standards in 1950 were already higher than in any other major country save the United States, and they rose to heights of prosperity unknown to the British people before.

Yet in relative terms it was not to last. With rival economies growing still faster – in the long boom between 1953 and 1973 Britain's 3.0 per cent per annum was outclassed by France's 5.3 per cent, Germany's 5.5 per cent, and Japan's 8.0 per cent – the British standard of living was overtaken in the mid-1960s by most of Western Europe and in the mid-1970s by Japan.[6] Britain's share of world manufacturing exports fell steadily from 25.5 per cent in 1950 to 16.5 per cent in 1960, 10.8 per cent in 1970, 9.7 per cent in 1980, and to 8.0 per cent by 1983.[7] All power and wealth are relative and, though Britain was in absolute terms richer than ever before, such statistics lie behind the decline of British power, the withdrawal from east of Suez, the break-up of the Empire, and retreat into Europe. By the 1990s Britain was a medium-sized member of the European Community, with national income per head below all but four of the member states: Ireland, Spain, Portugal and Greece.

In the swing from agriculture and industry to services Britain was second only to the United States, with nearly half the workforce by 1960 in services, and 70 per cent by 1991.[8] By no means all of these were Robert Reich's 'symbolic analysts', professional experts and the like; many of them were low-paid manual workers such as truck drivers, street cleaners and fast-food sellers, while most of the white-collar workers were women office workers, shop assistants, and lesser professionals like nurses and schoolteachers. Nevertheless, a growing number were high-paid professionals: doctors, lawyers, accountants, engineers, research scientists, academics, computer programmers, media workers, and civil servants and company managers. By 1971 professionals outnumbered 'employers and proprietors', 5.1 per cent of the male workforce, at 10.8 per cent; 'managers and administrators' were 10.9 per cent. Together, professionals in the broad sense outnumbered the old entrepreneurial class by four to one.[9] At the same time, the very term business man no longer meant the old-fashioned small enterprise owner but the employed company manager who usually earned far more. As the scale of corporations continued to rise and the professional managers' power with it, managerial rewards rose accordingly to astronomical heights, and the rivalry between these private sector professionals and the public sector ones became increasingly strident until it became the main issue in British politics.

This rivalry occurred in other countries and was perhaps the most striking effect of the restructuring of society into professional hierarchies, each competing for a larger share of the national income and/or the government budget, but nowhere was it so stark as in Britain. There the main cleavage between the political parties was their opposed attitudes to taxation and public spending. The Conservatives with their base in the private sector demanded lower taxes and less public expenditure (except of course for government contracts for defence, road construction, nuclear power, and other lucrative projects). The Labour Party, with many leading members either in the public sector or not-for-profit organizations like the trades unions and the universities, wanted more public spending on welfare, education, health, and the environment and less on defence and nuclear warfare. The problem was that these issues came to intermingle with and perpetuate the old class warfare between employers and trades unions and intensified the bitterness of industrial relations and class-based politics.[10] As we shall see, the survival of class conflict, reinforced rather than replaced by public/private sector professional rivalry, exacerbated the 'low-trust' relations in industry and the antagonism to government–business cooperation in economic and social policy which prevented Britain from reaping the gains of development elsewhere.

Britain also pioneered some degree of meritocracy, but its effects were limited by the same inheritance of class consciousness. The professionals, including the corporate managers, increasingly owed their careers to their formal education and training, and so to their human capital. More and more of that training was incorporated by the higher education system, with more professions such as accounting, business management, and new types of engineering drawn into university and technical college departments. Perhaps the most symptomatic change was the creation of business schools in the 1960s, in London and Manchester, and a host of new and old universities and polytechnics.

This was all part of an attempt to modernize British industry along American lines, and provide the meritocratic means to accomplish it. Britain had built an educational ladder from as early as the 1920s, with a small number of state university scholarships for the brightest examinees and student loans for those willing to teach. As a result British universities between the wars and for a generation after the Second World War had a larger proportion of working-class students than any other West European country except Sweden, more than one in four, and higher education expanded for all classes from the 1960s onwards. Yet because of the unequal size of the classes, this still left a working-class boy with a one in thirty chance of a university place (and his sister still less), compared with a one in four chance for a professional man's son, and a one in twelve chance for a boy from the intermediate class. Meanwhile, the ratio of chances between the top and bottom classes had slightly worsened, from 8.1:1 to 8.5:1.[11] The difference was due to the class segregation in British schools, sharper than anywhere else in the seven countries except West Germany, and reinforced by the public (fee-paying) schools that took about 7 per cent of the age group but provided about a quarter of all university students and about half those at Oxford and Cambridge, which dominated recruitment to most of the elite positions in government, the professions and business. Thus Britain's elite selection was much less meritocratic than most, and the neglect of talent showed itself in slower economic growth.

Britain pioneered women's emancipation and gave women, earlier than elsewhere, rights to custody of children (1839), separation and divorce (1857), their own earnings and property (1872 and 1880), the vote for school boards and other local government bodies (1870 and 1894), the parliamentary franchise (1918 and 1928), and entry to most professions (1870s onwards, confirmed by law 1919). Since the Second World War women have entered the workforce in much larger numbers than ever, rising from 33 per cent of adult women between the wars to 55 per cent in 1992 (71 per cent of those of working age, 16 to 59 years, compared to 86 per cent of men aged 16–65), second only to Denmark among European countries.[12] The 'permissive society' of the 1960s and 1970s with its demand for moral equality brought 'no fault' divorce and equal shares of the matrimonial property (1969 and 1970), equal pay for equal work (1970), and the Sex Discrimination Act (1975) which set up the Equal Opportunities Commission to secure equality in recruitment and promotion. Women now form 44 per cent of students in higher education, more than in Germany and Japan but less than in France and the United States. Much of the recent legislation was due to the women's movement of the 1960s and 1970s, but it was reinforced by the manifest need in modern society for trained expertise from whatever source.

None of these reforms has succeeded in ending inequality between the sexes in work and family and higher education. Employers find ways of circumventing the law and women earn only 70 per cent as much as men and still do most of the housework and childrearing. Recruitment to managerial and executive positions is still dominated by men, more so than in the United States but less than in continental Europe and much less than in Japan. Though women are nearing equality in student numbers there are progressively fewer in graduate school (38 per cent in 1980), in the faculty (14 per cent), and among the full professors (a miniscule 2.6 per cent).[13] The survival of the 'old boy' network in British business, government and the professions, though less monopolistic now expertise is at a premium, still tends to exclude outsiders, including both working-class men and women from all the classes. And the gender preference in executive positions is more powerful in Britain than in any major country except Japan.

Britain was also a leader, along with France and West Germany, in the post-war growth of government. Public expenditure as a percentage of GNP rose from 32.6 per cent in 1960 to 47.4 per cent in 1982, before falling back to 39.7 per cent in 1991 after the privatizations and contracting out of many public functions during the Thatcher era. Public employment also grew, from 26.6 per cent of the occupied population in 1951 to 31.4 per cent in 1981. Since then it has shrunk, due to the Thatcher government's privatizations, but is still the largest among the five nations.[14] Government provision of primary incomes, via central and local government salaries and transfer payments, became the highest among the five Western nations, rising from 33.9 per cent in 1951 to 56.3 per cent in 1981.

Margaret Thatcher began the campaign to reduce the size of government which has since been emulated in the United States and Europe, but it did not reduce the real cost of government, since the contracted-out services are notoriously unaccountable for their spending, especially on executives and their 'perks'.

Britain pioneered the post-war growth of the welfare state. Transfer payments for social security, pensions, and welfare were the fastest growing item of public expenditure, rising from 6.8 per cent of GDP in 1960 to 14.0 per cent in 1986. Transfer payments go back into consumption and help to explain why the state could take so much and still leave the private sector to generate most of the national income. All told, public expenditure on social security, social services, health, and education rose from 14 per cent of GDP in 1960 to 24 per cent in 1981, declining only slightly to 22 per cent in 1991. Much of this growth was due to the demand of public opinion for a full range of citizenship rights, needed in modern society where the extended family could no longer take care of its own and the cessation of income was beyond the individual's control and potentially disastrous. But it was also due in part to the self-interest of the welfare professionals, who not only had an interest in expanding their services, in health, education, welfare, and so on, but believed that they should be available to every citizen, regardless of ability to pay.[15]

The concept of social citizenship, the right to income support in the contingencies of life, was a by-product of what may be called the professional ideal of social justice. This ideal was defended by the public professionals, who stood to gain by its implementation, but came under increasing attack from the private sector professionals in the business community, who saw it as an open-ended commitment to taxation and public expenditure. Hence the backlash against the welfare state by the Thatcher and Major governments of the 1980s and 1990s, despite the opinion polls that showed that the numbers believing that 'government services such as health, education and welfare should be extended, even if it means some increase in taxes' rose from 34 per cent in 1979 to 59 per cent in 1985, while those favouring tax cuts and reduction of services shrank from 34 per cent to 16 per cent.[16]

The critics of welfare do not notice, or do not care, that most of the redistribution by transfer payments is horizontal, between those of working age, healthy and employed, and the same people when too young or too old to work, sick, disabled, or unemployed, rather than vertical, between the rich and the poor. In Britain, as in the United States, social security contributions are a heavier impost on the poorer part of the working population than income and wealth taxes, and are a form of regressive taxation paid more by the lower income groups than by the rich. Nonetheless, Britain has lost ground in the generosity of its welfare state and is now decisively behind most West European countries, though still ahead of the United States and Japan.

Britain was a pioneer, as we have seen, in opening the universities between the wars to able students who were unable to pay, and went so far by 1960 as to pay fees for all students regardless of income, plus maintenance on a parental means test (including a minimum allowance to all students, however rich). This meant that Britain spent more per student on higher education than any other advanced country. Unfortunately, this inhibited expansion of the universities, and Britain lagged behind in the huge surge of student numbers that took place all across the world between the 1960s and the 1980s. Student numbers in British universities and colleges rose from 9 per cent of the age group (only 7 per cent full-time) in 1960 to 20 per cent (13 per cent full-time) in 1981 and to about 25 per cent (17 per cent full-time) in 1990.[17] This was less than other European countries and far less than Japan, Canada and the United States, though it was mitigated by the lower drop-out rates and higher rates of graduation in British universities, and by the larger percentage of working-class and women students in the smaller British intake.

Not only was the quantity of higher education smaller than elsewhere but there were problems of kind and quality too: British students tended to concentrate in the arts and social sciences and avoid applied science and engineering, so that although Britain still produced pioneering scientists and more Nobel prize winners in proportion to population than any country except Sweden, there were not enough technologists and skilled workers to produce the industrial innovations required to compete in the more demanding global economy of the late twentieth century. Education was thought of as a cost to be kept down rather than an investment in the nation's human capital. This was one more reason for Britain's poor economic performance.

Britain also led the way, along with the United States and Germany, in the concentration of industry in a small number of great corporations. In Victorian Britain the largest 100 firms accounted for less than 10 per cent of manufacturing output. By 1909 they accounted for 15 per cent, by 1930 for 26 per cent, and by 1970 for 45 per cent. Today, 200 firms produce about 85 per cent of the output. By 1969 the ten largest firms in each major industry held two thirds of the assets in every major industry except non-electrical engineering (32 per cent), and more than three quarters in nine out of the fourteen industrial categories. Post-war Britain came to have the lowest number of small businesses with less than ten employees, 27,000 in 1963, which employed only 2 per cent of the workforce.[18] Many of these were subcontractors, franchisees, consultants, and sales outlets for the large corporations in that neo-feudal structure we have already seen in the American economy. In the tier above the industrial corporations are ranked the finance companies, banks, insurance companies, unit trusts, and pension funds, which own three quarters of the shares on the stock exchange, and in turn invest the savings of millions of small investors, depositors, premium payers, and pension contributors. All their flows of income and capital are concentrated in and through the major corporations which produce the goods and services. This complex web constitutes the sophisticated global economy of post-industrial society, in which Britain was a leading pioneer.

Britain was until recently the senior contributor, next to the United States, in the new multinational economy. In 1973 fifty of the 401 largest transnational corporations with over 20,000 workers were British, second only to the United States' 211, and ahead of West Germany's twenty-nine, Japan's twenty-eight and France's twenty-four. Several, including Royal Dutch/Shell, Imperial Chemical Industries, and General Electric, were in the top twenty. Yet by 1992 Britain had slipped to fourth place in the top 100, with eleven (two of them shared with the Dutch), behind the United States' twenty-nine, Japan's sixteen, and France's twelve, and just ahead of Germany's nine.[19] While some, like Imperial Chemical Industries, Unilever, Royal Dutch/Shell, and Glaxo and Beachams Pharmaceuticals can compete with the best, British car, electronics, computer, and machine tool companies are being outclassed by American, German, and Japanese manufacturers, and British banks and insurance companies, once the largest in the world, have been overtaken by Japanese and American ones. The British-owned mass-produced car industry has vanished, replaced by American Ford and General Motors, Japanese Nissan, Toyota and Honda, French Peugeot–Citroën, and now German BMW's acquisition of Rover; as has the production of television receivers and video recorders, personal computers and most domestic consumer durables. It is true that British investors own more investments in the United States than any other country including Japan, but this merely underlines their failure to invest sufficiently in domestic industry. Britain has squandered the lead it once had in a range of high-tech industries, from computers to bio-engineering, and without a sound domestic base in manufacturing industry it is difficult to see how it can maintain a significant place in the new global economy.

If Britain pioneered the third great revolution in each of these ten ways, why is it the least successful, the slowest growing, and the most vulnerable of the major post-industrial societies? Why has the country which inaugurated the second social revolution and looked poised to do the same for the next, failed to exploit its advantages and benefit from the third? Why, after leading the way in economic development, inventiveness and living standards for nearly two centuries, has Britain since the Second World War begun its seemingly inexorable, if relative, decline?

## THE DEBATE ABOUT ECONOMIC DECLINE

When the economic decline began is a matter of debate. Some historians see the 'climacteric', the top of the rise from which the road ran downhill, as early as the 'Great Depression' of 1874–96, when the rate of growth of industrial production slowed to below 2 per cent per annum for the first time since the Industrial Revolution began; some in the 1890s, when national income per capita, including services as well as goods, began to falter; and some in the Edwardian age, when economic growth fell to the same rate, about 1 per cent per annum, as population increase. Some see it in the interwar period, when Britain failed to take full advantage of the new consumer goods industries and persisted with the old staples of textiles, iron and coal, and shipbuilding, even though industrial production accelerated to mid-Victorian levels (3.4 per cent per annum in 1929–37), outpacing all rival countries despite the depression. Even after the Second World War, in which Britain suffered great destruction and lost most of its overseas investments, growth surged to the un-precedented level of 4.1 per cent per annum in the 1950s, and maintained a respectable average rate of 3.2 per cent per annum for the whole period 1950–73. This was the 'never had it so good' age of Macmillan, when the British people at last reached the plateau of high mass consumption, and began in large numbers to have cars, refrigerators, television sets, central heating, foreign holidays, and so on. It is not surprising, therefore, that, though they were acutely aware of the prosperity of the Americans, bruited daily in films and on television, it took some time to realize that they were not doing as well as Western Europe and Japan.

It is also not surprising that the debate about economic decline was fraught with confusion and disagreement. The paradox can be explained by the double helix of rising absolute living standards and relative economic decline which characterized the post-war period, particularly in the long economic boom from 1950 to 1973. Despite full employment and visibly rising real incomes, politicians and economists began to worry about keeping up with rival countries, and the failure of all at-tempts to 'go for growth', which always ended in a balance of payments crisis and a stop in what became the 'stop–go' cycle of economic policy. Successive governments looked with envy at the impressive rates of growth of the European Common Market, founded by the Treaty of Rome in 1957 but spurned at that time by British politicians obsessed with the American 'special relationship', the sterling area and the strength of the pound, and the remains of the Empire.

When first Harold Macmillan and then Harold Wilson applied to join the European Community in the 1960s, these very concerns, especially the Atlantic connection, which French President de Gaulle thought was an American Trojan horse, were used to veto British entry. By the time that Edward Heath took Britain in on 1 January 1973, the first oil crisis came within ten months, and the European 'economic miracle' came to a sudden halt. Average rates of growth fell abruptly in the OECD European countries from 4.8 per cent per annum in 1968–73 to 2.5 per cent in 1973–79, while Britain's fell from 3.3 per cent to 1.5 per cent.[20] By then it was too late to join the gravy train. Britain, overtaken in GNP per head by the mid-1960s, now began to fall further behind, ending in the 1990s as the seventh richest nation in the twelve-member European Union, ahead only of Spain, Ireland, Portugal, and Greece.

Whatever the absolute gains, there can be no gainsaying the relative decline. The puzzle is how to explain it. As *The Economist* pointed out in 1986, a world power that falls behind its rivals by 1 per cent per annum in economic growth can lose its place in the front rank in a single generation.[21] In 1900 Britain was still a superpower, head of the largest empire the world had ever seen, the largest exporter of manufactures, the owner of most of the world's shipping, the largest banker, insurer, and investor, and the dominant naval power, able to project its strength across all seven seas. By the Second World War, decisively overtaken in aggregate wealth and military power by the United States, Germany, and the Soviet Union, it was still second only to the United States in national income per head. By the mid-1970s it was a middling member of the European Community with no pretensions to superpower status. The gap of 1 or 2 per cent per annum in economic growth had done its work.

Why had this astonishing falling-off occurred? There are almost as many explanations as there are historians, economists, and political analysts, but they divide into two groups, or three if we count those who deny that there was decline, like Barry Supple, who emphasizes the absolute gains, and Donald McCloskey, who believes that Britain was as successful as it could have been given its limited population and resources.[22] This ignores the astonishing success of Japan, a similar over-crowded off-shore archipelago with fewer raw materials and less coal, gas, or oil reserves, and equally dependent on its human capital. Why did not the British, like the Japanese, find substitutes for their lack of resources through the ingenuity and trading opportunism of their people?

The two main groups are the economic and the cultural critics. Some economic historians, like Nicholas Crafts and Patrick O'Brien, blame a backlog of old plant and equipment left over from traditional industry, an attachment to older ways of producing goods, the lack of domestic investment, the diversion of capital to overseas markets where interest rates and profits were higher, the lack of enterprise in old family firms and the shortage of pushing new entrepreneurs, the preference for high profit margins per unit over low profit rates on large volumes. Sir Alex Cairncross blames the low ICORs (incremental capital output ratios): 'Britain required twice as much investment [as West Germany] to match a given increase in output' – mainly because of the foot-dragging tactics of the workers.[23] Some business historians, like Alfred Chandler and Daniel Shiman, have blamed British attachment to the family firm and its reluctance to delegate to more enterprising non-family managers.[24] Such explanations carry conviction, but they do not explain *why* British workers dragged their feet or British managers failed to innovate or persuade their workers to cooperate.

Other economic historians, like Malcolm Chalmers, W. A. P. Manser, and Sidney Pollard, in line with Paul Kennedy's theory of 'imperial over-stretch', have argued that Britain's balance of payment problems, which prevented governments from 'going for growth', were entirely due to government spending overseas, especially for defence. They point out that Britain's private trade was nearly always in balance in the post-war period and thrown into the red only by government spending, of which military expenditure for troops overseas was the largest component: between 1958 and 1981 the total deficit was £13,620 million but the private balance was a positive £16,710 million; the official deficit was £30,330 million, of which £9,790 million was for military purposes. They argue that if West Germany and Japan had had government outflows of these dimensions, they too would have incurred deficits, and Britain would not have declined relative to them.[25]

There is much truth in this argument. The costs of maintaining the army of the Rhine and fighting colonial wars in Malaya, Cyprus, Kenya, Aden, and other places, and of the final lunacy of the Falklands War in 1982 (on behalf of 1,800 people and 18,000 sheep) – still costing £1 billion a year in occupation costs and transport charges – were beyond Britain's diminished powers, and contributed to its decline. But this is an excuse rather than an explanation, since it was deliberate government policy, the choice was made by the political and financial elites, and it is part of the indictment against them. It is also doubtful, given the global pretensions of those elites, whether the positive balance would have been invested in British industry rather than overseas. The squandering of the windfalls from North Sea oil and the £50 billion from privatization in the 1980s do not suggest that the profits would have been used to rehabilitate the British economy. By 1991 the domestic manufacturing base had shrunk to 27 per cent of the workforce (from 38 per cent in 1980), exports of goods to 18 per cent of GDP, and investment in machinery and equipment to 2.8 per cent of GDP.[26] Thatcher's belief that invisible exports would fill the gap proved to be a tragic fantasy: though by 1991 invisible exports overtook goods by £107 billion to £103 billion, they had actually declined, from 2 per cent of GNP in 1977 to 1 per cent in 1991.[27] The best that can be said is that foreign investment might have provided a small cushion of invisible income to soften the fall.

Each of these economic causes can be viewed as a cultural problem. The lack of investment and the sluggishness of entrepreneurs have been seen as stemming from a peculiarly English (rather than British) attitude to dirty-handed industry, an aversion inculcated by old-fashioned aristocratic values imbibed by business men and their sons at public schools and the older universities, and the snobbish disdain towards engineers and applied scientists not educated as 'gentlemen'. Martin Wiener argues that English culture was fundamentally aristocratic and from at least the mid-nineteenth century was anti-industrial, infecting the brightest young people with a preference for the professions, the civil service, imperial government, and clean-handed work in finance and commerce rather than manufacturing. His thesis has been attacked by economic historians, who argue that business men until recently were rarely educated at the public schools and Oxbridge, that the anti-industrial critics had little influence on their behaviour, and that entrepreneurial failure, where it occurred, had purely economic causes.[28] Others have objected that the values taught at the reformed public schools and Oxbridge when future business men did begin to attend were not aristocratic but professional, the ideal of public service rather than 'mere money making'.[29]

W. D. Rubinstein counters that rival countries also had their anti-industrial critics, like Americans from Thoreau to Ralph Nader, Frenchmen from Tocqueville to Sartre and Althusser, and Germans from Goethe to Günther Grass. But he unwittingly underscores Wiener's thesis by arguing that finance and commerce were where Britain's comparative advantage lay, and that avoidance of manufacturing industry was a rational choice.[30] There are problems with both theses. Wiener ignores the fact that English aristocrats, from the eighteenth-century Earl of Derby who ran a cotton mill in Preston to the twentieth-century Earl of Shrewsbury who manufactured Talbot cars and sold them in London, Paris, and Monte Carlo, were eager to profit from industry, and became far richer from the rents and profits generated by the Industrial Revolution than ever before.[31] They now go, as Rubinstein suggests, into the City, 'where the money is'.

Rubinstein overlooks the fact that finance and commerce have not enabled Britain to stay ahead, and that the French, Germans, and Japanese, who have outdone the British in foreign investment as well as industry, have sent their best students to engineering schools (*Ecole Polytechnique*, *Technischehochschulen*, etc.) whereas English students have avoided them. British industry is largely run by accountants and arts graduates with little or no understanding of manufacturing processes, who treat engineers and scientists as servants rather than executives, and pay them accordingly. This is due, as Wiener suggests, but for the wrong reason, to the class differences in British education and business, where executives are assumed to be 'gentlemen' educated in the 'right' kind of subject at the 'right' kind of school and university and, until recently at least, engineers and applied scientists were second-class citizens to be used at lower levels of management and research.[32] The social causes of Britain's economic decline are at the heart of the problem.

## THE SOCIAL CAUSES OF ECONOMIC DECLINE

Britain's relative economic decline comes down in the end to a problem of productivity, which lags most strikingly behind all its rivals. Since the Second World War, British real GDP per employee has grown more slowly than that of every major competitor except the United States and Canada, which were already far ahead in absolute terms: between 1960 and 1987 by 2.2 per cent per annum compared with West Germany's 3.1 per cent, France's 3.4 per cent, Italy's 3.9 per cent, and Japan's 5.4 per cent. Since then, despite the further reduction of the manufacturing base and the closure of less efficient factories, which automatically raises productivity, the growth rate of GDP per person employed has sunk still further, to 1.2 per cent per annum, and industrial production has stagnated at the same level for 1993 as 1988.[33] As we have seen, the problem is only partly a matter of low investment in machinery and equipment; it is mostly a problem of low returns on what investment there is, the low ICORs that Cairncross complained of and blamed on the obstructionism of British workers and trade unions.

The question arises: *Why* do British workers, unlike American, German, French, and Japanese, drag their feet and oppose innovation, and British managers look for scapegoats instead of solving the problems of industrial cooperation which lie in their path? And why did they not do so during the earlier industrial revolution when Britain raced ahead in technological innovation and became almost the sole workshop of the world? Why the dramatic change from industrial world leader to post-industrial world laggard?

The short answer is that Britain had the right kind of society to pioneer the second, Industrial Revolution but the wrong kind of society to exploit and benefit from the third, post-industrial revolution. British society in the late eighteenth and early nineteenth century was an open aristocracy based on property and patronage, which meant that nearly all ranks of society stood to gain by innovative economic growth. The landlords had fought the Crown, the Church, and the peasants over several centuries to impose their concept of absolute property in the land, which enabled them, unlike their feudal counterparts elsewhere, to benefit in increased rents and land values from every kind of improvement, from agricultural enclosures and mining to factory building and town development. The most successful business men, apart from gaining profits from the new industries and trade, could hope to emulate the landowners and claim the status that went with their new wealth (like lottery punters, it did not take many winners to stimulate the rest). The populace, made up not of peasants with little propensity to consume but of wage-earners in agriculture and domestic industry who spend as they earn, were attracted into the mines and factories by the hope of higher wages and the new consumer goods. Above all, nearly everybody was drawn into the market by the emulative spending that went with 'keeping up with the Joneses' in an open and dynamic society.[34]

Britain is still paying the penalty of that early success. British society, never having suffered defeat in war or revolution, did not have to change sufficiently to accommodate the next great transition in social organization. It continued to contain what Pareto called 'residues' of the society created by that earlier revolution, the class attitudes that militated against further innovation.[35] The West German Chancellor Helmut Schmidt put it succinctly, if unkindly, when he visited Britain in the 1970s: 'As long as you maintain that damned class-ridden society of yours, you will never get out of your mess.'[36]

It is not ignorance of the means of economic growth that holds Britain back but the class conflict and mutual suspicion in industry and politics that frustrate innovation. 'Snobbery is the religion of England', Frank Harris wrote in 1925, and it is still as true as ever today.[37] Class differences are built into the fabric of British society and industry. The social distance between management and workers, expressed in different hours and conditions of work, different schooling, accent, and language, separate canteens, lavatories, and car parks, and different structures of reward – rising monthly salaries and careers for managers, weekly or hourly wages and the static 'rate for the job' for the workers, 'golden handshakes' and stock options for the directors, small or no redundancy pay and bonuses for the rest – lead to an 'us versus them' mentality that makes production a struggle for income and control rather than a cooperative endeavour.

The result is what Alan Fox, doyen of industrial sociologists, has called 'low trust' industrial relations, the mutual suspicion between managers and workers that frustrates collaboration for common profit and innovation. Instead of a cooperative effort in pursuit of a larger cake to be fairly shared between both parties, the two haggle over the size of their respective shares and do not trust each other to play fair. Ralf Dahrendorf, a sympathetic outsider, has called it a 'zero sum game', in which one side's gain is the other side's loss.[38] Whereas in a German or Japanese factory a new machine that will do the work of three with only two workers will be welcomed and the gain shared between the firm and the remaining two – with the hope that lower prices will lead to expansion and more employment – in Britain the fear is that the firm will take all the gain and one in three workers will be unemployed. Whether or not this is true, the general belief is that management is out to 'screw the workers' and the workers play 'ca'canny' and do as little work for as much pay as they can get. British workers operating the same machines as those in the United States, Germany, or Japan produce only half as much output.[39] It is said that in a British car factory when the assembly line stops the maintenance men have to be fetched from the back room; in a German factory the maintenance men are circulating around the line ready to spot the trouble; in a Japanese factory there are no maintenance men: all the workers descend on the problem to get the line restarted as fast as possible.

Bad industrial relations, then, are the source of the trouble. Bernard Alford has written that 'anyone with even the slightest interest in Britain's economy since the Second World War can hardly fail to recognize in this a major, if not the single most important, factor in industrial performance – or lack of it'.[40] Cairncross blames the trade unions:

> The evidence suggests that when British management sought to raise productivity by the use of modern methods and equipment they found themselves obliged to accept conditions as to manning, operation or pay that cancelled out much of the advantage of making changes and were not insisted upon by the employees of their competitors abroad.[41]

This became a wonderful excuse for scapegoating the workers, which was seized on by the Thatcher government in the 1980s to pass the anti-trades union legislation which has been condemned, as we shall see, by all the international organizations dealing with workers' human rights.

Yet blaming the workers is like a defeated general blaming his troops. It is management's job, as the employers' associations insist, to manage, but they have to manage with the workers they have, not with some ideal type of loyal, disciplined retainer custom-designed to the managers' taste. The proof is the experience of Japanese factories operating in Britain, whose managers are able to get high productivity out of native workers without either breaking the unions or firing the recalcitrant. Sony at Bridgend, Hitachi at Aberdare, Nissan at (the original) Washington near Sunderland, Canon at Guildford, and over 100 other Japanese-owned factories in Britain practise Japanese methods of 'single status', with managers and workers having the same hours, uniforms, and facilities.[42] To everyone's surprise, British workers proved capable of responding to good management with willing cooperation and nearly the same high trust industrial relations as in Japan. The Japanese managers had one great advantage: they were not trapped inside the British class system, and were therefore not resented by their British employees.

This suggests that it is not British workers who are responsible for the resistance to technological change but British managers who cannot escape from the apartheid mentality of the British class system. Artificial barriers and authoritarian attitudes breed resentment and low trust relations. The test of good management is the extent to which it invokes willing cooperation to raise productivity and expand output. Japan with its high trust industrial relations has raised its real GDP more than eight-fold since 1950 (admittedly starting from a lower base); Britain has had to struggle to more than double it.[43]

Class-ridden industrial relations in Britain are compounded by politics. More than in any other country, the political parties are anachronistically based on a conception of class more appropriate to Victorian society than to the third social revolution. The Conservative Party, despite its claim to represent all the people, is far more closely wedded than its counterparts in Europe to big business and has become identified with confrontation against the trades unions and the working class. It no longer has the compassion of a Churchill or a Macmillan, and regards the welfare state, the health service, and education as costs upon private industry rather than as investments in the creation and maintenance of human capital. Labour, on the other hand, despite the efforts of the late John Smith and Tony Blair to change its image, is still seen as tied to the old manual working class, a declining sector in the new society, and invites the charge that it only cares for the underdog, the poor, the homeless, the sick, the elderly, and the victims of society. It is therefore vulnerable to the electoral ploy that it intends to tax the middling classes, including the 'C1s and C2s', the non-manual and skilled workers who form the critical centre, to support the undeserving underclass. These anachronistic images are very powerful, and the gut reactions they provoke sway elections, while the real problems of the country are neglected. But one party has been in power two thirds of the time since 1951, always with a minority of the popular vote. To the dangers and temptations of minority government, which have exacerbated class hostility and accelerated Britain's economic decline, we must now turn.

## THE PERILS OF MINORITY GOVERNMENT

The British electoral system, unlike in the rest of the European Union where proportional representation is the norm, is based on the 'first past the post' principle, which allows a party with a minority of the popular vote to elect an overwhelming majority of MPs in the House of Commons. In Tory Lord Chancellor Hailsham's term, it is an elective dictatorship. Since 1911 when the House of Lords' veto was reduced to a delaying power, whichever party has a Commons majority can do whatever it likes. Minority government is therefore built into the system. Indeed, it is even more undemocratic than that: whichever faction can capture not the party membership in the country but the minority of constituency activists who control the nomination of candidates, can dominate the party in the Commons and so control the government. Once in office, the minority faction can select the prime minister, who in turn appoints the ministers and determines government policy and legislation. Democracy in effect is turned upside down. Instead of the voters selecting and controlling the MPs and the MPs selecting and controlling the government, the prime minister selects and controls the Cabinet, which in turn through the Whips' Office controls the party's MPs and so both the executive and the legislature. It is government by a minority of a minority which, in the absence of a written constitution, a bill of rights, or a supreme court, is able to impose its will upon the people.

During the 1970s democracy was further undermined by the disenchantment of the electorate with politics as usual, and the inability of the politicians to stop Britain's slide into mediocracy (government by the mediocre). Voting for the two major parties had declined from 77 per cent of the electorate in 1951 to 55 per cent in 1974 and only recovered to 61 per cent in 1979, and party memberships were halved.[44] The result was that the extremists on both sides were able to take over the constituency parties. Left-wing socialists, Trotskyists, and ex-communists like the Militant Tendency nearly succeeded in electing Tony Benn as deputy leader of the Labour Party under the moderate but ailing figurehead, Michael Foot, while followers of Enoch Powell, the anti-immigration and free-market populist, came – after the defection of Powell himself to the Ulster Unionists – to dominate the Tory constituencies and elect Margaret Thatcher to the leadership.

Once in office the Thatcherites, with never more than 43 per cent of the popular vote, began to put into practice the programme of the minority who, in the words of one Tory cabinet minister, had hijacked the party, the free market ideologists who boasted of having put them there. Their aim was to 'roll back the state', to 'wither the welfare state', and to cure their 'evil of evils', inflation, by squeezing the money supply and taming the trades unions so as to halt inflationary wage increases. This was paradoxical, since their policies entailed increasing the powers of the state over any institution they deemed a threat. As Kenneth Morgan has pointed out,

> In all these areas – the trade unions, the local authorities, the Church, the media, the universities and the schools – the paradox was that a government dedicated to extending individualism and the private ethic became the champion of greater centralization and state control ... [T]he conversion of the population to a market philosophy needed direction on a massive scale.[45]

Far from reducing state spending (excluding capital investment and privatization yields), they actually increased it, from 43 per cent of GDP in 1978 to 48 per cent in 1985, partly because of the trebling of unemployment from 1 million to 3 million and the resultant rise in welfare costs.[46]

The powers of the police were increased to cope with the reactive militancy of the trades unions, especially the striking miners in 1982 and 1984; the Official Secrets Act was strengthened to silence critics within the Civil Service (the occasional civil servant, like Sarah Tisdall, was jailed *pour encourager les autres*); and top civil servants were politicized to ensure they were 'one of us'. Taxation was actually increased, by the legerdemain of reducing income tax (from 33 to 30 per cent and eventually to 25 per cent, and the top rate from 75 to 60 and eventually to 40 per cent) but more than doubling VAT (from 8 per cent to 15 per cent and eventually to 17.5 per cent), thus making the average consumer pay for tax breaks for the rich.

The irony was that free-market practice did not fulfil the promise of free-market theory. Neither massive unemployment nor monetarism, tight control of the money supply, succeeded in curing inflation, which fell from the heights of 16 per cent per annum in the oil crisis years of the later 1970s to 8 per cent per annum in the 1980s but rose to 10 per cent in 1992.[47] The government therefore turned to its second strategy, 'bashing the unions'. In five acts of Parliament between 1980 and 1990 the entire basis of industrial relations was changed: to end the unions' immunity, enjoyed since 1906, from civil suits arising out of trade disputes; to enforce a postal ballot of the whole membership before a strike could be called; to criminalize unofficial strikes and 'secondary picketing' against other employers; to prevent victimization of non-striking workers and non-union members; to require electoral ballots every five years for union officials; to ban the single union workplace and the closed shop; and even to forbid union membership in specified government services like GCHQ, the intelligence gathering centre at Cheltenham.[48] Some of these changes were ostensibly democratic, limiting the power of despotic officials to coerce members and non-members, and of militant shop stewards to call unofficial strikes, but the general effect was to handicap the unions and prevent workers from evening up the balance with the employers, now largely concentrated in great corporations, by collective bargaining.

The Thatcherite labour legislation was condemned by all the international bodies concerned with workers' human rights. The International Labour Organization declared in May 1989 that it was in breach on nine counts of ILO Convention No. 41, 1948, as undermining the right to strike and other rights of trade unionists. The Council of Europe's Committee of Independent Experts challenged parts of it as in breach of the European Social Charter of 1961. The European Court of Justice pointed out that Britain was 'the worst law breaker' in cases concerning human rights: twenty-six out of ninety-one adverse judgments (some concerned with Northern Ireland) were against the United Kingdom. The European Commission in Brussels accused Britain of breaking a series of directives, on equal pay for women, sex discrimination in employment, the safeguarding of workers' rights in business transfers, and on hazardous materials in the workplace, and of blocking a directive requiring consultation with workers on management proposals concerning them. The OECD ranked Britain along with the United States as bottom of the league of member nations in labour standards, and invoked collective bargaining, recognition of trade unions, and workplace consultation – all rejected by the British government – as a means of promoting market efficiency.[49]

The Thatcher government's response was to condemn all criticisms and to reject the European Community's Social Charter of 1988 guaranteeing workers' rights, including decent wages and living and working conditions, consultation of workers by employers, the right to strike, vocational training, the health and safety of workers, equal treatment by gender, race, and age, and special measures for the young, the old, and disabled. This modest document, containing much that was already British law, was condemned by Thatcher as 'a socialist charter' which would undermine the competitiveness of British exports – to the disgust of other EC members, who accused Britain of practising unfair competition.[50] Finally, her successor John Major ratified the Maastricht Treaty in 1993 without the Social Chapter, thus confirming Britain's role as the main opponent of citizens' and workers' rights. The European Union countered by passing the Works Council Directive by which all large companies with more than 1,000 employees operating in more than one European country will by September 1996 have to appoint works councils with the right to be consulted about all changes in company policy, which the British government cannot veto.[51]

The Thatcher government's determination to strengthen the private sector and 'roll back the state' went much further than the attack on the trades unions. It set out to impose the free market on every activity that could be privatized. Denationalization of the great state industries was at first a pragmatic policy, initiated to plug the gap in the government budget caused by the artificial boom before the 1983 election, but became an article of faith as it succeeded. Success was defined as popularity with the investors, who received public property at knockdown prices and enjoyed windfall capital gains; and with the managers, who immediately began to pay themselves outrageous salary increases and share options. The chairmen of privatized industries like Lord King of British Airways, Sir Roland Smith of British Aerospace, Sir Iain Vallance of British Telecom, and Cedric Brown of British Gas not only vastly increased their salaries but gave themselves generous stock options which escalated in worth as the shares climbed from the artificial launching price to their real market value. Edward Wallace, for example, chief executive of PowerGen, one of the two main electricity generators, stood to gain £1.2 million from stock options in 1995. The CEOs of the ten privatized regional water companies, who raised their average salaries from £46,400 to £149,000, took stock options worth more than £500,000 each. Bryan Townsend, chairman of Midlands Electricity, having trebled his salary over three years, took a cut on going part-time from £197,000 to £165,000, but then received a pension said to be £125,000, which took him to £290,000 a year.[52]

Still more questionable, some of the ministers responsible for privatization resigned to become directors and even CEOs of the very companies they had privatized. Lord Tebbit, the Industry Secretary who privatized British Telecom, now sits on its board; Lord Walker who privatized British Gas is on its board; Sir Norman Fowler who as Transport Secretary privatized National Freight is now a director; Norman Lamont, a successor at the Treasury, is a director of N. M. Rothschild which handled many of the privatizations; while Lord Young of Graffham, regulator of Cable and Wireless as Industry Secretary, became its chairman, at a salary of £883,000 plus stock options.[53] Thus did the new private monopolies reward their benefactors.

The Thatcherites have also rolled back local government. A large part of the public housing owned by local councils has been sold off at bargain prices to sitting tenants, who can after three years make large capital gains on their resale. The policy at first benefited many poor families, until depression and unemployment struck and they found they could not meet their mortgage payments and had their homes repossessed. Many local authority services have been privatized, including street cleaning, waste disposal, old people's homes, and the like. Many other public functions have been turned over to more than 5,500 unelected 'quangos' (quasi-non-governmental organizations) with over 42,000 members appointed by central government from among its loyal supporters, who spend £46 billion a year and are accountable to no one.[54] These quangos include private hospitals which have opted out of the National Health Service, regional purchasing bodies for the NHS, one of which spent £43 million on a computerized patient record system that did not work;[55] parent–teacher committees for schools which opted out of local education authority control to operate their own budgets, who find themselves having to choose between firing teachers and maintaining the buildings; private prisons which have failed to prevent prisoners from escaping; and a whole range of civil service functions like car and driving licensing and school inspection which have been outsourced to private contractors. A national curriculum designed by politicians who do not trust teachers to teach politically correct subjects has been imposed on the schools, bringing central government control into education for the first time. The universities in 1980–84 were forced to shed one in six of the faculty, on the grounds that academics were anti-business, even though Thatcher employed more academics, chiefly free-market economists, than any previous government. Only when the 'brain drain' of professors to the United States and the English-speaking dominions became notorious, and the gap between Britain and its rivals in science, engineering, and biotechnology became a scandal, was the decrease in student numbers and research reversed, but then without a commensurate increase in government funding. The BBC and ITV companies have been forced to shed most of their programme making to independent production companies, often with the same producers and technicians, who are now self-employed and without sick leave, social security, pension rights, or career structures.

Above all, they tried to roll back the welfare state, by letting inflation erode benefits, removing whole categories of claimants such as young people between 16 and 18 years old. They inveighed against teenage mothers (a tiny fraction of single mothers, who are mostly divorced or widowed in middle life) and set up the Child Support Agency which harries absent fathers, often with a second family to support, to save money not for the first family but for the state. The 'No Turning Back' group of influential MPs, including cabinet ministers Peter Lilley and Michael Portillo, proposed to reduce social security to a minimum safety net for the poorest groups by targeting the 'needy', defined by means tests, and removing all benefits from the better off, however much they have contributed to the scheme.[56]

All this was done in the name of the 'enterprise culture' and 'Victorian values'. Such values would not be recognizable to most Victorians of any of the three great traditions of social thought in the nineteenth century, all of which contributed to the origins of the welfare state. The classical economists, to whom the Thatcherites look back, developed exceptions to *laissez-faire*, like factory, mine, and public health legislation, and it culminated in Alfred Marshall's belief in raising the working class into salaried 'gentlemen', and welfare economist A. C. Pigou's demand for a minimum standard of life. T. H. Green, Arnold Toynbee and the Idealist school of philosophy believed in society as an organic community in which people were responsible for one another and property had obligations to those in need. And the socialist tradition from Robert Owen to the Fabians was dedicated to the proposition that society existed for people not people for property, and the community should guarantee the basics of life for all.[57] All three streams belonged to what I have called the professional social ideal, the belief in public service for the sake of social justice, a belief that the private sector professionals of the late twentieth century seem to have lost. The three streams were united in R. H. Tawney, the Fabian Christian Socialist and product of Green and Toynbee's Balliol College, who rejected the 'tadpole philosophy' by which one tadpole out of thousands could become a frog and preach the blessings of competition to the rest. A consummate Victorian professional, he believed in a 'functional society' in which professionals, including managers and workers, provide expert services for all who need them. He was indeed the first prophet of professional society.[58]

Some Victorians, it is true, believed in extreme individualism, like Herbert Spencer of *The Man versus the State* (1884), who invented 'Social Darwinism' and 'the survival of the fittest', and thought that the sick labourer, the poor widow and her orphaned children 'should be left to struggle for life and death' in 'the interests of universal humanity'.[59] His followers, the 'absolute philosophical anarchist' Wordsworth Donisthorpe, W. H. Mallock, and the Earl of Wemyss of the Liberty and Property Defence League, continued to believe in undiluted individualism, but they were repudiated even by the Conservative Anti-Socialist Union in 1911 as 'a reactionary group' who proclaim 'a policy of negation'.[60] Spencer's survival of the fittest was transformed by his more enlightened followers, Karl Pearson and Benjamin Kidd, who came to believe that the struggle was between nations, not individuals, and that welfare measures were vital to produce the competent workers and fit soldiers for the international competition of the twentieth century.[61] The Spencerians were the true precursors of the free-marketeers, but in the end even they could not face the full destructive implications of their theory.

It is a travesty of the Victorians, who were imbued with the ideal of public service and initiated most of the collectivist measures in factory legislation, public health, education, clean air, municipal gas, water supply, electricity, trams, and buses, to saddle them with the anti-statism of the Thatcherite free-marketeers. They had a keener sense of man's responsibility for man, and a higher view of social morality than the latter's devil take the hindmost philosophy. As the Archbishop of Canterbury has commented,

> The privatization of morality threatens to undermine a sense of social cohesion as society itself is broken down into a multiplicity of individual atoms ... We have witnessed a powerful ideological attack during the 1980s on the value of public goods, together with a strong affirmation of private values and individual choice.[62]

This is the indictment of the free-marketeers: they are willing to sacrifice social cohesion to the theory that everyone is an isolated individual motivated by material self-interest and personal greed. They are surprised when people do not behave as the theory predicts but demand instead a more humane morality that sees society as a great mutual insurance trust in which we are all members one of the other. Their creed is a crude, reductionist ideology that appeals to the worst and most selfish in human nature, and then they are perplexed when people do not cooperate to produce profits for the already rich and privileged.[63] Willing cooperation is the *sine qua non* of economic growth, and a system that works by fear and discipline instead of consent and mutual concern is doomed to frustration. That, rather than the obstructionism of British workers, which is simply the understandable reaction to a selfish philosophy, lies at the heart of Britain's economic decline.

The supreme irony is that the very people who preach the free market do not themselves believe in it. The professional corporate executives believe, with Alfred Chandler, that the corporation exists to control the market and to internalize the transactions that were once left to the uncertainties of market forces.[64] They resist the attempts of free-market libertarians to enforce competition by proscribing cartels and restrictive practices, and pressurize the government to limit the intervention of the Monopolies and Mergers Commission. They pretend that their own remuneration is determined by the market, while in fact they fix it themselves in a circular process by which the directors decide the chief executive's pay and the CEO then decides theirs, with no relation whatever to the profitability of the company or to the pay structure of the rest of the workforce. That is why the gap between executive pay and the average worker's has widened under the Thatcher/Major regimes to unprecedented size.

The scandal of executive greed has produced a backlash in Britain as in the United States. Big business responded with the Cadbury Committee on executive governance, chaired by Sir Adrian Cadbury, Quaker ex-chairman of Cadbury Schweppes, which has recommended the use of independent non-executive directors to determine corporate appointments, rewards, and promotion. But only five companies out of the top 100 have accepted its Code of Best Practice, and given that most non-executives are well-paid directors of other big companies it is unlikely to make much difference.[65] The Major government appointed the Nolan Committee on Standards in Public Life to inquire into the standards of conduct of all holders of public office and the appointment of ex-ministers and civil servants to company boards. The response of the government was to accept its modest recommendations, on full disclosure of MPs' outside interests and earnings, a delay of two years (like civil servants) before ex-ministers are normally allowed to join companies with which they have had official dealings, and the appointment to quangos by merit, but they have been opposed by Tory and Liberal Democratic MPs unwilling to reveal their earnings from consultancies or to cut their ties with lobbying companies.[66] The

Confederation of British Industry was similarly forced by public opinion to appoint the Greenbury Committee on executive pay, consisting of five corporate executives whose salaries alone add up to £4 million. Its recommendations, unsurprisingly, were completely voluntary, and relied on full disclosure and shareholder pressure to police outrageous remuneration packages, limit stock options particularly for newly privatized companies, and relate rewards more closely to performance.[67] The CBI and the government still cling to the fiction that executive pay is determined by the market (when it is clear that it is fixed if not by by the executives themselves then by their friends from the same unaccountable background). Companies like British Gas and PowerGen that have come under fire for their overpayment of senior executives claim that Greenbury justifies their practices, which is a measure of the report's ineffectiveness. This confirms the logic of the free-market ideology, that the individuals with the greatest power in the market use it to exploit the rest of the community.

The application of free-market principles on a very selective basis, as in the United States, is responsible for the widening gap between rich and poor. The 'enterprise society' and the Thatcher and Major governments' consumer tax increases to balance income tax reductions, especially on the higher rates, have benefited the rich far more than the poor. Before tax, the share of disposable income of the top fifth of households has increased from 43 per cent in 1979 to 50 per cent in 1988, a bonus of one-sixth, while that of the bottom fifth has halved, from 4 per cent to 2 per cent. Even after tax the top fifth has increased its share from 37 to 44 per cent, while that of the bottom has shrunk from 10 to 7 per cent. On top of this, the Institute of Fiscal Studies in 1994 found that the tax reforms since 1985 had taken £3 a week from the poorest tenth of families and added £52 a week to the richest tenth.[68]

These gross figures do not measure the real exploitation by the dominant elites, who are far fewer than the top 10 or 20 per cent. In 1991–92 thirty directors of British companies were paid more than £1 million, exclusive of expense accounts, stock options, and pension rights.[69] Even failure was handsomely rewarded: Sir Ralph Halpern, after profits fell at Burtons the clothiers, was given a 'golden handshake' in 1990 of £1.6 million, plus a pension of £465,000 a year; his successor Laurence Cooklin, who lasted little more than a year, was given a leaving present of £773,000. Dr Ernest Mario of Glaxo Pharmaceuticals was said to have been paid three years' salary totalling £2.9 million to take his leave. Peter Scott was paid £2.2 million to leave Aegis, the advertising agency. Sir Peter Parker left the fading shipping and property empire Trafalgar House for £1.3 million. Don McCrickard was paid £763,000 to leave the loss-making, recently privatized Trustee Savings Bank. The egregious Sir John Cahill, an American resident who chaired British

Aerospace and spent only ninety days a year in Britain, presided over the loss of £237 million and 25,000 jobs and the sale of Rover, the last British-owned car company, to German BMW; he was rewarded for his twenty-one months of part-time work at a salary of £540,000 with a 'golden handshake' of £3.2 million.[70]

At the same time, the application of 'market principles' to the public service, which meant minuscule pay increases for most public servants – except, significantly, the police and the armed forces – gave massive increases to the top echelons, including top ministry officials, judges, generals and admirals, and ministers themselves. On the advice of consultants from the private sector like Sir Mark Rayner of Marks and Spencer, these top officials were paid what they were supposedly worth on the open market, without any evidence to test that belief.

Meanwhile, according to the *Inquiry into Income and Wealth* by a London School of Economics team for the Joseph Rowntree Trust in 1995, the gap between rich and poor had become so wide that it was damaging the cohesiveness of society without any attendant economic benefits. Income inequality in Britain had grown faster since 1977 than in any comparable industrial country, and the proportion of the population with less than half the average income had trebled. While average real wages had increased by 35 per cent, wages for the lowest paid, both men and women, were lower in real terms than in 1975. The position was worse for the non-white groups: while 18 per cent of whites were in the poorest fifth of the population, more than a third of the non-whites were in that group, including 40 per cent of West Indians and half the Pakistanis and Bangladeshis. The report stated:

> Regardless of any moral arguments or feelings of altruism, everyone shares an interest in the cohesiveness of society. As the gaps between rich and poor grow, the problems of the marginalized groups which are left behind rebound on the more comfortable majority.[71]

Their view is borne out by the enormous increase in homeless beggars on the streets, produced in part by government policies of denying welfare to teenagers and emptying the mental hospitals; by the accelerating wave of crime, which has more than doubled since the mid-1970s; and by the riots in once quiet places like Oxford, Bristol, and Newcastle, instigated by the bleakness of life on the drab, forlorn housing estates full of unemployed teenagers.[72] The filthy streets, broken pavements, and delapidated public transport of London and the great cities bear witness to the 'private affluence, public squalor' that John Kenneth Galbraith saw as the inevitable consequence of the unregulated free market. Margaret Thatcher's belief that 'There is no such thing as society' is coming true in a sense she did not bargain for. That philosophy is close to Hobbes's definition of the state of nature, 'a war of all against all'.

At the other end of the social scale the effects are just as dire. In the unregulated free market the opportunities for fraud and dishonesty have become notorious. The Bank of England, which is supposed to regulate the banking system, failed to warn the public about the fraud practised by the Bank of Credit and Commerce International or the reckless gambling on the Singapore and Osaka stock exchanges by Barings Bank. Lloyds Insurance has been accused by its own 'names' of defrauding them of millions of pounds. The Scott Inquiry has revealed how the government prosecuted three directors of Churchill Matrix for illegally exporting arms-making machinery to Iraq, which had been secretly authorized by ministers, including Alan Clark, Lord Trefgarne, and William Waldegrave, minister for open government, and had then tried to cover it up by denying the documentation to the court![73] All these instances occurred without anyone resigning, a sign of how far public standards have declined since the governments of Attlee and Churchill.

The British criminal justice system, once the envy of the world, has been condemned by the international community for its conviction and long imprisonment of innocent people like the 'Maguire Seven', the 'Guildford Four', and the 'Birmingham Six', Irish men and women accused on falsified evidence of IRA bombings. The government's response to the problems of obtaining unpopular convictions has been the Runciman Commission's proposals to end the accused's right to silence and in certain cases to trial by jury.[74] The Chief Inspector of Police for England and Wales has blamed 'malpractice' by the police (doctoring evidence to obtain convictions) on the whole judicial system, which is run for the benefit of judges, court administrators, lawyers, and policemen rather than the victims of crime.[75]

All this suggests that a governing elite that has been in power with only 43 per cent of the popular vote through four general elections has become a law unto itself. Like the professional managers of the great corporations who are responsible only to the shareholders, which in practice means to no one but themselves, the British government has become unaccountable to the majority of the voters. Like the *nomenklatura* of the Soviet Union, they are victims of the corruption of near-absolute power. They are in danger of suffering the same fate.

Britain's decline from its superpower status at the beginning of the century is entirely due to the failure of its political and business elites. At the start of that decline the ruling elites were largely aristocratic and capitalist, landed politicians who eventually lost an empire because they did not understand the aspirations of its peoples, and entrepreneurs who, with some exceptions, could no longer compete in the new high-tech industries of the twentieth century. Before and after the Second World War they were progressively replaced by professionals, chiefly

75

professional politicians, bureaucrats, corporate managers, and their academic allies, who claimed to be able to cure the 'British disease' if only they had the freedom to do so, but instead found scapegoats and excuses in the workers, the trades unions, the growth of the state, the burdens of welfare, and the threat of socialism. If the Duke of Wellington had blamed his troops – 'the scum of the earth', as he called them – instead of beating Napoleon at Waterloo, he would have been laughed at. The professional and managerial elites who have led Britain down the primrose path to mediocrity have no excuse. It is their fault and no one else's that Britain has become the poorest and least successful of the major post-industrial societies on the Western democratic model.

# 4

# FRANCE
## A planned meritocracy

France pioneered at least one characteristic feature of professional society. From the French Revolution onwards it was designed to be a meritocracy. The revolutionaries, and Napoleon despite his abortive empire and Bonapartist nobility, set out to replace the hereditary principle of the *ancien régime* with *la carrière ouverte aux talents*. The state suppressed the education system run by the Church and abolished the universities, and replaced them by the government *lycées* and *grandes écoles*. These secular high schools and advanced colleges were highly selective institutions, open in theory to everyone with sufficient brainpower and stamina to pass the competitive entrance examinations, but in practice confined to those who could afford the fees, the private cramming, and the opportunity costs in foregone income, which limited them to the prosperous bourgeoisie.

Even so, the competition was severe, the places at each next level fewer, so that only the most intelligent and diligent of the sons of the upper bourgeoisie – no daughters in this male-dominated system until very recently – made the grade. Even those who made it to the *Ecole Polytechnique*, the premier *grande école* founded in 1794 to provide military engineers for the revolutionary armies, or to the *Ecole Normale Supérieure*, its humanities equivalent refounded in 1808, still had to compete throughout their careers. Only the best, the top third or so of each class, were accepted at the next level, the postgraduate *Ecole des Ponts et Chaussées* founded in 1747, the *Ecole des Mines* its near contemporary, or the *Ecole Libre des Sciences Politiques*, the only private *grande école*, founded in 1871 in the aftermath of the Franco–Prussian War, and replaced by the state *Ecole Nationale d'Administration* in the aftermath of the Second World War. Finally, only the *crème de la crème*, the very best alumni of the *grandes écoles*, found admission to the *grands corps*, the elite institutions of the civil service from which all the top bureaucrats and, increasingly since the Second World War, most of the top managers of the nationalized industries and the big corporations have been recruited.

77

## A SKEWED MERITOCRACY

The meritocracy was a government-sponsored and state-planned one. The main purpose of the education system was to provide the state with efficient and reliable officials. The French invented bureaucracy, from the *bureau*, the green baize cloth on the official's desk which gave its name to the office and so to the man occupying it. The first bureaucrats were Louis XIV's intendants, themselves a device for outflanking the venal, hereditary officials who purchased their offices and passed them on to their sons. Even the Sun King could not defeat them, and it took a revolution to abolish proprietory office holding. Napoleon established modern bureaucracy on 17 February 1800, when the First Consul appointed Prefects for most of the *Départements* throughout France, and so created the Paris-centred local government which is still the country's hallmark. Since then France has always been governed from the centre, and every institution which has stood between the state and the individual has been subordinated to the will of Paris, whether that meant the king, the emperor, or the president of the republic.

Hence, for example, the paradox that in this most professional of traditional societies the liberal professions – law, medicine, engineering, architecture, and so on – have been denied self-regulation on the Anglo–American model and are entirely dependent on the state for their training and qualifications. They are for the most part educated at the universities, state institutions revived by the Third Republic in 1896; there were separate, scattered faculties of the Napoleonic university throughout the nineteenth century, but they were isolated, poorly staffed, and underpaid.[1] Uniquely in the modern world, they were not at the head of the higher education system but took second place in prestige and the employability of their graduates to the *grandes écoles*, as they still do. The expansion of the universities since the Second World War has only increased the gap between the two systems, and intensified the competition to get into the *grandes écoles*, where aspirants outnumber places by more than twenty to one.

The liberal professions, aside from the few engineers and social scientists educated at the latter, nevertheless take their social standing and economic opportunity from their university degrees, not from their membership of professional associations, and slot into the social hierarchy below the *cadres* (executives) of the civil service and the corporations. Many of the professionals, indeed, are employed by the state, in the courts, the schools, the universities, the hospitals, the public engineering works, and so on, and are in effect public functionaries. But there is practically no movement from the civil service to the professions, and none at all in the reverse direction.

The universities are currently being squeezed not only from above by the *grandes écoles* but also from below by new forms of higher education. Leaving aside the CP-GE (the courses preparatory for entrance to the *grandes écoles*), two new channels are syphoning off potential students from the traditional universities. The IUTs (*Instituts universitaires de technologie*) founded in the 1960s on the lines of the British polytechnics (now universities) or the German *Fachhochschulen* (vocational high schools), have not been a great threat. They have failed to live up to their promise and in 1987–88 took only 8.7 per cent of higher education students against the universities' 53.4 per cent.

The other, more surprising route was an extension of secondary education, unknown elsewhere. The *lycées*, the selective high schools, began to offer the STS (*Sections des techniciens supérieurs*), the equivalent of the first two years of higher education, in preparation for the later cycles taken at the university, thus preempting about half the normal university undergraduate course. In 1987–88 they took no less than 21.8 per cent of the students, three times the CP-GE students and over twice the IUTs'. The universities have been described as the poor relations of the system, and have lost some of their research functions to separate research bodies like the *Centre nationale de la recherche scientifique*, which handicaps them in the global competition with foreign universities. Unlike the latter in most of the advanced countries, they are not at the head of the system but strictly second best to the *grandes écoles* and the national research institutions.[2]

The *grandes écoles*, despite their functional names, do not in fact prepare specifically for professional careers but offer a general education to a social elite. As an OECD report on French higher education at the time of the 1968 student unrest asserted, 'the different *grandes écoles* dissimulate, under an academic definition of their function, their real function as instruments perpetuating cultural advantage among the privileged classes or even of recruiting an administrative elite on behalf of the ruling classes.' The entrance examinations and grading system of each school

> were no more than the technical expression of its social function of providing a trained and dedicated caste of specialists for the economy and of general practitioners for the machinery of the state. It is therefore not surprising that the recruitment for the Grandes Ecoles is even more bourgeois than the recruitment for the Faculties.[3]

This illustrates how powerful the French state is, not only in relation to education but to French society as a whole. By controlling and manipulating education, the state controls and manipulates recruitment to all positions of power and prestige in the public sector and increasingly, via secondment of top government officials, to a large proportion of those in the nationalized industries and the private corporations. Colonization of the private sector is facilitated by the traditional practice of *pantouflages*, literally 'taking one's slippers' in early retirement but in reality moving sideways into highly paid employment in the mixed economy of national- ized enterprise and government agencies and, especially since the Second World War, into high executive positions in the private corpora- tions. As early as 1972 61 per cent of the directors of the nationalized industries and 47 per cent of those in partially state-owned companies (*sociétés d'économie mixte*) were ex-civil servants.[4] At about the same time 68 per cent of the PDGs (*Presidents Directeurs-Généraux*) of the 475 leading private firms, and 74 per cent of those in the most prestigious industries, were graduates of the *grandes écoles*, 42 per cent of them from the *Ecole Polytechnique*.[5] An earlier study in 1959 showed that over the previous eighty years between a quarter and a half of the *Inspection des Finances*, the most prestigious corps in the service, and about the same proportion of the *Corps des Mines*, had moved into the private sector. The numbers passing over have increased since the war, as industries were national- ized and semi-independent agencies were set up, and private business has become concentrated in fewer and larger enterprises which are worthy employment rivals to the state. Moreover, those migrating are doing so at younger ages, some even in their twenties, since the rewards in the private sector have far outgrown those in the public. There they assisted the collaboration between government and business which played a key role in the post-war national plan and French economic growth.

The *cadres* do not just join the civil service. They each belong to an institution peculiar to French government, the *grands corps*. Each recruit is inducted into a *grand corps*: the *Inspection des Finances*, the *Conseil d'Etat*, the *Corps des Mines*, and so on. The corps are club-like institutions which exist within and beyond government service. Once a corps member you are always a corps member, whether you climb the internal ladder to *chef de cabinet*, like Pierre Laroque or Jacques Delors, go into politics like Giscard d'Estaing, Georges Pompidou or Francois Mitterand, or *pantoufle* into business as PDG of a national bank or great corporation. The corps even pays your salary while on secondment or between jobs, and will always find you a new position if you need one. In British terms it is rather like a prize Fellowship of All Souls College, Oxford, except that it continues for life.[6]

The corps are almost all recruited from the *grandes écoles*, and particu- lar corps are symbiotically connected with particular schools. The top graduates of the ENA (*Ecole Nationale d'Admistration*) go into the *Inspec- tion des Finances*, the *Conseil d'Etat*, the *Cour des Comtes*, *Administrateurs civils*, the Diplomatic Corps, or the Prefectoral Corps. The best graduates of the *Ecole Polytechnique* and *Ecole des Mines* go into the *Corps des Mines* or *Ponts et Chaussées* (whose functions go far beyond mining and road building and embrace most scientific and technological activities). The best students at the *Ecole Normale Supérieure* staff all the institutions of higher education from the *grandes écoles* themselves to the universities, research institutes, the IUTs, and CP-GE colleges. Although only about 2 per cent of all graduates, they monopolize most of the top positions in politics, the civil service, and big business, and so they have been able over the last hundred years to block every attempt to reform the *grandes écoles* or open their recruitment to a wider public. Mitterrand, himself a double graduate of ENS and ENA, came into the presidency with the goal of democratizing their intake but was soon sidetracked by his own ministers and civil servants. Both left and right, Socialists and Gaullists, come from the same select stables and are unlikely to open their doors to any but those they consider the best bloodstock. The OECD Report of 1970 on French higher education in the wake of the 1968 troubles forecast that, despite the creation of separate and independent universities out of the unitary Napoleonic University of France, the reforms would not touch the *grandes écoles* and so would change nothing.[7]

The result is a governing elite more integrated and interconnected than any in the world, save perhaps in Japan. There, as we shall see, a handful of universities play much the same role in recruitment to top jobs as the French *grandes écoles*, migration from the bureaucracy into private business takes place on much the same lines, by *amakudari* ('descent from heaven') instead of *pantouflages*, and the networking between 'old boys' (*jinmyaku*, 'veins in the rock', or telephone networks) gets things done in much the same way. The two societies are remarkably similar in their values and goals. Both the French and Japanese postwar economic 'miracles' owed a great deal to the networking which, rather than any cut and dried plan, brought all the decision makers together in pursuit of economic growth, united them all in a common goal, and enabled them to cut corners in achieving it. The common educational background of the politicians, civil servants, and leading business men, their common feeling of having climbed the same highly competitive ladders, and their consciousness (whether justified or not) of being the very best of their generation gave them a self-confidence – to outsiders, an arrogance – in their own capacity to succeed. They were, if not born, then selected by their brainpower to rule, and they were confident that only they could create the future. Their arrogance is epitomized by President Jacques Chirac, the Gaullist 'bulldozer', who is willing to oppose the whole of world opinion and put French exports at risk to revive nuclear tests in the Pacific of no possible use to France or anyone else.

Like the Japanese, the French elite were helped by other factors: the yearning of a battered and defeated nation for a better, more peaceful and prosperous life; the hope, fostered by elite bureaucrats like Jean Monnet and Robert Schuman, that European integration would ensure prosperity and abolish war; the faith in new technologies like nuclear power, computers, and telecommunications which solved France's problems of resource scarcity; and, to turn a burden into a driving force, the rapid fall of the peasant population which had always been a drag on progress but now became a blood transfusion of fresh human labour.

They were also opposed by a French intelligentsia based in the universities but led by graduates of the *grandes écoles* like Jean-Paul Sartre and Louis Althusser, who were anti-capitalist, anti-clerical and anti-statist, a largely left-wing movement of the disenchanted and *enragés* who despised the technocracy and anti-intellectualism of the ruling elite. They themselves were a product of the same system, the Adlerian younger brothers deprived of their birthright, who envied and criticized their elder brothers and fomented destructive philosophies and political demonstrations. Their main function, however, was to divert the attention of the young from materialism and economic growth while the bureaucrats and corporate managers pursued it and, to a degree, marginalized them. The irony was that it was the very prosperity of the first quarter-century after the war that gave the radical students and their brilliant but ineffectual mentors the means to protest. In 1968 they had their chance and even managed to tire out General de Gaulle and provoke his eventual resignation, but their protests failed to change the fundamental structure of the meritocracy, to which indeed they were as attached as its defenders and paid it the compliment of envy.

What underlay the protests was the fact that meritocracy is, or seems to be, an ideal system for successful meritocrats but a less than ideal one for the rest. In fact, there are decided limits to its efficiency for the meritocrats themselves. Although the civil service and the *grandes écoles* have made half-hearted efforts to incorporate late developers, for example by admitting promising middle-ranking civil servants in their thirties to the ENA, it fails to pick up and utilize a mass of late-blooming talent, which then becomes frustrated and resentful. University students know they will always be treated as second best, and their periodic demonstrations are an expected, even cherished, feature of French life. Within the service, rigid barriers are allowed to grow up between ministries and between their *grands corps*, which compete for power and prestige in bitter turf wars at the expense of the general good. A distinguished Inspector of Finance, Simon Nora, told John Ardagh in the early 1980s:

> Our elite system was a great asset until about a decade ago – that is in the post-war years when our politics were unstable and France was fast modernizing and industrializing. The technocrats were then a dedicated *clergé*, the secular priests of progess, pulling France forward with autocratic zeal. Today France is largely

modernized and what is needed is something else, the emergence of a more open and egalitarian society where ordinary people can participate more.[8]

One might add that an elite is more likely to be trusted and admired when it succeeds, but when, as from the oil crises of the 1970s, growth slackens and the elite is seen to be fallible, disillusion sets in and the merit of the meritocrats begins to be questioned. When the race is to the swift, and the swift are seen to be no longer superhuman, the slow begin to resent the prizes the swift award themselves.

The resentment of the also-rans was increased when some of the cleverest of the intelligentsia, including Pierre Bourdieu, J.-C. Passeron, Raymond Boudon and Alain Girard, demonstrated how skewed the meritocracy was.[9] 'Cultural capital' in the shape of family-based *savoir-faire*, knowledge of the ropes, command of the right kind of language, together with superior economic means and social connections, gave bourgeois children a decisive advantage in the race and handicapped the rest.[10] These advantages were self-reinforcing, and helped to transform natural talents, which might be very modest, into major social and psychological attributes. Their cultural inheritance imperceptibly became embedded in the personality, and was recognizable as kith and kin by the existing inhabitants of the culture. 'People like us' has always been the main principle of elite recruitment. In this way, the elite products of the *grandes écoles* convinced themselves that their high positions and large salaries were simply the just reward for their exceptional abilities. In Bourdieu's terms, a social inheritance was transformed into a 'natural gift' (*le don*).[11] They hold power and wealth because, in their own eyes and to the extent that they can persuade the rest of the nation, they are by nature the most gifted and talented of their generation.

Even the great expansion of higher education since the war, from 180,000 students in 1965 to 1.7 million in 1992, has in no way changed the social structure. The *grandes écoles* have successfully resisted expansion and therefore admit a decreasing percentage of the age group, thus increasing the competition for the same number of places. In 1991 70,000 students enrolled in CP-GE courses preparatory for the *grandes écoles*, competing for about 3,000 places, including only about 300 in the *Ecole Polytechnique* and about 100 each in the ENS and ENA, the most prestigious of the schools.[12] Of the successful entrants the great majority, four out of five, still come from the upper and middle classes, about half of these from the families of business managers, high executives, senior civil servants, and the liberal professions, who constitute about 10 per cent of the population.[13] Children of artisans, shopkeepers, white-collar workers, manual workers, farmers and farm workers, about 80 per cent of the population, constitute less than 20 per cent of the intake. As elsewhere, the expansion of higher education has increased the chance of education in every class, but more or less proportionately, so that life chances between the classes remain much the same.

For all that, the system is still a meritocracy, if a skewed one. No more than a small minority of the children of the upper bourgeoisie make the grade and not all the children of the peasants and working class are excluded. In 1980 three quarters of the children of *cadres supérieurs* (top executives) obtained the *baccalauréat*, the ticket of admission to higher education, compared with three fifths from the *cadres moyens* and white-collar workers (*employés*), two fifths from the artisan class, and one quarter from the blue-collar working class.[14] The best and brightest – in terms of passing examinations and the *concours* for the *grands corps* – from each class win the glittering prizes, and merit is merit whether acquired by natural endowment or cultural advantage. The remarkable thing is that, apart from a few French intellectuals who are themselves meritocrats and beneficiaries of the system, the great majority of French people still accept it not only as fair and natural but as proof of the superiority of French society, education, and culture.

## L'ÉTAT, C'EST NOUS

Given the central role of the state in French society at every level and the consequent dominance of the *cadres supérieurs* (senior executives) who run the government, the growth of the French state comes as no surprise. Before the First World War government expenditure averaged about 13 per cent of Gross National Product, between the wars about 25 per cent. Since the Second World War it has risen from 42 per cent in 1947 to 52 per cent in 1971 and, on a different scale, from 38.3 per cent of Gross Domestic Product in 1972 to 51.8 per cent in 1987. This compares with an average rise between the last two dates in the OECD countries from 32.1 per cent to 40.9 per cent.[15] Since then, the social welfare cuts and privatizations under the latter-day Mitterrand have lowered it to 47 per cent in 1991, but the state still remains the largest single employer of labour. In 1991 the government still controlled 107 enterprises, including 58 public corporations such as the major banks, the Renault car firm and the Elf oil company, employing with their more than 2,000 subsidiaries some 1.3 million workers. Adding to these the 4.5 million 'functionaries' in central and local government, the post office, the police, the school and university teachers, the government employed about one in every four French workers.[16] This does not include the pensioners, the un-employed and other welfare beneficiaries dependent on the state for their incomes, which would raise the numbers to more than one in three.

The main reason for the more than average growth of French govern-ment expenditure, apart from defence, on which France spends more than most European countries but less than Britain and the United States, is the generous welfare state. Transfer payments, to the retired, the sick, the handicapped, and the unemployed, plus housing and family support, amount to 28 per cent of GDP and constitute no less than 32 per cent of the disposable income of the average family. Since French income taxes are relatively light, at about 9 per cent of income, due to the curious French practice of dividing the family income by the number of members before taxing it, most of the money is raised through the social security contributions, paid more by the employers, which amount to 30.5 per cent of income. Thus the redistribution is largely horizontal, between the active, healthy, and employed and the same people when too young or too old, too sick or disabled, or otherwise unable to work, or have a large family. Retirement pensions and child and family support are exceptionally generous. Housing subsidies, for example, bring down the average cost of accommodation from 42 to 28 per cent of disposable family income. And for those whom the indexed minimum wage (SMIC – *salaire minimum d'insertion*) fails to raise above the poverty line, the guaranteed family income (RMI – *revenu minimum d'insertion*) introduced in 1988 makes up the difference.[17]

The rise of so generous a welfare state – though it stopped growing in the late 1980s under a revisionist socialist president – in a country traditionally ruled by right-wing governments, is at first sight somewhat puzzling. Jean-Pierre Jallade in his comparative study of European welfare states places France in the tradition of Bismarck's conservative attempt to 'dish the Socialists' and consolidate the workers behind a paternalist, caring authoritarianism.[18] Certainly, social security expanded faster under de Gaulle and his epigoni than under the socialists and Mitterand. The explanation is that the French, despite their assertive individualism, are exponents of *solidarité*, a sense of community, of dedication to the good of *la nation*, that sees national power and survival in a hostile world in the strength and stability of the individual and the family.[19] This stems in part from the Roman Catholic tradition of charity and corporatism, partly from the republican tradition of the integrity and defence of the nation, and partly from the connected fear of population decline which reduced France in the nineteenth century from Number One in Europe to Number Three, behind Britain and Germany. But mostly, in the pragmatic terms of those who made the decisions to expand welfare provision, it stems from the ideology of a ruling elite who harnessed all these pressures to the paternalist concept of *La France* as one great family responsible for all its citizens. It was a version of the same ideal of social citizenship preached by R. H. Tawney and T. H. Marshall that influenced its growth in Britain, but infused with nationalist emotion and French pride.

Even more important than their ideology was the direct role of the *cadres supérieurs* in the building of the welfare state. They, more than the politicians, were responsible for creating the policy, framing the legislation, and putting it into operation. The 'French Beveridge', Pierre Laroque, president of the General Inspectorate of Social Affairs, was the architect of the welfare system. Later pioneers, like Robert Boulin who reorganized the state pension scheme in 1971 on the basis of one half of lifetime earnings, and Jacques Delors, the socialist who integrated social, wage, and industrial policies under Gaullist President Pompidou (himself an ex-bureaucrat) before migrating to the presidency of the European Commission, were in the same tradition.

Laroque would have prefered a single insurance fund (*caisse unique*) but, under pressure from the mutual aid societies and trades unions (cf. the British friendly societies and trade unions under Lloyd George in 1911), accepted a system of shared responsibility between government and those institutions. It culminated in what one comparative historian of welfare states has called 'a complex system of multiple and partially administered plans in which the boundaries between public and private, state and society, were blurred'.[20] Retirement pensions, for example, might be paid to the same person from three different sources, a state-backed *mutualité*, a trade union fund, and an employer's occupational scheme. Such fragmentation, in a country renowned for its centralization in everything else, reflects the fragmentation of French society. The persistent divisions between peasants, manual and white-collar workers, and *grands* and *petits bourgeois*, and the power of different groups to demand separate treatment, down to the level of individual occupations such as the miners and the railway workers, all contributed to the complexity of contemporary welfare provision.

The only group that represented society as a whole and could square the circle of conflicting interests was the government bureaucracy, whose ingenuity built the rambling house out of the diverse materials thrown into the circle by the competing parties, groups and institutions. Their paternalism, based on the public professional ideal of social citizenship and social efficiency in the face of centrifugal forces, accounts for the peculiar combination of decentralized provision and bureaucratic supervision that characterizes the French *état providence*. Finally, it also rewards them with the increased functions and powers required to operate so complex and convoluted a system.

The most striking success of the bureaucracy was the series of national plans which have been credited with the French post-war 'economic miracle'. The General Planning Commission set up in 1946 was not solely concerned with economic growth. Indeed, its first concerns were with social, health, and demographic policies, to provide an ailing France with a growing, healthy, and socially secure population. Its subsidiary Commission on Consumption and Social Modernization under the presidency of trade unionist Henri Raynaud, secretary of the General Confederation of Labour, aimed at an optimum population of 50–60 million: to enable France to compete with neighbouring countries, to satisfy labour needs for production and defence, to provide enough young workers to support the aging population, and to spread the burdens of society across a wider base of support. The Commission on Manpower was also concerned with making more use of womanpower, by equalizing male and female wages and salaries, increasing women's access to education, professional training, and employment at all levels, and by providing more help and child care for working mothers, thus reversing the old natalist policy of 'the mother at home'.[21]

Economic policy, moreover, has been questioned in its effectiveness by free-market economists, who argue that the French economy grew in spite, not because of it. Growth was due, they argue, to the general boom in the global economy which swept the French, like all the rest, along with it, and to special French advantages including the largest pool of cheap rural labour in Western Europe and, from 1959, the 'unfair' protection and support of the European Common Market, and the immense subsidies and price supports of the Common Agricultural Policy.

It is true that the French agricultural workforce, the largest in Western Europe, shrank from 27 per cent of the occupied population in 1954 to a mere 6 per cent in 1991, providing an invaluable human resource for industry and the service sector. But similar if smaller shifts were occurring in all the other advanced countries, while the French economy was surging ahead even faster than free-market West Germany and much faster than Britain: at 5.5 per cent in 1960–73 and 2.2 per cent in the oil crisis years 1974–87, compared with 4.5 per cent and 1.9 per cent in West Germany and 3.2 per cent and 1.7 per cent in Britain.[22]

The free-market argument, based on an obsessive distaste for every kind of planning, misses the point of the French variety. This was not the central state planning with rigid production quotas of the Soviet command economies, but a flexible type of indicative planning that merely suggested possible goals and opportunities in particular industries and committed the government to providing the financial and fiscal environment in which they might be attained. The corporations, however much they disliked state direction, had in any case to plan their own production targets and budgets, and it made their job easier if the government indicated how it saw the broad economic situation in the immediate future. If expectations were shared by all or most of the parties involved, they had a much better chance of being fulfilled. The government's commitment to growth assured business managers and encouraged them to invest in the most promising directions. And it was the permanent officials rather than the ephemeral politicians, especially in the period of unstable governments under the Fourth Republic, who gave that assurance.

More important than the plan itself was the networking between the ministries, the banks, and the corporations facilitated by the common education and experience of the graduates of the *grandes écoles* and the members of the *grands corps* that ensured the success of the system. As in Japan, where a telephone call between old classmates and colleagues could unblock a bottleneck and ensure that things got done, the French bureaucrats and corporate managers could foster growth with or without a national plan, but the existence of the plan simplified cooperation and helped everyone to pull in the same direction.

*Le Plan* was essentially the symbol of the common determination to rebuild France and restore its pride among the nations. It began as a rescue operation but succeeded so well that it overshot the target and pushed France into the lead in European economic growth. It worked best while it flowed with the general tide of the European and global economic boom from 1945 to 1973, but in the harsher world of the oil crises and the collapse of communism when even a socialist president lost faith in central planning and nationalization, it faltered. But by then it had done its work and restored France to second place in Europe, behind only a united Germany with a third more population and two thirds more production. Unlike the more diverse and diffuse elites of Britain and Germany, the French bureaucracy with its offshoots in the private sector can truly say *L'état, c'est nous*.

## THE SERVICE REVOLUTION

The traditional predominance of government service, on which, as we have seen, about one quarter of the workforce depended by the 1980s for their incomes, prepared France well for the service revolution, the transition from agriculture and industry to service occupations. The French were traditionally suspicious of industry and looked with disdain on mere money making. Economic historians like David Landes have attributed the slowness of French industrialization before the mid-twentieth century to the attitude of business men themselves towards ambitious competitors as cannibals (*mangeurs d'hommes*) who were not prepared to live and let live for the sake of a quiet and therefore less innovative life. Although fear of ruthless competition may have been due to slow population growth and a sluggish market in a largely peasant society with little propensity to consume, the attitude was real enough and led industrialists to be rationally cautious about innovating, to transfer surplus capital into passive investment like land or foreign stocks and bonds, and to send their sons into government service and the professions. It also led others to look askance at business and to ascribe more honour and prestige to state officials and professional men. The French were therefore readier than most nations for a further increase in an already large and powerful service class and, paradoxically, for their takeover and professionalization, through corporate management, of big business itself.

The proportion of the active population engaged in service occupations increased from 34 per cent in 1946 and 38 per cent in 1960 to 55.3 per cent in 1980 and 63.5 per cent by 1990. Those in agriculture fell precipitately from 38 per cent in 1946 to 8.8 per cent in 1980 and to 5.8 per cent in 1991, while those in industry, stimulated by what may be called the completion of the French industrial revolution, at first rose, from 28 per cent in 1946 to 35.9 per cent in 1980, and then fell back to 29.5 per cent by 1991.[23]

As in other countries experiencing the service revolution, not all service workers were highly paid professionals, officials, or managers. In 1991 only 11.6 per cent, one in nine, were *cadres et professions intellectuelles supérieures* (senior executives in government, business and the professions); another fifth, 20.1 per cent, were *professions intermédiaires* (middle managers and officials and lesser professionals); while the rest were office workers, policemen, military personnel, shop assistants, catering staff, transport workers, and the like. As elsewhere, the service revolution did not bring improvement to everyone and may even have made things worse for many, as well-paid jobs in manufacturing were replaced, if at all, by low-paid ones in Robert Reich's 'in-person services', like fast-food catering, supermarkets, garbage disposal, and so on.

Nonetheless, while merchants and industrialists of the traditional kind declined in numbers from 1,045,000 in 1962 to 895,000 in 1989, the *cadres et professions superiéures* decisively overtook them, growing from 892,000 to 2,318,000.[24] Moreover, with comparatively few exceptions the executives who run the big business corporations, whatever their provenance, are now highly educated, salaried employees rather than owners, though their rewards may be far greater than the profits of the old owner-managing entrepreneurs.

Besides nearly trebling their numbers in a quarter of a century, the *cadres supérieurs* have until very recently increased their take-home pay faster than the rest of the population. Or, rather, a new class of senior executives is emerging from the mass of top professional workers who, while the rest have suffered a slight setback in the recent recessions, have surged ahead in wealth, prestige, and power. While the average increase for the top 10 per cent has decelerated in the last few years, those at the very top have enjoyed increased prosperity and have begun to separate themselves from the rest. This explains how the top decile of salary earners with at least twice the average family income could gain slightly less in percentage terms of the national income in the 1980s, while the richest 1 or 2 per cent have been gaining ground over their fellows and the whole population.[25] They are becoming a new, higher elite, what has been called a *nomenklatura à la francaise*, a modern aristocracy based not on birth but on success, power, and money. While some in the salaried middle class and the self-employed professions are becoming a sort of neo-proletariat with precarious living standards and no security of tenure, this new elite chases not only higher incomes but also privileges and fringe benefits, including expense accounts, private health care, company cars, longer holidays, bonuses and stock options, and contracts that give them 'golden handshakes' (huge lump-sum payments) when they leave.[26] This is one more example of members of a ruling elite looking after themselves.

After the United States and Britain, France has one of the most unequal distributions of income and wealth in the advanced world, at least before welfare benefits are taken into account. Ten per cent of households receive 28 per cent of the national income, and the same percentage own 54 per cent of the property.[27] Most, though not all, of these overlap with the ruling elite of senior executives in government and business. (Some old wealth still exists in the landholding aristocracy.) The business executives have more access to the sources of wealth than the government bureaucrats, but the latter have increasing opportunities to join them via *pantouflages* or secondment. Meanwhile, more of the graduates of the *grandes écoles* are bypassing government service altogether and going straight into business. In this way a new social framework (*un nouveau découpage social*)[28] is emerging with a higher summit and a larger gap between it and the lower ranks. The very peak of the meritocracy is becoming more detached and remote from the society it dominates, with disturbing consequences for the future of both.

## THE SECOND SEX

When Simone de Beauvoir wrote her manifesto *The Second Sex* in 1949 she launched the liberation of the French woman. This was much needed and overdue, since women there had only just achieved the vote and were still subject to a massive burden of oppressive laws. Women still had no right to custody of their children and a married woman could not sign a cheque without the concurrence of her husband. At the same time, although the French natalist ideal was *la femme au foyer*, women worked outside the home to a greater extent than their neighbours, and were still expected to shoulder all the chores of the household. Moreover, like Mary Wollstonecraft before her, de Beauvoir still seemed to believe in marriage as a partnership in which the husband was the natural head, and recent biographies have shown her to have been abjectly subordinate to the sexist and less intelligent Jean-Paul Sartre, a typical product of the *Ecole Normale Supérieure*, who stole some of her best ideas on which he based his existentialism.[29]

Since then French women have liberated themselves to a surprising degree, based on their expansion in nearly all areas of the workforce. Women have taken over jobs in industry and the professions, including old male monopolies like telephone engineering and plumbing, and proved their ability to compete. In the 25 years to 1990 women in the workforce increased by 3 million to 42 per cent, compared with only 1 million men. Of women over 15 years of age (including students and pensioners) 46 per cent are in employment. Between the ages of 25 and 49, the main childrearing years, three out of four women now have a job outside the home. The obvious reason is the demand from the service sector, in offices, shops, and personal service, where women are often preferred, in which they have increased their numbers from 66 per cent in 1962 to 76 per cent in 1989.[30] In the *professions intermédiaires*, which include teachers, nurses and technicians, they have increased from 34 per cent to 43 per cent. Even among the *cadres et professions intellectuelles supérieures* they have increased from 16 per cent to 29 per cent.[31] The feminization of large areas of employment is a major aspect of the service revolution. While traditional blue-collar work for men has been declining, and light industry has offered more work for women, white-collar work is dominated by female workers.

It has not been all gain for the women, however. In France as elsewhere, women are paid less for the same work; they are less often promoted to higher posts, even with the same qualifications; they are more likely to work part-time; they have less security of tenure and are the first to lose their jobs in recessions; and because of interruptions due to maternity and childrearing they are much less likely to have a career. Although income differentials between the sexes have narrowed somewhat since the war, men still earn on average a third more than women. Even in the same occupations, women earn less: 8 per cent less in white-collar work, 29 per cent less among *cadres supérieurs*, mainly because men occupy the higher positions.[32]

Women outnumber men in higher education, where France has proportionately more women students than any other major country save the United States, but few go to the *grandes écoles* and fewer still enter the magic circle of the privileged elite. Their chances of breaking into the 'old boy' networks and using them to advance their careers are therefore attenuated. A very few, like Edith Cresson, briefly Prime Minister, or Nicole Questiaux, Secretary of State for Social Affairs and National Solidarity, in the 1980s, make it to the top, but they are as rare as the Margaret Thatchers or Janet Renos in Britain and America.[33] The service revolution has opened up more jobs for women but far more in the lower echelons than at the top.

## THE INCORPORATION OF BIG BUSINESS

As we have seen, since the Second World War the state bureaucrats and graduates of the *grandes écoles* have successfully colonized the management of the nationalized industries and the private corporations. Rather than assimilating government to big business through the 'revolving door' as in the United States, or the Thatcherite recruitment of like-minded executives in Britain, the French bureaucracy has quite deliberately set out to incorporate big business into the unified elite. This is in line with the French tradition of government involvement in industry, stretching back to Colbert under Louis XIV. Modern incorporation began fairly naturally with the nationalization programme after the war, when 90 per cent of the banks and a large number of industrial corporations, like Renault, Elf Aquitaine, Paribas, and the Suez investment group, were taken into public ownership, some because of collaboration with the Nazi occupation but most to control the 'commanding heights of the economy' in the interests of French recovery. The mixed economy was natural to France. As experts on international business structure have noted, national government in France 'is intimately involved in business organization and governance. It participates significantly in economic endeavour . . . and in *la société d'économie mixte*.'[34]

The nationalized banks and industrial corporations were staffed from the beginning by seconded civil servants, whose success in turn eased the way for others to migrate into the private sector. By no means were all the top executive positions filled by ex-bureaucrats, and there are many great companies, like Carrefour, Moulinex, and Bouygues, founded and managed by tough self-made men, though their number fell from 31 to 21 per cent between 1983 and 1993. But the proportion of *grands patrons* recruited via the *grandes écoles* and the *grands corps* increased at the same time from 41 to 47 per cent, and there were always enough to create the symbiosis that gave birth to the national plan and the economic 'miracle'.[35] In the last two decades *pantouflages* from the civil service into the private sector has accelerated. A study of the inspectors of finance in 1990 showed that between 1974 and 1989, 'Never since the Liberation have the high functionaries so often quitted the state, and never have they left so rapidly.' Many were leaving government after only two to four years, often below 30 years of age, for top jobs close to the directorate in the big corporations. They were valued less for their experience of government than for their intellectual success at the ENA and their proven ability to adapt to new situations.

The authors, Michel Bauer and Dominique Danic, argued that, paradoxically, while the state was disengaging from its direct role in the economy, it was producing a new and brilliant economic elite which the corporations could not provide for themselves. The young *'Enarques'* (graduates of the ENA) were displacing 'les X' (the polytechniciens) who dominated industry in the past, and were also colonizing distribution, the press and publishing, communications and information services, and even construction.[36] There they were meeting up with other graduates of the grandes écoles who, as we have seen, constituted two thirds of the PDGs of the largest corporations and most of their director colleagues.[37]

A further study by Michel Bauer with Benedicte Bertin-Mourot published in 1995 showed that nearly half the heads of the largest corporations had been recruited from the state bureaucracy: 'the corporation has simply subcontracted recruitment to the state'. A full half had attended the same two schools, the ENA and the Ecole Polytechnique. Far from reducing this flow, the new free-market policies had increased it: 'The privatizations only reinforced this elitism' by moving public servants to the private sector. Not only did this intensify the homogeneity of the ruling elite, it produced 'a total absence of alternative views and complete uniformity of thought on everything from the 'franc fort' to unemployment'.[38] The resultant networking between classmates in government, the nationalized industries and the corporations is central to French social policy and economic growth. The privatizations – twenty-one more great enterprises were sold in 1993–94 – have made little difference to collaboration between industry, government politicians, and the bureaucracy. The same integrated elite runs all three.

The government in any case retains considerable powers to guide and influence private industry. Through the Centre des bilans it voluntarily collects and exchanges information with 28,000 business firms on their relative performance and profitability. Through the Centre des risques it exchanges information on company debts. And through the related Fichier bancaire des entreprises it provides free credit ratings (cotations) on 750,000 companies to the banks as potential lenders, plus information on 700,000 managers. The Trésor directorate in the Ministry of Finance wields even more influence than its counterpart in Japan, encouraging finance companies to invest in promising companies and saving firms in trouble by holding off creditors and rallying institutional shareholders. And, until recently at least, government investment and aid to nationalized and private corporations, like the £590 million it provided for Machines Bull and Thomson–CSF in information technology, came near to breaking international rules against unfair trading.[39]

Such help and guidance has enabled French companies to claim third place, after the American and Japanese, in the global economy, with twelve of the 100 top asset-holding transnational corporations in 1992.[40] Eight French companies (Renault, Elf Aquitaine, Electricité de France, Alcatel–Alsthom, Usinor–Sacilor and Pechiney) are in the first fifty of the London Times list of the top 1,000 European industrial companies by turnover, though they do not rank very high, between eleventh and thirty-seventh.[41]

For a country traditionally renowned for its abundance of small businesses, this is a remarkable change. Moreover, some of the largest French holding companies, such as the Suez company, Paribas, Pargesa, and the Franco–Belgian Groupe Bruxelles Lambert, sit at the centre of galaxies of European banks, insurance companies, utilities, mining, transport, and manufacturing companies. Given the importance of institutional shareholdings in the larger companies, 36 per cent according to the Banque de France in 1991,[42] here is an example of corporate neo-feudalism to match what we have already seen in the United States and Britain.

Company structure, however, is different from the Anglo–American, in which the shareholders are the nominal owners and controllers but the real power rests exclusively with the professional executives. It is true that a French PDG can be a 'little Napoleon' and run his company with an iron hand without even consulting the board of directors. But in practice he operates within an environment that restricts his initiative far more than any Anglo–American CEO. He is beholden to the institutional investors, who form a hard kernel (*noyau dur*) of professional watchdogs, two thirds of whom must be non-executive directors owing allegiance to their institutions rather than the PDG, and who maintain a permanent interest and can (but rarely do) dismiss the PDG if they so wish. He has to liaise with the civil servants in the appropriate ministry, or forego the information, subsidies, contracts, and other benefits they can offer. And, unlike his British or American counterparts, he has to deal with a *comité d'entreprise* which all large corporations have to have, on which the workforce and the trades unions are represented. The *comité* sends one or two members (six in a nationalized industry) to board meetings and has the right to appoint a financial adviser with power to examine the accounts and confirm the firm's profits – an invaluable factor in wage negotiations.

A small number of firms have taken advantage of Method II, the two-tier system introduced in 1966 in consequence of the European Community's German-inspired Fifth Directive, with a supervisory board (*conseil de surveillance*) to oversee the directorate. This has proved useful as a vehicle for certain mergers, where the amalgamating partners want to see what the new company is up to, but has not proved popular elsewhere. Neither system, *comité d'entreprise* nor *conseil de surveillance*, goes so far as the German device of codetermination, in which a supervisory board with legal representation for workers and their unions oversees the main executive one. Yet it bespeaks a European rather than an Anglo–American attitude to company law and structure, one in which the stakeholders include not only the shareholders and by extension the management but also the major creditors in the form of the regular bankers and, to some extent, the workforce as well, not to mention the state as a kind of permanent nurse or watchdog. And the new industrial directive under the 1992 Maastricht Treaty will require the appointment of works councils in all large companies (with more than 1,000 workers, operating in two or more European countries) by September 1996.[43]

Consequently, the French corporation is much more proof than the Anglo–American against hostile takeovers, and therefore much less obsessed with short-term profits and share price, and can plan and invest in research for the long-term health and expansion of the company without looking over its shoulder for the predatory raider. It is not so proof against management buy-outs, fifty-two of which took place between 1985 and 1990, more than in any other country – a further confirmation, if any were needed, of the professionalization of French business.[44] As with the state bureaucracy, there is in French business a culture of paternalism and solidarity that takes pride in working for the good of the nation. This does not of course prevent the managerial elite, like others who control the flow of income, from steering more of it their own way, which brings us to the Achilles' heel of all post-industrial societies, the question of corruption.

## OVER-REGULATION AND CORRUPTION

Most French people believe, with some justice, that they live in an over-regulated society. This is the downside of bureaucracy and a state-sponsored meritocracy. Almost every activity of the individual, from farming to investing, is subject to close scrutiny by public officials. It is, for example, almost impossible to buy or sell agricultural land except to existing farmers or their offspring, and at prices which are in effect fixed by the state. The slightest error in a tax return will bring in an inspector who will not only go through every document in sight but will supervise every transaction until the wickedness is purged. Nothing can be built or repaired without a host of applications and permissions. Foreign payments in and out of the country are treated as suspect and have to be explained and justified. In such an atmosphere suspicion is often justified, because the French, beset by red tape, seek to avoid officialdom and regard regulations as made to be broken. The chief reason for the low income tax, at an average of 9 per cent, is that tax evasion is a national sport that the state cannot hope to stop.

According to public opinion surveys, the French over the last few years have come to feel even more uneasy about the state. Since 1970 the number considering it something far removed from themselves and their interests has risen from 51 per cent to 74 per cent. Two out of three, 69 per cent, believe that politicians do not concern themselves with what their constituents think. Only 12 per cent, less than one in eight, believe that politicians have integrity. People have lost confidence in the capacity of the political system to solve major problems and scandals, like the contamination of the hospital blood supply with the HIV virus and the consequent 'homicide' [sic] of thousands of people. They protest against the dishonest financing of the political parties, the manipulation of justice, and alleged wastage of FF100 billion a year in maladministration and inefficiency, subsidies to industry and agriculture, the mismanagement of the national debt, and the failure to use the receipts from privatization to reduce it. The moves towards the free market seem only to have brought recession and a new precariousness to life, and there has been a reaction back to the values of equality and solidarity. That means, ironically, that people look to the government to solve the very problems they attribute to government. It is a very good example of the French love–hate relation with the state.[45]

Such an attitude both invites and feeds on corruption. Until recently the bureaucracy had a reputation for honesty and integrity. Now the media are full of tales of scandal, kickbacks, corruption, and official greed. 'Two years ago,' wrote Judge Thierry Jean-Pierre in 1994, 'I thought political corruption existed in France but that it was marginal. Yet the more you delve, the more you realize it's completely systematic. It is not linked to the Mafia, like it is in Italy – but it is everywhere.' His investigators showed that, from the smallest commune to the Presidential Palace, from left-wing socialists to the Gaullist right, kickbacks were regarded as normal, even commonplace, in bargaining for public contracts. The politicians and their friends were powerful enough to prevent prosecutions: 'Judges are always blocked; they never get to the bottom of these affairs. That's what makes you despair.'[46]

In 1993 Jean-Pierre and his colleague Judge Renaud van Ruymbeke found evidence that for twenty years every socialist-run local authority had asked for a 2–4 per cent commission on public works contracts, recovering hundreds of millions of taxpayers' francs for the party funds. He also alleged that the late Roger-Patrice Pelat, a close business friend of President Mitterrand, had received FF25 million (£2.9 million) for negotiating a deal between a French construction firm and North Korea to build a hotel in Pyongyang, and that Pelat had, during accusations of insider dealing in 1989, made payments to Mitterrand's son Gilbert. For his pains Jean-Pierre was transferred from his Le Mans office and not replaced, so that his files there gathered dust. He has since resigned and been elected to the European Parliament on an anti-corruption, anti-bureaucratic, and anti-European ticket.

Such reformers have been labelled by their critics *imprécateurs* (cursers) and accused of being self-serving, politically ambitious, and unpatriotic. But the flood of political scandals continues to rise, on both sides of the political spectrum. In the late 1980s Henri Emmanuelli, secretary and former treasurer of the Socialist Party, was charged with running fictitious consultancies, but the dossier was buried by the Prosecutor's office and not pursued. On the other side, van Ruymbeke found in 1993 that the Parti Republicain which controlled Nantes city council had received FF4.4 million (£530,000) commission for awarding a waterworks contract to the Pont à Mousson company, with specifications for pipes produced only by that company. In 1987, the Parti Republicain government's Industry Minister, Gérard Longuet, granted a licence to the SFR mobile telephone network which conveniently used the party's public relations agency GRR and placed expensive advertisements in the party's publications. While out of office Longuet is said to have made FF2.4 million (£290,000) from deals with Compagnie Générale des Eaux, the parent company of SFR; back in office, he ordered France Télécom to reduce its charges to SFR, saving the latter about FF200 million (£24 million) a year.[47]

These are but a few examples of the political corruption now said to be rife in France. Much of it is not individual graft but, as in American politics, 'for the good of the party'. There is, of course, plenty of personal chicanery too, like the notorious allegations of fraud and tax evasion against Bernard Tapie, the left-wing media tycoon and owner of the Marseilles football team under investigation for buying match wins. Yet this type of corruption, for personal gain or political advantage, is much less important than the 'structural corruption' built into the system, as in most post-industrial societies, like Italy or Japan. The power of an entrenched elite to direct more income towards its members is reinforced when they themselves believe to be indispensable, uniquely talented, and deserving of unlimited rewards. Convinced that their contribution to society's prosperity is by definition greater than everyone else's, they measure their own worth by their rewards and compete with each other in a sort of Dodo's race, in which everyone in the circle of privilege gets more and more prizes. Even though the state bureaucracy may be personally uncorrupt, they are always open to the temptation to accept offers of lucrative jobs from private business corporations with whom they do business. In a state-dominated economy like the French, in which relations between civil servants and big business are necessarily close, it would be less than human for the officials to ignore the golden opportunities on offer via *pantouflages* into the private sector and, consciously or unconsciously, to adjust their decision making accordingly. This kind of tacit understanding is neither illegal nor technically corrupt, but it has profound effects throughout the society.

The unsurprising result is that France has, before allowing for transfer payments at least, one of the most unequal distributions of income in Europe, and one of the most unequal in the First World, though it has been overtaken recently by Britain. In 1970 it was the most unequal of ten major OECD countries, with a Gini coefficient (1.0 = equality) before tax of 4.16, compared with an average of 3.68. The top 20 per cent of income earners received 10.9 times the average of the bottom 20 per cent, compared with an OECD average of 7.1 times. In 1984 the top 10 per cent received 14.3 times the income of the bottom 10 per cent. After tax, given the light weight of French income taxes, there was little change in the ratios, but welfare benefits reduced the gap to the OECD average. However, since the transfer payments were paid not by the lightly taxed rich but mainly by the ordinary workers, this only slightly reduced the real income of the elite.[48]

The consequences of inequality are manifold, in terms of rising crime, drug-taking, unrest and cynicism. One side effect is on race relations. Amongst the poorest in France are the recent immigrants, especially those from North Africa, who increased from one seventh of all resident foreigners in 1954 to nearly half in 1990. The 1990 Census reported the immigrants as 3.6 million, 6.3 per cent of the population, but the Ministry of the Interior puts the real figure at 4.5 million, 7.9 per cent.[49] Until 1962 and the end of the Algerian war France had a reputation as a racially tolerant society, especially towards French-speaking black Africans. But the influx of some 200,000 Moslem Arabs from Algeria, Tunis, and Morocco with very different culture, religion and life-style has produced a backlash, exacerbated by recession and unemployment, and fuelled the neo-Fascist right under Le Pen. This has been further exacerbated by the Moslem fundamentalist anti-French terrorism in Algeria and France itself, which peaceful Algerian immigrants fear will make life untenable for them.

The immigrants are blamed for many social problems, including crime, unemployment, housing shortages, slum dwelling, and so on. One in five convictions are of immigrants, three times their weight in the population, though they are far more likely to be arraigned and convicted than the native French. Crime has independently increased: in the forty years to 1991 it multiplied six-fold, reaching 3.7 million offences, four out of five of them offences against property, the rest mainly drug trafficking and the like. These suggest a social malaise not unconnected with poverty, unemployment, and, perhaps, envy of the affluent life-style of the rich. French social surveys put the crime wave down to the worsening of the social climate, worldwide as they see it, including new dangers such as political terrorism, information systems piracy, and the international drug trade. All these are exacerbated by global recession and mass unemployment, of which France has had more than its share.

France thus exemplifies both the benefits and social costs of meritocracy. The administrative efficiency and economic growth, the high living standards and longer, healthier lives, the increased leisure and longer holidays, for most of the people, testify to the success of the ruling elite of state bureaucrats and corporate executives, united by a common education at the *grandes écoles* and the old boy networks. But these have been bought at a high cost, in over-regulation and government intervention, the arrogance of officialdom and the hauteur of business tycoons, their self-aggrandizement in rewards and power, the temptations for abuse and corruption, and in the social consequences of the unequal distribution of income. All these combine to produce the cynicism that infects French society today.

The worst effect of a skewed meritocracy, if it pushes its exploitation and greed too far, is its suicidal tendency to undermine its own survival and that of its society. If it takes too much power and resources to itself, it incurs the risk not only of increasing social unrest, crime, and disorder, but of starving the mass of the people of the means to buy their own products. The economy will then begin to implode, and drag the elite down with it. France has not gone so far down this slippery slope as, say, Italy or Britain, still less as far as the late Soviet Union and its East European satellites, which have already self-destructed into ruin. What still saves France from its own excesses is the ideology of *solidarité* and mutual responsibility which infuses *la nation*. As long as that remains, the skewed meritocracy will justify its complacent self-esteem.

# 5

# GERMANY
## Two versions of professional society

Within twenty-five years of defeat in the Second World War the two Germanies had become the most successful post-industrial societies in their respective halves of Europe. West Germany became by far the largest economy in Western Europe, the fourth largest in the world after the United States, the Soviet Union, and Japan, and the model of a democratic, prosperous 'social market economy' uniting the free market with a generous, caring welfare state. East Germany became the most stable and productive member of the communist bloc, ostensibly (according to its own unreliable statistics) the eighth largest economy in the world and, in theory at least, an egalitarian meritocracy which catered for its citizens' every need. Situated on either side of the front line of the Cold War in political and military confrontation with each other, they constituted the most objective test of the competition between the two rival versions of professional society, the libertarian, democratic capitalist free market and the totalitarian socialist command economy. Both claimed of course to be democracies, the West of the traditional, pluralist, multi-party kind, the East of the collectivist, single-party variety in which freedom lay in obedience to the historical will of the working class, as interpreted by its self-chosen vanguard, the Socialist Unity Party. (In fact, since the Communist Party could never achieve a majority, there were four parties but they were totally submerged in the Socialist Unity Party, which the minority Communist Party used as its instrument of domination.) Both, in practice, were dominated by ruling elites who in their different ways contrived to extract an exceptionally good living from their societies.

## THE BURDEN OF THE PAST

The two Germanies inherited the weight of too much history. They had to live not only with the immediate Nazi past with its burden of war guilt, gratuitous aggression, and mass murder but also with centuries of oppression and humiliation by bellicose neighbours, followed by close on 100 years of fruitless revenge. Locked in the centre of the continent, broken into fragments by the medieval struggle between Empire and Papacy, scourged and divided by the religious wars of the Reformation, crippled by the Thirty Years' War of the seventeenth century which killed a third of the population, and trampled and humiliated by the armies of the French Revolution and Napoleon, Germany was a geographical expression rather than a country. The thirty-nine German states that emerged in 1815 felt victimized and abused. Except for Prussia, keeper of the eastern frontier against the Slavs, they were renowned for music, literature, philosophy, and fine craftsmanship rather than militarism, and no one could have forecast their future as a great, unified economic and military power. That fork in the road was taken in 1815 at the Congress of Vienna when Prussia was made keeper of the western frontier, too, against further incursions by the French, the unintended consequence of which was that Germany would be united under a military aristocracy rather than a modernizing bourgeoisie.

The German industrial revolution began even before the country came to be united, commercially from 1834, politically in 1871. Unification came, unexpectedly, by force, through Bismarck's three blitzkriegs against Denmark, Austria, and France, under Prussian and therefore military aristocratic leadership. The Second Reich rapidly became the most powerful, yet psychologically insecure, empire in Europe. Its fears of encirclement became self-fulfilling, alienating its near neighbours France and Russia, and provoking it into a bid, first, for mastery on land and then, fatally, for overlordship at sea. Whether Kaiser Wilhelm II wanted a war, and whether for world conquest, still provokes acrimonious debate, but there is no doubt that he challenged the hegemony of the powers in possession and left a legacy for Hitler and the Nazis to exploit in their fatal attempt to conquer Eurasia and the world. This led to the legend of Germany's innate military aggression that careered it down the road from Bismarck through two world wars to Hitler, the conquest of Europe, and massive defeat. That legend of a peculiar German disease of mindless militarism, however unjustified, was a disastrous past for the two post-war Germanies to live down.

It was not the only legacy from the past. There was also an exaggerated respect for the state, the result of centuries of dependence on it for disciplined defence and for the encouragement of economic growth; a 'habit of obedience' in Ralf Dahrendorf's phrase that found comfort and excuse in superior orders;[1] a rigorously disciplined and disciplinarian bureaucracy with greater prestige than the industrial and commercial bourgeoisie; a remarkably efficient and substantially free education system extending upwards to the technical high schools (polytechnics) and universities; and a surprising paternalism descending from Bismarck's social insurance of the 1880s to the welfare states on both sides of the post-war border.

The two Germanies dealt with these legacies in different ways. The West accepted guilt for the Nazis and paid compensation to victimized individuals and their families and to the state of Israel as surrogate for the six million Jews murdered in the Holocaust. The East denied any such guilt, arguing that Nazism was a disease of late capitalism which oppressed the working class, destroyed the trade unions, and crushed the Social Democratic and Communist parties, none of which could be held responsible for the sins of their oppressors. Both Germanies inherited the bureaucratic tradition, if not the bureaucracy itself since so few Nazi officials were purged, but put it to different uses. The West set out to democratize and subordinate it to elective political control, and successfully harnessed its paternalism to an enlarged welfare state. The East purged more of the Nazi officials but took over the tradition of bureaucratic control lock, stock, and barrel, down to the heirs of the Gestapo, the dreaded Stasi, who employed tens of thousands of informers and kept files on at least a quarter of the population. In most respects except racism and political orientation, on the left instead of the right, the German Democratic Republic mirrored the Third Reich: a totalitarian state which controlled the work, leisure and, as far as it could, the thoughts of its citizens, and abolished every institution that stood between the individual and the dictatorship – except, fatally for itself, the Lutheran Church, which became the only important, if cautious and cooperative, centre of dissent. Perhaps because of the Nazi inheritance of ruthless oppression and the German habit of obedience, the GDR after the one small rising of June 1953, mostly confined to East Berlin, was the most stable and quiescent member of the communist bloc, until it was destabilized by Gorbachev's *perestroika* and withdrawal of Russian support in 1989.

The quintessential legacy for the rapid recovery of both Germanies after the war was the German people themselves. There is no better proof of the importance of human capital in modern society than the speed with which the two Germanies (as, indeed, Japan) recovered from defeat and the massive destruction of their physical industries and infrastructure. The skills produced by a highly successful education and training system enabled them not only to recover their pre-war levels of production within five or ten years of collapse, but to overtake most of their erstwhile enemies within twenty-five years. By 1970 West Germany had surpassed every ex-enemy country except the United States in GNP per capita; by 1980 East Germany claimed to have overtaken Britain and was certainly the most productive country in the Soviet sphere. By 1991 united Germany, despite the costs of reunification, had by far the biggest and strongest economy in the European Community and had the third largest aggregate GDP in the developed world, after the United States and Japan.[2]

Other factors no doubt helped their recovery. What Arnold Toynbee called the moral advantage of defeat, the manifest need to subordinate every other desire to the rebuilding of the country – its cities reduced to rubble, its factories, roads, and railways destroyed or worn out, and the population starving and humiliated – forced their peoples to pull together, first to survive the terrible winters of the late 1940s, then to restore pre-war production in the 1950s, and finally in the 1960s to over-take their conquerors in economic growth. The Cold War was a blessing to them both. Marshall Aid and American investment put West Germany on its feet, and the continued presence of Allied forces brought more foreign spending than it cost and provided cheap defence, half the percentage of GDP of the United States and two thirds that of Britain, which allowed the West Germans to invest more than their Cold War allies in civilian industry.[3] East Germany became the front line against what was perceived as Western aggression, the base for the largest concentration of Russian troops and, despite Russian extraction of the spoils of victory in the early years, the most loyal and favoured satellite of the Soviet empire.

After a shaky start in which the Russian occupiers stripped its industry of nearly everything moveable and set up Russian controlled 'joint ventures', the East Germans found a central role in the communist alliance as the most productive and reliable supplier of high-quality machinery and instruments to the rest of the Warsaw Pact, aided by funds from West Germany to allow elderly people to migrate and a higher level of Western loans than the rest of the Eastern bloc. The Soviet Union was the only empire in history to allow its colonies, above all East Germany, to attain a living standard higher than the metropolis. This was in spite of the high expenditure on defence, in a vain attempt to match the West with only a quarter of the population and a fifth of the productive capacity, and of the drain on skilled manpower of the 2.6 million refugees who escaped to the West before the Berlin Wall was built in 1961.[4] None the less, in the 1960s and 1970s the GDR conducted its own 'economic miracle' which matched the West's earlier one in speed if not in scale. When the non-communist economies slowed down with the oil crises of the 1970s, East Germany actually surged briefly with the aid of cheap oil from the Soviet Union, though after 1977 it began its long terminal decline.[5] It was not the inherent inefficiency of the command economy that caused the East German collapse in 1989 but the corrup-tion of the ruling elite and the disillusion of the people, who voted with their feet as soon as Gorbachev, the reforming communist Tsar, allowed the Wall to be outflanked via the already self-emancipated Hungary.

Meanwhile, both economic miracles were entirely due to the resilience and skills, both technical and organizational, of the German people – in short, to their human capital. Other factors may have offered them the opportunities, but it was German know-how and determination that took advantage of them. This is the answer to those who doubt whether the two Germanies, and especially the East which seemed to be stuck at the industrial stage in terms of heavy industry and fewer workers in services, were strictly professional societies. The West undoubtedly compared in every respect with the most advanced countries in the world: the high living standards, the service revolution, a modest degree of meritocracy, professional hierarchies in government and business, the emancipation of women, the growth of government and the welfare state, the concept of social citizenship, the explosion of higher education, the concentration of industry in great corporations, and involvement in the global economy.

The East by comparison looked backward, with large percentages of the workforce still locked into agriculture and old-fashioned industry – although the regime's ideology led it to regard many white-collar workers in industry as working-class and reported them as such – but in other respects, notably the self-conscious abolition of class and the re-structuring of society in career hierarchies recruited by merit (as defined by the regime), and the professional and biological emancipation of women, it was more advanced, in its own peculiar way, than the West.

Both societies had substantially collapsed and been forced to rebuild themselves from scratch. The democratic social market in the West and the command economy in the East changed the whole environment in which the old institutions worked, which thus became substantially different. The major trends of professional society operated with as much force there as elsewhere but, as elsewhere, they were influenced and modified by the historical and cultural tradition and assumptions in which they operated. It was as if the German road, or rather the two roads, had taken a new turn, no longer militarist or megalomaniac, but towards two peculiarly German versions of professional society, both of which are worth exploring further for the lessons they can teach.

## TOWARDS PROFESSIONAL MERITOCRACIES

By all the criteria both Germanies became fully-fledged professional societies in the forty-four years of their separate existence, the West more overtly than the East but the latter no less so in its underlying structure. In the transition from agriculture and industry to services the West surged ahead, but still retained a larger manufacturing sector than other major Western countries. Agriculture shrank from 14.0 per cent of the workforce in 1960 to 3.4 per cent in 1991, industry from 48.2 per cent to 39.2 per cent, while services rose from 37.8 per cent to 57.4 per cent.[6] This last figure was smaller than in most Western advanced countries, but in fact disguised the large numbers of white-collar workers, clerks, managers, technicians, and the like in German factories, more numerous than in comparable countries except perhaps Japan, which accounts for their greater productivity and export success. West Germany built up its export trade more in manufactures than in services, and in 1991 manufactured exports outgrossed those of every other OECD country, including the United States and Japan.

In the East meanwhile, where recent figures are less accessible, agriculture shrank from 17.2 per cent of the workforce in 1960 to 11.4 per cent in 1980, industry actually increased from 48.3 to 49.5 per cent, while services rose slowly from 34.5 to 39.1 per cent[7] – probably too low a figure considering the numbers of managers and clerks employed in the command economy factories and collective farms, especially in the latter where most of the men were bureaucrats and foremen and most of the fieldwork was done by the women. In both countries, as elsewhere in the developed world, the rise of productivity in mechanized industry increased the ratio of white-collar and managerial employees to direct production workers, so that even these figures of service occupations were understated. The West Germans, who believed that as much as possible should be produced at home rather than abroad, deliberately maintained a large manufacturing sector, which was the basis of their large exports of sophisticated engineering and chemical products and of their mounting balance of trade. The East Germans were also involved in large exports of machinery and high-quality consumer goods to their communist partners, since except in space research and nuclear energy, which the Russians kept to themselves, they were the vanguard of technological development for the Soviet bloc.

More importantly, both countries experienced a shift in social structure from a class-based system towards a meritocratic one based more on professional hierarchies. In the West this was a natural progression with the gradual widening of educational ladders and the opening of careers in government, both national and regional, and the concentration of industry in large corporations noticed below. Class, or what the Germans prefered to think of as estates (*Stände*), was still a powerful factor, and in 1967 the child of a government official had thirty-nine times more chance of obtaining a university place than a worker's child, and thirty-two times more chance of being elected to the *Bundestag*. Since a university degree, preferably in jurisprudence, was the ticket of entry to government service and the professions, this ensured that social mobility was always strictly limited and continued to be so under the Federal Republic. The tripartite secondary school system, with the *Gymnasium* or *Oberschule* for the children of the educated class, the *Mittelschule* for the middle ranks, and *Hauptschule* (main school) for the ordinary workers, deprived all but a few workers and lower middle-class children of a higher education. Students with working-class fathers rose from 5 per cent in 1955 to 15 per cent in 1978.[8] Moreover, as the nineteenth-century bourgeois recruits to the bureaucracy and the professions disguised their origin by pretending to aristocratic mores, so now the occasional working-class son who climbed via the *Gymnasium* and university to the middle class adopted bourgeois airs and graces. Class attitudes also infused the trades union movement, revived, surprisingly in view of the American attitude to unionism back home, by the Allied Occupation in the form of industry-wide unions, but they were tempered by corporatism in the form of the German system of legally regulated industrial relations, with workers' representation on corporate supervisory boards and labour courts to enforce wage bargains and other contracts (see below). This ensured that West Germany had, until reunification at least, the most peaceful industrial relations and the fewest strikes in Western Europe.

East Germany deliberately abolished the old class system, expropriating the Junker landlords and the capitalists, and squeezed out private enterprise altogether, except for a small percentage, 3.4 per cent by 1970, of small craftsmen and shopkeepers. The regime created a self-conscious meritocracy, based on education and training as well as political loyalty and proletarian credentials. Merit was defined as intelligence and expertise, backed by Marxist–Leninist ideology and unquestioning loyalty to the regime. At first, the meritorious came overwhelmingly from the families of industrial workers and peasants, who had first call on higher education and party membership, but as time went on party members and especially the *nomenklatura* (to use the Russian term), the elite of top politicians, bureaucrats, and managers, tried to perpetuate themselves in their children, as all elites tend to do. In the second generation an expanding percentage of university places and top jobs went to the offspring of officials and managers in what was becoming a single hierarchy of power. During the 1960s the children of workers shrank from 50.3 per cent of full-time university students to 38.2 per cent, and the children of the intelligentsia rose from 15.6 to 20.4 per cent and had three times the chance of entering higher education.[9]

The *Volkskammer* (an advisory rather than decision-making parliamentary body) did not report its membership by occupation but by parents' occupation: by that criterion three quarters of its members in 1971 were from workers' and peasants' families. More significantly, in the Central Committee of the Socialist Unity party, the real power in the government, only 4.7 per cent were genuine workers, the rest being party and government officials and intelligentsia. An ordinary worker could not get to the top except by changing his or her occupation and becoming part of the elite. Nevertheless, in East Germany a worker's child still had a far better chance of rising than in the West: six times the chance of getting to university, and nine times the chance of becoming a member of parliament.[10] To that extent the GDR was a more egalitarian meritocracy than the FRG.

In West Germany, by contrast, the old bourgeois and professional classes maintained their grip on the selective educational system and therefore on selection for most leading positions in government, the professions, and business. The traditional status groups – the nobility, who recovered much of their property and status after the war and soon found their way back into politics and big business to merge with the plutocratic *Oberschicht* (upper crust), the *Beamten* or high civil service, the *Angestellten* or white-collar salariat (upper and lower), and the *Arbeiter* or blue-collar working class – remained as strongly entrenched in their respective positions as ever. They were in a sense official categories, since the social security system provided different pension funds for wage and salary earners, and even a separate fund for miners, who were thought to be a separate 'community', isolated from the rest. Even impoverished *Angestellten*, clerks and shop assistants earning less than many manual workers, clung to their middle-class status. The only difference now was that still more emphasis was placed on competition via the educational system, and the FRG became a self-conscious 'achievement society' (*Leistungsgesellschaft*), in other words a committed meritocracy.[11] The West German elites were certainly more open than, say, the French or Japanese, which were meritocratic in principle but skewed towards those who could pay for cramming to get into the *grandes écoles* or into Tokyo, Kyoto, and a handful of other Japanese universities. All German universities were equal in status, confirmed by the student habit of migrating from one to another to sit at the feet of different gurus. The patron-professor was more important for one's career than his institution. This made for a wider social provenance of the elite, drawn as it was from the whole stratum of university graduates rather than from the tiny minority like the Oxbridge, *grandes écoles*, and Todai graduates of Britain, France, and Japan.

Nevertheless, the traditional German tripartite secondary education system, with only the highly selective *Gymnasium* preparing for the university, ensured that middle-class children had a far better chance of higher education than the rest, and qualified for the best jobs. Student numbers exploded from the 1960s, from 5.6 per cent of the age group in 1960 to 27.5 per cent in 1987, but working-class students, who increased from 5 per cent of the student body in 1955 to 15 per cent in 1978, declined again to 12 per cent in 1987, compared with their parents' half share of the labour force. More reached the vocational high schools, rising to 28 per cent of their students in 1975 but falling again to 22 per cent by 1987, but their graduates took fewer of the top jobs and earned on average 14 per cent less than university graduates. On the other hand, while graduates filled the civil service and the professions, they did not monopolize business management: in a 1972 survey only 40 per cent of top managers came from universities and 18 per cent from the *Fachhochschulen*, while the rest, 42 per cent were non-graduates.[12]

In brief, West Germany, like France but much less narrowly, was a skewed meritocracy, in which cultural capital and educational advantages gave the middle class most of the prizes, and there were what Dahrendorf regards as barely surmountable barriers between the different strata.[13] Hartmut Kaelble's comparative studies of social mobility confirm that in this West Germany mirrored other advanced societies in the Western world.[14]

Paradoxically, the incomplete meritocracy may have been one more reason why the West was so attractive to East Germans, who escaped there whenever they could. The children of workers and peasants or collective farm workers could more easily get an education in the East but exploit it more profitably in the West, where salaries and career prospects were better and not limited by ideological strings. The pull of Western rewards and affluence added to the push of Eastern material privation and political discontent.

## THE SURVIVAL OF PATRIARCHY

Both Germanies inherited a patriarchal belief that women's place was in the home. Goebbels' slogan '*Kinder, Küche, Kirche*' had a long history of women's subordination behind it, as in most Western countries but nowhere so dogmatic as in Imperial and Nazi Germany. In 1963 one international survey of five countries found Germany second only to Mexico in authoritarianism within the family.[15] The two post-war Germanies could not hold this line: in both because of the imbalance between the sexes due to the unequal slaughter of war, in the West because of its commitment to democracy, and in the East because of the Marxist ideology which stressed theoretical equality, though both in practice lagged far behind theory. In East Germany, partly because of its shortage of labour and partly because of its belief in work for everybody, half the adult women, the largest proportion in any advanced country, were at work. For this reason it also provided more generous facilities for working mothers: twelve months' maternity leave on full pay (eighteen months for the third and subsequent births), free crèches and kindergartens, and after-school centres for school children. The West, with only a third of the women working and very few mothers of young children, was much less generous: only fourteen weeks' maternity leave on state benefits, and almost no provision for child care (only 26,245 crèche places for half a million mothers of under-3s in 1982).[16] In both countries, more so in the East, the double burden of paid outside work and unpaid housework for working mothers made motherhood a declining option. Hence the fall in the birth rate and the rate of population growth, in the West from 2.4 children per family in 1960 to 1.4, less than the replacement rate, in 1991, while in East Germany, which introduced abortion on demand in 1972, the population suffered an absolute decline (partly due to emigration) from over 18 million in 1945 to under 17 million in 1975. The united German population of 80 million in 1990 is projected to fall to 75 million by 2025 and to level out at 65 million by the mid-twenty-first century.[17] German women, it seems, are taking their silent revenge on patriarchy.

They still have a long way to go to achieve equality. In both Germanies they generally earned only 70 per cent of the male average (much like Britain, France, and the United States), and held progressively fewer jobs higher up the scale. They began to approach equality in higher education, but only at the lower levels. In the West they increased their share of *Abitur* passes (the entrance qualification for university) from 42 per cent in 1973 to 49 per cent in 1987, but fewer went to university, 41 to 43 per cent, and still fewer to the vocational high schools, 25 to 33 per cent. But they were only 20 per cent of university faculty and 28 per cent of vocational high school staff, and a miniscule 5 per cent of the professors.[18]

The educational situation was very similar in the East, where women held more skilled jobs, 15.5 per cent as against 6.2 per cent in the West, and more positions in government service and management, but fewer of the top positions: 3.2 per cent as against the West German women's 5.5 per cent. There were more women in the East German *Volkskammer*, 31.8 per cent as against the *Bundestag*'s 6.4 per cent, though, as was said before, the former was not a decision-making organ and they formed only 4.2 per cent of the party leadership.[19] The latter included women like Margot Honecker, education minister and wife of party leader Erich Honecker.

## THE LEGACY OF THE GERMAN STATE

Ever since Frederick the Great, and later Hegel, the state had played the major role in Prussian and then in Imperial German society, and its divide and rule domestic policy and external aggression had been the main ingredient in the concept of the *Sonderweg*, industrialization by the alliance of iron and rye, of capitalists and Junkers. Given the 'democratic centralism' of Marxism–Leninism, it is not surprising, therefore, that the state continued to dominate society in the GDR, where the legacy was taken over intact and came to control the whole economy and most of political, social, and cultural life. By 1973 93 per cent of the occupied population worked in the public sector, and only 7 per cent in private and mixed business, so that virtually all production was planned by the command economy.[20] The whole of education, the media, publishing, entertainment, and even sport, in which with shameless state support and the use of steroids East German athletes excelled at the Olympics, was controlled by the government. Modelled on their Russian masters' regime, it was a more efficient totalitarian state than the Nazi Third Reich in that it managed to control more of people's lives, including their working days, their leisure time, and their consumption: it was like a permanent war economy. The *quid pro quo*, however, was the state provision of welfare, health services, subsidized housing, public transport, and leisure facilities that surpassed anything in the West. At reunification many East Germans expressed their ideal to be a West German salary with East German welfare and subsidized food and rents.

The Federal Republic was less heavy-handed in its statism, and ostensibly dedicated to a pluralist democracy consciously, if not compulsorily, modelled on the American and the British. Yet, as elsewhere in the post-war West, government came to play a much larger role in civil society than ever before, even under the Nazis, as measured by peacetime levels of taxation and expenditure. Public expenditure rose from 32.5 per cent of Gross Domestic Product in 1960 to 49.4 per cent in 1980. It fell back to 44.2 per cent in 1991,[21] owing to tighter social budgeting and a change in social policy from permanent support of the exigent to prevention, but it was still far higher than in Bismarck's or Hitler's day, and considering the smaller expenditure on defence, more than in most other Western countries. In part, of course, this registered the greater complexity of life in post-industrial society and the increased demands on government for managing the economy, building and maintaining the infrastructure, and providing a sophisticated range of services for the population, from education and health to housing and social work. Two thirds, 67.6 per cent of Federal expenditure or about 30 per cent of GDP in 1991, went on social security, welfare, housing, health, and education, a measure of the generous West German welfare state.[22]

The growth of the welfare state is one of the defining features of post-industrial society. Since people can no longer be self-supporting, a modern sophisticated society cannot exist without social provision for the exigencies of life, notably unemployment, sickness, disability, old age, widowhood, in fact the cessation of income for whatever reason. There is also the continuing need for the ruling elite to insure themselves against discontent, leading to crime, alcoholism, social breakdown, strikes and slow-downs, and rebellion. Preventing these by 'dishing the socialists' was Bismarck's motive when he pioneered social insurance in the 1880s, and has been a marked feature of German social policy ever since. Even Hitler, before war brought rationing and deprivation, claimed, disingenuously perhaps, to put butter before guns and welfare before warfare and maintained most of the welfare system intact. Since 1945 West German social policy has been based on the 'social market economy', defined as the free market combined with social protection against its arbitrary effects. The phrase was coined by Alfred Müller-Armack, the senior civil servant behind Economics Minister Ludwig Erhard's 'economic miracle', who was a member of the seminar at the University of Freiburg in the 1930s where the idea originated. However, its roots go back even further, to nineteenth-century Catholic social thought under Pope Pius IX and the tradition of corporatism.[23]

The Federal Republic extended the welfare system with its 'magic triangle' of social policy: the law of 1957 indexing retirement and other pensions; the Social Welfare Act of 1961 which provided a safety net for all citizens; and the Employment Act of 1969 which adopted a full employment policy with industrial retraining and unemployment benefits up to 90 per cent of previous earnings. By 1979 West Germans derived one quarter of their incomes via the state, in child support, pensions, subsidized housing, family income support, and other social income. Social benefits amounted to 60–100 per cent of previous income, far more than in most Western societies, though the system was largely self-supporting with contributions up to more than a third of insurable income. It was decentralized, and managed by more than 1,500 separate funding bodies (1,350 for health insurance) employing in the 1970s some 175,000 staff administering about DM200 billion, one fifth of total GNP.[24] Participants were equally represented, including trades unions and employers, an arrangement which effectively removed it from the political arena and the conflicts over welfare spending so familiar in the United States and Britain. It thus allowed both contributions and benefits to be cut back in the recessions of the 1980s without the major struggles over resources that occurred elsewhere. By concentrating on prevention rather than cure, West Germany and the Netherlands were the only West European countries in the 1980s to reduce welfare spending as a percentage of GNP.[25]

Allowing for its lower standard of living, about two thirds of that in West Germany, East Germany had an even more generous welfare state. With the exception of unemployment, which in Marxist–Leninist theory could not exist under socialism, provision was made for every contingency of life. Indeed, the whole standard of living was in effect provided by the state, in the form of administered wages and salaries, subsidized basic foods, housing and public transport, child care and leisure facilities. All this was at a lower standard than in the West – compare the smoky, smelly Trabant and Wartburg cars with Mercedes and BMW, or the bustling shops and restaurants of the Kurfürstendamm in West Berlin with the drab monumentalism of Karl Marx Strasse in the East before 1991 – and even affluent workers outside the elite had to wait years for a car, refrigerator, or telephone, yet the East Germans were so much better off than their communist neighbours that many considered themselves to be well blessed. The television beamed from the West showed them how much better their blood brothers were doing, which played a part in the collapse of the GDR. But reunification was to give them not an instant rise in living standards but massive unemployment, a sharp rise in prices, and cuts in welfare benefits and subsidies.

Yet both countries in their different ways had a concept of citizenship that emphasized community and belongingness. The individual had claims upon the state and fellow citizens that went beyond the contractual obligations of the market place. Social citizenship, we have seen, is a necessary feature of post-industrial society, since the isolated, self-sufficient individual can no longer survive in a complex, interdependent economy. In the German case the concept also had its roots in the legacy of nationalism, the fiercely intense belief in the unity of the *Volk*, and the right of all Germans everywhere to a place in the *Heimat*, expressed in the right of return that still welcomes even non-German speaking refugees of German descent from as far afield as the Ukraine and the Crimea. This has its downside in the rejection of foreigners, the labelling of Turks, Slavs and other aliens as temporary 'guestworkers' with no claim to citizenship, and in the crude xenophobia of neo-Nazi thugs, mercifully few but always a temptation for right-wing demagogues to exploit. Arson attacks on foreign workers and refugees are the price that is still being paid for the scapegoating electoral appeals of right-wing politicians like Franz Josef Strauss of Bavaria in the past and some neo-Nazis in the present.

## HIGHER EDUCATION AND SOCIAL MOBILITY

An increasing share of public expenditure has gone in both Germanies into education, especially higher education, the main source of the human capital so necessary to professional society. Education played a larger role in the German industrial revolution of the nineteenth century than almost any other and helps to explain its remarkable rapidity. As we have seen, it was not an egalitarian system but a highly selective, tripartite one, preparing a small minority in the *Gymnasium* for the university, the chief path to high-level employment in government and the professions, another in middle or vocational school (*Mittelschule* or *Fachhochschule*) for the technical high schools (polytechnics) and skilled or managerial work in industry, and the majority in the *Hauptschule* (secondary modern school) to become ordinary workers and farmers. The assumption was that intelligence was already, with a few exceptions, distributed according to class, which schooling could only reinforce, and this attitude persisted down to the 1950s in the West, though it was turned upside down in the East, where the proletariat became the vanguard class.

Curiously for such an authoritarian country, the universities enjoyed

112

the tradition, derived from Wilhelm von Humboldt and the University of Berlin he founded in 1810, of freedom of teaching and research, except of course for the Nazi period, and they came to be renowned centres of research attracting students from all over Europe and the United States. Even more useful to industrial development were the technical high schools, in effect polytechnics, which produced some of the finest engineers and chemists and gave Germany the edge in the second phase of the industrial revolution with fine chemicals, electrical engineering, and the internal combustion engine. This was, as elsewhere in Europe, the elitist system that survived the Nazis and was revived after the war.

Such a traditional system, confined to a minority of the age group, was not adequate to the needs of post-industrial society, and both Germanies, in common with other advanced societies, enormously expanded their higher education systems from the 1960s. The number of West German students entering universities and vocational high schools (*Fachhochschulen*) rose from 6 per cent of the age group in 1960 to 20 per cent in 1986, and (after the high drop-out rates of 16 per cent in universities and 14 per cent in the *Fachhochschulen*) those graduating rose from 4.8 per cent to 13.6 per cent.[26] This was on a par with most West European systems, but a long way behind Japan, Canada and the United States, which catered for a third to a half of the age group. Despite the doubling of student admissions between 1960 and 1986 from under 9 to over 20 per cent of the age group, it was still a very unequal system, heavily skewed towards the middle class. Working-class children increased from 6 per cent of the student body in 1962 to 11 per cent in 1973 and 15 per cent in 1985, but fell back to 12 per cent in 1987. They took more of the places at the vocational high schools, 26–28 per cent throughout the period 1973–87. But the latter, although qualified in the more technical subjects, found more difficulty in getting jobs and were paid on average 14 per cent less when they did. University graduates monopolized government and the professions, but less so business management. As we have seen, in 1972 only 40 per cent of high-level West German managers were university graduates, 18 per cent came from the vocational high schools or their predecessors, while 42 per cent were non-graduates.[27] Most, however, were drawn from the middle class: in a similar survey of social origins in 1965, 45.3 per cent of top managers had fathers in the upper middle class, 49.6 per cent in the lower middle, and only 5.1 per cent in lower strata.[28] Although opportunities for workers' children were increasing, Dahrendorf's barely surmountable class barriers were still very much in place.

By contrast, East German higher education was deliberately far more egalitarian, at least at first, with workers and peasants given priority over the old middle classes, who had to prove their loyalty to the regime before being admitted to higher education at all. It soon, however, began moving in the opposite direction. In 1958 53 per cent of the student body came from workers' and peasants' families, but by 1967 they had dropped to 38 per cent, while the children of officials, managers, and the intelligentsia (many themselves of proletarian parentage, no doubt) increased their share accordingly.[29] Very few class data are available for the GDR, which would not admit that classes survived there, but, as we have seen, while workers' and farmers' children formed three quarters of the *Volkskammer* in 1970, only 4.7 per cent of the Central Committee of the party, the chief governing body, were workers in their own right.[30] The rest were officials, managers, and intelligentsia, so the East German meritocracy was becoming skewed in favour of the emerging elite at quite an early stage. Thus, while the FRG was a traditional society moving reluctantly towards a more open meritocracy, the GDR was a self-conscious meritocracy moving the other way.

## GERMAN INDUSTRY: VOLUNTARY VERSUS COMPULSORY COOPERATION

Imperial Germany had been one of the pioneers of large-scale enterprise and, indeed, had far fewer hang-ups about monopoly capitalism than the United States or Britain. This was mainly because big business worked closely with government, and some of the early cartels and mergers, like the salt union and the coal cartels of the 1840s, included government undertakings. In the 'marriage of iron and rye' in Bismarck's day, when the Junker landlords and bureaucrats joined together with the industrialists to oppose the Social Democratic Party and build up a powerful defence industry, the notion that large corporations were any threat to the state or society was unthinkable. Big business, while not as implicated in the rise of Hitler and the Nazis as was once thought, undoubtedly worked with and for them once in power, and in the case of firms like Krupp and I. G. Farben even worked concentration camp labour to death in the war effort.[31] Some of these giant corporations were broken up by the Allies after the war, but in the West either came together again, like Krupp and Thyssen, or the fragments themselves became large entities like BASF, Bayer, and Hoechst, giant children of the gargantuan I. G. Farben empire.

Both post-war German economies were characterized by large enterprises. The East German economy consisted of a series of nationalized industries and state or collective farms, in which, since capitalism had been abolished, the workers were supposed to be free and equal partners with the state managers. What this meant in practice was that the workers were expected to work enthusiastically and accept whatever wages and conditions the government laid down, for the good of the whole community and the utopian future of socialism. Complaint or resistance was tantamount to disloyalty and political incorrectness was

114

punishable in extreme cases by loss of job or imprisonment. The trades unions became puppets of the management, whose role was not to protect the workers but to force up production and raise productivity. In the workers' republic there was no such thing as workers' involvement in decision making. Cooperation was compulsory, and the workers' only role to fulfil the central state plan.

As in the Soviet Union, where Lenin had learned from Henry Ford and F. W. Taylor the virtues of large-scale organization, continuous mass production, and managerial control over the work process, the giant state enterprise was the ideal. Nothing was allowed to stand in the way of intensive production, neither the trades unions nor the health and safety of workers and the public. A visit to East Germany before reunification was like a return to the most fog-bound and polluted regions of Victorian Britain. On the east side of the border the same pretty towns, clean, sparkling, and glowing with colour in the West, looked like abandoned film sets, devoid of paint and ringed by factories belching brown smoke from the lignite they burned. The state corporations were almost immune from regulation and allowed to pour out filthy outflows at will. The paradox of the planned economy was that it was effectively subject to no controls except the purely economic requirement to meet the central planning targets at whatever cost.

By contrast, West German corporations, larger than the state enterprises of the East because of their four times larger home market and their European and global ties, were far more responsible to their workers and the public. By 1970 40 per cent of the workforce was employed by firms with over 1,000 workers, 70 per cent by firms with over 200. Of these, 475 firms alone employed a fifth of the workers. One hundred firms in 1991 dominated the market, and within them ten giant corporations (including Siemens, Daimler Benz, Volkswagen, Bayer, Hoechst, Thyssen, VEBA, and Krupps) employed half the workforce and sold nearly half the turnover.[32] In 1973 twenty-nine of the 401 largest multinational corporations were West German, and in 1992 thirty-three of the top 500.[33]

Yet because of the German tradition of responsibility to the state, unalloyed by Marxist ideology or by extreme free-market theory, the corporations prided themselves on working for the public, including their customers and workers. Article 14(2) of the West German Constitution of 1949 declared that 'Property imposes duties. Its use should also serve the public weal.' Companies exist not just to make profit for the shareholders but to produce reliable, high-quality goods and services on a long-term basis. Even the idea of ownership is qualified. A corporation belongs not to the shareholders alone or even to shareholders and managers. It belongs in a sense to all the stakeholders: shareholders, managers, employees both white-and blue-collar, and creditors all have rights in law and therefore claims upon the property. This structure has been called 'cooperative managerial capitalism'.[34] It mirrors in industry the social market in the wider society.

The creditors in particular are more important as the source of capital than the shareholders, since four fifths (81 per cent) of it is in the form of long-term debt and less than one fifth (19 per cent) in equity held through the stock market (in Britain it is half and half: 49 to 51 per cent).[35] This means that companies are not, as in Britain and the United States, nervously obsessed with their stock exchange yield and valuation and can take a more long-term view of their investment and production schedules. Research into new products and methods of production does not have to pay off before the next balance sheet, and long-term development with a view to future market share is the watchword. German company directors say that they would never pay dividends out of capital or retained profits just to keep up the share value, nor would they sell a major industry to foreigners, as British Aerospace sold the Rover car company to BMW in 1994, just to maintain cash flow. Their banks would come in long before to ensure that their long-term investment was secure. The banks themselves play a key role in the system, control 50 per cent of the shares of the big companies (most of them, 36 per cent, through the proxies they hold on behalf of individual shareholders) and have about 10 per cent of the seats on the supervisory boards. They believe in 'relationship' rather than 'transaction' banking, have a long-term stake in the firm, are partners rather than creditors, and have an ongoing relation which looks to the future, not just to the next day's share price. This means that hostile takeover bids are almost unknown, since the banks as major shareholders and creditors are rarely interested in quick profits at the expense of future growth.

Free-market economists complain that the German bank-based system of industrial investment and company control is by no means as efficient as it is claimed to be, and that the fall of the Metallgesellschaft and Schneider groups in 1994 showed that the long-term investing banks are not as sound as their Anglo-American counterparts.[36] (This was before the fall of Barings' merchant bank in February 1995 poured cold water on the City of London's and Wall Street's optimism.) But their main objections seem to be that the banks and other large shareholders monitor corporate performance too closely and through the supervisory boards restrict the freedom of managers to do what they like; and that they also enforce coordination with the macro-needs of the economy. This is exactly what the German system intends, with results for productivity and profitability that most Anglo-American corporations can only envy.

It also means that German companies can take a more relaxed view of industrial relations and think in terms of cooperation between workers and management. Indeed, 'codetermination' (*Mitbestimmung*) is built into industrial law. It has its roots in the workers' committees of the First World War which established a new framework for industry under the Weimar Republic. The Works Council Law of 1922 gave elected workers in large companies including but not exclusively trades union representatives, a role in overseeing collective agreements, health and safety regulations, and in nominating, along with the shareholders, members of the supervisory board. The latter became part of the two-tier system of control over the corporation, with a supervisory board (*Aufsichtsrat*) on which workers are represented alongside shareholders, management, and major creditors, especially the banks, to oversee the managerial executive (*Vorstand*) which is responsible for day to day operations.

Participation was resisted at first by the employers but eventually came to be accepted as a way of inducing worker cooperation in production. The Nazis crushed the trades unions but not the system, which was revived in 1951 when the Codetermination Law established that supervisory boards would have equal representation for workers in the coal, iron, and steel industries, which became the goal of the trades unions for all companies. The following year the Works Constitution Act extended the system to other large companies, but with only one third representation for workers, and the Personnel Representation Law of 1955 introduced a similar system in the public service. A further law of 1972 covered 98 per cent of firms in manufacturing and 75 per cent in wholesale and retail distribution. In all firms employing more than five workers it required works councils, which must approve all hirings, dismissals, transfers, work allocation, plant closures, and alterations in the scale or speed of production. It also provided for schemes of alternative employment, retraining, or severance pay in the event of lay-offs, and gave individual employees access to their personal files. Finally, in 1976 an act gave workers equal representation on the supervisory boards of all large companies with over 2,000 workers, though with a shareholders' chairperson to ensure an employers' majority.

The system was enforced by the industrial courts set up in 1953, which underpin the works councils and codetermination and settle conflicts arising from them, define the rights of workers and employers, uphold individual labour contracts, and lay down rules for hiring and firing.[37] Codetermination and state-encouraged partnership between workforce and management are the secret of the German corporation's strength, productivity, high-quality output, long-term growth, market share, and export success. The system is perhaps the most important reason why West Germany became, and united Germany remains, the locomotive of the European Union's economy.

There are of course costs to this system, and with the world recession of the early 1990s added to the problems of reunification, many

117

complacent economists of the free-market orientation began to forecast the downfall, if not of the German economy itself, then of its expensive social overheads. Codetermination builds in resistance to wage-cutting, downsizing of plants, the erosion of fringe benefits, and reduction of the social security contributions which add up to 35 per cent to the wage bill.[38] Free-marketeers confidently predict that the Germans will be forced to come into line with other advanced countries (meaning Britain and America) and either reduce these overheads or begin to export operations to low-wage countries where social welfare, health and safety regulations, and pollution controls are much worse or non-existent. As we have seen, West Germany in the 1980s reduced the size of its social budget in terms of GDP. A survey of 10,000 large and medium-sized firms in 1994 suggested that a third of them were planning to export at least part of their operations abroad in the next three years, to Eastern Europe or Asia,[39] though this differs little from other Western multinationals' plans.

Germany, despite its strength and power, cannot escape the pressures – or the short-sighted temptations – of the global economy. As the senior partner in the European Union, however, which may grow much larger as applicant countries queue for admission, Germany has the best chance of persuading the rest to resist competition from the countries with cheap labour, poor health and safety regulations, and reckless environmental policies. It has to decide whether to resist this trend or whether to sacrifice its people, as Britain and the United States are doing, to the unpatriotic profit-seeking of the few. There is no reason why Europe should let the rest of the world reduce its living standards by allowing the free market – strictly, the transnational corporations – to reduce wages and salaries to Third World levels. Unless the TNCs use their strength to raise the living and working standards of Third World producers to acceptable levels rather than reduce home-base standards to theirs, the benefits, even to the profits of the corporations themselves, could only be short-lived, and in the end, as workers at all levels below the profit-seeking elite could no longer buy the goods and services produced overseas, would be suicidal.

In the early 1970s West Germany persuaded the European Community to accept the Fifth Company Law Directive, which recommended co-determination, participative management, for all large companies, but this failed against British and other employers' opposition. The same formula has now been written into the Maastricht Treaty of 1992, and will be imposed on all member states by the end of 1996. It requires large companies with 1,000 or more workers (8,447 in 1992) and at least 150 workers in two different member countries (1,162 of these) to appoint works councils with representatives of the employees. The works council will have the right to full information on the company's economic and financial situation, business development, investment plans, employment prospects, relocation, closures, and collective redundancies. It will thus be able to share in the management and policies of the company and ensure that all partners in the enterprise are consulted about its future direction.[40] This is a large step on the way to the kind of stakeholder capitalism which has enabled Germany to become the economic giant of the Union.

## A COMPARISON OF ELITES

We are now in a position to compare the roles of the elites in the two post-war Germanies and in particular the extent to which they fostered or exploited the people under their care. The comparison, it may be argued, is redundant, since the West undoubtedly won and the communist regime in the East was not only beaten but completely discredited. Nonetheless, the East claimed to be a more egalitarian meritocracy and its failure could, perhaps, be attributed to its generosity towards the workers and its utopian attempt to give them the whole product of their labour. Marxist–Leninist theory held that once capitalist enterprise and private profit had been abolished exploitation was no longer possible. Certainly in the GDR wages and salaries were confined within a very narrow band so that, even if material rewards were lower than in the West, officially they were more equal. Indeed, there was some reversal of the old scale of values, since many professionals such as doctors and teachers were paid less than skilled manual workers. One possible excuse for failure is that talent and effort were not adequately rewarded, with dire consequences for the economy. 'To each according to his needs' discouraged and overwhelmed 'From each according to his ability'.

Official incomes are not the only measure of equality, however, and exploitation can take many forms. All ruling elites are obliged to extract a surplus from the people they govern if they are to provide the services and protections necessary to maintain a civilized society. The question is how much they extract and whether it is a reasonable reward for their function or whether it is motivated by greed and self-interest. In both free-market and Marxist ideology it is assumed that capitalism exists to make profit for the owners of the means of production, and that every partner in the productive process bargains for the most he can get. Marxism, curiously, has no theory to explain how surplus is extracted under communism or how its reasonableness can be measured. It simply assumes that once the means of production are owned in common, the problem no longer exists. It makes no provision for the possibility that human greed is not confined to capitalists and denies that the officials and managers who control the distribution of income under communism may be tempted to take more than their share.

We now know that the *nomenklatura*, the Russian term for the unified elite of party bosses, industrial managers and intelligentsia, received income in kind worth far more than their official salaries: vouchers for the purchase of luxury goods in the state shops and in shops exclusive to them and their families, high-quality accommodation at nominal rents, chauffeur-driven cars, domestic servants, special schools for their children, private clinics for their families, country clubs and leisure resorts, foreign travel facilities, and so on. Though we know less about their hidden rewards than we do about the Russian *nomenklatura*, since they were more skilful or careful in concealing it – much of it came to light only after the 1989 revolution, and the West Germans are disinclined to expose managers and bureaucrats they still have to work with – it is abundantly clear that most of them were enjoying life-styles far beyond their official salaries. The problem is how to measure their rate of extraction from the populace, and how to compare it with the degree of 'capitalist exploitation' in the West.

One scholar who made the attempt is Jaroslav Krejci, a Czech economist and sociologist who was imprisoned for six years for criticizing the Novotný regime's economic policies and escaped during the 'Prague Spring' of 1968 to work in Britain. In 1976 he made a careful comparison of the extraction rates in East and West Germany. For lack of statistical data on the GDR he was forced to make some heroic estimates and substitutions, but his figures, from an informed observer who knows both sides of the Iron Curtain, are convincing. His method was to add up all the returns to labour in earned and social income and to treat the rest, whether profits, rent, interest, or taxes, as surplus value, i.e. the difference between the produce of labour and its reward. He came to the conclusion that the extraction rates by the early 1970s were not very different in East and West, that is, the return to labour (including, presumably, salaries as well as wages) was slightly higher in the West than in the East, but that the gap was narrowing fast and looked like being reversed shortly. The extraction rate by his definition (surplus value divided by labour income) had declined slightly in the FRG from 0.77 in 1960 to 0.72 in 1973, while in the GDR it had increased steeply from 0.45 to 0.68. In more traditional terms, the labour share of the national income had risen in the West from 56.5 per cent to 58.2 per cent, while in the East it had declined from 68.8 per cent to 59.5 per cent. Further analysis of the statistics showed that, since in absolute terms the East German worker received 38 per cent less for his work than in the more prosperous West and was only 28 per cent less productive (a difference of 10 per cent), extraction of 'the surplus in the GDR was of a higher intensity than in the FRG'.[41]

In other words, exploitation was greater in the communist East than in the capitalist West. And this was in the visible terms measured by official statistics: in practice the East German *nomenklatura* extracted far more in invisible ways, in special rations and shopping coupons, privileged housing, cars and servants, special schools and clinics, private leisure facilities and holiday resorts, much like their Russian masters but, with German efficiency and ruthlessness, much better hidden until the collapse of the GDR revealed all to a horrified and disillusioned population.

The explanation is that the communist elite in the East, not being answerable to anyone but themselves for their administration of incomes, had begun by adhering to their egalitarian ideology and had fixed a reasonably fair distribution, but soon had been tempted by their irresponsible power to steer more and more of the available income towards themselves. Although we must not put too much weight on extrapolation, it is clear in what direction the extraction rate was headed, and why despite the high rate of economic growth in the GDR the return to labour was so poor and so slow to increase. It was the structure of rewards, discouraging initiative and enterprise and encouraging bribery and corruption, that hobbled economic progress. The point is not merely theoretical. It could be seen in the manifestly poorer quality of life in the pre-unification GDR. It is not surprising that, when they saw how well their leaders lived and how much better their neighbours across the border were rewarded, the East Germans escaped at the earliest opportunity and, finally, overthrew the regime.

Though the return to labour in the West was proportionately little greater, it was a share of a much larger cake, and one which was growing more confidently. There were no long queues in the shops, no waiting years for a substandard car or refrigerator, no overcrowded housing with little chance of moving to better, no restrictions on foreign travel or holidays confined to dreary communist resorts, no state-controlled news service and entertainment, no censorship of publications, above all, no constant propaganda from leaders who preached hard work and equality but themselves practised hypocrisy and privilege. The West German elite, too, had the advantages of pluralism, of being split into a number of separate divisions, and thus made a more difficult target for critics to hit. More importantly, they delivered the goods, not only in the material form of a high standard of living with all the luxuries, gadgetry, cars, foreign holidays, of modern consumerism, but in the psychologically satisfying form of a meaningful vote in the political process and a say in the running of the companies that employed them. They also offered the pride of a defeated country which had beaten its opponents in the one race that mattered. They had lost the war but handsomely won the peace.

Above all, West Germany offered an alternative model of professional society, a third way between the extremes of individualism and collectivism, between soulless communism and the mindless and materialist free market. The social market, a carefully regulated free market with all the choices that an affluent person could reasonably want plus the protections and benefits that the same person might need in the exigencies of life, is a concept that chimes with the philosophy of professional society. It squares the circle of combining individual ambition to rise as high as one's abilities will reach with collective insurance against falling to the depths of poverty. It liberates the talents of individuals and challenges them to do the best they can for themselves and for society without exacting the unacceptable risk of total failure. It achieves the best of both worlds, competitive efficiency and a concern for every citizen, not only the poor and underprivileged but the rich and successful too, who never know when through bad luck, ill health, or act of God they might need the help of their fellows. Society, in fact, is a great insurance company against the ill winds of life which only the most reckless and overconfident of free-marketeers would be foolish enough to reject. The social market is the best compromise between the adventure of risk taking and the safety net of community. The Germans, now united, have discovered a political economy that exactly suits the future of professional society and can steer between the Scylla of free-for-all capitalism and the Charybdis of totalitarian communism.

It is a model, too, that is favoured by the European Union, and is supported by the Brussels Commission, with its Works Council Directive requiring codetermination in industry by September 1996, and by the Strasbourg Parliament, with the Social Chapter protecting the civil rights of workers and citizens. Alone among the member countries only the British government, with its politics of confrontation, its belief in a low-wage economy open to the unfair competition of a world economy run by offshore manufacturing multinationals, and its ill-informed imitation of the American free market, stands out against it. The fear is that the pressures of the global economy will force Europe into competitively beating the social market down and out of existence. The countervailing hope is that the strength of united Germany, now recovered from the trauma of reunification, will haul Europe into a prosperous twenty-first century and prevent the sabotage of its model of professional society by the extreme free-marketeers.

# 6

# SOVIET RUSSIA
## Gulliver's giant

The Soviet Union a post-industrial society? How absurd – the country that Brezhnev left, unwittingly, to Gorbachev and Yeltsin had scarcely completed its drive to mature industrialism. And yet, paradoxically, it was in some ways the first professional society. If that society is defined as the rise to dominance of the professional elites and the displacement of their landed and capitalist rivals, then the bureaucratic state and command economy that Lenin and Stalin built between the 1917 Revolution and the Second World War must qualify as the pioneer of one extreme, admittedly pathological, species of professional society. For over seventy years before its ignominious collapse in 1991 it formed the far pillar of the great arch, the state-centralized version of post-industrial society.

Some elements of the bureaucratic model were inherited from its predecessor. New communist commissar was but old Tsarist imperial official writ large – larger than life, we may say – with more extensive powers and greater penetration into what passed for civil society in that huge despotic empire. Indeed, the Western concepts of landlord and capitalist had never become firmly established in the old Russia. The feudal aristocracy, the serf-owning *pomeshchiki* and their successors, had never completely escaped from their personal dependence on the Tsar or from their obligation, abolished in law but not in custom or mentality by Catherine the Great, to serve the state as officials and military officers, while the tiny merchant class were a cringing herd alternately milked and pampered with contracts and subsidies by the bureaucracy. Such industrialism as existed – and it was more considerable than Lenin admitted or the proletarian Revolution could not have occurred – was largely government-induced and driven, and was only less in degree and efficiency, not in kind or intent, than the Stalinist five-year plans. The Tsarist regime bequeathed a legacy of state-centralized economic planning under Counts Vishnegradsky and Witte to their Gosplan successors whom the 'democratic centralism' of the communist party only raised to a higher power.

123

It was still, however, for half a century or more, a traditional 'Asiatic despotism' with a thin skin of educated officials and managers overlaying a mass of peasants and workers. In 1913 peasants and industrial labourers composed over 90 per cent of the occupied population, in 1939 over 80 per cent, and as late as 1970 still 75 per cent, nearly a third of whom worked on the land.[1] From Nicholas II through to Khrushchev the main problem of government was how to control and motivate a large mass of poor, ill-educated manual workers through a small, if growing, educated class of 'employees', officials and managers. It was the classic picture of Gulliver as the sleeping giant, pinned down by the feeble ropes of the Lilliputians, and given to shattering heaves and restless thrashings from time to time that crushed thousands and sometimes millions of victims – as in the revolutions of 1905 and 1917, Stalin's forced collectivization of agriculture in the 1930s, and the 'Great Patriotic War' of 1941–45. When the giant finally awoke, would he allow himself to be harnessed to the task of economic revival and democratic progress, or would he crush his tormentors and lay waste about him? For a long time, until Gorbachev in fact, the controllers did not dare to slacken the ropes. When they did, the giant surprised them, for it was a different giant from the one they had tied down.

## A QUALITATIVE CHANGE IN THE MERITOCRACY

Between the death of Stalin in 1953 and that of Brezhnev in 1982, the Soviet Union had evolved swiftly from a raw agrarian and heavy industrial society into a much more sophisticated and occupationally differentiated one. The urban population grew from less than half to more than two thirds of the total, and the number of cities with over 100,000 inhabitants from 125 to 231.[2] The percentage of workers in agriculture halved, from about 40 per cent to about 20 per cent, industrial workers increased from 32 to 39 per cent, and the number of service workers expanded from 15 to 26 per cent (probably more, since so many service workers not directly producing goods were concealed in the management of the collective farms and factories).[3] This last increase, though less than in Western countries, was the key to social and political as well as economic change for the future of the regime. The quality of the workforce had improved dramatically, and so had their social and political outlook. Not only were more of the manual workers skilled and better educated – by 1984 four out of five had secondary schooling or better – but the non-manual employees had doubled, from 16 million, only half of whom were 'specialists', to 32 million, virtually all of whom were so termed, over two fifths of the latter with higher education and the rest with vocational training. Nearly half, 15 million, could be described as 'intelligentsia', that is, professionals, officials, managers,

124

administrators, and so on. They had grown four-fold since 1960, compared with a two and a half-fold increase in the occupied population, and included an important contingent, 1.5 million, of scientists and engineers. This produced a qualitative change in the social structure, which began to create for the first time a civil society independent of the state and party.[4] In the words of one well-informed Western observer, Moshe Lewin, this was 'a momentous development': the USSR had leapt into the twentieth century. 'In the USSR today [1988], the professional classes and the intellectuals direct all spheres of economic, political and social life.' As government and party officials and managers of state-owned productive units, they were the instruments through which the party controlled every aspect of society and the economy.[5]

In the absence of capitalists and landlords, this was the class from which the ruling elite of party officials and government politicians were drawn. In 1981, as we saw in Chapter 1, the 17.5 million members of the Soviet Communist Party came nearly equally from the manual and white-collar occupations (43.4 and 43.8 per cent) and the rest from the peasantry (12.8 per cent).[6] What these offical figures fail to reveal is that, whatever their original family or occupation, those who mattered were in effect career bureaucrats who had spent most of their lives in the party's service. About half a million of them belonged to the leadership group (less than 0.5 per cent of the occupied population, significantly equal to the landed and bureaucratic elite of Tsarist Russia), and perhaps half of that number to the party machine and the organs of central, regional, and local government. According to one estimate for the early 1970s, some 227,000 belonged to an elite of party and government officials, trades union leaders, large enterprise managers, leading doctors, judges, journalists, writers, and artists. They earned over 450 roubles a month, a measure of their status compared with skilled workers on 300 roubles a month, but not of their subsidized standard of living which was much higher. Most junior members of these hierarchies earned less, though they were still privileged by comparison with the ordinary citizen. But the real ruling group were the 80,000 or so individuals who were named as occupying or candidates for posts on the official list drawn up by the party's Central Committee – the so-called *nomenklatura*.[7]

The political elite were increasingly recruited from the intelligentsia, since only they had the education and managerial skills necessary to direct an increasingly sophisticated economy and society, though they were a much narrower group and, curiously, less stable and secure. Though the *apparatchiki* did not depend on public opinion or, save in formal and easily manipulated terms, on popular election, they could be removed at the whim of their superiors and were therefore prone to please and flatter them, if not to grovelling sycophancy – not unlike the middle managers of big Western corporations, with the difference that there was no escape from the state monopoly. Khrushchev's famous excuse that when Stalin said 'Dance!' everyone danced, may no longer have been true of Brezhnev, but the career open to flattery and, as we shall see, to bribery and influence, was still the rule. Talent still counted for something, and since running a large enterprise, political or economic, was thought to be the best preparation for running the state, most of the top leaders had been industrial plant or collective farm managers or local party cadres before climbing the ladder of city, regional, and ministerial government to the inner circle[8] – an interesting parallel with the American penchant for high government appointees from corporate business, city and state govenment, or the military. It was in effect a meritocracy, in which merit was defined in terms of education, experience, but above all loyalty to the regime and lip service to its ideology as defined by the prevailing party line, or rather to the arbitrary keepers of the ideology and line, one's superiors and patrons. Ideology, however, increasingly took second place to the self-interest of the *nomenklatura*, whose younger members increasingly began to challenge the old practices as being unworkable and self-defeating.

The problems of such a meritocracy are three-fold. First, there are never enough top jobs for those educated, qualified, and ambitious for them, and so self-generating discontent is built into the system. The intelligentsia outside the system, or even the more intelligent within it, are motivated by personal autonomy, especially those in science, scholarship, or the arts, and are driven to question the system and demand its reform. They resent those they perceive as incompetent or dishonest who reach the top and lord it over them. Equality for them means equality of opportunity, and a generational rivalry provokes secret contempt for the old reactionaries above them. Second, the successful meritocrats, old and young, are apt to steer more and more of the resources towards themselves, at first by legitimate means for their supposedly superior effort, which is at odds with the egalitarian ideology, and then, as opportunity offers, by chicanery, fraud, and bribery, the Danegeld always offered to people with arbitrary power. They are thus drawn imperceptibly into a vortex of corruption, when they find that even their legitimate goals of production or administration cannot be accomplished without *blat* – bribery and influence – and merely to fulfil the plan requires cutting corners and being economical with the truth. Hence, even the upright operators are forced to pay, if not to receive, *blat* in order to get things done.

Finally, when corruption itself becomes self-destructive, not merely immoral and unjust but exploitative to the point of transferring so large a share of society's resources to the elite as to deny the populace sufficient purchasing power to maintain the planned rate of economic growth – milking the cow to dryness – then even the meritocrats themselves, or the more intelligent among them, become disillusioned with its failure, particularly in international competition, and for the sake of self-preservation seek to reform it. Ironically, Marx's 'contradictions of capitalism', the economic failure arising from the workers' inability to gain their fair share of surplus value, applied even more severely to communism. This scenario, the greed, exploitation and corruption of a single, integrated elite with absolute power, rather than the theoretical shortcomings of the ideology (which admittedly made exploitation easier), explains the collapse of communism and the Soviet Union under Brezhnev and Gorbachev.

In short, it was professionalism itself, in the pathological form it took in the Soviet Union, that undermined the only autonomous, self-generated professional society on the state-centralized, bureaucratic model. As the late Alexander Simirenko, a Russian emigré sociologist at Penn State University, showed before Brezhnev died, it was the very professionalization of Soviet society that was its downfall. The party had become the profession at the head of all the professions, whose function was 'therapogenic', to offer therapy to troubled believers in the ideology, to calm fears, and solve problems arising from the disjunction between the egalitarian ideals and the manifest inequalities of the system. When belief failed, because of the greed and exploitation of the professional elite, it was bound to collapse.[9] In other words, communism had become a church and the party a clergy, which like the pre-Reformation Roman Catholic Church existed to sell indulgences and extract material tribute from a gullible congregation. It was to provoke the same outraged protest and to meet much the same dilemma: either revolution or reform.

In 1986, only one year after Gorbachev's accession to power, two sociologists, L. A. Gordon and V. V. Komorovsky, analysed the evolution of Soviet occupational structure through three generations: those born before the revolution, between the wars, and in the 1950s. Manual workers and peasants had declined from about 90 per cent of those born around 1910 to about 60 per cent of those born in the 1950s; the rest, about 40 per cent, were officials and 'specialists', including a tiny minority of the professional elite of top bureaucrats and managers. They forecast that there would arise 'social trouble of great magnitude' from 'a socio-professional structure adequate to the needs of a scientific–industrial system . . . strait-jacketed into a productive system that is still stuck in an earlier technical and technological age'. There were 'too many well educated people and not enough challenging, demanding jobs'. In the absence of reform, professionalism would create widespread social crisis: job dissatisfaction among educated youth, low morale in the work-force, under-utilized engineers and scientists, a shortage of competent technicians, a wasted generation of frustrated talent, and disastrous back-sliding for the whole country.[10] The next five years were to prove them right.

127

The problem, however, began long before. It was endemic in the bureaucracy bequeathed but kept in check – by sheer terror – by Stalin. This is not the place to explore the sheer brutality and immensurable bloodshed of the Stalinist terror, the casual murder of hundreds of thousands, if not millions, of alleged opponents of the regime, whose major offence was merely to question Stalin or his policies or to be arbitrarily suspected of doing so. This has been documented by Roy Medvedev, Robert Conquest, Alexander Solzhenitsyn and others, whose horrific statistics of death and destruction are still subject to bitter dispute under Gorbachev and Yeltsin.[11] The terror was counter-productive: party officials and economic managers spent more time and effort guarding their backs and passing the buck than performing effectively, and resorted to reporting what their bosses wanted to hear rather than the real state of affairs. Nikita Khrushchev tried to reform the system and had some successes, lifting the terror and reining in the political police, the KGB, and the arbitrary system of justice, and to some extent stabilizing the bureaucracy to improve the state planning and production machinery. But the entrenched *nomenklatura* defeated him, and replaced him with the arch-*apparatchik* Leonid Brezhnev, under whose eighteen-year rule the bureaucracy was allowed a hand free of accountability to exploit the system to its decline and defeat.

## THE REASONS FOR *PERESTROIKA*

And exploit it they did. As Tatyana Zaslavskaya, 'the woman who invented *perestroika*', explained in 1990, 'the socially degenerate stratum of officials nominated by the Party apparatus had a definite tendency to turn into a ruling class, exploiting the rest of the people'. They presented 'a picture of shameless theft of public property by the ruling stratum, colossal swindles, systematic use of office for personal enrichment, and accumulation of multi-million rouble fortunes, the unjustifiable and illegal acquisition of privileges and advantages'.[12] Zaslavskaya is one of those strong Russian women who did most of the work and got least of the credit in the Soviet Union. She is against Western-type feminist 'liberation' because she believes that Russian women have had too much freedom to work and therefore carried the double burden of badly paid labour and all the household chores and childrearing.[13] As Tatyana Tolstaya has put it, 'Russian men have been lying down for years, and Russian women have been bemoaning this state of affairs.' Men sat around complaining of the long night of the Russian soul, while women got on with doing the work, queuing for food, cooking, raising the children, and making ends meet.[14] But the men occupied all the top positions and got most of the rewards. Above all, they composed both the *nomenklatura* and the mafia with which they were intertwined.

A rural economist and sociologist in the Akademigorod think-tank at Novosibirsk, Zaslavskaya wrote a famous report on the state of the Russian economy discussed at a high-level conference in 1982. She and her boss, Abel Aganbegyan, Director of the Institute of Economics, were reprimanded by the Politburo, not for criticizing the system, which was allowed to privileged insiders, but for leaking it to the *Washington Post* (3 August 1983), which they both denied. The report, which was couched in obscure Marxist jargon, complained of 'the substantial lagging of production relations in Soviet society behind the development of its productive forces'. By this she meant that the economy had become too complex and sophisticated to control from the centre and that the Marxist theory that class conflict (theoretically non-existent under official ideology) was impossible under socialism was out of date. The system had ignored the importance of human behaviour and the workers' resentment of all work and no play for low rewards and empty promises. The poor morale and low productivity that ensued from the conflicts between 'class groups' were responsible for the slowing down of economic growth, the declining birth rate, the frequency of divorce, the breakdown of the family, the lack of enthusiasm for education and vocational training, the reluctance of workers to move to new jobs in new areas, the low quality of output, poor discipline at work, preference for moonlighting in the private sector, and difficulties in allocating resources between distribution, exchange, and consumption. The answer was to motivate the workers to work more enthusiastically by offering them more choice, more freedom, and more opportunity, so as, in Yuri Andropov's words, to 'stimulate top quality productive labour, initiative and enterprise' and relate material rewards to work performance. The urgent need was for the reconstruction (*perestroika*) of the system of state management to fit the new economic system and the new, better educated and more complex workforce that had come into existence. She offered no specific means to escape the 'economic labyrinth' of declining productivity, low consumption, and hopelessness, other than the ritual academic request for more research, but the report, obscurely written as it was, was so germane to the current malaise that it made an impact on the leadership just at the moment that Brezhnev died and was succeeded by Andropov, Gorbachev's patron, and shortly, after the brief interregnum of the corpse-like Chernenko, by Gorbachev himself.[15]

Zaslavskaya became an adviser to Gorbachev as Minister of Agriculture under Andropov, and when he became General Secretary he made her the first director of public opinion surveys ever to be appointed in the people's democracy. Under the freedom of *glasnost* and *perestroika* she went on to write *The Second Socialist Revolution* in 1990, an extension of her critique of Soviet society and a blueprint for *perestroika* itself. Her analysis of the crisis which Gorbachev faced was devastating.

The original revolution had been betrayed by the party, which had turned itself from a functional social group into a new ruling class. She was shocked by the dichotomy between the official ideology of social equality, with all incomes kept within a tightly controlled band, and the reality of an immense gap between the luxurious living standard of the elite and the poverty and deprivation of the average worker. She argued not for a Western-style free market but for a return to true socialism: not the authoritarian state capitalism of Stalin and Brezhnev, but democratic socialism, the absence of exploitation, more equal incomes, the elimination of poverty, freedom of expression, democracy in the workplace, respect for human rights and the rule of law, a higher level of morality, and more equality between the nations of the Soviet Union and its satellites. Social ownership did not mean state ownership but workers' control over public industries; it was not an end in itself but only a means to the end of social democracy.[16] The Fabian Society could not have said it better.

The party, or rather the *nomenklatura* who governed in its name, had seized absolute power and had exploited it for their own gain. They had tried to impose their will on the environment and ended by destroying it. Stalin and his successors thought that they could command the forces of nature, both human and physical. They had begun by forcing industrialization at the expense of human suffering and environmental pollution. In nothing was this so obvious as in the vast water engineering programme for irrigation and hydro-electric schemes, which entailed damming the great rivers, devastating vast stretches of agricultural land, and extracting huge quantities of water for irrigation that dried up lakes and rivers and ruined fisheries and neighbouring communities.[17] One of Stalin's schemes was to reverse the flow of the northern Siberian rivers, which would have changed the geography of the tundra and perhaps brought the Arctic ice nearer, with detrimental effects on the climate. Another was the irrigation of large areas of Uzbekistan and Kazakhstan for cotton production, which led to the shrinking of the Aral Sea by 40 per cent, turning an area as large as New England into salt flats, destroying the fishing industry, salinating the surrounding region, stinging the eyes and harming the kidneys of the neighbouring population, raising the infant mortality of the Uzbeks to 43.3 per cent, and making 70 per cent of the adults and 80 per cent of the children chronically ill.[18]

Even worse than the exploitation of nature was the exploitation of human beings. Under Brezhnev the command economy was no longer harnessed to economic growth – except in so far as the arms race forced ever-expanding investment in the military–industrial complex, which dominated the economy even more than in the United States – but, ironically in the face of Marxist theory which attributed it exclusively to capitalism, to the extraction of surplus value from the populace for the benefit of the elite. As Zaslavskaya observed and sociologists like

Gaetano Mosca and Milovan Djilas had predicted, the party had become a new ruling class living on the backs of the people. As Mosca put it in the 1930s, 'It is inevitable that a new bourgeoisie should eventually emerge in Russia from the ranks of the very men who carried the revolution through, and that private property should be reestablished in substance if not in form.' Milovan Djilas, dissident aide to Yugoslavia's Marshall Tito in the 1950s, said much the same: 'More than anything else, the essential aspect of contemporary communism is the new class of owners and exploiters.'[19] Not only did the Soviet elite steer more and more of the national income towards themselves, in disguised ways that did not appear in the official records, but they used state property as if it were their own, in the form of privileged accommodation, country *dachas*, personal cars, railway coaches and planes, the use of exclusive holiday resorts and hunting reserves, and even secret country clubs for drinking, gambling, and sex. One view, indeed, of *perestroika* is that it was seized on by the *nomenklatura* to turn their use of state property, notably houses, land, and factories, into outright ownership, at give-away prices.[20]

## THE PRIVILEGED MARXIST ELITE

What incensed Zaslavskaya and other reformers was the hypocrisy of a system that preached equality and collective responsibility and practised exploitation and individual greed. In theory all incomes fell within a very narrow range, with skilled manual workers, the ideal citizens of socialism, paid more than clerks, teachers, doctors, and lawyers, unless the latter headed institutes or the like, in which case they were paid as managers and thus *nomenklatura*. In the early 1970s – up to date figures are hard to come by – the average monthly wage was 135 roubles, though peasants on the collective farms might earn as little as 60 roubles; Brezhnev as General Secretary officially earned only 900 roubles a month, while the highest party officials earned between 450 and 600, and most managers of factories and collective farms earned between 200 and 400.[21]

Basic salary, however, was no measure of the elite's standard of living. The system of elite privilege made them as rich, in comparison with the average worker, as the wealthiest classes in the West; indeed, in certain respects even richer, since they commanded more labour and greater access to exclusive state resources. First, their basic salary was supplemented by the 'thirteenth month', an annual bonus often given on the eve of vacation, plus a 'personal salary' for selected individuals and/or a fictitious job for the spouse, which might together more than double the official salary. Then came the 'Kremlin ration', a package in kind or vouchers for the state shops, nominally worth about 50–70 roubles but in fact much more since it gave access to supplies of scarce food and drink, such as caviar and whisky, unobtainable by the ordinary consumer. Some of them received a monthly envelope which might contain a second salary equal to the first. Private restaurants in party or government offices or exclusive hotels, with access by official lapel badge, supplied luxury meals at subsidized prices and even take-home packages of cooked food. The elite also had access to the *berezka*, the foreign currency shops that sold imported and other luxuries, and to the tourist hotels and restaurants closed to ordinary citizens. They were allocated high-class apartments of up to 75 square metres, when the norm was 6 metres per person, at nominal rents half the average, including heating, lighting, telephone, use of elevator and cleaning of the common areas, plus of course the summer *dacha* in the country. They were often provided with domestic servants for cooking, cleaning, and child care, a practice condemned by the ideology. They had free use of large cars, when the smallest Zhigli (Fiat 125) cost over three years' income for the ordinary citizen, if they could obtain one after years of saving. On retirement they received pensions of 300 roubles a month as against the norm of 120.[22]

The material advantages were the least of the *nomenklatura*'s distinction. They were in effect an aristocracy as well-endowed and powerful as their Tsarist predecessors. When Len Karpinsky, dissident son of Lenin's aide and copy editor in exile in Switzerland, was rehabilitated in 1959, he recalled later:

> I was part of the elite again, and not merely as my father's son but as a real member. I was part of the top nomenklatura, and the nomenklatura is another planet. It's Mars. It's not simply a matter of good cars or apartments. It's the continuous satisfaction of your own whims, the way an army of bootlickers allows you to work painlessly for hours. All the little apparatchiks are ready to do everything for you. Your every wish is fulfilled. You can go to the theater on a whim, you can fly to Japan from your hunting lodge. It's a life in which everything flows easily . . . You are like a king: just point a finger and it is done.[23]

It was the life of an *ancien régime* French duke, an American senator, or a Saudi prince. Their rarefied existence was hermetically sealed off from the experience of the mass of the people.

Meritocracy always tends to make itself hereditary, and the children of the elite found it much easier to gain places in the more prestigious schools and universities, notably those specializing in foreign languages, mathematics, engineering, and the arts. Admission to the Moscow Institute for International Relations, for example, the gateway to the Ministry of Foreign Affairs and access to foreign travel, required high-level references and influence with the Central Committee of the party. Elite families were issued special TASS Agency summaries of the foreign press, including articles critical of the Soviet Union, to be destroyed after reading. While health care was free to all but very basic, the elite were treated in special hospitals and clinics under the Fourth Department of the Ministry of Health. The Writers' Union for prestigious and loyal authors, for example, had its own polyclinics in nine cities. There were also fee-paying clinics for those still unsatisfied and able to pay. In addition to their private *dachas*, there were state compounds of low-rent *dachas*, vacation hotels and clubs on the Black and Caspian Seas, in hunting reserves across the Union, and in ski resorts in the Urals or the mountains bordering Afghanistan and China. The Writers' Union had seventeen 'creative houses', three holiday hotels, twenty-nine writers' clubs, and its own compound of *dachas*. Foreign travel, especially to the West, was a rare privilege, and the elite were at the head of the queue for exit visas, delegations, fraternal missions, cultural exchanges, and the like. And when privilege alone failed to suffice, *blat* – bribery and influence – might do the trick, in getting a child into the best school or college, obtaining a room in a full hotel, or jumping the queue for a car or other luxury purchase.[24]

All these advantages added up to a life-style far above that of the ordinary Russian, and reinforced the sense of hierarchy and respect for rank which pervaded this purportedly egalitarian country. Yet it must be seen in perspective. Mervyn Matthews, who made a special study of privilege in the Soviet Union from which the above details are drawn, concluded that, unsurprisingly, it was no worse than in the six East European satellites. More to the point, 'The Soviet elite family in the early seventies enjoyed a living standard equal to, or perhaps somewhat below, that of an average American household.'[25] It could only be seen as privileged in a country where nearly all the commodities and services taken for granted in the West – good quality food and drink, housing space, comfortable furniture and domestic appliances, a family car, regular holidays, foreign travel, reliable medical treatment, and high-grade education – were luxuries allocated by the state or rationed by voucher, and had to be saved and scrimped for by the ordinary citizen for years on end.

It must also be seen against a universal if low-grade welfare system, with guaranteed employment, subsidized basic food, housing and public transport, universal secondary education, and a larger percentage of students in higher education than most West European countries, not to mention, despite all the privileges, more upward mobility for the working class than in the West. There was also, before the collapse, no visible poverty, no beggars on the streets, no overt racism, and none of the riots and hooliganism which have become common features of Western life – all this of course before 'reform' unleashed the free market in aggression, gangsterism, violent crime, prostitution, guns, drugs, and ethnic intolerance of the post-Gorbachev era. There was also a surprisingly lively and thriving culture, in poetry, theatre, opera, ballet, and sport, all subsidized by the state as long as it kept within ideological bounds, and even critical writing thrived in the form of *samizdat* publications often winked at by the government. To Western visitors it was manifestly not a Third World country: people were adequately if boringly fed, warmly if unfashionably dressed, and it was considerably less depressing than the decaying areas of many Western cities, such as the South Bronx or South Chicago, Brixton (London), Moss Side (Manchester), or Nanterre (Paris). The distribution of income, even allowing for all the hidden perks of the elite, was probably no more unequal than that of the United States or Britain. The destructive nature of the inequality lay in the structure of rewards and the encouragement it gave to systematic, all-pervading corruption and to the political psychology of resentment.

## SELF-DESTRUCTION BY CORRUPTION

Zaslavskaya gives many examples of corruption, notably in the non-Russian republics where it was reinforced by the traditional nepotism of extended family networks. In Georgia, Azerbaijan and Uzbekistan the pickings from the oil, fruit, and cotton industries were plentiful, and the 'shadow economy' run by the mafia was intertwined with the official command economy. Even she seems unaware that the so-called mafia and the party apparatus were one and the same thing, and rose as high as the Central Committee of the Communist Party of the Soviet Union. Arkady Vaksberg, a courageous investigative journalist with the Moscow *Literaturnaya Gazeta* who began his exposures of corruption under Brezhnev, is a better informed guide. His book on the *The Soviet Mafia* published in 1991 declared that 'the whole political regime of the country – in all its guises – for the last seventy years is itself a mafia: a despotic totalitarian regime cannot be otherwise'. He argued that whereas Stalin was not a rich man, contenting himself with the ruthless power he exercised over 'an enormous country with its untold wealth and tens of thousands of slaves' (which of course is the reality of property without the symbolic title), Brezhnev and his henchmen were ignorant cynics and vulgarian self-seekers who 'managed to squander their inheritance, ruining the country in the process'.[26]

The mafia, Vaksberg asserted, was not, as in Italy or the United States, a set of hidden criminals organizing crime outside and parallel to the state, even though they might influence officials, judges, and the police with bribes, blackmail, and threats where they could. In the Soviet Union they were an organized network of politicians, enterprise managers, and operators in the shadow economy, who controlled the party, the government apparatus, and the economy and turned them to their own profit.

This usage was well understood by ordinary Russians, who used the term interchangeably for both official and extra-legal corruption. As Hedrick Smith, the American sovietologist, has put it,

> In Soviet parlance, the mafia is a stratum of society that includes powerful Party and government officials, economic managers, and criminal elements, an amorphous, privileged layer held in popular contempt for its corrupt life-style and evil tentacles that reach into all walks of life.[27]

Although few Russians were willing to define it or name names, they were in no doubt that the term almost always linked political power and illicit economic benefits. Vaksberg concentrates on the mafia's operations in five areas, chosen perhaps because under Brezhnev exposure of corruption was allowed as a warning to lower-level delinquents, especially far from the centres of power in European Russia. These were: the Krasnodar district on the Black Sea which included the Sochi resort favoured by the Moscow elite, and the Republics of Uzbekistan, Kazakhstan, Azerbaijan, and Moldavia (now the breakaway republic of Moldova). Each had its 'uncrowned king', who usually united the leadership of the local party with command of the local mafia.

In Krasnodar the local boss was Sergei Medunov, a close friend of Brezhnev who until his illness in 1976 spent his summers in Sochi. Just one of the local scams, with the aid of Rytov, Deputy Minister of Fisheries of the Union, was the Okean chain of specialist seafood shops, which purveyed delicacies like caviar, crab, and smoked salmon to the *nomenklatura*, with vast profits syphoned off through the local Sochi bank. They were caught out through excessive greed, exporting thousands of cans of caviar labelled as sprats in tomato sauce or herrings in brine. It took all of Medunov's influence with Brezhnev for him and his gang to survive the trial and closure of the operation. The lieutenants of the Sochi mafia under Medunov were Alexander Myerzly, First Secretary of the Krasnodar party, whose wife Valentina was Medunov's mistress, and the mayor of Sochi, Vyacheslav Voronkov. Their main racket was skimming the cream off the lucrative tourist trade. The pay-mistress, Bella Borodkina, known as 'Iron Bella', whose lover Nikolai Pogodin was Medunov's chief assistant, was in charge of all the bars and restaurants in the main tourist area of Gelendzhik, and took 250–300 roubles from every visitor, totalling a million tourists a year.

Medunov's main Moscow patron was Nikolai Shcholokov, Minister of Internal Affairs, whose opponent, Yuri Andropov, head of the KGB, decided to intervene. He sent prosecutor Viktor Naidenov to investigate the racket, but Medunov appealed to Brezhnev, who had the Central Committee dismiss Naidenov for 'insulting the party'. After Brezhnev's death his successor Andropov made Naidenov Deputy Prosecutor of the

Soviet Union and reopened the investigation with a new prosecutor, and the whole gang was arrested. Under interrogation Myerzly revealed the secret of the 'Sochi Belvedere', a palatial club and brothel for the local mafia and their friends. He was sentenced to fifteen years and Voronkov to thirteen years in prison, though they served only five. Iron Bella, who knew too much, was sentenced to death and shot. Her lover, Pogodin, disappeared and may have been killed to silence him. Medunov was dismissed from office but retained his VIP pension and all his privileges, though he was later removed from the party by Gorbachev. His patron, Shcholokov, fell foul of Andropov and Chernenko, was tried for corruption, stripped of office and party membership, and finally, in 1984, shot himself.[28]

In Tashkent 'the father of the Uzbek people' was Sharaf Rashidov, First Secretary of the Republic's Party, friend of Brezhnev and his son-in-law Churbanov, Shcholokov's deputy at the Ministry of Internal Affairs. He was a would-be literary star whose novels were ghostwritten by two Moscow writers. He was also a friend of Ygor Ligachev, the Kremlin's ideologue, who was to become the main critic and opponent of General Secretary Gorbachev. By means of lavish gifts Rashidov replaced Medunov as Brezhnev's chief favourite, and won ten Orders of Lenin for his services, which included promising to deliver 6 million tons of cotton a year to overfulfil the Gosplan target. 'Uzbekistan was a bottomless well of phantom riches'.[29] The cotton was grown, picked and processed by poor Uzbek women and girls, some as young as 6 years old, who were paid 16 kopeks (22 US cents) an hour and overworked to the point of exhaustion. Some Moslem teenagers were forced into prostitution; other women (360 in eighteen months) committed suicide by drenching themselves in kerosene and burning themselves to death – though this may have been due to their Moslem bridegrooms denouncing them as non-virgins.[30] The 6 million tons of cotton a year were never achieved, since in the Alice in Wonderland world of Soviet central planning the producers were paid not for what they delivered but for what they reported on paper. The Uzbek authorities therefore made enormous profits out of thin air to spend on luxuries, gold and jewellery, on the flow of gifts to Moscow patrons, and on the *dolce vita* in 'rest houses' with every modern convenience including nubile girls.[31]

Brezhnev's death left them vulnerable, and under Andropov KGB General Melkumov arrested eight of the Uzbek leaders in Bokhara. Chernenko tried to save them by transferring Melkumov to another post, but despite that a young and vigorous prosecutor, Telmar Gdlyan, pressed on with the arrests. Rashidov died and was given a state funeral, but his lieutenants were either caught or committed suicide. The 'Emir of Bokhara', Abduvakhid Karimov, was arrested nude in the arms of his mistress, and was found to have salted down 100 kilos of gold, over

5,000 Imperial gold coins, 12,000 items of diamond jewellery, five cars, twelve television sets, twenty-two stereo systems, plus hundreds of furs and leather clothes, tableware and teasets, chandeliers, and 1 million roubles in cash. The Uzbek Minister of Internal Affairs and his deputy, Kudrat Ergashev and Gennady Davydov, committed suicide, as did another official, Rais Gaipov, who left behind half a million roubles and a chest full of gold rings and bracelets. The real godfather of the Uzbek mafia was a mere 'pub-owner' and director of a modest agricultural machinery depot, who from his outside base pulled the strings of the rest, 'recommended' (i.e. ordered) appointments to senior posts, and arranged for the murder of disobedient *nomenklatura* and potential witnesses. When Vaksberg wrote his book, Gaipov was still in prison awaiting trial – an event feared by many of the Uzbeks' Moscow protectors for what it might reveal about their own connections.[32]

The biggest fish caught in the Uzbek net was Yuri Churbanov, Brezhnev's son-in-law, out of favour with all Brezhnev's successors, who survived only as long as the Brezhnevites had sufficient clout in the Politburo. He was finally brought to trial in September 1988, accused of taking 657,000 roubles in bribes, and sentenced to twelve years in the Gulag. One of the accused, Rashidov's successor as First Secretary of the Uzbek Party, Usmankhodzhaev, gave evidence that he had personally given Ligachev a bribe of 60,000 roubles – which Ligachev, a strong opponent of reform but reputedly a 'straight arrow' who claimed that he was framed by his enemies, strongly denied – and that sixteen other high Moscow officials had been similarly bribed. Whether true or nor – and some observers are sceptical of prosecutor Gdlyan's charges – the fact that they were accepted by the court shows how high up the hierarchy the corruption was thought to reach.[33]

The adjacent republic, Kazakhstan, shared with its neighbour the Aral Sea and its environmental problems as well as the cotton belt and the corruption. There the mafia was divided between rival gangs, who were anxious to use the Moscow prosecution service against their opponents. The main rivalry was between the Alma Ata and the Karaganda mafias, led respectively by Dinmukhamed Kunaev, First Secretary of the Kazakhstan Party, and Nursultan Nazarbaev, leader of the Karaganda District Party and also a protégé of Gorbachev. The Kunaev gang's corruption, according to Nazarbaev, was staggering. In that extremely poor and thinly populated country, nearly as large as Europe, one of the main income flows was from public transport. By issuing bus tickets to only 25 per cent of the passengers the mafia were able to extract 75 per cent of the proceeds. Every government transaction cost a bribe: a student place in higher education cost an incredible 40–60,000 roubles, and most places went to sons of the third of the population who, like the mafia, were Kazakh. The proceeds supported a mafia life-style that included Kunaev's palaces and immense sporting gun collection, a private plane for every member of the republic's Politburo, and a vacation house in the Tien Shan range on the Chinese border where maids acted as 'personal carers' for the guests in return for double salaries and high school certificates without attending school. When Gorbachev came to power, Nazarbaev engineered the fall of Kunaev and his replacement by Gennady Kolbin, a Russian, who for that reason was unwelcome to the Kazakhs, and so the Kunaev gang were able to play the nationalist card. Kunaev managed to keep most of his loot, and after the violent anti-Russian disturbances in Alma Ata in 1986 he was able to survive until Kazakhstan gained independence as a nuclear power within Yeltsin's Commonwealth of Independent States.[34]

The same nationalist card was played even more successfully by Geidar Aliev, the 'Monarch of Azerbaijan', who had milked the profits from the lucrative oil, fruit and vegetable, seafood, and transport industries of this Caspian Sea republic. Though secret head of it, he posed as the scourge of the mafia, prosecuting rivals, especially the small operators of the illegal workshops packing cans of caviar and other delicacies for the black market. Surrounded by female 'volunteers' whose services were mainly sexual, he ingratiated himself with Brezhnev by a stream of gifts, including a 'Sun-king' diamond ring worth 226,000 roubles and a jewel-encrusted framed protrait of the great leader. (The jewelled frame, apparently, had previously been offered, with his own portrait, to Khrushchev, who had refused it.) Aliev's generosity paid off: when two Moscow prosecutors investigated the Azeri mafia, one was tried and expelled from the party, the other convicted and shot. At a cost to the Azeri mafia, it was said, of 4 million roubles in bribes, Aliev was promoted to the Moscow Politburo, where under Andropov he became first deputy prime minister. There he planned an 'All-Union Curative Centre' on the Caspian Sea for tired and sick *nomenklatura*, which would have brought great prosperity to the republic and profit and influence to the local mafia. Unfortunately for him, his patrons, Andropov and Chernenko, both died and under Gorbachev he saw the writing on the wall. The subsequent investigation by prosecutor Gamboi Mamedov – despite the persecution of all his relatives in Azerbaijan – produced a wave of suicides among the Azeri mafia and some mysterious deaths among Aliev's lieutenants. Aliev himself suffered a heart attack at his desk, and was retired to a government consultancy with full privileges.[35]

Aliev was not finished yet, however. The conflict between the Azeris and the Armenians over Nagorno–Karabakh flared up, stirred perhaps by the mafia, sparking anti-Armenian pogroms in Baku and the bloody suppression of the Azeri rioters by the Red Army. This played into the hands of the Azeri mafia, who promptly turned themselves into Azeri nationalists. Aliev thrust himself to the head of the Azeri People's Front, and was elected to the Supreme Soviet of the republic in time for independence in 1991. After a coup in June 1993, he finally became President of Azerbaijan.[36]

The same trick was turned by Ivan Bodyul, 'King of Moldavia', another personal friend of Brezhnev, Chernenko, and Shcholokov, who profited from embezzlement in the bakeries, wineries, and transport system of that western republic on the borders of Romania, and from the lucrative smuggling of Western products such as computers. They survived the arrest and imprisonment of their Moscow patron, Viktor Smirnov, when his release back to the Kremlin gave them a second wind. The local mafia knew when to turn nationalist. Along with Georgia and the three Baltic Republics, they refused to join Yeltsin's Commonwealth, and declared independence as Moldova. Unfortunately for them, the eastern part of the breakaway republic is full of ethnic Russians, who are now calling on Moscow and the Red Army to rescue them from the Moldovan nationalists.

Although most of Vaksberg's evidence comes from the peripheral, non-Russian regions, he insists that corruption was endemic throughout the old Soviet Union, and was condoned and profited from up to the highest levels of government: 'literally everywhere from top to bottom those in authority were criminals directly or indirectly connected to the powerful and far-flung mafia network'. It was not a chance phenomenon: 'Its roots are deeply embedded in the political culture which gave it birth and thus a change in the situation will only be brought about by a change in the whole system.' Official statistics estimated the black economy at 150–200 billion roubles, but better informed observers put it as high as 400 billion. It was in fact the free market gearing up to take over. Specialists estimate that there were 200,000 millionaires in the old Soviet Union, of whom perhaps 300–400 were in the arts as star performers, artists, composers, and film makers, but the rest were leading *nomenklatura* and *mafiosi*.[37] Their numbers compare well with 180,000 millionaires in the United States in 1972 (though there are far more American ones now, as indeed there are many more Russian dollar millionaires now, under a far more ruthless and greedier free-market mafia who are buying property in the West). The difference is that under socialist theory there should have been none at all.

The black economy was in fact to all intents and purposes the real economy of the country. The command economy could not have operated without the aid of private entrepreneurs and contact men to supply scarce materials and capital, unblock bottlenecks, motivate managers, keep production running, and make the meeting of Gosplan targets even proximately possible. But such a system had its costs. Because the operators, both official and *sub rosa*, had to cut corners, pay bribes to officials to turn a blind eye and sweeteners to suppliers to obtain strategic parts, and often engage in crude barter to keep things running, the cost of doing business was unnecessarily high. The system was therefore incredibly inefficient. As one example of waste and incompetence, the First Secretary of the Kazakh Party, Alexander Protozanov, reported to Brezhnev in 1981 that the excellent grain harvest was rotting in the fields for lack of harvesting machinery, grain stores, and transport. Brezhnev replied: 'Never mind. Just get on with the work – we have complete confidence in you.' On one occasion the railway minister, Ivan Pavlovsky, sat up all night on the telephone just to get one goods train through. Meanwhile, the mafia bosses were piling up gold, jewellery, roubles, and foreign currency in attics, cellars, and garages, photographs of which Vaksberg prints.[38]

The system was thus atrophying from within long before Gorbachev came to power and tried to clean up the mess. It is now fashionable in the West to blame the collapse on the Marxist–Leninist ideology and/or the command economy, but both these explanations, so flattering to Western politics and free-market thinking, are beside the point. Indeed, it is widely believed in Russia that the American advisers from universities like Harvard and Chicago have done more to harm than help the Russian economy, since they failed to diagnose the problem and did not allow for the lack of experience and understanding of the self-discipline and framework of regulation required of an operational free market. By Brezhnev's time no one of any consequence in the Soviet Union believed in the ideology, and individualism of the most cynical kind motivated the people in charge. The party had become a self-perpetuating institution, much like the medieval Roman church or the Chinese mandarinate, and existed to receive the tribute of their tied dependants. The *nomenklatura* no more believed in communism than the executives of Alfred Chandler's Western corporations believed in the unregulated free market.[39] The command economy was inefficient and self-defeating not simply because it was planned but because it was unreal: it existed mainly on paper, and measured performance not by actual goods and services produced but by reports and declarations of the managers, whose rewards depended on exaggerating them.

A real command economy, like the 'war socialism' that Churchill practised in both world wars, can be efficient, but only if it has the confidence and enthusiasm of the people for a recognized common purpose. After half a century of promises unfulfilled and of cynical exploitation by a hypocritical elite, the Soviet people had neither confidence nor enthusiasm for the vision of socialism for their grandchildren. But after the scandals perpetrated by capitalist elites – the Maxwells, Milkens and Boeskys, the Bank of Credit and Commerce International, the Vatican Bank, the Banco Nazionale di Lavoro, the Keatings and Neill Bushes of the American savings and loans industry,

Japanese 'money politics' and Yakuza gangsters, to mention only a few –
who is to say that communism has a monopoly of corruption? The far
more naked corruption, violence, blackmail, and crime which has
succeeded its collapse and the return of the free market can hardly be
said to be an improvement. As Lord Acton so presciently said, 'All
power tends to corrupt; absolute power corrupts absolutely.' That is as
true under capitalism as under communism. In the absence of democratic controls, which have completely failed to operate on Western corporations as on the Soviet *nomenklatura*, corruption, legal or otherwise,
always wins. In the Soviet case, the problem was the absolute power of a
monolithic elite, uniting both government and economy, with no rival to
compete for power. The Soviet elite was responsible to no one but itself.
The same might happen in the West if the corporate elite could attain its
aim of completely controlling government. Once the fear of Stalinist
terror was removed, members of *nomenklatura* were like children in a
candy store, completely free to grab everything in sight, without stop-
ping to think what this would do for their own legitimacy and survival.
In the end, after seventy years, they paid the price.

The chief reason for the collapse of the Soviet Union, then, lies in the
flawed structure of rewards, which is indeed the key to the success or
failure of any system. The *nomenklatura* were paid not to make the
system work but to undermine it. Given the false egalitarian ideal of 'To
each according to his need', which assumed that all incomes should be
nearly equal, 'From each according to his ability' became an exhortation
with little material incentive to perform honestly. The result was that
those who controlled the flows of income found increasingly ingenious
ways of steering more and more of it towards themselves. If this could
not be done legitimately because of the ideology, they did it corruptly,
by skimming off the cream. In short, it paid them to be corrupt, to take a
cut from every transaction, to demand *blat* for every permission, licence,
concession, and to take their rewards in kind, in privileged accommodation, luxury food and drink, cars, schooling, clinics, vacation facilities,
travel, and the like. This became an enormous tax on production, increasing the cost and reducing the output, so that little was left for the ordinary consumer except the dregs. The people, too, had little incentive to
work productively or accept change or innovation except the promise, in
the words of the old Marxist slogan about capitalist religion, of 'pie in
the sky by and by'. No wonder they turned to alcohol, absenteeism and
'going slow'.

Zaslavskaya explains the moral decay in two well-known slogans,
which might be the epitaphs of the system: 'If the bosses steal, we'll steal
too,' and 'If they only pretend to pay us, we'll only pretend to work.'[40]
They encapsulate the demoralization of Soviet society that finally
brought it down. Paradoxically, Gorbachev's *perestroika* made things

worse. He tried to introduce freedom of speech and a free economy without giving up central political control, which left the *nomenklatura* in place to sabotage his reform programme. As Aleksandr Solzhenitsyn put it, 'The corrupt ruling class – the many million party–state *nomenklatura* – is not capable of voluntarily renouncing any of the privileges they have seized. They have lived shamelessly at the people's expense – and would like to continue to do so.'[41] A Yugoslav cartoon summed up the situation: it showed a train labelled *Perestroika* bearing down on a barricade of office furniture manned by bureaucrats, saying 'Comrade Gorbachev does not know what he is up against!'[42] It seems that the bureaucrats won. The mafia, no longer reined in by the KGB, became more shameless and demanding, acquired guns often from the Red Army, openly traded in gambling, prostitution and pornography, and began to operate crude protection rackets on all the small business men in the new free market. Robbery and murder, rare under the old regime, exploded, and the streets became unsafe for the first time since the revolution. The bureaucrats resisted the reforms and clung to the remnants of the command economy. As Boris Yeltsin saw before he came to power,

> I suddenly became aware of what a morass we had sunk into and how immeasurably difficult it was going to be to haul ourselves out of it. For it was precisely this body of people – the party bureaucracy – which is doing its best to put new obstacles in the way of *perestroika* and *glasnost*; and they were not prepared to surrender to anyone their right to do so.[43]

Gorbachev knew this well enough. When he launched *perestroika* in April 1985, he announced

> an effective offensive against bureaucracy and its uglier manifestations, such as diktat, arbitrary administrative actions in the economy and in the social, intellectual and cultural spheres, bureaucratic indifference to the people's rights and needs, and high-handed dismissal of public opinion and of the social experience of working people. Against the background of stagnation and restraints on democratic institutions bureaucracy grew to dangerous proportions and held back social progress.[44]

But instead of abolishing it and starting again, he tried with the instincts of an old apparatchik to work through it, with disastrous consequences for his reform programme and for himself.

The resentful bureaucrats fastened on to the traditional Russian envy of people who were more equal than themselves. 'That psychology of intolerance of others who make money, no matter why, no matter whether they work harder, longer, or better,' Anatoly Sobchak, a reformist Deputy of the Supreme Soviet said, 'that psychology is blocking economic reform on the collective and state farms. Peasants smash the machinery and burn the barns of other peasants who try to work their own land to make a better living.' 'The blind, burning envy of your neighbour's success,' a reform economist, Nikolai Shmelyov wrote in *Novy Mir*, 'has become the most powerful brake on the ideas and practice of *perestroika*.'[45] This, added to the sheer weariness of queuing endlessly for the means of life, gave the opponents of reform what they thought was their chance.

## THE FINAL COLLAPSE

In August 1991, while Gorbachev and his family were on holiday in the Crimea, the old guard in the Kremlin made their last throw. The self-appointed 'State Committee for the Extraordinary Situation' under Gennady Yanaev and Mikhail Suslov seized power and sent the tanks into Moscow to overawe the Parliament of the Russian Republic, headed by Boris Yeltsin. They were met by unexpected resistance from the people of Moscow, who poured into the streets in their thousands to block the tanks and persuade the troops to join the people against the leaders of the coup. Yeltsin bravely addressed the crowd from the top of a friendly tank, persuaded the troops to support him, and with the help of the army and the KGB restored the legitimate government. But the violent means by which he defeated the Russian Parliament, with the 'White House' in flames and billowing smoke, may have undermined the fragile democracy introduced but never consolidated by Gorbachev, and may yet bring Yeltsin himself down.

Whatever the outcome, it was too late for Gorbachev and his version of *perestroika*, which had never grasped the nettle of real reform and true democracy. By December Gorbachev was gone and the USSR with him, to be replaced by Yeltsin and the Commonwealth of Independent States. Twelve of the fifteen republics joined, leaving out the three Baltic republics which had only been added by the Hitler–Stalin Pact of 1939, though they were followed later by Georgia and Moldova. This was only the beginning of Yeltsin's difficulties, however. Armed clashes were already taking place between old nationalist enemies – the Armenians against the Azeris, the Ossetians against the Georgians, the Tatars and Chuvash against their fellow Moslem neighbours, the Latvians, Lithuanians, Estonians, Moldavians, and Chechens against the ethnic Russians, who numbered 25 million outside the Russian Republic itself. This in turn provoked a backlash from the Great Russian nationalists united behind the *Pamyat* ('memory') movement and stirred up by demagogues like Zhirinovsky, who revived the old Russian xenophobia and condemnation of the Jews. The nationalities, held together under both the Tsars and communist overlords only by terror, now fell to fighting each other like starving dogs over meatless bones. While most of the conflicts stemmed from old ethnic animosities and incompatible claims on the same territory, there is little doubt that the local bureaucrats and mafiosi used them to divert attention from their misdeeds, to avoid trial, and to hang on to power. In one republic after another they thrust themselves to the head of the nationalist movement and got themselves elected as presidents and ministers of newly independent governments. In this way they were able to preserve their privileges, continue their exploitation, and yet gain a popularity they had never had before. New nationalist was but old mafioso writ large.

Meanwhile, even the genuine reformers, and those who paid lip service to *perestroika* in order to stay in office, rushed to take advantage of the end of collectivism. In some ways this was inevitable, since only they had the knowledge and experience to take over the state enterprises. Most of the new businesses were run by their old managers, who also began to buy up the shares issued to small investors who were only too glad to cash them in. Many became millionaires overnight, and can now be seen in Western capitals buying huge quantities of consumer goods, spending freely at the best hotels and restaurants, and investing in real estate in the most expensive areas. In addition, the *nomenklatura* hastened to purchase their apartments and *dachas* at bargain prices and to turn state property, as Sergei Shishkin observed in 1994, into their own private real estate. Nikolai Ryzhkov, Gorbachev's prime minister and Yeltsin's opponent, who expressed shock at the very mention of privatization, nevertheless tried, unsuccessfully, to buy his state villa and 1.5 hectares of woodland.[46] 'Tens of marshalls, hundreds of generals and thousands of apparatchiks' managed to buy properties with twelve to fifteen-room 'palaces' with swimming pools and ancillary buildings worth 30–40,000 roubles, while the ordinary citizen had to pay over 20,000 roubles for a small two-room flat.[47] Mosca's prediction that the revolutionaries themselves would restore private property for their own benefit was borne out in fact.

Perhaps the best hope of creating a thriving, but regulated, market economy lies with the mafia themselves, not the bureaucrats who simply milked the system without contributing anything to it, but the entrepreneurs of the shadow economy who made the system work as well as it did. They had the true entrepreneurial instinct for making a quick profit and supplying a need that the original small-scale free market of Adam Smith's day thrived on. Small operators and individual peasants from their private plots had supplied the cities with about a quarter of their fruit, vegetables, and flowers. You could see them selling them out of suitcases at the curbside, and in the spring peasant women with huge bunches of gladioli bigger than themselves stood at bus stops all around Moscow and Leningrad. Now the danger is that these same small operators are being milked by 'protectors' from the new mafia, thugs who do not hesitate to maim or murder those who do not cooperate. The first thing any reforming government needs to do is to restore law and order and to suppress the gangsters who are battening on society in cruder ways than the old *nomenklatura*. But how to do that without threatening human rights and undermining democracy is the dilemma that must be solved by Yeltsin or his successors.

The 74-year history of the Soviet Union is an object lesson in the achievements and dangers of professional society on the centralized command model. It transformed an ancient agrarian despotism into one of the two great superpowers of the modern world, able to threaten the survival of the human race and the destruction of the planet. It did this by creating a society of professional experts, scientists, engineers, managers, and bureaucrats who, when given their head and absolute power, turned their intelligence and powers of organization to exploiting the system for their own benefit. It was a more nakedly pathological version of professional society than the rather primitive one they set out to overturn and defeat. In the process they reduced the mass of the people to helotry, to a species of wage slavery more oppressive than the capitalist one from which they claimed to rescue them and which they used as a bugbear to frighten the helots into supporting them.

Their exploitation, of course, went too far. It backfired and destroyed the system, in two ways. First, the extraction of too much surplus value caused the contradictions, ironically imputed by Marx to capitalism, by which the economy failed to produce and the impoverished proletariat lacked the means to consume the products of the system, leading to a lethal combination of unsatisfied demand and lack of purchasing power. This in turn provoked discontent and disillusion which, in a classic Habermasian crisis of legitimacy, meant that the people had no reason to want to save the system from collapse. Second, the exploiting elite had to work through and came to depend for control on an increasingly educated class of professionals not all of whom could be employed, rewarded, or corrupted by the system, and saw salvation for themselves in reforming or overturning it. Thus the system contained the seeds of its own destruction, and produced both the moral decay and the men and means to attack it.

Whether a viable, honest, and fair professional society can be salvaged from the present chaos remains in doubt. The unregulated free market recommended by naive Western advisers, who seem to have no conception of how their own system works and how it depends on a self-regulating culture which they do not recognize, still less understand, is only intensifying the chaos in a country which has never known a free enterprise system under either the Tsars or the commissars, and certainly does not know how to operate it. Freedom now seems to mean only freedom for the bully and gangster. The positive freedom that comes from self-regulation under a benevolent government dedicated to fair play for all is beyond their ken. A political culture that respects the rules of the game which alone guarantee that the market is conducted fairly and honestly to the mutual benefit of all is not constructed overnight, though it can, given the greed and selfishness of some operators, be demolished in a day.

The Soviet Union was an experiment in professional society on the centralized command model that failed spectacularly. That does not mean that the alternative model, the so-called free-enterprise model which is really freedom for corporate managers, is therefore vindicated. The triumphalism of free-marketeers like the followers of Friedrich von Hayek and Milton Friedman or pseudo-Hegelian 'end of history' tub-thumpers like Francis Fukuyama is premature, to say the least. If they were more perceptive they would not preach to the Russians but ask themselves what lessons should be learned from their mistakes for the salvation of the West. The chief lesson would seem to be that professionals, whether public or private, are good servants but bad masters, and that to give absolute power to any group, whether government bureaucrats or corporate managers, is to invite them to divert the resources of society to their own gain, at the risk of undermining the economy, demoralizing the populace, and imploding the society. Like the Soviet Union, Western professional societies have the choice between a regulated market based on social justice and fair (not equal) shares for all and a pathological one dedicated to the greed and selfishness of an irresponsible ruling elite. In a post-industrial world where life, health, and prosperity depend on professional expertise, what both East and West do not have is the choice of no professional society at all.

# 7

# JAPAN
## A floating world

Japan, at first sight at least, is an ideal version of professional society. It is on the face of it a meritocracy in which people find their way through a relentlessly competitive educational and selective system to career ladders in government and the best corporations. Vertical hierarchies in the administrative and corporate bureaucracies have replaced 'class' – or what passed for class after the feudal castes or status groups of Tokugawa Japan – and this vertical structuring (*tate shakai* in Chie Nakane's formulation)[1] reaches down to the blue-collar workers. The employees of the large corporations are guaranteed lifetime employment at salaries rising with seniority and length of service. The *wa* or harmony arising from the resulting high-trust industrial relations has enabled Japanese industry to create an 'economic miracle' and make 'Japan Number One', if not in aggregate GNP then in national income per capita at current rates of exchange (though not, as we shall see, in purchasing power). The consequent massive trade surplus is enabling Japan, despite the world slump of the 1990s, to buy up factories, mines, forests, banks, and real estate in the United States, Europe, Asia, and Australasia and build up some of the largest multinational corporations in the world.

Japan indeed seems to embrace both ends of the great arch stretching from the most free-market oriented to the extreme state-directed version of post-industrial society, in a unique combination of private enterprise and administrative guidance. Or rather, since nothing in Japan is quite what it seems, it sails high above the great arch in a floating world of its own in which a supposedly unique Japanese culture of consensus, harmony, team spirit, and voluntary subordination of the individual to the goals of the group contrives to produce social cohesion, political unity, and enormous economic success.

Just as Britain pioneered the second great social revolution into industrialism because it had the right kind of society for it, so Japan seems – or seemed until the 1990s – to be forging ahead in the third, the rise of a global professional society, because it has the right kind of society for that further change in human development. As in Britain in

147

the eighteenth century, not all of the appropriate features were in place when the transition began. The famed paternalism of the Japanese corporation, often traced back to the *ie*, the Japanese family or household which embraced only co-resident members including adopted ones like incoming sons- and daughters-in-law, was in fact a modern invention, a pragmatic response to the disruptive, and allegedly socialist-inspired, industrial unrest before the First and soon after the Second World War. The 'three sacred treasures' used to explain the economic miracle – lifelong employment, promotion by seniority (*nenko*), and the company union – were similarly an 'invention of tradition', a solution to problems of factory discipline and labour shortage in the same periods. The three treasures never applied to more than the third of the workforce employed by the large corporations, and only then to their permanent, full-time, mainly male employees.[2] Lifelong employment, often ending at age 55 or earlier, allied to tacit agreement by the corporations not to employ each other's 'deserters', could become a device for enforcing company loyalty; seniority salary scales, not transferable to other companies, were a prophylactic against desertion and a pressure for early retirement; and the company union was an ally of the employer against the worker. That they are not so viewed in Japan bears witness to the success of the Japanese elite in selling their ideology to the people, and to the difference in Japanese thought between form or principle (*tatemae*) and reality or practice (*honne*), between appearance, what is in plain view (*omote*), and what is hidden (*ura*).

That difference between appearance and reality is vital for understanding Japanese society. Since forms, concepts, and institutions, however, exist chiefly in the mind, the Japanese view of themselves and of the outside world is itself an objective fact, whatever the reasons for it. If they think of themselves as an extremely homogeneous people who dislike conflict, pursue consensus, put group interests before the individual, have little sense of solidarity with people on the same level in other companies, industries or countries, and feel immense loyalty to those above and, to a less extent, below them in the same corporate, administrative, academic, or other hierarchy, that is a social, economic and political fact to be explained – not a 'cultural excuse' (*Wakatte kudasai* – 'Please understand') for having it both ways, as many 'Japan bashers' believe. The explanation is not that the Japanese are hypocrites, but that they truly believe their own ideology, which happens to fit perfectly both the interests of the elite and the prerequisites of a modern professional society.

The paternalist ideology was not established without opposition. In the early years after the Second World War the power of the elite was challenged by recusant rivals: by the socialist parties, which briefly formed a government in 1947–48; by the connected labour movement which, with the short-lived encouragement of the American Occupation administration, re-established the trades unions and opposed the big corporations in a series of disputes culminating in the self-destructive coal miners' strike against the Mitsui Corporation in 1960; and by the right- and left-wing opponents of the American alliance and the Cold War down to 1960 and beyond. It was only after the consolidation of the conservative parties in the Liberal Democratic Party in 1955, midwifed by the Americans to prevent a socialist victory at the polls, that the ruling elite was able to negotiate the 'social contracts' with the farmers, small business, and the moderates in the trades unions, through which the characteristic social order of the next four decades was set in place.

## THE CHANGING ROLE OF THE BUREAUCRACY

At first the elite was almost completely dominated by the bureaucracy, the only element of the pre-war system to survive defeat, loss of prestige, and the Occupation's purges of war criminals. As Milton J. Esman of the Public Administration Division of SCAP (Supreme Commander for the Allied Powers) put it in his famous memorandum to the Chief of the Government Section in 1946,

> Of all the major bulwarks of feudal and totalitarian Japan, only the bureaucracy remains unimpaired. The bureaucracy will undoubtedly outlast the occupation and will play a decisive role of molding the future of Japan.[3]

He was right. Although the conservative politicians re-emerged in the LDP in 1955, and the proscribed *zaibatsu*, the 'money trusts' which dominated the pre-war economy, were resurrected in the *keiretsu*, the closed rings of mutually shareholding companies that play the same role in the post-war period, it was the bureaucracy that provided continuity and formed the brain and spinal cord of Japanese recovery. The bureaucrats reached their zenith in the second post-war period, in the era of rapid economic growth between 1955 and 1973, when they were credited, too generously perhaps, with masterminding the 'economic miracle'. Only when they had successfully re-established the other elements in the structure, notably the professional politicians and the *zaikai*, the top corporate managers, did they relinquish some of their power to them in what became the most unified and integrated elite in the non-communist world. Their changing role is best viewed from that central period, which transformed Japan from a marginal nation into a world trading power.

If we take the official, popularly accepted version of Japanese society and contrast it with the underlying reality in the light of the well-established tendency for professional elites to profit disproportionately from the system, we find that Japan is not so very different from other professional societies, except in its spectacularly greater success in terms of economic growth, if not so clearly in quality of life. Its success stems from the most characteristic feature of all professional societies. All professions live by persuasion, by persuading clients, citizens, corporations, governments, and society at large to believe in and pay for their often invisible, evanescent, fiduciary services. The clergy promise to save your soul, the doctor to save your health, the lawyer to save your property, liberty, and life itself. When they fail, it is too late for redress. Government bureaucrats and corporate managers are even more remote and unaccountable, and their failure is even more disastrous for the whole society, as the sorry condition of the ex-communist states of the Soviet empire or corrupt capitalist regimes like Italy or Nigeria bears witness. Professional societies are as good or bad as their ruling elites, who promise political justice, economic growth, and a civilized social life, whether they deliver the goods and services or exploit them for their own exclusive use. Until the recent corruption scandals, the Japanese ruling elite of state bureaucrats, Diet politicians, and corporate managers, have been overwhelmingly successful in convincing the Japanese people to accept their ideology of a free, harmonious, consensual, paternalistic, prosperous, and above all economically accelerating society, one that has become the envy of the world. Whether they can continue to succeed in the depressed and politically fragmented 1990s remains to be seen. Corrupt politicians who have been in power far too long, as in Russia or Italy, have been defeated and may yet meet their nemesis. Outrage against corruption overthrew the LDP in 1993 and ejected its successor, the Hosokawa coalition, in 1994, and the final outcome is not yet in sight. Meanwhile, have the elite justified their propaganda, delivered on their promises, created an equitable meritocracy, and at what cost?

First, in this self-consciously classless society in which 90 per cent of respondents regularly claim to be middle-class, who are the elites and what are their sources of wealth and power? Even Karel van Wolferen, doyen of the 'Japan bashers', who claims that there is no sovereign Japanese state, no centre in ultimate control of policy, no clearly demarcated group of power holders, admits that 'Japan has a clearly discernible ruling class. Its members – mainly bureaucrats, top businessmen and one section of the LDP – are all basically administrators . . .' [4] Given its consciously meritocratic recruitment, it is a fairly open elite, though like all meritocracies it tries to perpetuate itself and is skewed, in that the sons (rarely daughters) of the bureaucrats, politicians, and businessmen have the best chance of success. To an extent even greater than the French with their *grandes écoles* and the British with their public schools and Oxbridge, the bureaucrats and politicians, and most of the top businessmen are recruited from a handful of universities, most of all from Todai, the University of Tokyo, and from one division of it, the Law School.

Since so many politicians and business executives have until recently been recruited via the ministries, the bureaucracy is the key to the system. While one third of the successful candidates in the higher civil service are Todai graduates, a pass does not guarantee a job, and about two thirds of those actually appointed to Grade 1 posts in the ministries are from Todai, three quarters of these from the Law School. The remainder come largely from Kyoto, Waseda and Keio universities, although recently there has been a rising but still miniscule percentage from other universities. Since the ministries recruit independently from the pool of successful examinees, Todai graduates dominate still more the most prestigious departments: 77–85 per cent of the annual hirings in the Ministry of Finance, 75–100 per cent in the Home Ministry, 76 per cent in the Foreign Ministry, 69 per cent in the Ministry of Transport, and so on. And because the main principle of promotion in any meritocracy is 'people like us' (i.e. people with the same kind of merit defined by ourselves) 'the higher the position, the greater the proportion of Todai graduates'. In 1986 73 per cent of the bureau chiefs and 86 per cent of the administrative vice-ministers (chief civil servant in each ministry) were Todai graduates; 5.5 per cent and 9.2 per cent were from Kyoto; and the rest, 11.0 per cent and 4.6 per cent, from other universities.[5]

Todai graduates were less numerous but no less important in the rest of the 'administrative ruling class'. Only a minority went into the civil service, the rest into the corporations, public or private, local government, banking, insurance, and only a small minority, 9 per cent of law graduates, became practising lawyers. But they became leaders in every field of activity. In the Diet they constituted one quarter of the members, including one third of the ruling LDP; all but two of the LDP prime ministers (the self-made construction tycoon and political godfather Kakuei Tanaka and his disloyal protégé Noboru Takeshita, both brought down by allegations of corruption from their equally corrupt rivals); most of the chairmen and vice-chairmen of the *Keidanren*, the main employers' organization, the chief executives in forty-three of the fifty largest business corporations in the mid-1970s, and 401 presidents of the 1,454 largest companies in 1985 (plus another 140 from Kyoto University).

Like the *Polytechniciens* and *Enarques* in France and the Oxbridge products in Britain, Todai and Kyodai graduates are able, self-confident, like-minded types, conscious of their success in the educational rat race that has brought them to the top, with a conviction that they alone can run any enterprise that has the good sense to recruit them. It is no surprise therefore that, despite the rivalries between ministries, between the factions (*habatsu*) of the LDP and between the top managers of the large corporations, they speak the same language, pursue much the same goals, and are a much more integrated ruling elite than any in the West.

Their integrity is reinforced by a system of relationships not unknown elsewhere but raised to a higher power in Japan. By means of 'old boy' connections (*kone*) similar to but more intense than the 'old school tie' network of the English public schools or the more intellectual links of the French *grandes écoles* and civil service *grands corps*, they keep in touch across the boundaries between politics, ministerial bureaucracies, and the private corporations. Each politician, bureaucrat, and corporate executive has his own *jinmyaku* (literally 'veins in the rock'), a network of connections to cronies in other institutions, which enables him to pick up the telephone and 'get things done' by short-circuiting the formal channels.

It is not a universal access system but highly personal, selective, and particular. Ministry of Finance officials have buddies in the Diet prepared to push through unpopular budget proposals, with managers in the Bank of Japan and other leading financial institutions, and particularly with the banking arms of the *keiretsu*, the rings of companies owning each other's shares and sharing overlapping directors, like the eighty companies that make up Mitsubishi. The officials of the mighty MITI, the Ministry of International Trade and Industry credited by Chalmers Johnson and others with masterminding the post-war economic miracle, have connections with all the main export industries, and schedule some, like car production, electronics, and bio-technology, for expansion and others, like textiles, steel, and shipbuilding, for winding down or offloading on to overseas subsidiaries.[6] The bureaucrats of the ministries of Construction and Transport are closely involved with the big contractors for roads, bridges, harbours, airports, and urban development, where the profits from licences and permissions are the greatest and the opportunities for corruption unbounded. Construction takes 15–16 per cent of GNP per annum and the ministry commissions or licenses virtually all private development. The ministry plays godfather to the *dango*, the bid-rigging ring of construction contractors, which excludes all outsiders including foreign firms, and spent some 636 billion yen in 1985 in 'entertainment' and helping LDP politicians to get elected with pork barrel projects in their constituencies.[7]

With the cost of land in Japan soaring to stratospheric heights – the land under Greater Tokyo became more valuable than the whole area of the United States – the rocketing collateral is used to fund massive investments in Japan and still more overseas. In the 1980s Japan overtook every country except the United States and Germany in the number of dollar billionaires, and many of them, like Tanaka and Kanemaru, were in the construction industry. The role of the *jinmyaku* in smoothing the path to urban development cannot be exaggerated, nor can it in every other field of activity, whether manufacturing, banking, insurance, transport, overseas commerce, and so on. This explains why foreigners, however well-financed, like T. Boone Pickens who tried to take over a Toyota satellite, find it so hard to break into the magic circle. Without the connections that spring from climbing the exclusive ladders of Japanese competitive meritocracy it is next to impossible to deal on equal terms.

There is another practice that cuts across the boundaries between the tripartite elites and helps unite the administrative ruling class. By the custom of *amakudari* ('descent from heaven') senior bureaucrats migrate on retirement to leading positions in the LDP, to executive posts in the many government agencies, and most of all to directorships in the private corporations. This migration is stimulated by two civil service requirements: early retirement, usually at about age 55 (maximum age 60 since 1985), which means that pensions are low and retirees still have many years of useful life ahead of them; and the *nenji* rule by which members of the same entering class must, when one of them is promoted over their heads to bureau chief or vice-minister, retire immediately so as not to suffer the humiliation of taking orders from their peers.

Although ex-civil servants are not supposed to take employment within two years of retirement with any firm with which they have had close connections while in office, very few (3–7 per cent in the 1980s) are refused exemption from the rule, and the number of senior officials moving to private corporations has more than doubled since 1965. In 1985 318 retired officials (178 technical, 140 administrative) were granted exemptions and became either directors (*yakuin*) or advisers (*komon*) to corporations. Of the twenty most senior officials, one became president of a company, two managing directors, six directors, and eight advisers. The recently privatized Japan Telegraph and Telephone Corporation hired five of them, three as directors. Not all of them went to large corporations but enough did so to reinforce the *jinmyaku* between each ministry and its client companies. The Ministry of Finance was the most prolific source of recruitment. Of twenty-nine senior officials retiring in 1984 only one did not seek employment: six went to government affiliated institutions, nine to public corporations, two to private banks, eight to other private firms, and three became licensed tax accountants. Of the total, sixteen went as directors and five as advisers. Similarly, Ministry of Transport officials found employment with airlines and harbour and road construction companies, construction ministry officials with property and development companies, MITI officials with manufacturing and export–import companies, and so on.[8]

Sometimes the official negotiates his own appointment directly with a company or agency he knows well, or the firm asks for any retiree with the appropriate expertise, experience, and contacts, but most 'marriages' are arranged by the vice-minister or chief secretary of the ministry with firms it has regular dealings with. It is true that similar recruitment of ex-civil servants takes place in the West. The French practice of *pantouflages* – migration of young civil servants into nationalized industries and private corporations – is a parallel device, though it generally takes place at a much earlier age and requires the ex-official to climb the corporate ladder before reaching the top. There are also many examples of British civil servants moving on retirement at age 60 to banks and other large corporations, not to mention the American 'revolving door' between the federal government and the private sector. But nothing occurs on so regular and organized a scale as in Japan.

Most of those who do not parachute down into the private sector 'slip sideways' (*yokosuberi*) into the many public corporations, agencies, and entities, some 111 of them employing nearly a million people in 1980, including nearly 800 in executive positions. Since then many of these agencies have been privatized, with no visible effect on *amakudari* except to require retirees to seek exemption, which they do not need for public agency employment. According to an unofficial report in 1987, over three quarters (379 out of 489) of the executives in eighty-three public bodies were retired bureaucrats. About one quarter slip sideways several times from one agency to another, collecting separation allowances each time amounting to a maximum of 36 per cent of their total earnings while in post. To take an older example, Funayama Masakichi, Vice-Minister of Finance, retired in 1953 to become successively a director of the Bank of Japan, deputy governor of the Japan Export-Import Bank, and finally governor of the Smaller Business Finance Corporation, collecting 'golden handshakes' totalling 27.5 million yen on the way. Again, individual ministries place retiring officials with client agencies. The Housing Agency, for example, found six of its eleven executives from the ministries of Construction and Finance, the Economic Planning Agency, and the Prime Minister's office; and the Highways Agency found seven out of twelve from the Construction, Finance, Transport and Home ministries. Even consumer protection bodies and women's organizations recruit retired bureaucrats for their *jinmyaku* links to the policy makers in their fields of interest.[9]

Finally, a small but significant number of retiring officials migrate into politics. They have of course to get themselves elected, and less than half of them (42.3 per cent) succeed. In recent years they have also had to climb the internal career ladders of the LDP, which has become increasingly dominated by professional politicians, and the most successful ex-bureaucrats have migrated in their forties rather than their fifties. Those who do, have the best *jinmyaku*, with business men in the constituencies with whom they have had dealings, and with established politicians who have the most effective *koenkai*, the personal followings which, in the usual absence of constituency parties, undertake to get out the vote. In 1986 eighty ex-bureaucrats were elected to the House of Representatives, making up one quarter of the ruling LDP's members there, and twenty-four to the House of Councillors, one in three of the LDP members of the upper House. They came mainly from the more prestigious ministries, notably Finance, MITI, Construction, and Agriculture, and nearly all were graduates of Todai.[10] With their immense experience of government from the inside, their manipulation of the political ministers who spend only a few years in any particular office, their continuing contacts with the business world and, surprisingly, even with the opposition parties, the ex-civil servants in the LDP and in government are at the heart of the Japanese system and of the administrative ruling elite. Even the Hosokawa coalition government of 1993–94 had to rely on them to survive as long as it did. But their main power now lies in the serving ministry officials rather than the ex-bureaucrats. In Prime Minister Uno's 1989 government only five cabinet ministers out of twenty-one were ex-officials, and only one of them had been an administrative vice-minister at the head of a ministry; the rest were career politicians.

The system obviously lends itself to corruption, but while in office the bureaucrats are scrupulously upright and personally uncorrupt. Only a miniscule number, two to five in 10,000, have been caught out in bribery or embezzlement, even fewer at the senior levels of national government. The stakes are too high for individuals who hope to benefit far more from what Chalmers Johnson has called 'structural' or 'institutional corruption'.[11] Long-term dealings with business men from whom lucrative jobs may be expected and with LDP politicians who need constituency projects to get themselves re-elected are far more valuable than any immediate cash pay-off. Retiring bureaucrats are recruited by corporations, public agencies, and LDP factions less in gratitude for past favours than for the value of their *jinmyaku*, their contacts with former colleagues and clients, which can smooth the way to lucrative policies, contracts, licences, research grants, and subsidies. For example, one of the keys to the LDP's past success lies in the small rural constituencies, where one vote counts for three in the large cities, and which provide the party with 45 per cent of its vote. There the ex-officials of the Ministry of Agriculture staff many of the farmers' organizations and work to maintain the tariffs and administrative devices which make beef twice and rice five times as expensive as on the world market. This is not personal corruption, since they do not themselves make money from their operations, but it helps the farmers, who now constitute less than 10 per cent of the Japanese population and are now mostly part-time, to maintain their hold on import policy and ensures their allegiance to the LDP. That they operate at great expense to the Japanese consumer, who also suffers from the complex, lengthy, and inefficient distribution system, is one more demonstration of the success of the ruling elite in persuading the Japanese public to vote against their pockets.

155

The bureaucrats and their *amakudari* ex-colleagues have a foot in all three camps of the administrative ruling elite. They are the leading thread in the tapestry, the reinforcing rods in the concrete, the hard drive in the computer of the Japanese system. In the third post-war period, since the oil crisis of 1973, in which despite slower economic growth affluence and routine have entrenched rival leaderships in politics and business, the central role of the bureaucracy has declined but has not disappeared. Rather has it become more diffuse again, involving more actors in decision making and requiring greater skill in uniting the elite in agreed policies. Yet the common educational background and the continuing integration through the *jinmyaku* have kept the elite together, even through and beyond the revolt against the LDP. This explains why it can seem so fragmented and decentralized to many experienced observers and yet appear to act as one self-directed, goal-oriented organism.

## MANAGED CAPITALISM AND THE ECONOMIC MIRACLE

The idea that the Japanese bureaucracy planned in detail and meticulously implemented the post-war 'economic miracle', notably through the Ministry of International Trade and Industry, successor to the all-powerful and infinitely resourceful Ministry of Munitions, is now recognized as too simple. So, however, is the naive notion of a Japanese phoenix rising from the ashes in the tempering fires of an American-imposed free market. Post-war Japan had no master plan beyond a determination to rebuild its economy and a flexible opportunism that amounted to genius. Indeed, the early post-war years were marked by conflicts and disputes over such questions as investment versus welfare and rearmament versus domestic consumption. Many mistakes were made, such as putting too much faith in the heavy industries like steel and coal in which the country had little comparative advantage, but Japan learned to abandon failing experiments with a ruthlessness unknown in the West.[12] But there is no doubt that the Japanese elite practised a variety of 'managed capitalism' which, while falling short of a centralized command economy like the Russian, relied on the tacit understanding between the politicians, the ministerial bureaucracies, and the leading corporations that certain developments were good for the economy and the country and should be encouraged, protected, and if necessary subsidized so as to make Japan rich, independent, and commercially successful.[13] 'Administrative guidance' together with extraordinary luck and an eye for the main chance, rather than a fortuitous reliance on the unguided free market, set Japan on the road not only to recovery but to economic leadership in the global economy.

There was no shortage of luck. Japan, despite its devastating collapse had many advantages: the advantage of defeat itself, which destroyed all illusions, vested interests, and the unproductive burden of the military; the advantage of a post-war world starved of exports which the old enemies could not fully supply and a rock-bottom exchange rate to exploit it; a docile labour force, once the Americans had given up their attempt to enforce trade unionism, banned the 1947 general strike, and helped the employers suppress labour unrest; the windfall of the Cold War in general and the Korean and Vietnam wars in particular, which made the erstwhile American enemy a firm friend and patron who offered cost-free military protection and abundant hard currency for army supplies and bases; and the blessing of a defence budget of 1 per cent of GNP when the United States was spending an average of 7.3 per cent, Britain 6 per cent, France 5 per cent, and even the other defeated enemy, West Germany, 3.8 per cent.[14]

Japan, with its astonishing private savings rate of up to a third of GNP – not an inborn feature of the Japanese but a product of growth itself in a community unused to having surpluses to spend – was able to pump massive amounts of capital into civilian industry, commerce, infrastructure, and marketing. It was helped by cheap capital from the Fiscal Investment and Loan Programme which collects the household savings of the people and directs them into public and private ventures at the behest of the bureaucracy. The result, once post-war recovery had been achieved, was a surge of economic growth in the 1960s and early 1970s twice as fast as its competitors: 10.2 per cent and 8.7 per cent per annum compared with an average of 5.0 per cent and 4.4 per cent for the other six members of the G7 leading economies. It even weathered the oil crisis of the 1970s and the world recession of the 1980s far better than they did, with growth rates of 3.6 per cent and 3.8 per cent compared with their averages of 2.7 per cent and 2.6 per cent.[15]

One advantage was the structure of industry. Whereas in the West – apart from Germany and possibly France – the corporation was controlled by management in the sole interest of the shareholders, the Japanese *kaisha* is regarded as a family and responsible to all the stakeholders, including employees, subsidiaries and subcontractors, and customers. The goal is not immediate profit to maintain the equity price on the stock market but long-term growth and market share in the interest of keeping the firm together and serving all parties to the enterprise. This is the ideology behind the 'three treasures' of lifetime employment, seniority-based incomes, and company unions, limited as they are only to the more permanent, and mainly male, employees. The system is not simply altruistic: it is taken as axiomatic that secure and stable employment ensures a cooperative workforce, loyalty to the firm, high-trust industrial relations, higher productivity, flexible production and easy innovation, longevity for the company, and prosperity for all. There are of course costs: stable employment means carrying an unnecessarily large workforce during recessions, difficulty in getting rid of redundant workers, and rising wage costs as the workforce ages, but these were easily borne while the economy expanded, and it was found possible during recessions like those of the 1970s and 1980s to offload some of the problems by dropping temporary workers, especially women, cutting orders to subcontractors, and transferring older and redundant workers to satellite companies.

In effect, Japanese corporations pioneered outsourcing almost from the beginning, relying on tied subcontractors for a large part of their operations. This encourages a species of legerdemain which safeguards the larger companies at the expense of the smaller, and makes Japanese industry a two-tier system, with large differences in wages and conditions between those employed by big and small business. Critics have pointed out that the success of the minority rides on the backs of the majority of medium and small suppliers whose workers are downtrodden and exploited. Nevertheless, all bosses and workers benefit from the economic growth led by the few, and from the doubling and redoubling of income which enabled the Japanese to rise from a nearly Third World living standard in 1945 to a leading First World standard in a single generation.

Japanese management as well as the workers also have the advantage of a stable environment. Even more than in the West, companies are embedded in a system of corporate neo-feudalism. Companies are ostensibly owned by their shareholders, but most shareholders are other institutions: 70 per cent of shareholdings are 'stable', with banks, insurance companies, and related companies, especially customers and suppliers, having a long-term stake and looking not to immediate profit but to ongoing dealings with 'their' company. This leads to the formation of *keiretsu*, groupings of companies holding each other's shares and having a permanent interest in each other's success.

There are two kinds of *keiretsu*. The vertical kind, like Hitachi or Toyota, consists of a pyramid of companies manufacturing a finite number of similar products. Hitachi, for example, is at the top of a hierarchy of suppliers, subsidiaries, subcontractors, and the like, numbering between 800 and 1,000, most of whom will have some shares in the main company and in each other. The cross-shareholdings may be small, averaging 1 or 2 per cent, but they are meant to show 'sincerity' and a continuing trust and partnership. The other is the horizontal *keiretsu*, the famous successors of the pre-war *zaibatsu*, usually with the same names, like Mitsui, Mitsubishi and Sumitomo, rings of related companies in different industries, often linked to a holding company and one or more major banks. Mitsubishi, for example, consists of about eighty companies, including four banks, three insurance companies, trading and shipping companies, and a range of industrial companies from cars and computers to coal and steel. Although the groupings are loosely structured and steered only by occasional presidents' meetings, the cross-shareholdings and shared directorships, plus continuous informal networking, ensure common policies and guarantee an impenetrable defence against hostile takeovers. The companies can therefore concentrate on long-term research and development, innovation and market share without nervously looking at the share price in fear of hostile raiders. If one company finds itself under threat, the others rally round, buy more shares, and freeze out the invader, refusing him representation on the board even if he holds a quarter of the equity, as T. Boone Pickens found in his bid for a Toyota satellite.

In theory Japanese business is less concentrated than British or American. In 1992 188 companies held 17 per cent of the capital, 19 per cent of the assets, and 16 per cent of the sales among the nearly 2,000 quoted on the stock exchange, which in turn did only 29 per cent of the national turnover. Japan has more small businesses than most Western countries: small and medium sized firms constitute 98 per cent of the total and produce more than half the output. But this is seriously misleading, since most of these enterprises have more or less permanent links with the large firms, as suppliers, subcontractors, outlets and franchises. While it is too simple to talk about 'Japan Inc.', the whole economy consists of overlapping networks of related companies with a long-term involvement in each other's activities.

To a greater extent even than in Britain or the United States, neo-feudal capitalism, with its hierarchies of permanent connections and its intense rivalries between feudal groupings, operates to make Japanese business at once more cooperative and more competitive than elsewhere. This gives it a competitive advantage which the Japanese have exploited to make themselves the second largest economy in the world and Number One in trading success and international credit.

The greatest advantage, of course, is the Japanese people, and the success of the administrative ruling elite in persuading them to accept the elite's version of Japanese culture. This is neither the ideology of the free market as preached by Friedrich von Hayek, Milton Friedman and the Chicago school of neo-classical economics, nor that of the bureaucratically administered central plan envisaged by Chalmers Johnson, Kioyoaki Tsuji and the 'bureaucratic dominance' school of Japanese interpreters, but something far more subtle. It is the belief system of a partnership between bureaucrats, politicians, and *zaikai*, the top business functionaries. They operate without any blueprint other than the flexible goal of economic growth, but with the tacit agreement and collaboration of men who, in whatever sector, know each other's minds because they are the same kind of people from the same educational and social background, who have fought their way up the same career ladders with the same competitive spirit and determination. Indeed, in many cases they are, through *amakudari*, the very same people. The bureaucrats and ex-bureaucrats, in politics, the ministries, and the corporations, form the *jinmyaku* of all *jinmyaku* and are the nerves that unite and energize the whole system.

The system can best be described as managed capitalism, as long as we accept that its management is both decentralized and light of touch. (The Japanese themselves speak of *kanri shakai*, a 'managed society', which takes still further the idea of manipulation by the elite.) It differs in important ways both from the 'visible hand' of Chandler's 'organized capitalism' in which American multinational corporations lobby the government for contracts, subsidies, and other favours, and from the discredited state capitalism of Soviet Russia in which the central plan replaced the market. In the American system the corporations control the market as far as they can and try to persuade the state to loosen its controls. There are some common values and exchange of personnel, but the public and private sectors are still distinct and thought to be adversaries. In the defunct Soviet system the Gosplan bureaucrats called the tune and the enterprise managers danced to it, or twisted their steps to outwit the Muscovite planners and make the system work to their own advantage, but private enterprise was officially anathema.

In the Japanese system by contrast the distinction between public and private scarcely exists and is little valued or understood. The interpenetration of the three sectors – politicians, bureaucrats, and business men – is so inextricable that it is almost impossible to know who pulls whose strings. The three elites work together almost imperceptibly to achieve unspoken common goals of perpetuating their joint hegemony and expanding the economy and Japanese power because it is their own. From one point of view this looks like a tightly organized and centrally ordered system. As a former president of the Mitsui Bank, Sato Kiichiro, put it, 'During and after the war . . . Japan's economy was controlled until it became second nature to uphold a planned, controlled economy.'[16] From another point of view, since no single controlling agency exists, it looks like the kind of free market the American corporations would ideally prefer, freedom for corporate managers to do as they please but with plenty of help and encouragement, not to say insurance against failure, by the state. It is precisely in this sense of having the best of both worlds that Japan embraces both pillars of the great arch of professional society.

## INDIVIDUALISM IN THE ARMS OF COLLECTIVISM

This paradox, however, is puzzling only to unsubtle Western minds and unreconstructed Marxist ones which think in terms of the dichotomy between public and private enterprise. It derives from the Confucian tradition that Japan took over from China and 'naturalized' with infusions of Buddhism and Shinto, to create the ideal of the 'golden mean', social harmony, and mutual responsibility within the group (family, clan, firm, nation) that explains the unity of the Japanese against outsiders. The truth is that the Japanese mind floats in a world high above the great arch, disdains dichotomies, and finds no difficulty in embracing contradictions as long as they are fruitful. The only dichotomy that matters is between 'us' and 'them', between my *ie* (household) and yours, my working group and its competitors, my company and its rivals, my country and the rest of the global economy. This explains why the Japanese can be at once individualists and collectivists, personally ambitious to the point of suicide when they fail an exam or production schedule, and totally loyal to the team, glowing with pride in the group's admiration when they succeed and suffering shame and humiliation when they fail the group. Some years ago, after giving a lecture at Yale, I met a young Japanese academic who was pleased to meet me because, he said, 'I translated your book.' I asked him if he minded his head of department getting the credit on the title page as the translator. He replied, 'Professor S. did not get the credit. Everyone in the group knew I translated your book.' His reward was the approbation of his colleagues and a research trip to America. He is now head of the same department. That illustrates the peculiar mixture of personal ambition and selfless subordination to the group that characterizes Japanese team work (*shudan shugi*) – individualism in the arms of collectivism.

Although there is little objective continuity between Tokugawa Japan and its modern successor, today's Japan mirrors the attitudes and values of pre-industrial feudalism, in which the *samurai* (retainer) rose in the service of the *daimyo* (great lord) by fighting or administrative skill and achieved individual satisfaction through the *han* (clan). The link was personal and lasted until death. It was vertical, between lord and follower, and was meant to preclude any alliance between followers to oppose the lord. It was directed against outsiders, not on grounds of policy or principle, which would have invited argument, but simply in the competition of one clan against another, over land, peasants, and power. Thus individual ambition and team spirit (*shudan shugi*) dissolved into each other, to satisfy goals of both lord and follower in overcoming and replacing rival clans. It is easy to see why the ministries, corporations, and LDP factions should emulate and wish to revive their version of this traditional Japanese culture, which promises to expand their span of power without alienating their subordinates to the point of questioning their hegemony.

In the same way, then, as Tokugawa Japan – but for its own reasons, not because of tradition – modern Japan harnesses individual ambition and personal loyalty to group, company, and national ends. The junior official in his ministry, the novice manager in his office, the tyro politician in his faction, the assistant professor in his academic department, the young gangster in the *yakuza*, latches on to his superior, the leader of the team, foreman of the working group, research professor, or gang boss, and hopes to shine in his eyes, not so much for his individual prowess but for his contribution to the group's power and prestige in the sight of outsiders. His contribution is made through the *ringi* system, the practice of consultation within the office or workplace, or through *nemawashi*, the informal socializing in bars and restaurants after work, where the most junior member can throw in his two yen which, if accepted, becomes the decision of the group. Bonuses, fringe benefits, entertainment allowances, leisure facilities, are all collective to the group, and the individual who contributes most, even though his ideas or innovations go out under the leader's name, is the most appreciated. The system operates, *pari passu*, up and down through the organization, and involves institutions like quality control groups, company anthems sung before work, and breaks for communal exercises. It weakens as it reaches down to the smaller companies, and disappears altogether in the sweated workshops which underpin the whole economy.

Whatever its origins, in the vague memories of a romanticized feudalism or in the inspired invention of twentieth-century business, the culture of group loyalty has played the central role in Japan's success in war and peace. Viewed in this way, as a neo-feudal system of rivalries between ministries, between political factions, and between corporations in each industry for expansion and market share, the at once fragmented and goal-oriented groupings that make up Japanese society begin to make sense. Without any detailed plan or policy, the corporate managers are only too eager to follow up hints and suggestions from bureaucrats in the relevant ministry, either for expansion of new products and technologies or for the winding down of old ones, knowing that cooperation will lead to sales opportunities, contracts, subsidies, financial and other help with exports, and so on, and – a boon rarely available in the West – cheap capital from the Fiscal Investment and Loan Programme mentioned above, which accounts for 40–50 per cent of the government's capital budget. Between 1960 and 1986 Japan consistently invested twice as much in housing, infrastructure, preparation of sites for private development, and loans to private companies, as other major OECD countries.[17] What might be called spontaneous collaboration between the public and private sectors lay behind the phenomenal economic growth.

Corporate managers also know that if they do not take the hint their rivals will, since government policy is to make capital and research available to several if not most large firms in an industry and then make them compete for market share. This happened in car production, electronics, and now bio-technology. In computers, for example, the government collaborated with eight large corporations to set up a 1 billion dollar research project in artificial intelligence, on the understanding that all eight would receive the results and then compete to incorporate them in their own computers and software.[18] 'Administrative guidance', invented by Shigeru Sahashi, post-war vice-minister (chief bureaucrat) at MITI, and practised since by all the relevant ministries, was used to lead and sometimes bully corporations, even foreign ones, into expanding, or contracting, in directions useful to Japan as judged by the bureaucracy. Sahashi, for example, bullied IBM into licensing their patents to Japanese companies for no more than a 5 per cent royalty in exchange for allowing them to open a joint operation. He then controlled the leasing of computers throughout Japan through the Japan Electronic Company headed by an ex-official of the Ministry of Commerce and Industry, the immediate predecessor of MITI.[19] This was the launching pad for Japan's take-off into computing and so into automation, where it now has three quarters of the world's industrial robots.

This does not mean that initiative comes only from the bureaucracy or that the Japanese economic miracle was wholly state-led. In cars, for example, the first Japanese high-tech product to astonish the world, Honda, Nissan and Toyota all refused to follow MITI's advice to concentrate on specialist lines and opted to become full-range manufacturers of automotive vehicles. This necessitated a different approach from the world leaders: GM, Ford, and Chrysler in Detroit. Eiiji Toyoda, a young engineer in the family that founded Toyota in 1937, visited Ford's River Rouge plant in 1950 and realized that mass production of the traditional kind was beyond Japanese capabilities at that time. So he and his brilliant production manager, Taiichi Ohno, invented the 'just in time' or 'lean production' (*kanban*) system, terms which understate its originality and productivity. It was far more than a highly organized component delivery system, with hourly deliveries from the suppliers to save inventory and waiting time in production. It was, and is, an immensely flexible system that facilitates instant changes of model, colour, accessories, and so on, to meet individual customers' requirements. It has been called 'post-Fordist' production in that it abandons the long runs of identical models and the vast investment in prototypes and tooling-up for each new version, though that too is misleading: it simply takes mass production to a higher level of control and performance. It depends in part on flexible technology, quick changes of body press dyes, the use of general-purpose rather than job-specific robots, and electronic controls of every operation. But most of all it depends on the structure and flexibility of the workforce: instead of specialists in each operation strung out along the assembly line plus specialized mechanics ready to jump in as in the West, the whole team is multi-skilled and interchangeable, so that when the line stops the whole group descends upon the problem to get it moving again.[20] This could happen only with a workforce undivided by demarcation (who does what?) disputes, wholly dedicated to fast, efficient, high-quality production. Here team spirit, loyalty to the group, plant and firm, collective bonuses, 'single status' for workers and managers, and, at a remoter level, the 'three treasures' of lifelong employment, wages rising with seniority, and the enterprise union, all play their part. That depends less on organization than on attitude to work and the corporation, which means high-trust industrial relations, in a word, a culture of cooperation. However much such a culture is ultimately based on coercion and propaganda rather than on spontaneous belief, it is a measure of the success of Japanese corporations in persuading their workers to accept their paternalistic ideology.

The car industry offers an excellent example of how corporate neo-feudalism operates in Japanese business. Each major producer, whether a specialist in vehicles like Honda or Toyota or part of a larger *keiretsu* like Mazda (of Sumitomo) or Mitsubishi, has its own circle of satellite component suppliers, subsidiaries domestic and foreign, and tied consumer outlets. These act as *samurai* to the main company's *daimyo*, as permanent, loyal, dependable, but ruthlessly subordinated members of the team. Their prices and costs are determined by the central firm, and they bear the brunt of recessions and unemployment, taking price cuts, working short time, or laying off workers, to save the profits and permanent survival of the main corporation. The satellites in turn exploit their subcontractors, down to the small sweated workshops at the bottom of the heap.

This explains how Japan, with some of the largest corporations in the world, comes to have two or three times the proportion of small firms (with less than 100 workers) of the United States or Europe, most of them satellites of the major corporations. The central firm in turn has its obligations and loyalties, not so much to its individual shareholders as to its institutional backers and creditors, particularly in its own *keiretsu*, since Japanese companies, like European but unlike American or British ones, depend more on long-term institutional borrowing than on the short-term insecurity of the stock market. The whole edifice is suffused by mutual shareholding and interlocking directorships, which makes the individual company almost invulnerable to take-over raids and allows it to pursue long-term aims in research, new technology, capital investment, and above all, market share. As Akio Morita of Sony has remarked, while Western corporations have a time horizon of ten minutes, the length of time it takes the stock exchange computers to register a fall, Japanese corporations have one of ten years, long enough to outstrip any competition.[21] Even a pyramidal *keiretsu* firm like Toyota knows how to operate the interlocking group system: they were able, with only a 15 per cent holding in Koito, a partner firm, to beat off a raid by T. Boone

Pickens, who held 26 per cent of the equity but could not buy a single further share from other members of the group.[22] Such corporate neo-feudalism operates, as we have seen, in the United States and Europe, but the Japanese have raised it to a higher plane of organization and sophistication.

## JAPAN IN THE GLOBAL ECONOMY

Managed capitalism, market competition within a framework of administrative guidance, and corporate neo-feudalism, have enabled the Japanese to create a secure domestic base from which to expand into the global economy, in three main ways. First, by expanding their exports to the point where, despite having to import most of their raw materials, they were making huge surpluses on balance of payments. Surprisingly, however, the value of exports as a percentage of GDP has been much lower than in all major competitor countries except the United States: 10 per cent in the late 1980s compared with Britain's 16 per cent, France's 17 per cent, Germany's 26 per cent, and the United States' 6 per cent.[23] The surplus was based less on the astonishing export success, guided by the bureaucracy in its search for market opportunities, than on the restraint of Japanese consumers, who were content to prefer high-priced home products to low-priced imports (though with 'non-tariff' restrictions to discourage imports) and to save a larger percentage of disposable income than in any major country except Italy. Nevertheless, the annual surplus amounted to $80 billion by 1987, $130 billion by 1993. It had to be invested somewhere, so the second incursion into the global economy was by direct investment in overseas plants and subsidiaries, the well-known appearance in America, Europe, and South East Asia of Japanese factories making cars, television sets, transistor radios (Sony 'Walkmen'), computers, and other high-tech consumer goods, and the less well-known purchase of mines, forests, and other sources of raw materials. Some of these investments were aimed at securing reliable supplies of fuel and materials, some at bypassing potential retaliatory trade protection in the West, and some, especially in Asia, at offloading labour-intensive manufacturing such as textiles, steel, and shipbuilding to cheaper labour areas. They were followed by Japanese banks and securities institutions, now among the largest in the world. Such direct investment increased more than ten-fold during the 1980s, half of it directed to the United States, amounting by 1988 to nearly one quarter of the capital outflows within the OECD.[24]

Yet, again surprisingly, direct investment in subsidiaries consumed only a fraction of the trade surplus, and 80–90 per cent went into the third incursion, passive investment in equities, government bonds, and other securities. This was inevitable, for three reasons. The huge trade surplus had to go somewhere if it was not to bring commerce to a halt, and most of it went into funding the growing American deficit, which was larger than the Japanese surplus. The steady appreciation of the yen, which went from nearly Y300 to the dollar in 1975 to around Y100 in 1995, meant to encourage imports and reduce the surplus, instead not only encouraged the Japanese to become still more efficient and reduce prices further but enabled Japanese investors to buy far more investments for their money. And the low domestic interest rates and soaring price of land meant that Japanese investors could borrow cheaply on large collaterals at home and invest at high interest rates abroad. Nothing seemed able to stop the juggernaut of Japanese economic success.

It may be, as some Western political economists have gloated, that the world recession of the early 1990s and the astonishing appreciation of the yen to Y90 to the dollar in 1995 will at last stop the Japanese 'economic miracle' in its tracks but, given past experience of Japanese resilience, they should not bank on it. Their rivals would love to have their problems, their trade surplus, and the strong currency that goes with it! The world's appetite for Japanese goods is seemingly unlimited, and the West's capacity to outwit the Japanese in introducing consumer-friendly products, though recovering, is still on probation. Only in the very latest inventions, notably the electronic superhighway whose attractions for the mass of consumers have yet to be tested, have the Japanese been overtaken, and in this area, as in so much else, Japanese tardiness may be short-lived.

## THE PRICE OF SUCCESS: THE QUALITY OF LIFE

Japanese economic success should not be exaggerated, however. Although its world share of manufactured exports rose fourteen-fold between 1955 and 1988, it was still only 10 per cent compared with the United States' 12 per cent and the same for West Germany before re-unification (and much larger afterwards). And although Japan overtook the United States in GNP per head – in 1991 at $27,005 compared with $22,204 – and was the highest of all the major countries, this was at current exchange rates. In terms of purchasing power parities it was only $18,957, 15 per cent behind the United States and on a par with Germany and France. As the OECD Survey of Japan for 1987 noted, 'There is still a substantial discrepancy between the country's economic strength and the relatively poor quality of life.' The high cost of living, poor housing standards, the high price of land which raises housing costs and reduces public provision of amenities, 'the extraordinarily long average working time' and consequently short leisure breaks and holidays, not to mention the crowded housing and the congestion of the cities, all effectively reduce welfare and increase the costs of maintaining a civilized life.

Because of the elongated distribution system, with many layers of middle men between producer, whether domestic or foreign, and consumer, food prices are far higher than in the West. The high cost of housing – mortgages may now last a hundred years, to be paid off finally by grandchildren – the expense of commuting up to two hours each way to and from work, the high cost of education including *juku* and *yobiko* (special schools outside state school hours to cram for the best high schools and universities), and the need to save for sickness and old age, all make Japanese people's disposable income far smaller than that of their counterparts in the West, two thirds that of Americans and less than most West Europeans.

All told, at purchasing power parities (allowing for comparative cost of living) Japan's GNP per capita in 1991 was in sixth place among OECD countries, below the United States, Canada, Switzerland, Luxembourg, and Germany, only slightly above France, and not too far above Italy and Britain.[25] This equality with the West (astonishing enough considering where it started half a century ago) is obvious to any visitor, who finds it hard to believe that Japan is clearly the richest (in exchange rate terms) among the major countries. Though up to 90 per cent of Japanese claim, plausibly, to be middle-class and there is little poverty to be seen in the cities, the urban congestion, cramped accommodation, crowded trains and buses, lack of public parks and open spaces, absence of modern sewerage and water supply for two thirds of the population, and the improving but still disturbing pollution problems, all show that the Japanese have paid a high price for their impressive economic success.

## THE OUTSIDERS: FRINGE WORKERS, WOMEN, AND THE MINORITIES

Some Japanese, too, have paid a heavier price than most, or gained less from economic growth. In terms of earned income statistics Japan has a very egalitarian income distribution. In 1985 the top 20 per cent of households received 37.5 per cent of personal income, the lowest percentage of any OECD country, while the bottom 20 per cent received 8.7 per cent, the largest share of any. Only the Netherlands, Belgium, and Germany came near the latter figure, with 8.3, 7.9, and 7.9 per cent.[26] Yet once again we must distinguish between *tatemae* (appearance) and *honne* (reality). The extensive use of bonuses, the thirteenth month's salary, fringe benefits such as housing, education supplements, health and welfare benefits, and expense accounts, make it difficult to assess the final distribution, since these go disproportionately to managers and, to a greater extent than in the West, to the permanent employees, including the core of skilled blue-collar workers. An official report estimates that workers in large corporations receive 40 per cent more in non-monetary benefits than those in small firms with less than 100 workers.[27] The overworked and underpaid employees of 700,000-plus small businesses, many of them subcontractors and suppliers to the big corporations, are among the outsiders who pay for the high living standards of the corporate executives and core workers.

Women, who compose two fifths of the workforce, are notoriously underpaid, their full-time wages averaging only half of men's, and they rarely enjoy lifetime employment or promotion to management. They are more frequently employed part-time or at piecework, which is still lower paid. As in Russia and some Western countries, patriarchy thrives: a woman's place is deemed to be in the home once she marries, and the increasing number of married women who prefer to work carry the usual double burden of paid work and unpaid housework, increased by the virtual absence of the husband during daylight hours. The wife is expected to manage the household income, pay the bills, and in particular to look after the education of the children. The 'education mama' is a well-known character, spending her whole life planning and scheming and badgering her sons (much less the daughters) to work hard and pass their exams, while her 'salaryman' husband arrives home at midnight, departs at 6 am, and rarely sees his children. More perhaps than in any other developed country except maybe Russia, the economy has been underpinned by the underpaid and unpaid work of women.

Japanese women have responded to the pressures of modern society much as elsewhere, though more cautiously in so traditional and patriarchal a society, with an incipient feminist movement announcing the 'era of the woman' (*onna no jidai*). Women have certainly played a role in the recent political unrest over the scandals and corruption of the politicians. The redoubtable Takako Doi, leader of the Social Democratic Party and one of the 3 per cent of parliamentary deputies who are women, was elected in 1993 the first woman Speaker of the Diet, while Mayumi Moryama became the first woman to achieve administrative vice-minister rank as chief cabinet secretary. A few women, like Nobuko Sawanoburi, president of a Tokyo marketing firm founded by women, and Akiko Ryu, creator of a popular high-fibre drink aimed at women, have risen to the top in industry, where a survey in 1988 showed that 34,636 out of 791,362 Japanese companies (4.4 per cent) had women presidents, mostly founders of their own businesses, though only 1 per cent of managers are women.[28] One high-flying young woman who broke into the masculine corridors of the diplomatic service, Masako Owada, has married Crown Prince Naruhito and is in line to become empress; her friends think she was foolish to throw away a brilliant career for a purely decorative ceremonial role.

Women have helped to make the artificially high food prices a political issue, got the rejection of Prime Minister Nakasone's 3 per cent consumption tax (though it came back later by the back door), and brought down Prime Minister Uno over his treatment of his geisha-mistress as 'a piece of merchandise'. Their most effective protest has been the fall in the birth rate, which has plummeted, making Japan one of the fastest aging modern societies, a fact which will have more effect on Japan's economy and future welfare than the women's circles which the ruling elite has tried to discourage or incorporate.

Japan's few and small minorities have also paid a price for progress, notably the three quarters of a million people of Korean descent, a relic of imperialism, discriminated against after several generations of resi-dence. So, too, are the *burakumin* or 'hamlet people', an outcast group once connected with the slaughter of animals and the leather trades, who are rejected as neighbours and marriage partners and even as workers save in the lowliest occupations. Parents go to great lengths, even hiring private investigators to check on the family background of potential mates, to avoid their children marrying them.[29] Both these minorities have begun to protest vehemently against their pariah status and have had some success in obtaining legislative protection, but the curious Japanese fear of contamination still engenders the same sort of informal discrimination as does racism in the West.

The largest price, in aggregate, is paid by the two thirds of the work-force (including most women and minorities) who work for small and medium sized companies. If Japan has a class divide, apart from that between the administrative ruling elite and the rest, it lies between those who work for the large corporations and the rest, whether they are white- or blue-collar workers. Statistically, it is close to the division in Britain and Europe – though not in the United States where 'middle class' means the middle 60 per cent – between the middle and working classes. As elsewhere, it marks the line between security and insecurity, between stable careers with tenure, rising salary scales, and generous fringe benefits on one side, and low wages, poor welfare benefits, and constant fear of short time and unemployment on the other.[30] As in the West, employees above the line fear falling below it, as many do in later years because of early retirement and low pensions. Over 50 per cent of men and 25 per cent of women continue working after age 65, mostly for small firms at lower wages. This is two and a half times as many as in the United States and six times as many as in France and Germany.[31] To offset the aging of the workforce, many large firms offload their lifetime employees in later years into secure but lower paying jobs in their subsidiaries.

Another source of inequality, as elsewhere but magnified in Japan by the spectacular rise in land values and the stock market, is the division between those who live solely on earned income and those with addi-tional income from property, landed or mobile. With low tax rates on unearned income (nil until April 1988, a flat rate of 20 per cent since then) and a miniscule capital gains tax (nil before April 1989, 1 per cent on capital transferred since then), property incomes have rocketed, and constitute a much larger fraction of personal income than in the West.

This has of course benefited some poor householders and children of parents with houses on expensive sites, small farmers and individual investors, but the main windfalls have gone to the property developers and financial speculators. It has made dollar billionaires of families like Tsutsumi, Mori, Jinnai, and Kinnoshita, some of whom have become famous as purchasers of real estate and corporations in the West. Japan now has the third largest number of dollar billionaires, after the United States and Germany. Some of the super-rich, like Kakuei Tanaka and Shin Kanemaru who both made their fortunes in the booming construction industry, have become godfathers to large factions of the LDP and leading figures in the corruption scandals of the 1980s and 1990s. Land deals, the skyrocketing stock exchange of the 1980s, and the profits of corruption have made the real but hidden distribution of income in Japan more unequal than the ideology and official statistics suggest. Inequality and corruption are provoking a backlash against the politicians and their allies in the bureaucracy and the corporations they run that threatens to end the harmonious society that has prevailed since 1945.

## 'MONEY POLITICS' AND THE NEMESIS OF CORRUPTION

That backlash has already broken up the Liberal Democratic Party and brought to an end its thirty-eight-year reign of one-party rule. It may yet recover, of course, since nearly all the partners in the Japanese elite, the politicians, the bureaucrats and the *zaikai* (top business men) who belonged to it, come from the same social and educational background, and control all the main institutions of Japanese society. The main rump of the LDP has already joined the 1994 coalition headed by socialist Prime Minister Tomiichi Murayama. Like the Russian *nomenklatura* the Japanese elite have too much to lose to give up power easily. They are skilled at running the system, and above all know how to manage the 'money politics' upon which it turns.

Indeed, the LDP had its origins in secret money. It was midwifed in 1955 by the CIA, which persuaded the warring conservative factions to come together to prevent an anti-American and allegedly pro-communist government, and provided the funds to finance it. From 1958, when Finance Minister Eisako Sato asked Douglas MacArthur II, General MacArthur's nephew, the American ambassador to Tokyo, for financial help, to at least 1976 when the cover was nearly blown by the fall-out from the Lockheed scandal, the CIA regularly supplied the LDP with funds, ostensibly in return for information but actually to keep it in power. As the American ambassador from 1966 to 1969, U. Alexis Johnson, put it, 'We were funding a party on our side.' It was all part of the Cold War strategy of supporting anti-communist forces against their socialist opponents, whom the CIA believed were being funded from Moscow. Obstructing the Japanese opposition, one CIA officer said, 'was the most important thing we could do'. Ex-ambassador MacArthur told the *New York Times* in October 1994,

> The Socialist Party in Japan was a direct satellite of Moscow. If Japan went Communist it was difficult to see how the rest of Asia would not follow suit. Japan assumed an importance of extra-ordinary magnitude because there was no other place in Asia from which to project American power.[32]

With this background, the LDP was firmly tied both to American policy and to dependence on outside money. When it became wealthy enough to do without American funding, it pursued power by the same methods. 'Money politics' (*kinken seiji*) was therefore the heart of the system, to an extent that makes American lobbying or Italian corruption look childlike. As one political scientist, Ikuo Kabashima, put it,

> Decades of one-party rule have led to widespread corruption and popular distrust in government. The Recruit influence peddling scandal exposed the cancer in our political system. Political reform in Japan requires fundamental changes. First, we must eliminate bribery, often disguised as customary gift-giving. Politicians claim that cash gifts to constituents – presents for weddings and con-dolence money for funerals – force them to rely heavily on big business for funds. Citizens often vote the way they are told by local big shots and interest groups. Some blatantly sell their votes.[33]

This flow of money from business through the politicians to constitu-ents is highly organized. Each New Year the LDP leadership meets with top business men to request donations – in 1985 10 billion yen – which the *zaikai* then allocate to different industries. On top of that, 'encourage-ment parties' are held for individual politicians, at which 'payments for refreshments' range from 20,000 yen to 1 million yen (about $180-$6,000). From such parties one politician in 1984, Kazuo Tamaki, received 445 million yen ($2.6 million dollars), in addition to 1,230 million yen ($7.2 million dollars) in donations from supporters.

The politicians are more open in their dealings than the American lobbyists or the Russian mafia, and can be seen on public occasions accept-ing and distributing money in plain envelopes or brown paper bags. It is all part of the custom of gift giving that permeates Japanese life, and is essential to getting elected. Karel van Wolferen estimates that the cost of maintaining a constituency in the mid-1980s was 400 million yen per year. The cost to party leaders was much higher, in party membership fees for supporters, sweeteners to faction members, and the endless round of meetings and dinners, all lubricated with money. Tanaka's election as party president in the early 1970s cost 3–5 billion yen, Nakasone's re-election in 1984 1 billion yen.[34]

The business corporations which are the fount of this cornucopia obviously expect value for money. The commercial banks give most, about one third of the registered donations to the LDP in 1984, and have been virtually protected from foreign penetration of the domestic financial market. Engineering and telecommunications come next, and get both protection and lucrative contracts. Even the doctors and dentists get generous tax concessions and the right to sell medicines (bypassing the pharmacists) in return for their contributions. Car mechanics themselves pay to preserve their profits from the compulsory biennial motor vehicle tests. The Recruit scandal named by Kabashima above, involving a managerial employment and public relations agency which gave blocks of shares to politicians of all factions yielding huge capital gains, was only one of the recurring scandals which have bedevilled Japanese politics in recent years. Its exposure in 1989 toppled Prime Minister Noboru Takeshita and his finance minister Kiichi Miyazawa, though in typical Japanese fashion they both bounced back again, the former as leader of the powerful Tanaka faction in the Diet and kingmaker of prime ministers, the latter his protégé as prime minister in 1992. Miyazawa became the target of accumulated public wrath over decades of political corruption, which came to a head in the crisis of 1993 and forced him and the LDP from power, to be replaced by a coalition of seven parties (including four ex-LDP factions) under Morihiro Hosokawa. But Hosokawa was forced to resign in turn over alleged misdoings before he came to office.

The richest pay-offs have always been in the construction industry, where licences for development and contracts for public works yield golden profits. The king of the contractors and greatest of LDP godfathers was Kakuei Tanaka, who rose from building labourer to construction tycoon and prime minister (1972–74) – a most unusual career in Japanese terms. In 1976 he was arrested for taking 500 million yen (then about $1.7 million dollars) in bribes from the Lockheed Aircraft Corporation and, after a long drawn-out case, sentenced to four years' imprisonment in 1983. There is little doubt that he was singled out for revenge by his enemies in the LDP, who themselves indulged in precisely the same practices. Nor did his disgrace put him *hors de combat*. With his eighty-member faction in the LDP he remained a major force and continued to make prime ministers, including Takeshita, Nakasone and Miyazawa, until a stroke finally put him out of action.[35]

His successor as senior godfather, Shin Kanemaru, also came up through the construction industry and was leader of the *dango*, the bid-rigging system which allocated contracts to construction firms. He was equally scandal-ridden, but with his 110-member following in the Diet, larger even than the late Tanaka's, considered himself invulnerable. Accused of taking a 500 million yen bribe (about $36 million) in 1990 from the Sagawa trucking company (which indiscriminately distributed 'gifts' to most of the leading politicians), he was able to plea-bargain his punishment down to a 200,000 yen fine ($1,600) without going to court. This, however, was so insolent that it provoked outrage and proved to be his undoing and also that of his protégé Prime Minister Miyazawa, and indeed of the LDP in its old form. Kanemaru was expelled from the party by the Young Turks bent on reform, and the LDP broke up into five parts, including four new parties dedicated to reform. Kanemaru, now over 80 years old, lost his immunity and was indicted for evading $10 million in taxes and for the first time brought into court, in a wheelchair. His defence was that the 'income' was not for himself but was seed money for a new reforming party, the *Shinsei* (Renewal Party), which won fifty-five seats in the 1993 election and joined the Hosokawa coalition without, of course, Kanemaru.[36] With such origins in the ex-LDP factions of the coalition one wonders whether the 1993 revolt really marked the end of the old 'money politics' and the beginning of a new era of clean government.

What is most sinister in the Japanese way of corruption is the use of gangsters by politicians and corporations to intimidate and silence opponents. The *yakuza*, famed for their full-body tattoos, smart Western suits, and personal loyalty to the boss, are the nearest thing to modern *samurai*, and operate in clans like the feudal *han* of Tokugawa Japan. They run their rackets in mutual competition, notably in prostitution and protection, though they are said to eschew drugs and guns – except in the fighting over leadership which succeeds the death of the top gangster in the system. They are a kind of inverted or extramural meritocracy, recruited from the uneducated and outsiders like the *burakumin* for their toughness and violence. There are about 3,000 gangs with over 300,000 members. The police estimate that they 'earn' about 1.5 trillion yen ($12 billion dollars) a year from their illegal activities, but this is probably too low. They are protected by leading politicians and business men, who attend and send gifts to *yakuza* weddings and funerals and hire them for their own purposes. The politicians use them to keep order at meetings and rallies and to intimidate left-wing student radicals and trades union protests. The LDP hired 30,000 of them to suppress protest demonstrations against the American security treaty and keep order during President Eisenhower's visit in 1960. The *zaikai* (top business leaders) hire them to keep order at shareholders' meetings and to face down awkward questioners, to intimidate protesting victims of pollution, to 'persuade' tenants of buildings standing in the way of development projects to leave, using harrassment by noise, threatening phone calls, dump truck assaults, and even arson. Although such practices are universally condemned as illegal, the *yakuza* are an integral component of the system and cannot be dislodged.[37]

## AN IDEAL PROFESSIONAL SOCIETY?

How much then is left of the ideal of a meritocratic, harmonious, and increasingly affluent society? There are signs that many Japanese people are becoming disenchanted with the ideology they have been sold by the administrative ruling elite. Many salarymen, and still more their wives, are beginning to question the benefits of lifetime employment tied to a single firm, at the expense of long days of relentless work and long evenings of compulsory socializing with workmates, long commutes of several hours a day, short holidays, cramped accommodation, and little or no time with their families. 'My-home-ism', a pejorative term used by corporate executives for employees who do not take work seriously enough, is spreading through Japanese industry. Women, both workers and homemakers, are beginning to protest at their lot, at low pay, discrimination in appointment and promotion, and at the domestic burdens imposed by overworked husbands. The two thirds of the workforce outside the large corporations are beginning to see themselves as exploited by a system that promises prosperity and security to all but delivers only to the few. The oppressed minorities, the Koreans and the *burakumin*, are challenging their pariah status. The elderly, who are now a rapidly growing proportion of the population, are likely to become, as in the West, a powerful force in politics which, as the war generation who venerated the emperor dies out, will demand better treatment, in pensions, health and welfare, than they have traditionally enjoyed. Finally, if the Japanese 'economic miracle' does come to an end, as some economists and politicians, especially in the envious West, predict, then the justification of the system will evaporate and its costs will be increasingly resented.

The aging of the population is perhaps the most dangerous symptom of potential decline. As Bill Emmott points out in *The Sun Also Sets*, Japan's economic miracle depended on a young, vigorous, yet docile workforce with an exceptionally strong work ethic and an exceptionally high savings rate.[38] These were not unlike the features that characterized earlier developing countries in their 'drive to maturity'. Once reached, maturity invites relaxation and enjoyment of what has been achieved. High incomes, even when made factitiously by positive exchange rates, encourage foreign travel and luxury imports, raise prices, intensify foreign competition, and drive out labour-intensive industries to low-wage countries in Asia and – a reversal of fortune – to poor, depressed areas of

Britain and the United States. Above all, since old people save less and spend more on leisure, travel, and health care, the aging population will undermine the savings rate on which the whole economic rise depends.

Like Britain in the nineteenth century and America in the twentieth, Japan has been accumulating a nest egg on which to live when hard times arrive. As with its predecessors, the nest egg could easily be squandered by a spending spree, if not on armaments then on invisible imports and those self-harming overseas investments that 'hollow out' domestic industry by exporting jobs and capital abroad and destroying them at home. Perhaps Japan, with its flexible, quick-witted response to changing market opportunities, can afford for a longer period of time to avoid the slow-down that comes with economic maturity. But the shift from domestic manufacturing to overseas subsidiaries, still more to overseas service industries like banking, financial dealing, and invisible earnings from passive investments, suggests a climacteric similar to that experienced by Britain in the late nineteenth century and by the United States in the Reagan–Bush years. Living on capital benefits the owning elites at the expense of the mass of citizens. It may last a few decades, but what then? For a country with even fewer reserves of fuel and raw materials than its competitors, the sun indeed may set.

Meanwhile, however, there is no doubt that the Japanese have created an ideal version of professional society, even though it is flawed by inequality, corruption and political legerdemain. The danger is, as with all professions and the societies they dominate, that the persuasion may fail and belief in the ruling elite and its right to take a disproportionate share of the society's resources may be withdrawn. If that should happen, and there are signs in the political events since 1993 of a crisis of legitimacy, the whole precarious edifice could come tumbling down. Survival of the system depends on the ability of the administrative ruling elite to heed the warning signals: the break-up of the LDP and its cosy relations with the bureaucracy and big business, the outrage at 'money politics' and the almost continuous corruption scandals, the growing disillusion of the workforce including the privileged salarymen in the large corporations, the manifest exploitation of the small, dependent subcontractors and their insecure workers, the raised consciousness of women, increasingly aware of their own exploitation and that of their absentee husbands, and the general feeling that the costs of development have fallen disproportionately on the people and the fruits have gone unequally to the elite. As Michael Young argued in *The Rise of the Meritocracy*, the danger to meritocracy is that, when the race is to the swift, the slow majority may come to resent all the prizes going to the few, and turn and rend them.[39]

Professional elites, to repeat one of the lessons of this book, are good servants but bad masters. They tread a fine line between beneficial service and irresponsible power. Abuse of power can be disguised for a time by effective propaganda and disingenuous public relations. The Japanese elite have been brilliantly successful in selling to their people a belief in the uniquely benevolent, meritocratic, egalitarian, and harmonious culture. The best propaganda is based on truth, and the Japanese elite have delivered on their promises to a remarkable degree, in economic growth, a ten-fold rise in living standards, a measure of social mobility, and an orderly, civilized society. Yet the difference between appearance and reality, *tatemae* and *honne*, is at once the source of its strength and the threat to its integrity. If the professional elite pushes its luck too far, abuses its hidden, irresponsible power beyond a tolerable point, and opens the gap between propaganda and experience too wide, it will lose its credibility and its place. Then the floating world of the Japanese ideal, held aloft only by the breath of *nihonjinron*, the myth of Japanese uniqueness, may collapse, and the professional administrative ruling elite with it.

# 8

# TOWARDS A GLOBAL PROFESSIONAL SOCIETY

The third great social revolution in the history of the world has been dealt with so far as a largely national phenomenon. This is because it is in the nature of social revolutions to start in specific places and to spread to other venues as their advantages become too attractive to pass up and dangerous to avoid. Yet as it spreads, the revolution is forced to change and adjust to the political, economic, and cultural systems of the receiving areas, which take from it what best suits their goals and ambitions. The importing communities transmute its organizational and technological innovations to fit their own ideas of the purpose and values of life, and create something new and syncretic, which differs from the pioneers as translations of Goethe or Shakespeare differ subtly from the originals.

The third revolution, however, even more than the first two, is a worldwide phenomenon which is in process of embracing the whole world, partly through imitation but chiefly through the domination of the global economy by the giant multinational corporations that now operate across national frontiers and outflank governments in the corporate neofeudalism that is its most characteristic form. These are based mainly in the advanced countries of the West and East Asia, above all in the five leading professional societies we have identified: the United States, Britain, France, Germany, and Japan. Yet all five have absorbed the trends of professionalism in idiosyncratic ways, and they impact on the rest of world, chiefly through their home-based multinationals, in ways peculiar to themselves. Whichever of them comes to dominate the global professional society of the future will proselytize its own version of professional society, and it is therefore important to see how they differ from each other.

## DIVERSITY AMONG PROFESSIONAL SOCIETIES

Each of the six or seven leading nations in the transition has shaped the major trends of professional society to suit itself and the elites who midwifed the changes, according to its own political structure, economic resources, cultural inheritance, and system of values. All have enjoyed the benefits of professionalism in a dramatic rise of living standards, better health and longer life, superior education, greater mobility and access to leisure, sport and entertainment, and all the expert services that go with the new plane of existence. Some have enjoyed more of them than others, and some, notably the old Soviet empire, have gone into reverse and are suffering a decline in living standards, health and welfare, public safety and crime prevention, associated with the collapse of communism and the failure of the market to replace it in a prompt and orderly manner. There, in fact, professional society never took a firm enough hold or, rather, took a pathological form that was bound to fail. But this was only the most extreme example of the diversity of response to the major trends of the revolution, and all of them transformed themselves into their own versions of the new society.

Higher living standards, first of all, have been enjoyed by all, but the Eastern bloc countries fell behind in the race and went into catastrophic decline with the collapse of communism, though East Germany was rescued by its bigger Western brother. All the rest seem to be approaching the same plane of material existence. The United States is still ahead in real GNP per capita, but Japan and Germany are pressing it close (and have indeed passed it at current exchange rates), while Britain has slipped badly behind and is in the lower half of the European Union league. What differentiates them, however, is the distribution of income, wider in America, Britain, and France, narrower in Germany and Japan, and becoming horrifyingly wide in the ex-Soviet Union. Given the role of equity and egalitarian values in supporting social cohesion and encouraging cooperative effort, it is not surprising that the countries that uphold them and have the most equitable distribution of income are the most successful in terms of economic growth.

Second, the occupational swing to services affected every post-industrial society but at differing rates and with different emphases. The United States and Britain went furthest and fastest, the Soviet Union and East Germany much more slowly, but neither system enjoyed faster rates of economic growth than Western Europe or Japan. Many of the service jobs in Britain and America were in low-grade, low-paid occupations not open to fast rising productivity. Germany and Japan kept sizable workforces in manufacturing industry, where internal service workers concentrated in management, supervision, technical support, inspection, and quality control, and raised productivity spectacularly but were often overlooked in the statistics, whereas large numbers of Britons and Americans were engaged in administration, banking and finance, litigation, and real estate, which moved wealth about at great cost (increasing nominal GNP) without adding much to it.

All seven benefited from the rising productivity of manufacturing, in which a declining minority of workers could produce the consumer goods for all the rest, just as a shrinking minority of agricultural workers in the second, industrial, revolution produced the food for all the rest. Indeed, agriculture in the third revolution was able with an even tinier minority of workers to feed the rest at rising levels of both quantity and quality. But what the rest of the population found to occupy themselves differed sharply from one society to the next. All the societies had to have management and administration but some had much more than others. The United States had more doctors, lawyers, and teachers – ten times the number of lawyers per head, for example, as Japan – and their rewards were much greater, but it did not enjoy better health, longer life, lower infant mortality, less crime, less litigiousness, or better schooling, and the costs (also entering nominal GNP) were certainly greater. At the other end of the scale of pay and prestige, it also had the largest proportion of low-grade personal services, in fast-food catering, supermarket sales, garbage disposal, and the like. The Soviet Union, by contrast, which rejected the concept of unemployment, had the lowest proportion of service workers but much the largest contingent of underemployed workers, in every sector from agriculture through manufacturing and transport to catering – as anyone who has waited for the supernumerary staff in a Moscow restaurant to serve cold Beef Stroganov can testify. The trade-off between unemployment, the weapon of the free-marketeers against inflation, and underemployment, the state planners' substitute for unemployment, is a measure of the different approaches of the two cultures. The predominance of services is a good criterion of professional society but it means different things in different countries.

One effect of this transition everywhere has been the decline of the industrial working class, the backbone of the traditional class struggle. Professional hierarchy has to a degree replaced class as the chief matrix of the new society. Of course, both class and hierarchy exist in all but the most primitive societies, criss-crossing each other like the weft and warp in the social fabric, but which of the two prevails on the face of the cloth depends on which dimension is predominant in the incomes and attitudes of the people. Class does not disappear altogether in professional society, and its importance differs from one to another. Britain is by far the most class-conscious, and this infects the whole of social life, politics, education, and industrial relations. Its existence, or at least its importance, is hotly denied by right-wing politicians, who prefer to believe that the free market offers equality of opportunity for all, while making sure that it gives their own children a head start in the race. Attempts to stamp out class protest in industrial relations have manifestly failed in Britain and the United States, where industrial disputes persist despite the efforts of Reagan and Thatcher to hobble the trades unions by legislation and administrative orders. Germany and France have not lost their class dimension, which raises educational and career barriers between the working and middle classes, and breaks out from time to time in occasional strikes. In Russia, where it was supposed to fade away in the classlessness of communism, it has reappeared with a vengeance in the anarchy of the collapse, with a new class of entrepreneurs (some old *nomenklatura*) lording it over an impoverished populace. Only Japan seems to have largely escaped the class struggle, at least since the early years of the post-war Occupation, owing, it seems, to the power of its paternalistic ideology – although even there there is an underclass of immigrants and untouchables. But with the decline everywhere of the old manual working class and the rise of the professional segment of the service sector, class is becoming latent again, as it was before the second, industrial, revolution brought it to the surface.

Professional hierarchy favours meritocracy, fourth, which all professional societies espouse in varying degrees. They steer between the self-conscious versions of France and Japan and the more relaxed, *ad hoc* varieties of Germany and the United States, while Britain, as ever, is weighed down by its backlog of old class attitudes. Meritocracy is most institutionalized, but perhaps most skewed, in France and Japan, where the integrated political, bureaucratic, and economic elites come from the same handful of educational institutions. It was institutionalized in a different way in the Soviet Union and East Germany, where the integrated elite was ostensibly open to mobility from the lowest levels, but where political loyalty and ideological lip-service increasingly took the place of wealth and family connections elsewhere. Surprisingly perhaps, given the power of the dollar and the prestige hierarchy of universities, the United States is a more open meritocracy than most, and both politicians and corporate executives are drawn from a wider background than in Europe. The American dream still beckons, though it operates most effectively through the top universities and business schools. Britain was and is the least meritocratic, despite the Thatcherite love affair with self-made men of dubious origins, because of an education system where privileged education can still be bought for cash. Oxbridge still takes half its students from the private schools which cater for about one in twenty of the age group. But everywhere in professional society human capital still has to be earned, and it cannot be harnessed without some concession to merit wherever it can be found. The notion that it is concentrated in certain classes, groups, or races flies in the face of the evidence if individual success rather than factitious averages is measured.

Fifth, and for the same reason, all post-industrial societies have had to make concessions to able women, especially in higher education where they now form nearly half the intake though much less of the graduate students and teachers, but in none so far have women achieved equality in access to jobs or equal pay for equivalent work. The Japanese have been the most resistant to accepting women in the higher professional echelons and the Americans the most welcoming, though the current campaigns in the United States for 'family values' and against single motherhood and abortion rights have as subtext the return of women to domesticity. (One curious paradox is the number of rich women like Arianna Huffington, who campaign full-time to force women back into the home, while allegedly employing ill-paid immigrant nurse-maids.) Nonetheless, white males still make up over 95 per cent of top executives in American corporations, and an overwhelming majority in Congress and the bureaucracy. The French for a long time were schizo-phrenic on the question, having the largest percentage of women work-ers in the West alongside the most pro-natalist welfare state, while the West Germans, who still had a lingering preference for *Kinder, Küche, Kirche*, had one of the lowest percentages. But now the convergence is striking as women are making up half or nearly half the total workforce, and British (51.6 per cent in 1991) and German women workers (47.6 per cent) have overtaken the French (46.2 per cent). Many of them, however, are part-time workers, occupy the lower-paid levels of employment, and are found in very small numbers in managerial positions. Unifica-tion, meanwhile, has made things much worse for East German women, who have lost their generous maternity benefits, child care facilities, and abortion on demand. The Soviet Union and East Germany were commit-ted to sex equality, but this meant women's rights to the lowest-paid jobs, to the double burden of outside and household work, childrearing, and queuing for food, and almost no access to the *nomenklatura* except as spouses. Women in all post-industrial societies are still the great neglected source of human capital.

The growth of government, the sixth and one of the most powerful trends in professional society, seems to be levelling off with the collapse of the command economies and the backlash against public ownership and welfare in the West. It was always greater in Europe with its tradi-tions of state enterprise going back to the eighteenth century and welfare provision going back to Bismarck, than in the United States and Japan, where culture and ideology favoured private enterprise, though of differ-ent kinds. The collapse of communism and the wave of privatization in Europe, begun in Thatcherite Britain, have started to roll back the involvement of the state in the civil economy, but this has by no means reduced the scale of traditional government employment and expenditure. All the efforts of the Reagan–Bush presidency failed, as the Gingrich–Dole control of Congress is now failing, to cut back government spending. They are simply redirecting funds from welfare and public infrastructure to defence, crime 'prevention' (meaning more police and prisons), subsidies to industries like agribusiness, logging and mining on public land, and military programmes like the revival of Star Wars.

Bureaucracy is the exemplar of Parkinson's Law, and the American Federal agencies, like the CIA, the Food and Drugs Administration, the National Forest Service, and the Federal Board of Reclamation (which builds dams that nobody wants), are masters of the game of making work for themselves and saving their jobs. The CIA, for example, set up in 1947 to fight the Cold War, has lost its *raison d'être* but not its will to live high on the hog: it has found new 'dangers' to the American way of life in industrial espionage, new forms of religious fundamentalist and other 'terrorism', and nuclear proliferation. Such agencies cost far more than the uncovenanted welfare (not paid for by the recipients like social security) to the underclass. If this is the case with the nation most agonized about 'balanced budgets' and hostile to 'taxing and spending', how much more is it so with countries like France, Germany, and Japan, where government–business cooperation is the norm and welfare, either public or corporate, is a given.

Government services are the basis of a civilized social life, and those who reject public spending pay for it in other ways, in increased crime, drug addiction, unemployment, and the costs of maintaining society's casualties either in institutions or on the streets. Not least, the creation and maintenance of human capital, by education and training, employment policies, and social support for the unemployed, is a function that cannot be left entirely to the private sector. That is why government spending, while it can and should be efficient and economical, is necessarily high in professional society.

The welfare state, seventh, plays a large part in maintaining human capital, and it now costs on average a fifth of GNP, though nearly all of it is recycled into the economy. Unsurprisingly, it is now the prime target of the free-market economists and the politicians of the radical right, especially in Britain and the United States, where the think tanks are paid huge grants by the rich to blame the poor and cut their benefits. Yet their own policies create the very problems they complain about: unemployment as the chosen cure for inflation, poverty as the result of the widening gap between rich and poor produced by a deregulated market, crime, drug addiction, and mental illness in consequence of that poverty and the social malaise of the disinherited. All these cost far more money than the preventive welfare practised by the state in Europe and by the corporations in Japan. Right-wing solutions always turn out to be more expensive: the largest prison population in the world has not reduced the American crime rate, nearly twice as high as the European, up to five times as high for murder and rape (the United States now has 25,000 murders a year, compared with 29,000 in the anarchy and mafia wars of post-communist Russia);[1] and the Gingrich orphanages for the children of single mothers would cost ten times as much as outdoor relief. Unless society adopts Dean Swift's satirical solution for the children of the poor (eat them and tan their hides for leather), there is no escape from preventive welfare expenditure. Keynesian full employment, though it would not cure the problem of what used to be called the impotent poor, would reduce the cost of social security, but this is anathema to the right wing except when it subsidizes their friends in big business. To quote Lee Iacocca in another context, asking Congress for money to bail out his bankrupt industry before it created massively expensive unemployment, 'You can pay now or you can pay later!'[2] The cheapest and most rational solution is to treat welfare, as in continental Europe, as an investment in maintaining human capital, the mainspring of professional society.

Higher education, eighth, the chief creator of human capital, is one of the leading items in government expenditure. The United States, with the largest private university sector, still spends more public money per student than any other country: $13,639 in 1991, compared with Britain's $9,621, Japan's $7,570, West Germany's $6,322, and France's $5,871. Its enormous investment in higher education has produced the largest proportion of graduates to population in the world, 36 per cent, compared to 15–22 per cent in the other four countries, and has given it the leading edge in scientific research and in many high-tech industries.[3]

But money isn't everything, and the more focused meritocratic higher education of France, Germany, and Japan has enabled them to catch up with, and the last two to overtake, the United States in GNP per capita (at current exchange rates) by 1992.[4] In professional society it is the quality rather than the quantity of higher education that counts, and the expensive American system, with its diffuse liberal arts first degrees followed by graduate school for about the same proportion as the whole intake elsewhere, is no more effective than the fewer but more intensive first degrees in Europe and Japan. By contrast, the determined investment in higher education in the Soviet Union, which helped it compete in nuclear weapons and space research with the United States, wasted resources on ideological education (now abandoned along with the redundant ideologue professors) and did not save the Russian economy from collapse. Investment in higher education is undoubtedly the ticket of entry to professional society – South Korea's economic surge was predicated on a rise in government expenditure on higher education from 2.5 per cent in the 1950s to 22 per cent in the 1980s, and a 150-fold increase in enrolment[5] – but it is the kind rather than the quantity that matters.

The rise in the scale of organization is what ultimately gives professional society the leverage to perform its many functions. Along with the expansion of government, welfare, and education, the scale of operation in the economy, the ninth major trend, has to rise to produce the gigantic flow of goods and services. The huge dinosaurs of state industries in the command economies manifestly failed, more because of mismanagement and corruption than ideology, but in the free world business has

183

continued to concentrate increasingly in large corporations. In every advanced country in both West and East each major industry is led by three to five large companies that dominate production, employment, and prices; on average some 200 big corporations and their satellite subcontractors and suppliers account for the largest part of the Gross Domestic Product of each nation.

Yet industrial concentration does not stop at national frontiers. The globalization of the economy is the tenth and final major trend of the third social revolution. The world economy, as we saw in Chapter 1, is now dominated by some 37,500 transnational corporations (TNCs), which between them control 207,000 foreign affiliates. Nine out of ten are based in the developed countries of North America, Europe, and Japan. They employ directly at home and abroad around 73 million people, nearly 10 per cent of paid employees in non-agricultural activities worldwide, and close to 20 per cent in the developed countries alone. Indirectly, through subcontractors, franchisees and tied suppliers, they employ as many again, making a total of 150 million workers, or nearly one in five of the globe's non-farm paid workers. The largest 100 (excluding banking and finance) held $3.4 trillion in global assets in 1992, about a third outside their home countries, and employed 12.4 million people, nearly half of them overseas, about one in six (17 per cent) of the multinationals' total direct employment. Three quarters of them are based in the five countries addressed here: twenty-nine in the United States, sixteen in Japan, twelve in France, eleven in the United Kingdom (including two jointly with the Netherlands), and nine in Germany; another five were based in Canada, Australia, and New Zealand.[6] On a wider view, 386 (77 per cent) of the 500 largest industrial (manufacturing and mining) companies were based in the five: 157 in the United States, 119 in Japan, forty-five in the United Kingdom, thirty-three in Germany, and thirty-two in France. They controlled assets in 1991 of $4.5 trillion and employed nearly 20 million workers, and dominated the global economy.[7]

## GLOBAL PROFESSIONAL SOCIETY

Professional society, in short, has gone global. The different countries have different approaches to company law, long-term goals, decision making, and participation of employees and other stakeholders, which colour their operational style overseas as well as at home, but they are all caught up in the new global economy. As Robert Reich has observed, there is no longer any such thing as an American or other national product.[8] A car, television receiver, video recorder or personal computer may be designed in one country, financed in another, parts made in several others, and finally assembled wherever there is a domestic or adjacent market. Instant telecommunications, cheap and rapid transport, and just-in-time delivery systems enable TNCs to operate as easily across continents, oceans and time zones as in their home countries. Financial transactions like banking, insurance, foreign exchange, and credit card processing are even freer of national frontiers and circle the globe day and night, to the discomfiture sometimes of national governments and international banks who can no longer defend their own currencies against the attacks of speculators and rogue dealers. All this gives immense power to the executives of TNCs, often beyond the capacity of nation states to regulate or rein them in, and the temptation to abuse that power is as great on the international plane as within their own societies.

What we are dealing with is what I have called in this book corporate neo-feudalism, the convoluted structure of managerial capitalism with hierarchies of proprietorial interests above the level of the board of directors and of productive layers below it that is now the model of the national and international economies. A corporation is like a tree, with branches and leaves drawing sustenance and feeding back nourishment above, and roots reaching deep into the subsoil of the economy. In such an organism power concentrates in the trunk where all the veins converge and allow the corporate executive board to control the flows in both directions. Like the barons of medieval feudalism, company executives are based in specific countries and ostensibly owe allegiance to them, but in practice operate freely across national boundaries. The TNCs have become the 'overmighty subjects' of the modern world, who loom larger than their official overlord, the sovereign state. Their directors can move capital and labour from country to country, make or break communities by investing in or closing down plants, and allocate internal pricing and therefore profits to the most tolerant and lightly taxed jurisdictions. The top thirty have turnovers (total sales) greater than the GDPs of all but the fifty richest nation states.[9] If wealth is power, they are in a bigger league than three quarters of the countries in the United Nations.

The free-marketeers argue that this does not matter because the TNCs do not possess coercive power in the shape of military capability or lethal force. But that ignores two powers which they undoubtedly possess, the power to outflank and the power to seduce: the power to withdraw investment and the power to persuade governments, with inducements and favours legal or illegal, to do their bidding. Politicians in both developed and developing countries queue up to beg for direct foreign investment, running in 1986–90 at $168 billion a year worldwide ($115 billion from the leading five countries),[10] offering sweeteners like free land, ready-built infrastructure, and tax holidays, and seek re-election on the strength of their salesmanship. More sinisterly, some of them compete to pay the kickbacks without which business cannot be done in many developing countries and, judging by the Lockheed scandal in Japan and the British Aerospace purchase of Rover cars (before its resale to BMW) in Britain, not even in some developed ones.

Corruption takes many forms, from direct bribery to legal favours. Perhaps the latter kind is the most pernicious, since it is barefaced and unashamed, and the 'money politics' of Japan, the funding of politicians of both major parties through Political Action Committees in the United States, and the rewarding of ex-ministers and civil servants in Britain by appointments in businesses they have privatized, are all examples of 'structural corruption' without penalty. The danger is that the elites who were under temptation to over-exploit their national societies are now under the same temptation to exploit the world at large. The world, it seems to them, is their oyster.

In many ways, the imperialism of the last four or five hundred years, in which Europeans and their descendants came to dominate every continent, was a rehearsal for the current globalization of human society. As Edward Said, Immanuel Wallerstein, and Eric Wolf have shown, the peoples of the European and North American core societies have come to dominate and exploit those of the periphery, imposing their own cultural attitudes, taking raw materials at knock-down prices, buying or enslaving cheap labour, forcing trade at the point of a gun, and piling up mountains of debt beyond the means to repay.[11] The old means of exploitation, military conquest, and direct rule, have come to an end with the winding up of the European empires, but the economic imperialism pioneered by Britain outside the empire in China and Latin America and by the United States in the same and other areas has more than replaced it.

The principal instrument of domination is no longer the imperialist state but the TNC – though as in the Gulf War or Central America the nation state can still be called on to provide military back-up. This is not all bad: just as the old imperial powers built roads and railways, provided famine relief and modern medicines, the TNCs bring benefits, including investment, jobs at higher than local wages, training in skills and management, and higher standards of health, safety, and industrial relations, if not as high as they are obliged to maintain at home.[12] But that does not diminish, for better or worse, the domination of the global economy by a few hundred TNCs based to an overwhelming extent in the same ex-imperialist countries. The professional managers who control them have the means to benefit the world or to exploit it to their own benefit. Their conduct in their own societies therefore indicates how they will behave in the global economy.

## THE CONTRADICTIONS OF FREE-MARKET THEORY

Over-exploitation of their societies' resources has been the besetting sin of ruling elites in all regimes since the beginning of history. The military aristocracies and sacerdotal bureaucracies of pre-industrial society screwed all they could out of the peasants, traders, and craftsmen to support their pastime of internecine war or crusades against the infidel, and their lavish life-styles. They were often saved from self-destruction only by their own incompetence or the wily resistance of their subjects. Empires and churches still collapsed, more through the reckless weakening of their human resource base than from the assaults of opportunist conquerors or heretics. In the same way, industrial capitalists, though capable of generating more wealth and so buying off trouble, were also tempted to take more than their share of the community's resources, at the expense of almost continual class conflict. Marx's theory of revolution through the over-extraction of surplus value he called the contradictions of capitalism, but such contradictions apply to all societies in which the elite take so much of the surplus that the rest are unable to maintain their customary standard of life, or come to resent the resulting inequality. Both feudal and industrial society had the excuse that total resources were limited by nature and current technology, and that an equal distribution of income would leave everybody poor. The price of civilization was the extraction of sufficient surplus value to enable the ruling elite to organize it.

Post-industrial society has no such excuse. The whole point and purpose of professional society is to apply knowledge and expertise to the production of enough sophisticated goods and services to meet the needs of every citizen. Not just the material needs for food, clothing, and shelter but the cultural, intellectual, and experiential needs, including education and the arts, sport and entertainment, holidays and travel, and so on. For the first time in human history the economy is capable of producing enough 'created assets' to give everyone – in the developed countries, since that is what development means – access to the full range of satisfactions once open only to the rich and powerful, and many that were unavailable to anyone before the late twentieth century: simultaneous news and pictures of events as they happen, instant communication with anyone anywhere on the planet, immediate access to data banks of universal knowledge, jet travel to exotic destinations, medical cures for even genetic diseases, music, opera, drama, films, and sport worldwide at the touch of a button, a global village of news and gossip on tap twenty-four hours a day.

There are still, of course, 'positional goods', symbolic acquisitions or awards conferring prestige and status, like bigger houses, faster cars, titles and honours, trophy wives and mistresses (or husbands and toy boys), even fifteen minutes of tabloid or televisual fame, to distinguish celebrities from the *hoi polloi*. But these are comparatively harmless foibles that may encourage talent and effort without diminishing the satisfactions of the many. They might even increase the emotional satisfactions of envy and indignation.

And yet we have at present the astonishing spectacle, in some developed societies at least, of an intensified struggle for income, not so much by the poor or the middling classes, but by the already rich to swell their overflowing coffers at the expense of the rest. 'To him that hath shall be given,' they believe, 'and to him that hath not, even that which he hath shall be taken away.' The excessive greed of some ruling elites is remarkable to behold, as they simultaneously downsize their workforces, cut the wages of those who remain, reduce the security of tenure of everyone but themselves, outsource as many functions as possible to subcontractors and consultants forced to do the same work for lower pay and benefits, and disrupt the career ladders which were the chief difference between the secure middle class and the declining percentage of manual wage earners, who in a properly organized professional society would have the same security and rising incomes. Instead, the middle class of salary earners are being proletarianized. In a word, the top professional elites are trying to deprofessionalize the employed professions.

The paradox of an unprecedentedly productive society unable or unwilling to guarantee work and security to its core members can be explained only by one factor: an ideology that justifies the extraction of surplus value to a self-destructive degree. It is not a question of fairness or of the contrast between absolute riches and poverty. When the extraction rate becomes too great, it prevents the producers from purchasing enough of their own products to maintain the economy in full employment, and creates unemployment, resentment, and a breakdown in social cohesion. The original classical economists tried to rebut this by appealing to Say's law, that one half of the goods in the market buys the other half, so that gluts and depression are impossible – this in the midst of some of the worst slumps of the nineteenth century. They and their descendants, the neo-classical economists, ignored the Keynesian time-lagged role of money and its capacity to sleep in the hands of the rich and depress consumption.[13] That ideology is of course the theory of the unregulated free market.

The consequences of over-exploitation for society are disastrous. The social malaise it generates destroys the willing cooperation on which production and civility depend. Some workers go slow, some turn to alcohol or drugs, some to crime or, as opportunity offers, to collective protest or violence. The struggle for income intensifies as people strive to maintain their customary standard of living. Finally, the economy itself begins to decline, relatively to other nations if not absolutely, as the producers can no longer buy enough of their own output. The elite try to fill the gap by over-indulgence, but they inevitably fail, since they instinctively turn to luxuries and frivolities, to existing capital acquisitions like land and great houses, and accumulate savings which, by reducing effective demand, exacerbate the fall in production. The result is a downward spiral of under-consumption and unemployment which, if it is not heroically redressed, leads ultimately to economic implosion and collapse.

Vilfredo Pareto, in his writings on the circulation of elites, foresaw this vicious spiral, and the loss of legitimacy to which it leads:

> The declining elite becomes softer, milder, more humane and less apt to defend its power . . . It does not lose its rapacity or greed for the goods of others, but rather tends as much as possible to increase its unlawful appropriations and to indulge in major usurpation of the national patrimony . . . On the one hand it makes the yoke easier, and on the other it has less strength to maintain it. These two conditions cause the catastrophe in which the elite perishes, whereas it could prosper if one of them were absent.[14]

Pareto's diagnosis certainly fits the Soviet bloc's collapse like a glove. From Stalin through Khrushchev to Brezhnev, and from Ulbricht to Honneker, the *nomenklatura* became simultaneously less brutal in their despotism and more grasping in their greed. Does the diagnosis fit the rest, and are they likely to meet the same fate?

The Japanese are not immune to exploitation and corruption, but their underlying philosophy of social cohesion makes them less prone to overdo it. Japanese corruption is legendary, of course, and has become the biggest issue in their politics. Yet 'money politics' was always a societal lubricant, and the politicians were the channels through which gifts and favours flowed from big business to the local constituents in the form of wedding and funeral presents and the like. Only when the flow became grossly distorted, as in the Recruit and Lockheed scandals, did the voters rebel and terminate the governing monopoly of the Liberal Democratic Party. More important than 'money politics' is what Chalmers Johnson called 'structural corruption', by which the bureaucrats and politicians, via *amakudari*, received deferred rewards in the form of jobs for the boys in government agencies and the corporations, a byproduct of the old boy network that stems from the common educational background of the unified elite.[15]

Yet so far the Japanese elite have maintained the people's trust and social cohesion by offering a *quid pro quo* for their power and wealth in the form of a paternalism that looks after at least the core workers in the corporations and persuades the rest that the system of recruitment to the elite is fair and open to all. The immense gains in national income since the war have been shared with the population and the rise in prosperity is visible and widespread. The elite, recruited via education rather than by birth or wealth (though these clearly confer advantages) are accepted to be the most able members of society, and they project an air of responsibility and seem to live up to their ideals. As long as they deliver the goods in the form of rising incomes and national pride and maintain their stance of caring concern, they are not likely to suffer the fate of the Soviet leadership.

Similarly, the continental European elites have for the most part maintained the trust and cohesion of their societies, by emphasizing their meritocratic recruitment, their concern for the common welfare, and by modifying the beneficial ownership of big business. Despite the corruption that infects French politics on both sides, among the friends of both ex-President Mitterand and ex-Prime Minister Balladur for example, the French bureaucracy's reputation for upright public service has survived and spilled over via *pantouflages* to the executives of the corporations. The West German elite, too, has a long-standing reputation for public service and what Ralf Dahrendorf has called 'the habit of obedience',[16] and the scandals have chiefly concerned not personal corruption but clandestine relations with the East German secret police, the Stasi. Above all, trust and cohesion have been maintained by the 'social market economy', the modified version of the free market that offers co-determination, participation in corporate governance to all stakeholders including the employees, combined with a generous welfare state that guarantees security to all. Although unification has put a strain on resources and annoyed the 'Wessies' with the costs of rebuilding the East and the 'Ossies' with the loss of the food and rent subsidies and other social benefits, the German economy has already recovered, as shown by the strength of the Deutschmark, the largest trade balance in the world, and the highest rate of industrial growth among the larger economies.[17] It is once more the locomotive of the European economy and the standard bearer for the industrial and welfare directives of the Union. In their different ways, both the Japanese and continental European elites have offered guarantees that they will not grossly abuse their power.

## THE ORIGINS OF ANGLO–AMERICAN INDIVIDUALISM

The American and British elites have offered no such guarantee. Like the Soviet *nomenklatura*, they have been seduced by a crude, reductionist ideology into believing that they have the right to exploit their societies to the limit, without conscience or restraint. Free-market theory has convinced them that greed is good, that the market will give everyone their due, and that they have a moral right to whatever share of society's resources they can grab. By a brilliant intellectual stratagem, their guru Friedrich von Hayek equated political freedom with the free market and argued that any interference with the individual's right to make money at the expense of his fellows was the road to serfdom. The heart of his theory is a distinction between fundamental law, which gives the individual indefeasible rights to acquire whatever he can in this world, and mere rules, the political regulations by which government underpins that law with definitions of property rights, contract, theft, fraud, and so on, but has no right to go beyond that to redistribute income or tax the rich to support the poor. The concept of social justice he specifically rejected as a sentimental interference with the individual's right to maximize his or her share of society's resources: justice is what the market gives you, no more and no less. The state and the state alone is the enemy of freedom: threats to liberty from other directions, from 'overmighty subjects' like powerful corporations, he simply ignored. The idealist concept of positive freedom, of government as the protector of the weak and defender of all against the bully and the overbearing institution, he laughed out of court. The market balances all interests and allocates society's resources in the fairest possible way.[18]

It is difficult to imagine a theory more favourable to the rich and powerful, or more irresponsible in its encouragement of reckless self-interest. It not only perpetuates the existing distribution of property but gives those with the most purchasing power the edge in acquiring more. Ruthless ambition and the gambling instinct are given their head, and competition becomes, as in Hobbes's state of nature, a war of all against all. Public service and social cohesion are sacrificed to individual self-interest, and social justice to the mindless operations of the market. Any kind of social reform or moral progress is blocked by the argument that it is self-defeating and will make matters worse. Compassion is a misplaced luxury that kills with kindness: the poor are the victims of their own inadequacy and not of the system, and welfare will only encourage them to be idle and to breed, and so increase their poverty. The rich see themselves as the benefactors of society: the more they consume, the more good they do to the rest by providing work and income.

Why does this theory appeal to the English-speaking elites far more than to the rest of the civilized world? The answer is deeply embedded in English law and culture. It goes back, of course, to Adam Smith, Ricardo, Malthus and the classical economists, through to the near-anarchism of Herbert Spencer in *The Man versus the State*, but it can be found much earlier, in Alexander Pope – 'true self-love and social are the same' – and Bernard Mandeville – 'private vices, public benefits'.[19] It stems ultimately from a peculiar change in the English idea of property between the fourteenth and seventeenth centuries, from contingent property in which a hierarchy of owners, the king, church, barons, knights, and peasants, had claims to a share of the income, to absolute property, in which a single individual owned all the rights.[20] This concept the English carried with them wherever they went, and applied it in all the English-speaking lands and in Ireland, India, and the colonies. Elsewhere the concept of shared property, with overriding claims by the community, was the norm, but in Britain, the United States, and the English-speaking dominions the notion of individual absolute property rights held sway.

It is from this idiosyncratic concept of absolute property that Hayek and the free-marketeers derive their theory of individualism and the free market. If individuals have an indefeasible right to carve up the world into discrete parts and own them outright, not as contingent rights granted by the community but as absolute claims against all-comers, then it follows that they have an equal right to trade and exchange them without let or hindrance. But life in practice is not like that. 'No man is an Island, entire of itself,' as John Donne put it, 'every man is a piece of the Continent, a part of the main.'[21] A civilized society requires co-operation between all its members, and property is only a convenient device for rewarding collaborative effort which, if abused, will destroy cooperation and the very purpose for which it exists, to enable human beings to survive and live decent lives. The market is an excellent device in moderation for eliciting spontaneous cooperation, but when it is pushed to excess and the few find means to control it in their own favour it becomes counter-productive and self-defeating. Competition left to itself always ends in a zero sum game, where winner takes all and the rest lose everything. It is a Saturn that devours its own children.

## WIDENING ANGLO–AMERICAN INEQUALITY

This is the fundamental contradiction at the heart of extreme free-market theory. Far from allocating society's resources equitably, it tends to reinforce success and failure exponentially, and so to produce an ever-widening gap between rich and poor. The Anglo–American experiment with Reaganomics and Thatcherism in the 1980s has proved this empirically. As we saw in Chapter 2, in 1980 the ratio between the top and bottom quintiles of household incomes was twelve-fold in the United States and eight-fold in Britain, compared with nine-fold in France, five-fold in West Germany, and four-fold in Japan. Since then the gap has widened considerably. By 1987 the American top decile had gained 16.5 per cent in aggregate income (and the top 1 per cent, 49.8 per cent) and the bottom decile had lost 14.8 per cent.[22] In Britain by 1991 the top fifth of households received before tax 23.7 times the average income of the bottom fifth, and after tax and benefits (which doubled the poor's income and reduced that of the rich by a third) still 7.4 times.[23]

Such broad brush strokes do not measure the exploitation by the top elites, who are a much smaller group than the top 10 or 20 per cent.

During the 1980s, according to Kevin Phillips, Reagan's political adviser, the take-home pay of the CEOs of the 200 largest American corporations increased from thirty-five times the average wage to 135 times. In 1992 when the average wage was about $16 an hour or about $32,000 a year for those in full work, the top fifty companies in *Fortune* magazine's list paid their CEOs upwards of $5 million (156 times the average wage), rising to $11 million at Philip Morris and $15 million at General Electric. The previous year Michael Eisner of Disney Corporation took home $37 million, while making huge losses on the French Disneyworld venture. In his six years as CEO of Coca-Cola, Robert Gozueta accumulated a portfolio of $300 million.[24] British executives are not in the same league, but the row over executive pay in the privatized industries has revealed some very large incomes. The chairmen of the ten regional water companies trebled their average salaries from £46,000 to £149,000, about seventeen times the median household income; Sir Desmond Pitcher at North West Water took a 571 per cent rise to £315,000. Sir Iain Vallance of British Telecom took a rise to £663,000, twenty times the pay of the young hospital doctors than whom he claimed to work harder. Lord Young of Cable and Wireless, which as Minister for Trade and Industry he helped to privatize, took a 77 per cent rise to £883,000, while David Jefferies of the National Electricity Grid, sold to the regional electricity companies for £750 million but valued for resale to the public at £5 billion, realized £2 million in salary and share options in 1994.[25]

Such rewards, at the same time as the industries are downsizing their workforces, reducing the real incomes of their employees by cutting wages or giving increases less than inflation, and shaving service standards (British Gas, whose CEO Cedric Brown took a 75 per cent increase to £475,000 plus stock options worth nearly £500,000, has cut the company's safety budget from £9 million to £1 million), have produced a backlash in both countries. In the United States stockholders' organizations like United Shareholders and the Council of Institutional Investors, and pension funds like those for the public employees of New York State and California, have forced the resignation of the CEOs of major corporations like General Motors, IBM, Citicorp, and Sears Roebuck, but this has not reduced the pay and benefits of their successors. As Sarah Teslik of the Council of Institutional Investors writes, 'CEO pay is merely the symptom of a larger problem – the lack of accountability in corporate America.'[26] In Britain, John Major appointed the Nolan Committee to inquire into MPs' private earnings and ex-ministers' and civil servants' corporate appointments, and the Confederation of British Industry appointed the Greenbury Committee to look into corporate executives' remuneration, but their reports recommended substantially voluntary codes of conduct and the supremacy of the free market.

The irony of this is that what Alfred Chandler, doyen of business historians, calls 'managerial capitalism' is designed to control the market, not to be controlled by it. The 'visible hand' of the corporation, he argues, has replaced Adam Smith's invisible hand and has internalized market transactions so as to ensure an orderly production process and predictable profits.[27] Control of the markets in goods, services, and labour in order to prevent unexpected fluctuations and unwelcome surprises is the aim of big business. Chandler's critics, like Charles Perrow, go further and argue that evading market pressures by externalizing social costs such as infrastructure, pollution clean-up, and the support of redundant labour is the real corporate goal.[28] Thus the free market between individual producers, workers, and customers envisaged by Adam Smith and the classical economists no longer exists. Neo-classical free-market theory is an anachronism, appropriate to a world that has long passed away, and irrelevant to the corporate neo-feudal capitalism of post-industrial society. The free-marketeers are the Aristotelians of modern economics, who like the medieval schoolmen in the Scientific Revolution, continue to preach a doctrine that has no relation to contemporary reality.

The reality is reflected in what the professional managers of Anglo–American business are actually doing, turning their control of the flows of income into permanent property. The issue of executive pay is much larger than a mere struggle for income, a question of fairness, or the politics of envy. It goes to the heart of the question of who owns the corporation. In Europe company law and in Japan custom and culture, as we have seen, recognize other stakeholders than the shareholders, thus involving employees, bankers, and creditors in the benefits of ownership. In Britain and America and their offshoots, the ostensible owners are the shareholders, but they delegate their rights to the directors, who control the flow of income to them as well as to the other factors of production. In practice this means that the directors decide who gets what: they determine where the benefits of ownership go. As we have seen in the 1980s and 1990s under the Hayekian free-market regime, they have steered more and more of the benefits to themselves, not only in salaries, perquisites, and pensions, but in stock options. The latter are the clue to what is happening to the ownership of British and American business. The huge stock options which the directors have awarded themselves and each other are in the process of transferring the ownership of industry from the shareholders to the managers. As Robert Heller says in *The Naked Manager*,

Men who have never laid their own fortunes on the entrepreneurial line are making themselves multi-millionaires at the shareholders' expense, with no more trouble than it takes to arrange a bonus deal

194

or a stock-option scheme. If as much ingenuity had been spent on getting more productive collaboration from the rest of the work force they might have presided over fewer losses of jobs and markets.[29]

This throws a fresh light on the meaning of Chandler's 'managerial capitalism': the executives are turning themselves into the owner-managers of the new post-industrial society. Like the entrenched elites in feudal and industrial society before them, they are engaged in rent seeking, in transforming day-to-day control of income into permanent property, producing unearned income in place of salaries, all of course in the name of the free market. The freedom of the market is their own freedom to acquire gratuitously the ownership of the companies of which they are legally only the servants.

## DOES IT MATTER?

The question arises, does it matter? It can be answered in two ways, by economic and by social criteria. Economically, we can compare the period of Keynesian regulated capitalism from 1946 to 1973 with the period of deregulated free markets which followed in the 1980s and early 1990s, and we can also compare the performance of the more extreme free-market-oriented British and American economies with what may be called the more organic or community-minded economies of continental Europe and Japan. (The real turning point was not the election of Thatcher in 1979 and Reagan in 1980 but President Nixon's abandon-ment of the Bretton Woods system of fixed exchange rates in 1972.) In the Keynesian period of regulated welfare capitalism, 1960–73, the OECD countries on average grew in aggregate Gross Domestic Product by a remarkable 4.75 per cent per annum; in the subsequent period, 1973–87, it was nearly halved, to 2.6 per cent per annum,[30] proof positive that the regulated market performed better than the unregulated model.

The contrast between the United States and Britain and the rest was equally striking. In the period 1950–73 the American and British rates of growth of per capita GDP were not much more than half that of the other leading countries: 2.5 per cent and 2.2 per cent per annum, compared with France 4.0 per cent, Germany 4.9 per cent, and Japan 8.0 per cent. In 1973–89 all five suffered from slower growth, but Britain (1.8 per cent) and the United States (1.6 per cent) along with France (1.8 per cent) still lagged behind Germany (2.1 per cent) and Japan (3.1 per cent).[31] But that is not the end of the story. Although America and Britain made more rapid recovery from the recession of the early 1990s, they both in that second period became debtor countries on a massive scale, in terms both of national budget and of overseas trade. The American national debt rose to $4,083 billion by 1992, and the British to £207 billion ($327 billion), despite selling off some £50 billion worth of public property. In 1983–92 the American overseas trading deficit added up to $762 billion, and the British in 1988–92 to £74 billion ($117 billion) in an economy one sixth the size.[32]

Trading at a loss amounts to failure to compete, and in private business would soon lead to bankruptcy. Because of its vast market, its post-war lead, and its higher rate of population growth (mainly due to immigration), the United States still leads the world in real national income per head (at purchasing power parity), but if current trends persist it will shortly be overtaken by Japan and Germany; it has already been overtaken by them at current rates of exchange. The same trends have made Britain, until 1960 the richest country in Europe, the fifth poorest nation per head in the European Union, after Greece, Portugal, Ireland, and Spain.[33] If this is the 'bottom line' in the two countries most dedicated to the free market, it is clear that the extreme free-market experiment has failed. Hayek called Keynes 'the illustrious man, whose name will go down in history as the grave digger of the British economy'.[34] He was too modest: that title belongs to Hayek himself.

The social effects of the experiment have been no less dire. In both countries there has been a widening gap, as we have seen, between rich and poor, an increase in unemployment (ineptly disguised by adjusting the official figures), a rise in poverty and homelessness, a wave of crime and violence, an increase in racial tensions, a neglect of public infrastructure, the 'in your face' rudeness and incivility in the streets, and for the first time an upwelling of insecurity and discontent among the middle classes, who can no longer feel assured that their children will be as well off as themselves. Like Malthus and the classical economists before them, the right-wing politicians and neo-classical economists try to fob off responsibility by shifting the blame on to the victims, the poor, teenage mothers, 'welfare scroungers', immigrants, and racial minorities, even women who are blamed for taking white male jobs. This tactic has worked in the past, together with scaremongering about the 'tax and spend' opposition, but it cannot work for ever. Sooner or later the British and American people will wake up to the fact that the free-market ideology is simply a device for justifying exploitation of the many by the few, and demand a return to a responsible civil society. If they do not, the two societies may go the same way as the Soviet Union and East Germany.

## A GLOBAL RAY OF HOPE

Among those already waking up to the failure of the free-market experiment are, surprisingly perhaps, some of the big business professionals themselves. Some corporate executives, despite the adulation they receive from the free-market ideology as the heroes of post-industrial society, have to operate in the real world where theory does not always work as predicted. In particular, the transnational corporations have to function overseas, in countries that do not necessarily welcome Anglo–American ideas of individual property, company law, industrial relations, and business practice, and demand a higher standard of corporate behaviour.

The Japanese have never accepted that the self-interest of a few rogue politicians and greedy corporate executives should come before the national interest, and the Ministry of International Trade and Industry has been known to call in and reprimand the heads of the mightiest *keiretsu* suspected of acting against it. Their ideology treats core workers as part of the family, with a permanent interest along with top management in the long-term growth and prosperity of the company. The company union is consulted about each fresh initiative, and if it is not satisfied is apt to ask the directors, 'What are you doing with our company?' Participation is not guaranteed but it is an expected feature of the business culture, and acts as a restraint upon exploitative behaviour by the corporate board.

The continental Europeans have devised a more formal counter-ideology along the lines of the German social market economy and built it into the Maastricht Treaty. This includes the Social Chapter which guarantees social security for all citizens of member states and the human rights of workers and trades union members. It also underwrites the industrial directive which will require all large companies (with more than 1,000 employees including 150 in at least two member states) by September 1996 to appoint works councils. The British government has opted out of the Social Chapter, to the chagrin of the rest who consider that Britain is trying to gain an unfair competitive advantage, but British multinationals cannot opt out of the works council directive, even in their domestic plants, if they wish to operate in Europe. Some British companies, like United Biscuits and Coats Viyella, have welcomed this, and others, like ICI, British Aerospace, Unilever, Allied Lyons, British Petroleum, and Bass are negotiating schemes with their staff and trades union representatives. About a fifth of the 5,000 British manufacturing companies will be affected. John Edmonds of the GMB trade union commented, 'The Government can like it or lump it. Works councils are changing the face of UK industrial relations by giving employees a seat at the table.' The directive compels companies to report on their economic and financial situation, business development, investment plans, employment prospects, relocation, closures, and collective redundancies. Presumably, this will give the employees the opportunity not only to negotiate pay and conditions more effectively and to discuss alternatives to firing workers and closing plants, but to oppose gross overpayments to directors. Enlightened companies expect to gain better communication with workers, improved industrial relations, and speedier decision making. Others of course fear the loss of the executives' right to manage and, more particularly, their power to control the flow of income and to overpay themselves. Either way, if they wish to operate in what will soon become the largest market in the world, they have no choice.[35] Re-regulation of the market is returning to Britain through the back door of the European Union.

American big business was built on the free-market ideology and has been committed to it even longer, yet even there some business men are beginning to see that deregulation has gone too far for their own good. As in the nineteenth century when government was forced to intervene, rogue companies which do not apply the same levels of safety, pollution control, and quality of output and service gain unfair advantage over the honest ones, which in turn begin to demand common standards of behaviour. Companies that claim to provide honest service and model working conditions have to live up to their own propaganda. The CEO of one major finance company has called on American business 'to counter the excesses of greed and unfair advantage that threaten our concept of a just society' by means of 'a modern social contract':

> First, the system should be fair, with rules and conditions that apply equally to all. Second, the system should be open, with opportunity always possible for movement from any lower position in the society to one of greater power and wealth. Third, there should be a sense of general proportion between the haves and the have-nots . . .
>
> The inequities of insider trading scandals and the lionizing of individuals with inordinate wealth accumulated through single-minded exploitation of unfair advantage – these developments clearly undermine the covenants that are the foundation of our democracy. Corporate managements must accept responsibility for establishing ethical standards.[36]

Many American executives are beginning to share this outlook, and to see that equitable treatment of all partners in the enterprise is good business.

The key to good business is the creation, maintenance, and improvement of human capital, the one resource that organizes all the other factors of production. An equitable structure of rewards, high-trust industrial relations, provision for education and training, and partnership in decision making, are not just charitable concessions but the high road to profitability and company survival. The United Nations *World Development Report, 1994* shows that transnational corporations are beginning to realize this, and to issue statements of corporate responsibility along the lines of the European Union directives and the Japanese corporate philosophy. They have learned from experience that to operate in the global economy without condemnation or resistance they have to be seen to apply the same ethical principles in a variety of different cultures and political regimes. Their codes of conduct therefore emphasize their social responsibility to their local workforces and communities, their determination to pay the best local wages and maintain defensible conditions of health and safety, to encourage education and training, and to ban under-age child employment, prison, or forced labour, and other employment malpractices. The least they can do to ensure a welcome in the host countries is to offer better pay and conditions than their local competitors.

Even here there is a difference in approach between the British and American corporations and the rest. In line with their obsession with ownership, the Anglo–American codes of conduct tend to place the interests of the shareholders first and those of the employees, subcontractors, customers, and creditors a distant second. A typical American code states:

> The overall purpose of Caterpillar is to enhance the long-term interest of those who own the business – the stockholders.
>
> This in no way diminishes the strong and legitimate claims of employees, dealers, customers, suppliers, governments, and others whose interests touch upon our own – nor, indeed, of the public at large . . .
>
> We believe we can best serve stockholders and the long-term profitability of the enterprise through fair, honest, and intelligent actions with respect to all our constituencies.

Royal Dutch/Shell states its first responsibility to be to shareholders – 'To protect shareholders' investment and provide an acceptable return' – before going on to its responsibilities to employees, customers, and society.[37]

Japanese companies, by contrast, do not even mention the shareholders. Toyota's 'Guiding Principles' of 1992 declare:

> Toyota always has been a company devoted to enhancing the quality of life for people around the world by providing useful and appealing products. Toyota also is a company committed to addressing issues of common concern to people everywhere, such as safety and environment. In the years ahead, we must accompany our growth and development as a corporate citizen of the world with unflagging efforts to help resolve the pressing issues of our time.[38]

Both kinds of code are of course aspirational rhetoric, good public relations, but they demonstrate a different approach to business success, the first a belief in profits in order to do good, the second a belief that if you conscientiously do good, profits will follow.

The publication of such codes gives the TNCs something to live up to and affects their behaviour both overseas and in their home countries. They generally declare that employees are to be provided with safe conditions of work, competitive pay and conditions of service, equal opportunity employment for women and minorities, appointment and promotion by merit, and sometimes involvement in planning and decision making. Customers are to be offered value in terms of price and quality, and the local community and the public an assurance that the companies will operate as responsible corporate members of society. Some, like Royal Dutch/Shell's, are specifically designed to be consistent with the voluntary codes of international bodies like the OECD Declaration and Guidelines for International Investment and Multinational Enterprises and the ILO Tripartite Declaration of Principles. Similar codes have been adopted by Levi Strauss, Unilever, CIBA–Geigy, Johnson's Wax, Reebok, and other TNCs. Levi Strauss, for example, which sells $6 billion worth of clothing in sixty countries and has seventy-six plants with 36,000 employees in twenty-four countries, requires its business partners to operate a less than sixty-hour week with one free day, to pay fair wages by local standards, to have safe and healthy facilities, to employ no prisoners or child labour, and to be committed to a pollution-free environment.[39]

Going beyond good citizenship and obedience to local laws, the best TNCs husband their human capital by providing training and education. Japanese TNCs in 1989 trained one in twenty-four (4.1 per cent) of their employees worldwide, and continue the process every year. Nissan spent the equivalent of 7.6 per cent of its payroll on training in 1993. Nestlé and Alcan set up management centres in Europe which have grown into business schools. Citicorp/Citibank gives five days' training a year to all employees at home and abroad. Pepsi-Cola brings its overseas managers to the United States for up to three years' training. IBM in Scotland has invited local colleges to provide courses for its employees at its Greenock plant. Over two thirds of TNCs' foreign affiliates provided training in 1992. The *World Investment Report* comments that their main advantage to developing countries is the raising of technical and managerial skills, not only for their subsidiaries but for the rest of the host economies.[40]

These aspirations to good corporate conduct offer a ray of hope to the global economy and to professional society worldwide. But the enlightened self-interest of some TNCs overseas makes the short-sighted behaviour and unenlightened self-interest of much big business, notably in Britain and America, difficult to understand. The current wave of free-market triumphalism, the gross and shameless overpayment of corporate executives, the downsizing of workforces, the cutting of wages, the down-grading of conditions and fringe benefits, the outsourcing of functions to lower paid subcontractors and consultants, display a short-sighted neglect of social responsibility and long-term self-interest that can only end in disaster. The high-wage economies with long-term investment in human capital will inevitably outcompete the low-wage short-term profit chasers whose time horizon is the next company balance sheet. The free-market fundamentalists have led the two great pioneers of professional society, Britain and the United States, down a blind alley. One pillar of the great arch of post-industrial society, the Soviet command economy, betrayed by its ideologues, has fallen. Will the other pillar, the Anglo–American, led astray by its own brand of fundamentalist ideologues, be the next to crumble?

That takes us beyond history into the realm of speculation. It raises the vital question of what is to be done, which demands, if not a definitive answer, at least an extended epilogue.

# EPILOGUE
## What is to be done?

History never stops, but contemporary history finally hits a brick wall called the future. It is of course a receding wall, beyond which lies not history but speculation. The history of social forecasting, from Plato to Jules Verne, H. G. Wells and Herman Kahn, has a poor record of success, based as it nearly always is on extrapolation of existing trends, if only because existing trends when they become too threatening are evaded, diverted or rejected.[1] This, paradoxically, makes intelligent social forecasting all the more valuable, since to be forewarned *may* be to be forearmed, and to avoid the fate of the Gadarene swine. Its greatest hope is to be proved wrong, by making its warnings successful.

There are many existing trends in the present state of the world that may lead to disaster: global warming, the expanding hole in the ozone layer, the proliferation of nuclear weapons, fragmenting and competing nationalisms, rival religious fundamentalisms, the extinction of species of animals, plants, and bacteria vital to human survival, in addition to global overpopulation which exacerbates them all. Any of these could wipe us all out like the dinosaurs and give evolution a chance to do better next time round.

Our concern here is with a more immediate threat, stemming indeed from the same human genius for making the worst of a good job, the self-destructive tendencies of professional elites. The road to professional society is paved with good intentions, but some of the paving is in danger of collapsing into pitfalls. The specialized expertise that has raised living standards, lengthened lifespans, cured or prevented diseases as ineluctable as the biblical plagues of Egypt, offered comforts, pleasures, and entertainments beyond the dreams of the Pharaohs and intellectual excitements unknown to the Greeks, built engineering works beyond the skills of the Romans and imperial Chinese, raised monumental buildings towering over the medieval cathedrals and mosques, given access to all the world's literature and science at the blink of a CD-ROM, cracked the genetic code of life, and opened the way to the planets and the stars, has also created the means of its own destruction. The human

202

capital, ingenuity, and organizational skill that went into its making can just as easily be abused. The higher human intelligence climbs, the further it can fall. Like Icarus, the current generation is flying too near the unforgiving sun, the lifegiver/destroyer, and may be riding for a fall. It is too late to turn back. Only *more* intelligence, *more* ingenuity, *more* organizational skill can save us from the steep descent into the ocean of oblivion.

This book has been about the blessings and promise of professional society but also about its downside, the danger of exploitation by greedy elites and their propensity for corruption. Like most elites before them, the landlords and entrepreneurs in the societies created by the first and second great social revolutions of settled agriculture and industrialism, they have succumbed to the temptation to treat their fellow citizens as dairy herds to be milked to exhaustion. It is as if, in some cases at least, they have an unconscious death wish, to eat, drink, and be merry to heedless excess, for tomorrow they expect to die.

To end on this pessimistic note would be to sink into useless despair and to abandon the wonderful promise of professional society. It would also be unfair to those elites, particularly in Europe and East Asia but also among the more intelligent of those in Britain and America, who have seen the writing on the wall and are trying to rein in their exploitation by sharing their good fortune more equitably with their fellows. To redress the balance and rescue the benefits of professional society while lowering its social costs, we need to eschew suicidal selfishness and embrace enlightened self-interest. To do so requires us to go beyond history and ask: What is to be done?

Professional society is the most productive and potentially beneficial system ever attained in the history of mankind. Unlike previous systems, it is not (yet) limited by the niggardliness of nature and the exhaustion of human energy. Its immensely sophisticated goods and services need not be confined to a privileged minority but can in principle be extended to everyone. Production, which for the classical economists was hobbled by the law of diminishing returns, is no longer the problem. With the resources and technology at our command it can be extended almost indefinitely. The problem, as John Stuart Mill saw a century and a half ago, is distribution: 'That is a matter of human institution solely. The things once there, mankind, individually or collectively, can do with them as they like. They can place them at the disposal of whomsoever they please, and on whatever terms.' This is what the neo-classical free-marketeers have forgotten or rejected, that while the supply side may be limited by physical laws (and even those are more elastic than they suppose), the distribution of goods and services is a matter of human contrivance, and ultimately rests on man-made laws of property, contract, and exchange. As Mill put it, 'The distribution of wealth, therefore, depends on the laws and customs of society.'[2] The notion that it is based on some sort of natural law is what Jeremy Bentham rightly called 'nonsense on stilts'; it is a con-trick got up by those who stand to benefit most from the existing dispensation of property in its primary sense of claims upon the productions of others.

This is not to say that *any* system of distribution, *any* dispensation of property claims, is as feasible as any other, and will have no tangible effect on production itself. The structure of rewards is the primary determinant of the productive efforts people are willing to make (including non-monetary rewards such as prestige, job satisfaction, and time off), and the skill and enthusiasm they are willing to bring to the work. We saw in Chapter 5 how the structure of rewards in the old Soviet Union undermined the economy and brought ultimate collapse: 'They pretend to pay us and we pretend to work.' High-wage economies like the German and Japanese which share out rewards between stakeholders more fairly are more productive than the British, where the executives try to take all the cream and leave their employees the skim milk. All modern societies redistribute income in one way or another, by taxation, welfare benefits, subsidies and concessions, grants and contracts for every sort of public activity from defence and police to education and scientific research. There is no category of spending which is 'natural' as distinct from deliberately willed, so that all redistribution is political and not a result of market forces – except, perhaps, the market in influence. All modern politicians in professional society are big spenders, whatever their rhetoric, but some prefer to spend on defence or space research which generates contracts for their supporters while others prefer social programmes which favour theirs. That is why one of the major trends, the growth of government, does not decline significantly under the Reagans, Thatchers, Majors, and Gingriches.

If, then, the distribution of income is largely conventional and dependent on the structure of rewards and the current laws of property, we can envisage a range of conventional dispensations, with different consequences for production and economic growth, social justice, and the survivability of the regime. Indeed, different dispensations already exist, or have failed and ceased to exist, in the post-industrial world. The question is not a theoretical but an empirical one: which arrangement is the most successful, in the sense of being the most productive, offering the fairest spread of human happiness, and guaranteeing the most likely stability and survival of a viable regime?

The question is not to be settled by rhetoric or ideology, by Marxist theory or free-market triumphalism, still less by post-modernist relativism which takes refuge in 'texts' to avoid dealing with the raw brutality of the real world. This book has demonstrated that, while no post-industrial society is perfect and all elites are under the temptation to abuse their power and gluttonize themselves into the grave, some are more enlightened than others and more restrained in their exploitation of their societies. What is to be done is, in essence, very simple. It is to do what all good management schools and organizational theory recommend, to raise existing systems to the best practice of the most successful, which in this case means turning unenlightened, self-destructive self-interest into the enlightened, self-renewing kind.

As we have seen, there are two varieties of professional society which have shown themselves to be more successful than the rest in meeting the needs and ambitions of nearly all their members. Neither kind is perfect, and each can be faulted for neglecting the interests of some of their citizens, particularly those who drop out of the meritocratic race and those whom it regards as outsiders, immigrants, or untouchables. Yet, in different ways derived from their past history and culture, each has learned the lesson of harnessing the skills, intelligence, and willing cooperation of most members of society.

The two success stories among the leading professional societies are, of course, the continental European and the East Asian. That they both stem from the defeated side in the Second World War (including those defeated and occupied by the Nazis and the Japanese before their liberation by the Allies) is no coincidence. Defeat is the most salutary of historical lessons and confers the benefit of disillusion with the past, which the complacent victor fails to learn. The Germans and their European victims and the Japanese and theirs in what became the 'Little Tigers' of the Pacific fringe were forced not only to rebuild from scratch with the latest technology and management techniques, but to harness the cooperation of every citizen in the task of reconstruction. This experience gave them a lively sense of common purpose and mutual obligation that, inadvertently, prepared them for their role as exemplars of professional society. Yet their inheritance of community spirit and social responsibility goes back much further, to traditions of Christian corporatism and altruism in one case and Confucian harmony and self-restraint in the other, both deeply embedded in their history and culture.

## THE CONTINENTAL EUROPEAN ANSWER

As befits the heirs of the Western tradition of rationality and legalism, the continental Europeans have encapsulated their version of professional society in an explicit framework of law. The leading model is the German social market economy, a combination of regulated capitalist market with generous social welfare which aims at high productivity based on social cohesion. It rests, as we have seen in Chapter 5, on a structure of company law that guarantees the interests of all the stakeholders, not merely the shareholders and the directors but also the employees, the bankers, and other creditors, and indirectly even the suppliers, subcontractors, franchisees, and consultants. Codetermination (*Mitbestimmung*) ensures the involvement of all partners in the enterprise in decision making, thus engaging them in the long-term survival and profitability of the firm. The self-interest of all parties, not just quick windfalls for the few at the expense of the rest, is thus harnessed to the common benefit of all. Long-term investment, research and development, and the training of managers and workers to create human capital, are given priority over instant returns to the shareholders, and a fair share-out of rewards between shareholders, directors, managers, creditors, and employees is ensured by involving all of them in the oversight of the company.

If this means that property, in the sense of claims on the flow of income, is redefined, that is part of the intention. Society reserves the right, through the democratic process, to determine who has a stake in the enterprise, who has a claim to share in the flow of income, and thus who should possess part of the benefits of ownership. A company, in short, is not, as is commonly assumed in Anglo–American law, an 'object' owned by outsiders, the evanescent and revolving shareholders, but an organism owned, as it were, by itself in the persons of the collaborating parties. If this means that property rights are fragmented, so they are in the real world, and so they have always been except in the simplified theories of Anglo-Saxon lawyers and business men. Even in English law a company is a fictitious person and therefore not owned by anyone, but that fact has been replaced by a pragmatic belief in ownership by the shareholders, who can hire and fire the rest, and dispose of or dismantle it – a construct of English custom and the law courts, not of 'natural law'. A corporation is a creature of human law as interpreted by human custom, and what the law gives the law can take away. All states recognize this in their reservation of the right to tax property, to define company law, to regulate the market, and to safeguard the rights of creditors, customers, and employees. British and American law has defined those rights narrowly, to give one set of stakeholders, the shareholders and their proxies the managers, exclusive claims against the rest. Continentals have defined them broadly, to embrace the rights of all the stakeholders. History has already decided which is the fairer, more productive, and more socially cohesive system.

The German approach is gradually being extended throughout the European Union, except for 'opt out' Britain, by the Social Chapter of the Maastricht Treaty and its endorsement of works councils, trades union rights, and stakeholders' overview. The welfare state is part of the system, not 'a cost upon productive industry' but an investment in human capital and in the social cohesion upon which everything else depends. It is, at the very least, a cheap insurance against the crime, drugs, disease, squalor, and social malaise that come with poverty and neglect. More positively, in the continental thinking of both Catholic corporatism and Protestant altruism, mutual responsibility is a value above and beyond individual self-interest, and indeed enables self-interest to flourish without too much damage to other individuals. The German and now European social market economy embodies these values, and upholds capitalism without undermining the social contract on which a civilized society is based.

## THE EAST ASIAN ANSWER

The East Asian version of professional society does not stem from a tradition of rational law but from a different inheritance, an implicit belief in social balance. The Japanese call this *wa*, harmony or domestic peace, which ultimately derives from the Confucian belief in social congruity and the golden mean. (Buddhism, too, with its disregard for the material values of this world, contributes to this outlook: it too, para-doxically, offers a sublimated individualism – the ambition to rise to a higher plane in the next life – in the arms of collectivism – the search for an all-embracing Nirvana.) Since *wa* starts from the needs of the social whole rather than the autonomous individual, it does not seek to embody itself in individual rights or concrete rational law. From the individual's point of view it is an emotional attachment to the group – the family, community, working team, firm, nation – and an expectation that effort, cooperation, and loyalty will be rewarded by the group's perma-nent concern for one's welfare. It is not a matter of universally defined objective rights but of the warm embrace of belonging to the group.

The downside of course is that non-members of the group are out-siders, to be bargained or competed with but not accorded the same claims or privileges. To be sure, there is inequality within the group, and hierarchy between groups, one inside the next like a set of Russian dolls, and one's loyalties and rewards are inversely proportional to the emotional distance from each one. They may compete with each other for one's primary bonding, as family with firm, or corporation with nation. But fundamentally all insiders at each level have preferential claims over and against all outsiders. Western universalizing objectivity has no place, and the Kantian categorical imperative – to do unto *all* others as you would be done by – is not a meaningful concept.

Such an outlook – it is too diffuse and personal to be called an ideology – can be infuriating to rational Westerners, with their demand for equality of treatment for all, the application of objective standards, and a 'level playing field'. It makes doing business between East and West extremely frustrating and leads to misunderstandings and re-criminations, even to mutual accusations of bad faith. But from the point of view of the societies in the Confucian tradition it makes very good sense. The feeling of belonging to a group based on mutual concern, interactive loyalty, and shared rewards is an ideal foundation for operating a successful professional society. The productive unit, the working team or the firm itself, becomes a quasi-family in which each member has a role, works to the same end, and shares the same conditions and rewards in proportion to his/her status. The members are not equal, since the family is paternal, even patriarchal, but all can contribute, earn respect, and grow into new roles with age and experience. It is the emotional force of the familial bond, not the legal framework, that accounts for the 'three sacred treasures' of the Japanese corporation: lifelong employment, rising wage scales and promotion by seniority, and the company union. Without the team spirit (*shudan shugi*) and the mutual trust it generates, the 'treasures' are meaningless or counterproductive, as they no doubt would be in the West.

It is easy for Westerners to see the flaws in this system. It is unfair as between insiders and outsiders, and between natives and foreigners. It is unfair even inside the firm as between core workers with lifelong employment and the peripheral ones, including most women, the less skilled, and minorities like the Koreans and the *burakumin* or untouchables. And it is unfair as between the firm's internal workers and those in the subcontracting and supplying firms, who are paid much less, work much harder in worse conditions, and have no security. Since it is based not on binding law but on custom and usage, it could erode in hard times and economic depressions. And because it is stronger within the immediate working group and the company than in the wider community and the nation, it has neglected the welfare of the citizen at large. The welfare state is minimal, and it is only recently that so basic a provision as the old age pension has been extended to the people and this will not reach full value until the next century. Moreover, since the whole system is based on trust and trust can so easily be abused, it lends itself to corruption and manipulation, as we have seen in the 1980s and 1990s. Without a strong legal framework, the Japanese answer to the problem of restraining the elite is, from a Western point of view, extremely vulnerable.

However, the Japanese model has not only survived but has triumphed over difficulties which Western commentators forecast would be lethal: the oil crises of the 1970s and 1980s, the world depression of the early 1990s, and the corruption scandals of the last decade. In a country with almost no resources other than its human capital it has soared from collapse and defeat into first place among equals in half a century, to become one of the most successful professional societies in the world.

# ANGLO-SAXON ATTITUDES

What lessons do the two moderately successful large professional societies, the German-led continental and the Japanese-led East Asian, have, since the collapse of communism, for the now most vulnerable ones, the United States and Britain? On any objective view, the experiment under the Reagan–Bush and Thatcher–Major regimes with the deregulated free market has done more harm to their economic growth and social cohesion than either Hitler in the Second World War or Stalin, Khrushchev and Brezhnev in the Cold War. In both countries the widening gap between the rich and the poor, as great as in the time of Dickens and Malthus, the flaunting of excessive wealth in contrast to the homeless beggars on city streets, the rising waves of crime, drugs, and violence met only by hysterical demands for more prisons and more draconian punishments, the blaming of the victims of poverty and unemployment by the very people who have done most to cause them, the intolerance for those labelled 'other' whether immigrants, minorities, 'liberals', or different religionists, the attack on trades union rights and the rejection of participatory industrial relations, the obsession of the media with violence and the bloodshot propaganda of the American gun lobby, the disillusion with politics and the corruption of politicians by the special interests, the insecurity and incivility on the streets – these are all signs of a civilization in decline.

Instead of hastening to shore up the dikes of civil society against the rising tides of greed, crime, and violence, the ruling elites frantically tear down the protective walls of regulation, welfare, and mutual responsibility that stand between the people and Hobbes's 'war of all against all'. Like doomed elites before them, the pre-Reformation Church, the French *ancien régime* aristocracy, and the Tsarist autocracy before the First World War, they want to have their lovely cake and eat it, to indulge themselves to excess without paying the price, to exploit society without offering anything in return. So long immersed in the Cold War, which offered excuse and rationale for the extraction of ever more of the surplus, they are the mirror image of the enemy, the Soviet *nomenklatura* who abused their power to the point of system failure.

Fortunately, by no means all Britons and Americans, not even the whole of the political and managerial elites, are infected by this deadly virus. There is considerable evidence that the intellectual tide is turning against the extreme version of the unregulated free market. It has already done so much damage to the real economy on both sides of the Atlantic that many people in business, politics, and academe are becoming disillusioned with its failure to deliver on its promises. Far from offering faster economic growth, the 1980s and early 1990s have seen it slow to little more than half the rate of the Keynesian golden age of 1946–73, and the early 1990s have seen the return of depression on a scale not seen since the 1930s. Keynesian economics is enjoying a revival among the more intelligent economists and business journalists, not merely out of negative despair but because Keynes's responsible version of regulated markets is the best hope of saving capitalism from its own excesses. Lester Thurow and Robert Reich in the United States and Will Hutton and William Keegan in Britain have called for a more responsible approach that could produce more wealth, distribute it more fairly, and compete more effectively with the more cohesive societies of continental Europe and East Asia.[3]

Political scientists and philosophers like David Marquand and John Gray have begun to question the 'unprincipled society' created by the Radical Right and its consequences of social malaise and family and community breakdown. Marquand has called for a rejection of the 'reductionist individualism' that has overtaken the Keynesian post-war consensus and for a reform of our political institutions to make real, small-scale democracy work.[4] John Gray, an erstwhile Thatcherite, has seen that

> The policies of the New Right have left in their wake a trail of weakened institutions and shattered expectations. From Bart's Hospital to the Civil Service, institutions once animated by an ethos of professional commitment have been casually dismantled, or subjected to a callow culture of contract and managerialism. From pension provision to long-term care for the aged, expectations on which people have built their lives have been abruptly overturned. Working lives are dominated by suspicion of employers and fear of losing job security for ever. The legacy of the New Right is not a nation at ease with itself but a culture of anxiety and suspicion.

The answer is to challenge the global free market and 'this defunct world view' of the 1980s.[5]

Big business men like George Soros in Britain and Felix Rohatyn in America believe that responsible capitalism, a regulated market, and a constructive social policy would restore Britain and America to their accustomed leadership.[6] We have seen in Chapter 8 that many giant multinational corporations based in the United States and Britain have been convinced by their international experience to issue codes of social responsibility that voluntarily restrict the free market. And many British companies are finding that the directives of the European Union restricting their 'freedom to manage' are actually helping them to produce more efficiently with a more cooperative workforce. These are more than straws in the wind, and the wind is changing fast.

On the other side, the politicians blinkered by the free-market ideology who hijacked the Republican and Conservative parties in the 1970s have, like the Bourbons, learned nothing and forgotten nothing. They still control most of the media and the think tanks, and are too committed to their ideology to give it up without massive loss of face. (The think tanks contain the real 'welfare scroungers', 'consultants' who are paid handsomely by the rich to attack the poor and justify the rich.) Many of them have gone far beyond their gurus, Friedrich von Hayek and Milton Friedman, in the extremity of their views, and have committed themselves to laughable theories like the Laffer curve ('lower taxes produce more revenue') when it only produces massive budget deficits, and the 'trickle-down' theory ('tax breaks to the rich benefit the rest'), a euphemism for 'pissing on the poor'. There is little hope from them of self-correction and reform. We can only hope that they will run out of gas and grind to a halt; intellectually they are now running on empty. Unfortunately, too, they have 'sold off the family silver', as Harold Macmillan said of privatization, and piled up such colossal budget and trade deficits that their successors will have very small resources with which to put things right.

What then can be done to save the debilitated Anglo–American societies from the same fate as the Soviet Union and Eastern Europe? They must first show that they want to save themselves by cashiering the free-marketeers who have led them down the path of dalliance to the phantom cornucopia of a false prosperity. This will not be easy, since they control most of the media, and as their electoral propaganda has demonstrated, they do not believe in playing fair. They are prepared to promise almost anything to get themselves elected, including 'a balanced budget' with both lower taxes and higher welfare or defence spending ('The National Health Service is safe in our hands'; Stealth bombers the US Air Force does not want, made in the House Speaker's constituency), and to rubbish their opponents' tax and spending plans ('Labour will cost you £1,000 a year in new taxes') and their record on unemployment ('Labour isn't working' – before Thatcher trebled unemployment). They even intrude in their sex lives (Bill Clinton's and Paddy Ashdown's) when their own record of creating single-parent families is flagrant (Newt Gingrich and Cecil Parkinson). They are not above accusing them of spying for the KGB (Harold Wilson and Michael Foot), when their own record of trading with potential enemies is hidden behind 'national security' and Public Interest Immunity Certificates (arms for Iraq and Iran). They cynically arrange tax give-aways and engineer economic booms before elections and then take them back afterwards. And they wrap themselves in the flag and pretend that criticism of themselves is 'un-American' or 'letting Britain down' – cynical hypocrisy in politicians who have presided over the sale of great national properties like British Rover and Time–Warner to foreigners, and the massive export of jobs and capital.

211

Yet sooner or later their policies will find them out. The greed of some top executives of corporations and the corruption and sleaze of some politicians have already produced a backlash in both countries. The Major government is the most unpopular since opinion polls began, and the American public is so disillusioned with politicians that the only way to get elected is to 'run against Washington' – though the net result in 1994 was to put into Congress the very people most responsible for their discontents. Both governments are supported only by minorities of the eligible voters, and could be tumbled out of power if the majority exercised its will.

## A NEW STRUCTURE OF REWARDS

If and when they go, how can their successors put things right? It will not be enough to put the train in reverse and steam steadily back to the past. The past is dead, and after the Communist débâcle 'socialism' in any traditional form is not a viable choice. For one thing the massive budget deficits left by the 'anti-big government' parties will prevent a return to state enterprise or to expensive welfare programmes of the old kind. What must be done must be done on the cheap, with as little additional spending as possible.

### Reform of company law

The first priority is to change the structure of rewards. People must be paid for genuine creative effort, for producing real goods and services, not for moving money around at great expense, the financial manipulation Robert Reich has called 'paper entrepreneurialism' – dealing in junk bonds, unfunded derivatives, arbitrage, and the sleazier forms of what Will Hutton has called 'gentlemanly capitalism'.[7] The surest way to do this is to reform company law along the lines of the European Union so as to transform stockholder power into stakeholder power. If all the stakeholders in a company, including the shareholders, managers, employees, and long-term creditors, had some representation in the structure – by the German two-tier system, the French Method II, or some wider version of the European Union's works councils – then all would gain a long-term interest in the firm's success and an incentive to work towards it.

### Equitable rewards for all stakeholders

Second, all the partners in the enterprise should be rewarded on equitable terms. Not equally, for superior effort deserves extra reward, but fairly in accordance with their contribution to the success of the firm.

212

An example of this can be gleaned from an American Federal law of 1988: it required that company pension schemes should be equitable as between different categories of employee, i.e. the same level of premiums as percentages of pay should be contributed by employer and employee for salaried and waged, manual and non-manual, staff and shopfloor workers. (Unfortunately, it does not seem to have been applied to the directors, who continue to take massive pensions way out of line with the rest.) This principle should be extended to every kind of remuneration, to fringe benefits, bonus schemes, and stock options. Give or take exceptional payments for exceptional effort – which in the case of the directors should be justified to the works council or supervisory board as well as the shareholders – all parties should share proportionately in the profits of the firm. CEOs and executives should obviously be paid more than the rest, but not so outrageously that morale suffers and co-operation deteriorates, and their pay should not be increased when the company profits fall, nor should they be rewarded for failure with massive 'golden handshakes'. Every member of the enterprise contributes to the firm's profitability, and should be rewarded proportionately. All pay increases should be within the same but flexible percentage range, and if the executives get bonuses and stock options, so should the rest of the company's employees.

The managers and workers together are the active creators of wealth and they should have first call on the gains. Investment in the future, by means of new technology and development, and education and training to create and improve human capital, should have the next call. Only then should the passive partners, the shareholders who provide the material but not the human capital, receive the residue.

### Incentives for long-term stakeholding

Would the shareholders go on strike? Not if they are provided with better incentives than the frenetic gamble which they now enjoy. Continental European and Japanese shareholders have shown that they are content with long-term, steady profits rather than quick and uncertain returns, and look forward to capital gains over the long haul rather than in the next balance sheet. Most shares in Britain and America are now held by institutions, pension funds, holding companies, unit trusts, banks, and insurance companies. Their interest is in long-term provision for the pensions, endowments, annuities, and the like, that they will have to pay out into the distant future. They stand to gain from a stable, secure capital market rather than the minute to minute fluctuations that the stock exchange now throws up. Only the dealers, the brokers, the paper entrepreneurs, the arbitrage merchants, and the takeover raiders would suffer by the change, and they should in any case be encouraged to take a more long-term view. Long-term profitability comes from a stable, committed, highly skilled workforce, from long-term investment in useful and attractive products, from research and development, and from a company that is not nervously looking over its shoulder each working day for the next takeover raid or leveraged buy-out.

These features are, in different ways, built into the continental European and Japanese corporation, but they are almost unknown in the Anglo–American. The reason lies in the volatility of the Anglo–American stock market and its domination of corporate psychology. As Sony's Akio Morita has pointed out, a Japanese corporation's time horizon is ten years, the British and American corporation's is ten minutes, the time it takes for the stock exchange computers to register a fall in the share price. If shareholders could be guaranteed a steady return and the prospect of stable growth, and encouraged to make a long-term commitment instead of hopping in and out at the flicker of a VDU screen, they would become real stakeholders with a genuine concern for the prosperity and longevity of the company.

There are various ways of achieving this. One is to offer them, or at least the larger institutional investors, corporate representation, on the supervisory or policy making board, as the Germans are required to do and the Japanese do by custom. A second is to reward long-term shareholders for their loyalty with higher dividends or bonuses. A third, requiring government intervention, would be to tax long-term holdings at a lower rate and tax short-term capital gains at a sharply increased rate sufficient to discourage speculative dealing and takeover raiding. A punitive tax on gains from shares bought and sold within one accounting cycle would magically stabilize the market and stop rogue dealers from gambling on 3 or 4 decimal points of 1 per cent differential between different stock markets, like Nick Leeson who brought down Barings Bank in February 1995. None of this would be popular with Wall Street or the City of London, which make their living out of rapid turnover, but they are now part of the problem and should be made part of the solution by accepting an investor's rather than a gambler's role. They should be forced to earn their living by providing capital for real wealth creation instead of living off the backs of the wealth creators. In the long run they stand to gain more from an expanding real economy than from the present rake's progress of frenetic finance.

## Tax and limit political contributions

Having limited the temptation of corporate elites to overpay and corrupt themselves and convert other people's property to their own use, it is also important to discourage them from corrupting others, especially the politicians and bureaucrats of central and local government. Here a device which has already been imposed on British trades unions should be applied *pari passu* to themselves. If individual members can opt out of the political levy a trades union contributes to a political party, so should individual shareholders be able to opt out of political contributions made by a company. Such contributions should not be a business cost but taxed like any other distribution or dividend. And they should not be at the whim of the directors but approved by the highest supervisory body, to take account of the wishes of all stakeholders, including the employees, and endorsed at the AGM. The use of other people's money – the shareholders', the employees', the creditors', the taxpayers', and, at one remove, the customers' – to fund the directors' political friends is too tempting to be left to the executives' own decision, and is the chief means of corruption in British and American politics.

## A national structure of rewards

Finally, a new structure of rewards is urgently needed at the national as well as at the company level. Social policy should be directed to the creation of wealth, now and for the future. The creation and maintenance of human capital, the *sine qua non* of professional society, requires a combination of education and training with welfare measures and a full employment policy. Leaving aside the elderly and the busy mothers of under-school-age children – and even they should be encouraged to train for their future if they are able – no one of working age in good health should be allowed to be idle. The unemployed should be provided with jobs – in the present run-down state of the infrastructure in both countries there is more than enough work to occupy the whole reserve army of labour – or given an income on condition of training for work in the future. Beggars should be treated as truants and led gently back to school. Citizenship has its duties as well as its rights. The welfare state in professional society is not optional. It is the essential foundation of the community, an insurance against poverty, crime, violence, and anarchy, and the reserve maintainer and improver of human capital on which everything else depends. It is not a cost upon production but the most important investment in it.

It can, indeed, become a financial investment too. If social security is fully funded and the contributions invested instead of being merged with general taxation (with the temptation for 'balanced budget' fans, who do not understand the difference between income and capital accounts, to raid the social security fund to meet the deficit from time to time, as Senator Daniel Patrick Moynahan has demonstrated they have done in the recent past) it could become a major source of capital for industry and public works. The Japanese Fiscal Investment and Loan Program, until recently the predominant system of saving for old age, was the major source of cheap capital for the Japanese economic miracle and accounted for 40–50 per cent of the government's investment budget.[8] By such means social security, and particularly the state pension scheme, with the aging population in all developed countries causing concern about its future solvency, could become not only self-supporting but an important source of economic growth.

## Managing the global economy

There still remains the problem of managing the global economy. The real threat to communities comes, as John Gray says,

> principally from the globalization of economic life – from global free trade and from global and practically instantaneous mobility of capital, which have made the livelihood of every community more dependent than ever before in history on the fluctuations of the world market.[9]

The New Right, who value free trade above the welfare of their fellow citizens, argue that the social overheads of British and American industry raise labour costs and make their exports uncompetitive. They fail to explain how German manufacturers, for example, pay the highest hourly wages and social overheads in the developed world and yet export more manufactured goods than any other country, or how the Japanese, with high corporate social costs, have such huge trade balances. They seem to make the same confusion between wages and labour costs as the original classical economists with their naive wages fund theory which, if correct, would have prevented the Industrial Revolution. Adam Smith himself believed in a high-wage economy, because it would encourage hard work, generate demand, and force employers to invest in labour-saving innovations. The current British government in particular is trying to compete by turning Britain into a low-wage economy, a formula for ratcheting down to Third World status, instead of investing in skills and technology to support high wages and profits. The irony is that it is the British and American governments, with their attack on job security, wages, and trades union rights, which are guilty of unfair competition, while at the same time finding it more and more difficult to compete. The lesson, that long-term investment and an enthusiastic workforce are the best means of competing, seems to have escaped them.

In so far as Britain and America are suffering from unfair competition from countries with low wages, child and prison labour, little or no social security, poor human and trades union rights records, and non-tariff restrictions on trade, this once again argues the case for a regulated rather than a free-for-all world market. If domestic markets need regulation, how much more does the global economy. This is not easy, but the World Trade Organization which replaced the General Agreement on Tariffs and Trade at the Marrakesh Conference in 1994 is a step on the way.[10] It should not accept that 'liberalization of trade' is a panacea, but only admit to the game those countries that play by the rules. Countries that cheat by working children for overlong hours, by banning trades unions, or by using unfair bureaucratic restrictions on imports, should not be allowed free access to others' markets. As for TNCs which try to have it both ways by producing only in low-wage, low-standard countries and selling in the richest markets, the golden rule should be: 'If you don't invest here, you don't sell here.' The goal of the World Trade Organization should be fair trade not unrestricted free trade, and to raise the wages and conditions of all to the standard of the best.

The global economy is too important to be left to the economists, whose theories have consistently failed to live up to their promises. Whenever the free-marketeers have been given their head in the past, as in the 1840s, the 1880s, or the 1920s and 1930s, the economic consequences have always been disastrous. While a global free market is essential for world prosperity, it must be a regulated one, which rogue countries and over-mighty multinational corporations are not allowed to rig unfairly to their own advantage. Dumping exports below cost, undercutting competitors by exploiting sweated, child, prison, or forced labour, gouging wages by oppressing workers and trades unions, restricting imports by bureaucratic dodges, exporting pollution to under-regulated countries or pumping it into the surrounding atmosphere and aquifers – all such practices should be outlawed, along with piracy, brigandage, corruption, and white-collar crime. To do this the World Trade Organization needs much stronger powers to police the global economy. Like the European Common Market it could become a stage on the way towards a more perfect union, the precursor of a global regulatory authority. Like the European Union, it should respect the principle of subsidiarity, that all decisions should be taken as close to the citizen as possible, and should only deal with questions of international trade affecting everyone. World government in this strictly limited sense would ensure a level playing field for all competitors.

The world belongs to the whole human race, not just to those who claim to own the means of production, and to the vast diversity of species that support human life. Each generation only borrows it for a while, and if they exploit it beyond reason they can destroy themselves along with a large part of the biosphere. The third great social revolution in the history of mankind, the revolution of the experts and the creation of professional society, has enabled us to attain a higher plane of existence, with knowledge and power, health and longevity, comforts and enjoyments, the sheer ease and abundance of life – for those in the developed world at least – beyond the dreams of any previous generation. All this has been brought about by human ingenuity, in the form of science and technology, intellectual curiosity and artistic creativity, education and innovation – in a word, by human capital.

The magic key to this cornucopia is professional expertise, yet professionalism is also the major threat to its success. How can we prevent the professional elites, especially those in control of government and production and thus the flows of income, from abusing their power and exploiting their societies to the point of collapse? We cannot shirk, beg, or evade this question. If we do not solve it, it will destroy us and plunge future generations, shrunken perhaps to medieval size, back into the dark ages. The question is, do we *want* to solve it? Or are we content to let the false prophets of individual greed and unenlightened self-interest lead us down the primrose path to the everlasting bonfire?

# NOTES

## 1 THE THIRD SOCIAL REVOLUTION

1 John Kenneth Galbraith, *The New Industrial State* (Mentor, 1986); Daniel Bell, *The Coming of Post-Industrial Society* (Penguin, 1973); Alvin Gouldner, *The Future of The Intellectuals and the New Class* (Macmillan, 1979); Robert B. Reich, *The Work of Nations* (Knopf, 1991).
2 Cf. V. Gordon Childe, *Man Makes Himself* (New American Library, 1983).
3 Cf. Harold Perkin, *The Origins of Modern English Society, 1780–1880* (Routledge, 1969), Chapters 1 and 3.
4 Cf. Harold Perkin, *The Rise of Professional Society: England since 1880* (Routledge, 1989).
5 Cf. Bruce Kimball, *The 'True Professional Ideal' in America* (Blackwell, 1992).
6 James Burnham, *The Managerial Revolution* (Day and Co., 1941); Max Weber, *Economy and Society* (University of California Press, 1978); Vilfredo Pareto, *The Mind and Society* (Harcourt, Brace, 1935), Vol 4, pp. 1787–98; and *Sociological Writings* (Praeger, 1966), pp. 247–50; see also Samuel E. Finer's Introduction, 'The Theory of Elites', pp. 51–71.
7 Jaroslav Krejci, *Social Structure in Divided Germany* (Croom Helm, 1976), p. 24.
8 Jan Pen, 'Expanding Budgets in a Stagnating Economy', in Charles S. Meyer (ed.) *Changing Boundaries of the Political* (Cambridge University Press, 1987), pp. 324–37; Vicente Navarro, 'Welfare States and their Distributive Effects', *Political Quarterly*, vol. 9, 1988, p. 220; OECD, *Economic Surveys: USA, Germany, and Japan, 1993*.
9 Krejci, *op. cit.*, p. 24.
10 OECD, *Economic Surveys: UK, 1994*: Basic Statistics.
11 Cf. T. H. Marshall, *Citizenship and Social Class* (Cambrige University Press, 1950), pp. 10–20; R. H. Tawney, *Equality* (Allen & Unwin, 1931), pp. 108–15.
12 Leslie Hannah, *The Rise of Corporate Society* (Methuen, 1976), pp. 118–21, 216, 225; Leslie Hannah and J. A. Kay, *Concentration in British Industry* (Macmillan, 1977), pp. 85–96; S. J. Prais, *The Evolution of Giant Firms, 1909–70* (Cambridge University Press, 1976).
13 UNCTAD, *World Investment Report, 1994* (UN, 1994), pp. 1–8.
14 *Ibid.*
15 *Guardian*, 15 January 1994.
16 *World Investment Report*, p.12; cf. Herman van der Wee, *Prosperity and Upheaval: The World Economy, 1945–80* (University of California Press, 1978), esp. the Epilogue.
17 Cf. Ralf Dahrendorf, *On Britain* (BBC, 1982), pp. 84–85.

18 Ezra N. Suleiman, *Elites in French Society* (Princeton University Press, 1978), esp. Chapters 8 and 9; Jane Marceau, *Class and Status in France: Economic Change and Social Immobility, 1945–75* (Oxford University Press, 1977).
19 Ralf Dahrendorf, *Society and Democracy in Germany* (Weidenfeld & Nicolson, 1968), Chapter 16; Krejci, *op. cit.*, pp. 100–6; V. R. Bergahn, *Modern Germany: Society, Economy and Politics in the 20th Century* (Cambridge University Press, 1987), p. 209.
20 Krejci, *op. cit.*, pp. 104–5.
21 Chester Barnard, *The Functions of the Executive* (Harvard University Press, 1938), as interpreted by J. Rohr, *To Run a Constitution* (University of Kansas Press, 1986), and Terence R. Mitchell and William G. Scott, 'The Universal Barnard', three articles in *Public Administration Quarterly*, vol. 11, 1987.
22 Cf. Paul Kennedy, *The Rise and Fall of the Great Powers* (Random House, 1987), pp. 514–35.
23 Basile Kerblay, *Modern Soviet Society* (Methuen, 1983), pp. 248, 261–63.
24 Alexander Simirenko, *The Professionalization of Soviet Society* (Transaction Books, 1982), pp. 1–3, 12–15, 37–44.
25 Tatyana Zaslavskaya, *The Second Socialist Revolution* (Tauris, 1990), pp. 10–11; cf. Mervyn Matthews, *Privilege in the Soviet Union* (Allen & Unwin, 1978), Chapter 2, 'Special Elite Benefits'; see also Geoffrey Hosking, *The Awakening of the Soviet Union* (Heinemann, 1990), esp. Chapter 7.
26 Arkady Vaksberg, *The Soviet Mafia* (St Martin's Press, 1991).
27 Mikhail Gorbachev, *Perestroika: New Thinking for our Country and the World* (Fontana/Collins, 1988); Boris Yeltsin, *Against the Grain: An Autobiography* (Jonathon Cape, 1990).
28 John Lukacs, *The End of the Twentieth Century* (Ticknor and Fields, 1993), pp. 158–60.
29 Karel van Wolferen, *The Enigma of Japanese Power* (Macmillan, 1987), esp. pp. 43–49 and Chapters 4 and 5; James C. Abegglen and George Stalk, Jr., *Kaisha: The Japanese Corporation* (Basic Books, 1985).
30 Herman Kahn, *The Emerging Japanese Superstate* (Prentice-Hall, 1970); H. Kahn and Thomas Pepper, *The Japanese Challenge* (Crowell, 1979); Ezra F. Vogel, *Japan as Number One* (Harvard University Press, 1979).
31 Bill Emmott, *The Sun Also Sets: Why Japan will not be Number One* (Simon & Schuster, 1989).

## 2 THE UNITED STATES: A FREE MARKET FOR CORPORATIONS

1 *The Second American Revolution* (Mobil Corporation, 1987).
2 Adam Smith, *The Wealth of Nations* (1776; 1905 edn), Vol. 1, p. 134.
3 Olivier Zunz, *Making America Corporate, 1870–1920* (Chicago University Press, 1992).
4 Alfred D. Chandler, Jr., *The Visible Hand: The Managerial Revolution in American Business* (Harvard University Press, 1977); *Scale and Scope: The Dynamics of Industrial Capitalism* (Harvard University Press, 1990) .
5 Daniel Yergin, *The Prize: The Epic Quest for Oil, Money, and Power* (Simon & Schuster, 1991), p. 55.
6 Arthur J. Eddy, *The New Competition* (Appleton, 1912), Epigraph.
7 James Bryce, *The American Commonwealth* (1888; Putnam, 1959 edn), Vol. 2, p. 401.

8 Robert Wiebe, *The Search for Order, 1877–1920* (Hill & Wang, 1967).

9 Chester I. Barnard, *The Functions of the Executive* (Harvard University Press, 1938); Terence R. Mitchell and William G. Scott, 'The Universal Barnard', *Public Administration Quarterly*, Fall 1985, Spring 1987.

10 Joseph A. Schumpeter, *Capitalism, Socialism, and Democracy* (Harper & Row, 1950), pp. 77–80 .

11 Charles Perrow, 'Markets, Hierarchy, and Hegemony', in Andrew Van der Ven and William F. Joyce (eds) *Organization Design and Behavior* (Wiley, 1981).

12 Zunz, *op. cit.*, pp. 40–46.

13 OECD, *Labour Force Statistics* (Paris, 1960, 1977, 1990); Richard Rose, *Public Employment in Western Nations* (Cambridge University Press, 1985), p. 11.

14 Rose, *op. cit.*, p. 45; cf. UK 56 per cent, France 55 per cent, West Germany 51 per cent.

15 Cf. Joel D. Aberbach *et al.*, *Bureaucrats and Politicians in Western Democracies* (Harvard University Press, 1981), p. 55, where only the US has an additional column for 'political appointees'.

16 Kevin Phillips, *The Politics of Rich and Poor* (HarperCollins, 1991), pp. 175–77.

17 Alice Fleming, *Ida Tarbell: First of the Muckrakers* (Crowell, 1971), p. 96.

18 Yergin, *op. cit.*, pp. 97, 104.

19 Bill Moyers, 'Listening to America: Corporate Campaign Contributions', PBS TV, 6 October 1992.

20 Phillips, *op. cit.*, p. 180.

21 James B. Stewart, *Den of Thieves* (Simon & Schuster, 1991); Ken Auletta, *Greed and Glory on Wall Street* (Random House, 1986).

22 Bernard Mandeville, *The Fable of the Bees, or, Private Vices Public Benefits* (1714).

23 Phillips, *op. cit.*, pp. 10–14.

24 *Ibid.*, pp. 15, 17, 241; see also Bennett Harrison and Harry Bluestone, *The Great U-Turn: Corporate Restructuring and the Polarization of America* (Basic Books, 1988), pp. 39–43.

25 *New York Times*, 7 October 1994.

26 John K. Galbraith, *The Culture of Contentment* (Houghton Mifflin, 1992).

27 Cf. Haynes Johnson, *Sleepwalking through History: America in the Reagan Years* (Anchor Books, 1992).

28 Cf. Robert M. Solow, Review of Edward N. Luttwak, *The Endangered American Dream* (Simon & Schuster, 1993), in *New York Review of Books*, 16 December 1993, p. 11.

29 Robert B. Reich, *The Work of Nations* (Knopf, 1991), pp. 72, 114.

30 E.g. Stefan H. Robock, 'Jobs Exported Overseas? It's a Myth', in *New York Times*, 27 November 1994.

31 Emma Rothschild, 'The Reagan Economic Legacy', in *New York Review of Books*, 21 July 1988, p. 38.

32 OECD, *Labour Force Statistics*, 1968, 1991; see Chapter 1, Table 1.2, this volume, for comparison with other leading countries.

33 Reich, *op. cit.*, p. 174.

34 *New York Times*, 10 July 1994.

35 Harrison and Bluestone, *op. cit.*, pp. 26–32.

36 Shintaro Ishihara, *The Japan that Can Say No*, (Simon & Schuster, 1991), p. 86.

37 Quoted in Norman Jones, 'The Hollow Corporation', *Business Week*, 3 March 1987.

38 *Newsweek*, 10 July 1989.

39 Reich, *op. cit.*, p. 83.

40 Harrison and Bluestone, *op. cit.*, Chapter 2 and p. 25; Susan Strange, *The Casino Society* (Blackwell, 1984).

41 Francis Fukuyama, *The End of History and the Last Man* (Free Press, 1989); Joseph S. Nye, Jr, *Bound to Lead: The Changing Nature of American Power* (Basic Books, 1990); Henry R. Nau, *The Myth of America's Decline: Leading the World Economy into the 1990s* (Oxford University Press, 1990).

42 James Champy, *Re-engineering Management* (HarperBusiness, 1995); for his original scheme see Michael Hammer and James Champy, *Re-engineering the Corporation* (HarperBusiness, 1993).

43 Graef S. Crystal, *In Search of Excess* (Norton, 1991); Robert A. G. Monks and Nell Minow, *Power and Accountability* (HarperCollins, 1991.

44 *Ibid.*, p. 167.

45 Crystal, *op. cit.*, p. 73.

46 Monks and Minow, *op. cit.*, p. 166–67.

47 Ishihara, *op. cit.*, p. 82.

48 Phillips, *op. cit.*, pp. 179–80; *Boiling Point: Democrats, Republicans, and the Decline of Middle-Class Prosperity* (Random House, 1993), pp. xxii, 251.

49 *Newsweek*, 1 March 1993.

50 Adolf A. Berle and Gardner C. Means, *The Modern Corporation and Private Property* (Macmillan, 1932).

51 Henry Demarest Lloyd, 'The Story of a Great Monopoly', *Atlantic Monthly*, 1881, and *Wealth against Commonwealth* (1894); Ida M. Tarbell, *The History of the Standard Oil Company* (1905); cf. Yergin, *op. cit.*, Chapter 5.

52 Thomas C. Cochrane and William Miller, *The Age of Enterprise* (Harper & Row, 1961), pp. 192–202; Zunz, *op. cit.*, p. 75.

53 Forrest McDonald, *Insull* (Chicago University Press, 1962), p. 134.

54 Zunz, *op. cit.*, pp. 70–75.

55 US Senate Committee on Banking, Housing, and Urban Affairs, 15 November 1979, p. 666, quoted in Louis Galambos and Joseph Pratt, *The Rise of the Corporate Commonwealth* (Basic Books, 1988), p. 262.

56 Chandler, *Scale and Scope*, p. 19, Table 5; United Nations, *World Investment Report, 1994*, pp. 1–12.

57 Paul Kennedy, *Preparing for the 21st Century* (Random House, 1993), p. 295.

58 *World Development Report* (World Bank, 1992), pp. 218–19, Table 1.

59 *Economist*, 25 October 1986.

60 Cf. Paul Kennedy, *The Rise and Fall of the Great Powers* (Random House, 1987), and press comment arising out of it, plus the many defensive counterblasts, including Annelise Anderson and Dennis L. Bark (ed.) *Thinking about America: The US in the 1990s* (Stanford University Press, 1987); Mark Green and Mark Pinsky (ed.) *America's Transition: Blueprints for the 1990s* (University Press of America, 1990); Joel Kotkin and Yoriko, *The Third Century: America's Resurgence in the Asian Era* (Crown Books, 1989); Fukuyama, Nye and Nau, *op. cit.*, and many more.

61 Cf. Phillips, *Boiling Point*, passim.

62 In 1992 US taxation was 37 per cent of GNP, compared with Britain 40 per cent, Germany 44 per cent, France 47 per cent, and Japan 34 per cent; US social security transfers in 1987 were 11 per cent of GNP, compared with Britain 14 per cent, West Germany 16 per cent, France 22 per cent, and Japan 12 per cent (see Chapter 1 above, Tables 1.8 and 1.12).

## 3 BRITAIN: KEYSTONE OF THE ARCH

1 Cf. Jonathan R. T. Hughes, *Industrialization and Economic Growth: Theses and Conjectures* (McGraw-Hill, 1970), pp. 44–45; Ashok Guha, *An Evolutionary View of Economic Growth* (Clarendon Press, 1981); C. H. Lee, *The British Economy since 1700* (Cambridge University Press, 1986), pp. 21–22; N. F. R. Crafts, *British Economic Growth during the Industrial Revolution* (Clarendon Press, 1985); Patrick O'Brien, *Economic Growth in Britain and France, 1780–1914* (Allen & Unwin, 1978).

2 Alexander Gerschenkron, *Economic Backwardness in Historical Perspective* (Harvard University Press, 1962), Introduction.

3 Joel Mokyr, 'Was there a British Industrial Revolution?', in *The Vital One: Essays in Honor of J. R. T. Hughes* (JAI Press, 1991), p. 255; H. De B. Gibbens, *The Industrial History of England* (Methuen, 1895); Arnold Toynbee, *Lectures on the Industrial Revolution* (Rivingtons, 1884).

4 Harold Perkin, *The Origins of Modern English Society, 1780–1880* (Routledge, 1969), pp. 3–4.

5 Sidney Pollard, *The Wasting of the British Economy: British Economic Policy since 1945* (Croom Helm, 1982), p. 6.

6 Keith Smith, *The British Economic Crisis: Its Past and Future* (Penguin, 1984), p. 81.

7 Malcolm Chalmers, *Paying for Defence: Military Spending and Economic Decline* (Pluto Press, 1985), p. 125.

8 See above, Chapter 1, Table 1.2.

9 Guy Routh, *Occupation and Pay in Great Britain, 1906–79* (Cambridge University Press, 1980), pp. 6–7, 45.

10 For a fuller exploration of this public/private sector rivalry, see Harold Perkin, *The Rise of Professional Society: England since 1880* (Routledge, 1989), pp. 9–17, 436–54, 495–506.

11 A. H. Halsey *et al.*, *Origins and Destinations: Family, Class and Education in Modern Britain* (Clarendon Press, 1980), Chapters 10 and 11.

12 *Social Trends, 1994* (HMSO, 1994), pp. 57–58.

13 University Grants Committee, *University Statistics, 1980–81* (HMSO, 1982), vol. 1, p. 51, Table 25.

14 Richard Rose, *Public Employment in Western Nations* (Cambridge University Press, 1985), p. 11; *Social Trends, 1992*, pp. 76, 115, 117; OECD, *Historical Statistics, 1960–87* (Paris, 1989), p. 38, Table 2.13.

15 Cf. T. H. Marshall, *Citizenship and Social Class* (Cambridge University Press, 1950); Richard Titmuss, *The Irresponsible Society* (Fabian Society, 1960), pp. 10–20.

16 Dennis Kavanagh, *Thatcherism and British Politics* (Oxford University Press, 1987), p. 294.

17 World Bank, *World Development Reports, 1984, 1994*, Table 26, Education; *Social Trends, 1994*, p. 47.

18 Leslie Hannah, *The Rise of the Corporate Economy* (Methuen, 1976), pp. 13 and 216, Table A2; Leslie Hannah and J. A. Kay, *Concentration in British Industry* (Macmillan, 1977), pp. 85, 96 and 89–91, Table 6.2; S. J. Prais, *The Evolution of Giant Firms, 1909–70* (Cambridge University Press, 1976), pp. 10, 13.

19 UNCTAD, *World Investment Report, 1994*, pp. 3–9.

20 OECD, *Historical Statistics*, p. 44, Table 3.1.

21 *Economist*, 25 October 1986.

22  Barry Supple, 'Fear of Failing: Economic History and the Decline of Britain', in *Economic History Review*, vol. 47, August 1994; and 'British Economic Growth since 1945', in Roderick Floud and Donald McCloskey, *The Economic History of Britain since 1700* (Cambridge University Press, 1994 edn), Vol. 3, pp. 318–46; Donald McCloskey, *Enterprise and Trade in Victorian Britain* (Allen & Unwin, 1981).

23  N. F. R. Crafts, *British Economic Growth during the Industrial Revolution* (Clarendon Press, 1985); Patrick K. O'Brien, *Economic Growth in Britain and France, 1780–1914* (Allen & Unwin, 1978); William Beckerman (ed.) *Slow Growth in Britain* (British Association for the Advancement of Science, Bath, 1978); Sir Alex Cairncross, 'The Post-War Years', in Floud and McCloskey, *op. cit.* (1981 edn), Vol. 2, p. 381.

24  Alfred D. Chandler, *Scale and Scope: The Dynamics of Industrial Capitalism* (Harvard University Press, 1990); Daniel Shiman, 'The Decline of the British Economy in the late 19th and early 20th Centuries', Ph.D. Dissertation, Northwestern University, 1992.

25  Chalmers, *op. cit.*, pp. 128, 35–36; W. A. P. Manser, *Britain in Balance: The Myth of Failure* (Penguin, 1971); Pollard, *op. cit.*; Paul Kennedy, *The Rise and Fall of the Great Powers* (Random House, 1987).

26  OECD, *Labour Force Statistics, 1994* and *Economic Surveys, UK, 1994* (Paris, 1994), Basic Statistics.

27  *Independent*, 9 July 1993.

28  Martin Wiener, *English Culture and the Decline of the Industrial Spirit* (Cambridge University Press, 1982 edn) and references in the Appendix: 'British Retardation – The Limits to Economic Explanation'.

29  Cf. Perkin, *Rise of Professional Society*, pp. 363–76.

30  W. D. Rubinstein, *Capitalism, Culture and Decline in Britain* (Routledge, 1993).

31  F. M. L. Thompson, *English Landed Society in the 19th Century* (Routledge, 1964), p. 306–7.

32  For a fuller discussion of this change, see Perkin, *Rise of Professional Society*, pp. 366–75.

33  OECD, *Historical Statistics*, p. 4, Table 3.7; *Economic Survey, 1994*, p. 128, Table E.

34  For further exposition see Harold Perkin, *Origins of Modern English Society* (Routledge, 1969), especially Chapter 2.

35  Vilfredo Pareto, *Sociological Writings*, S. E. Finer (ed.) (Blackwell, 1976), pp. 215–37.

36  Anthony Sampson, *The Essential Anatomy of Britain* (Hodder & Stoughton, 1992), p. 64.

37  Frank Harris, *My Life and Loves* (Grove, 1925), p. 730.

38  Alan Fox, *Beyond Contract: Work, Power, and Trust Relations* (Faber, 1974); Ralf Dahrendorf, *On Britain* (BBC, 1982), p. 85.

39  Alan Sked, *Britain's Decline* (Blackwell, 1987), p. 37.

40  B. W. E. Alford, 'New Industries for Old?', in Floud and McCloskey, *op. cit.*, (1981 edn), p. 329.

41  Cairncross, *op. cit.*, p. 383.

42  Cf. *Independent*, 4 February 1990.

43  See Chapter 1 above, Table 1.1: GDP per head in 1984 dollars: Britain 1950 $5,000, 1984 $11,068; Japan 1950 $1,486, 1984 $12,235.

44  David Butler and Anne Sloman, *British Political Facts, 1900–79* (Macmillan, 1980), pp. 208–10.

45  Kenneth O. Morgan, *The People's Peace: British History 1945–89* (Oxford University Press, 1990), p. 481.
46  *The Economist*, 18 January 1986.
47  Leslie Hannah, 'Crisis and Turnaround? 1973–93', in Paul Johnson (ed.) *Twentieth-Century Britain: Economic, Social and Cultural Change* (Longman, 1994), p. 347.
48  John Hendy, *The Conservative Employment Laws* (Institute of Employment Rights, 1990); Keith Ewing, *The Employment Act, 1990* (*ibid.*, 1991).
49  Hendy, *op. cit.*; OECD, *Economic Outlook*, July 1994.
50  Hendy, *op. cit.*, pp. 27–33.
51  *Guardian*, 18 February 1995.
52  *Ibid.*, 6 January, 9 February 1995.
53  *Ibid.*, 4 September 1993.
54  *Observer*, 3 July 1994.
55  Wessex Regional Hospital Authority, headed by Sir Richard Buchanan, since promoted to head the privatized National Health Service Supplies: BBC 1, *Panorama*, 12 July 1993.
56  No Turning Back Group, *Who Benefits? Reinventing Social Security*, reported in the *Independent*, 3 August 1993.
57  For references see Perkin, *Rise of Professional Society*, pp. 123–41.
58  R. H. Tawney, *Equality* (Allen & Unwin, 1931), pp. 108–16; *The Acquisitive Society* (Harcourt, Brace, and Howe, 1920), p. 180.
59  Herbert Spencer, *Social Statics* (Williams and Norgate, 1851, pp. 322–23).
60  Cf. Perkin, *Rise of Professional Society*, pp. 141–49.
61  Karl Pearson, *The Grammar of Science* and *The Ethic of Free Thought* (Black, 1900, 1901); Benjamin Kidd, *Social Evolution* (Macmillan, 1894).
62  Archbishop George Carey, reported in the *Independent*, 6 October 1992.
63  Cf. David Marquand, *The Unprincipled Society* (Jonathan Cape, 1988).
64  Alfred D. Chandler, *The Visible Hand: The Managerial Revolution in American Business* (Harvard University Press, 1977).
65  Cadbury Report on Executive Governance, reported in the *Guardian*, 1 December 1992.
66  *First Report of the Committee on Standards in Public Life* (Chairman Lord Nolan, Cm 2850-I, May 1995); Commons votes, *Hansard*, 19 July 1995.
67  *Report on Executive Pay* (Chairman Sir Richard Greenbury, CBI, July 1995).
68  *Institute of Fiscal Studies Report* on the impact of tax reforms on distribution of income, 1994.
69  *Financial Times*, 16/17 July 1994; *Observer*, 1 August 1993.
70  *Observer*, 25 July 1993, 13 February 1994.
71  John Hills *et al.*, *Inquiry into Income and Wealth* (Joseph Rowntree Trust, 1995); *Guardian*, 10 February 1995.
72  *Social Trends, 1992*, pp. 150, 203–4.
73  *Independent*, 16 July 1993, evidence of Mark Higgins before House of Commons Select Committee; and Scott Inquiry into Churchill Matrix Affair, Evidence and Report.
74  *Observer*, 11 July 1993.
75  Sir John Woodcock to the International Police Conference at the Barbican Centre, London, *Guardian*, 14 October 1992.

## 4 FRANCE: A PLANNED MERITOCRACY

1 Ezra N. Suleiman, *Elites in French Society* (Princeton University Press, 1978), pp. 43, 45.
2 Jean-Pierre Jallade, *Les Premiers années d'enseignement supérieur dans la perspective de 1993* (Institut Europeen d'Education et de Politique Sociale, 1990), Vol. 1, pp. 34–36.
3 C. Grignon and J.-C. Passeron, *Innovation in Higher Education: French Experience before 1968* (Paris: OECD, 1970), pp. 30–44.
4 Suleiman, *op. cit.*, p. 110.
5 David Granick, *Managerial Comparisons of Four Developed Countries: France, Britain, United States. and Russia* (MIT University Press, 1972), p. 187.
6 Cf. John Ardagh, *France in the 1980s* (Secker & Warburg, 1982), pp. 82–92.
7 Grignon and Passeron, *op. cit.*, Chap. 5.
8 Ardagh, *op. cit.*, p. 90.
9 Raymond Bourdieu and J.-C. Passeron, *Les Héritiers: Les Etudiants et la Culture* (Editions de Minuit, 1964) and *La Réproduction* (Editions de Minuit, 1970); Raymond Boudon, *L'Inégalite des chances* (Paris: Colin, 1973); Alain Girard, *Le Réussite sociale en France* (PUF, 1961) and *'Population' et l'enseignement* (PUF, 1974).
10 Jane Marceau, *Class and Status in France: Economic Change and Social Immobility, 1945–75* (Clarendon Press, 1977), pp. 3–5, 117.
11 Bourdieu and Passeron, *Les Héritiers*; Marceau, *op. cit.*, p. 114.
12 Gerard Mermet, *Francoscopie, 1993: Qui sont les Francais?* (Larousse, 1993), p. 110.
13 Marceau, *op. cit.*, Table 5.6, p. 110.
14 Mermet, *op. cit.*, p. 109.
15 *Données Sociales* (Paris, 1990), p. 409; *OECD Economic Survey: UK, 1994*: Basic Statistics.
16 Mermet, *op. cit.*, p. 277.
17 *Données Sociales*, pp. 136, 412, 416, 425.
18 Jean-Pierre Jallade (ed.) *The Crisis of Distribution in European Welfare States* (Trentham Books, 1988), pp. 11, 223.
19 Cf. Bruno Jobert, 'Democracy and Social Policies: The Example of France', in John S. Ambler (ed.) *The French Welfare State* (New York University Press, 1991).
20 Douglas E. Ashford, 'Advantages of Complexity', in Ambler, *op. cit.*, pp. 27–28.
21 Remi Lenoir, 'Family Policy in France since 1938', in *ibid.*, pp.153–55.
22 *OECD Economic Surveys: UK, 1994*: Basic Statistics; and OECD, *Historical Statistics, 1960–87*, p. 44, Table 3.1.
23 Mermet, *op. cit.*, p. 275; *OECD Economic Survey: UK, 1994*: Basic Statistics.
24 *Données Sociales*, p. 31.
25 *Ibid.*, pp. 140–41.
26 Mermet, *op. cit.*, pp. 208–9.
27 *Données Sociales*, p. 169.
28 Mermet, *op. cit.*, p. 208.
29 Simone de Beauvoir, *The Second Sex* (1949); Kate Fullbrook and Edward Fullbrook, *Simone de Beauvoir and Jean-Paul Sartre: The Remaking of a 20th-Century Legend* (Basic Books, 1994), Chapter 5.
30 Mermet, *op. cit.*, p. 263.
31 *Données Sociales*, p. 31.

32  Mermet, *op. cit.*, pp. 321–32; *Données Sociales*, pp. 332–34.
33  Jobert, *op. cit.*, p. 244; Ashford, *op. cit.*, pp. 46–47.
34  Jeremy Bacon and James K. Brown, *The Board of Directors: Perspectives and Practices in Nine Countries* (New York: Conference Board, Report No. 728), quoted in Jonathan Charkham, *Keeping Good Company: A Study of Corporate Governance in Five Countries* (Clarendon Press, 1994), p. 120.
35  Michel Bauer and Benedicte Bertin-Mourot of CRNS, reported in the *Guardian*, 11 March 1995.
36  Michel Bauer and Dominique Danic of CRNS, reported in *Le Monde*, 23 May 1990. I owe this reference to my friend Jean Lajudie of Paris, retired civil servant.
37  Granick, *op. cit.*, p. 187.
38  Bauer and Danic, *op. cit.*
39  Charkham, *op. cit.*, pp. 122–25.
40  UNCTAD, *World Investment Report, 1994* (United Nations, 1994), p. 8.
41  Charkham, *op. cit.*, p. 125.
42  *Ibid.*, p. 127.
43  *Ibid.*, pp. 28–38; *Guardian*, 18 February 1995.
44  *Ibid.*, p. 150.
45  Opinion survey data from Mermet, *op. cit.*, pp. 218–19.
46  Report by Adam Sage in the *Observer*, 17 July 1994.
47  *Ibid.*
48  Malcolm Sawyer, *Income Distribution in OECD Countries* (OECD, 1976), Tables 3, 4, 5; *Données Sociales*, pp. 141, 151; Kevin Phillips, *The Politics of Rich and Poor* (HarperCollins, 1991), p. 9.
49  Mermet, *op. cit.*, pp. 209–10.

## 5 GERMANY: TWO VERSIONS OF PROFESSIONAL SOCIETY

1  Ralf Dahrendorf, *Society and Democracy in Germany* (Weidenfeld & Nicolson, 1968).
2  OECD, *Economic Survey: UK, 1994*: Basic Statistics (for West Germany only but true even without the Eastern *Länder*).
3  Alan Sked, *Britain's Decline* (Blackwell, 1987), p. 33, Table 2.5: average percentages of GDP spent on defence 1950–83: USA 7.3; UK 6.0; France 5.0; West Germany 3.8; Japan 1.0.
4  Jaroslav Krejci, *Social Structure in Divided Germany* (Croom Helm, 1976), pp. 20, 118, Table 3.18.
5  V. R. Bergahn, *Modern Germany: Society, Economy and Politics in the 20th Century* (Cambridge University Press, 1987), p. 227.
6  OECD, *Labour Force Statistics, 1969, 1981, 1994*.
7  Cf. Chapter 1 above, Table 1.2.
8  Wallner/Funke-Schmitt-Rink, *Soziale Schichtung und Soziale Mobilität* (1980), p. 27, cited by Angi Rutter, 'Elites, Estate, and Class in West Germany since 1945' in Arthur Marwick (ed.) *Class in the 20th Century* (St Martin's Press, 1986), p. 155.
9  Krejci, *op. cit.*, pp. 96–97.
10  *Ibid.*, pp. 96–97, 104–5.
11  Cf. Angi Rutter, *op. cit.*, *passim*.

12 Ulrich Teichler, 'The First Years of Study and the Role Played by *Fachhoch-schulen* in the FDR', Report presented to the European Institute of Education and Social Policy, July 1989, pp. 22, 24, 30, 51.
13 Dahrendorf, *op. cit.*; cf. Angi Rutter, *op. cit.*
14 Hartmut Kaelble, *Social Mobility in the 19th and 20th Centuries* (St Martin's Press, 1985), esp. Chapter 1.
15 G. A. Almond and S. Verba, *The Civic Culture: Attitudes and Democracy in Five Nations* (Princeton University Press, 1963), p. 275; Krejci, *op. cit.*, p. 167.
16 Mary Fulbrook, *The Divided Society: A History of Germany, 1918–90* (Oxford University Press, 1991), p. 240.
17 World Bank, *World Development Report, 1993*, Table 26.
18 Teichler, *op. cit.*, pp. 24, 51.
19 Krejci, *op. cit.*, pp. 165–66.
20 *Ibid.*, p. 24.
21 See Chapter 1 above, Table 1.8.
22 *World Development Report, 1994*, Table 11.
23 Peter J. Katzenstein, *Policy and Politics in West Germany* (Temple University Press, 1987), p. 86.
24 *Ibid.*, pp. 66–67, 169, 176–79.
25 David Cameron, 'Continuity and Change in French Social Policy', in John S. Ambler (ed.) *The French Welfare State* (New York University Press, 1991), p. 60.
26 Teichler, *op. cit.*, p. 22, Table 4.
27 *Ibid.*, pp. 24, 30–31.
28 Krejci, *op. cit.*, p. 101.
29 Fulbrook, *op. cit.*, pp. 231–32.
30 Krejci, *op. cit.*, p. 105.
31 Peter Hayes, *Industry and Ideology: I. G. Farben in the Nazi Era* (Cambridge University Press, 1987), p. 377.
32 Katzenstein, *op. cit.*, p. 134; Bergahn, *op. cit.*, p. 283.
33 Alfred D. Chandler, *Scale and Scope: The Dynamics of Industrial Capitalism* (Harvard University Press, 1990), p. 19, Table 5; see also Chapter 4, 'Germany: Cooperative Managerial Capitalism'; *Statistical Abstract of US, 1994*, p. 871.
34 Jonathan Charkham, *Keeping Good Company: A Study of Corporate Governance in Five Countries* (Clarendon Press, 1994), pp. 8, 10.
35 *Ibid.*, p.51.
36 Cf., *inter alia*, Jeremy Edwards and Klaus Fischer, *Banks, Finance and Investment in Germany* (Cambridge University Press, 1994).
37 Katzenstein, *op. cit.*, pp. 64–65, 129–34.
38 *Ibid.*, p.169.
39 *Guardian*, Letters (Colin Hines and Tim Lang), 22 February 1994.
40 *World Investment Report, 1994*, pp. 363–69; *Guardian*, 18 February 1995.
41 Krejci, *op. cit.*, pp. 29–30.

## 6 SOVIET RUSSIA: GULLIVER'S GIANT

1 Basile Kerblay, *Modern Soviet Society* (Methuen, 1983), pp. 212–13.
2 Moshe Lewin, *The Gorbachev Phenomenon* (University of California Press, 1988), pp. 31–32.
3 OECD, *Labour Force Statistics,1968–91* (Paris, 1992), pp. 68–91.
4 Cf. Geoffrey Hosking, *The Awakening of the Soviet Union* (Heinemann, 1990), Chapter 4.

5 Lewin, *op. cit.*, pp. 47–50.
6 Kerblay, *op. cit.*, p. 249.
7 Mervyn Matthews, *Privilege in the Soviet Union* (Allen & Unwin, 1978), p. 31.
8 Kerblay, *op. cit.*, pp. 262–63.
9 Alexander Simirenko, *Professionalization of Soviet Society* (Transaction Books, 1982), Chapter 2.
10 L. A. Gordon and V. V. Komorovsky, 'Dinamika sotsial'no-professional'nogo sostava pokolenii', in *Sotsiologicheskie Issledovania*, vol. 3, 1986, cited by Lewin, pp. 50–55.
11 Roy Medvedev, *Let History Judge* (Columbia University Press, 1989); Robert Conquest, *The Great Terror* (Macmillan,1968) and *Harvest of Sorrow* (Oxford University Press, 1986); Aleksandr Solzhenitsyn, *The Gulag Archipelago* (3 Vols, Harper & Row, 1974–78); cf. David Remnick, *Lenin's Tomb* (Vintage, 1994), p. 129. Estimates of those killed range from Conquest's 14 million to Medvedev's 40 million and to Solzhenitsyn's 60 million.
12 Tatyana Zaslavskaya, *The Second Socialist Revolution* (Tauris, 1990), p. 10; for the epithet, see my review, 'La Perestroika' and report on the interview with her in the *London Review of Books*, 24 January 1991.
13 Interview with Zaslavskaya, Moscow, July 1990.
14 Review of Frances de Plessix Gray, *Soviet Women: Walking the Tightrope* (Doubleday, 1990), in *New York Review of Books*, 31 May 1990.
15 'The Novosibirsk Report, with a Comment by Philip Hanson', *Survey*, vol. 7, no. 1, Spring 1984, pp. 88–108.
16 Zaslavskaya, *op. cit.*, pp. 13–14
17 Thane Gustafson, *Reform in Soviet Politics: Lessons of Recent Policies on Land and Water* (Cambridge University Press, 1981); James Brennan, 'Water under the Arch: Bureaucracies and Water Policy in the United States and the Soviet Union', unpublished paper, Northwestern University, 1994. For a similar destruction of the environment see Marc Reisner, *Cadillac Desert: The American West and its Disappearing Water* (Penguin, 1987), esp. Chapter 12 and Epilogue.
18 Zaslavskaya, *op. cit.*, pp. 7–8; Hedrick Smith, *The New Russians* (Random House, 1990), pp. 311–12.
19 Gaetano Mosca, *The Ruling Class* (McGraw-Hill, 1939), p. 485; Milovan Djilas, *The New Class* (Praeger, 1957), Chapter 3.
20 Sergei Shishkin, 'The Russian Ruling Elite Redividing Property among Themselves', Lecture to the Woodrow Wilson Center, Princeton University, 25 October 1994.
21 Kerblay, *op. cit.*, pp. 88, 130; Matthews, *op. cit.*, pp. 21–23.
22 Matthews, *op. cit.*, pp. 36–46.
23 Remnick, *op. cit.*, pp. 172–73.
24 Matthews, *op. cit.*, pp. 47–55.
25 *Ibid.*, p. 178.
26 Arkady Vaksberg, *The Soviet Mafia* (St Martin's Press, 1991), pp. 18–19.
27 Hedrick Smith, *op. cit.*, p. 91.
28 Vaksberg, *op. cit.*, pp. 3–17.
29 *Ibid.*, pp. 108–14.
30 Hedrick Smith, *op. cit.*, pp. 312–15.
31 Vaksberg, pp. 121–23.
32 *Ibid.*, pp. 116–36.
33 *Ibid.*, pp. 124–30.
34 *Ibid.*, pp. 138–68.

35  *Ibid.*, pp. 174–76, 181, 188–92.
36  *The Independent*, 28 July 1993.
37  Vaksberg, *op. cit.*, pp. 13, 133, 258.
38  *Ibid.*, pp. 77–78, and illustrations nos. 5, 7 and 16.
39  Alfred D. Chandler, Jr, *The Visible Hand: The Managerial Revolution in American Business* (Harvard University Press, 1977), as we have seen in Chapter 2, argues that the corporation came into existence to escape and control the market.
40  Zaslavskaya, *op. cit.*, pp. 17–18.
41  Vaksberg, *op. cit.*, p. 261.
42  Reproduced in Valerie Bunce, 'Gorbachev and Reform', *Northwestern University Arts and Sciences* (magazine), Fall, 1988.
43  Boris Yeltsin, *Against the Grain* (Jonathan Cape, 1990), p. 3.
44  Mikhail Gorbachev, *Perestroika: New Thinking for Our Country and for the World* (Fontana/Collins, 1988), pp. 290–91.
45  Hedrick Smith, *op. cit.*, pp. 204–5.
46  *Ibid.*, pp. 231–32.
47  Vaksberg, *op. cit.*, pp. 258–59.

## 7 JAPAN: A FLOATING WORLD

1   Chie Nakane, *Japanese Society* (Penguin, 1973), Chap. 2; for different views of the 'class-ridden' nature of Japanese society, see Tadashi Fukutaki, *The Japanese Social Structure* (University of Tokyo Press, 1983); and Roy Steven, *Classes in Contemporary Japan* (Cambridge University Press, 1983).
2   Ronald Dore, *British Factory – Japanese Factory* (Allen & Unwin, 1973), esp. Chapters 10 and 12.
3   B. C. Koh, *Japan's Administrative Elite* (University of California Press 1989), pp. 37–38.
4   Karel van Wolferen, *The Enigma of Japanese Power* (Vintage, 1990), p. 109; cf. also Chalmers Johnson, *Japan: Who Governs?* (Norton, 1995), and Eamonn Fingleton, *Blindside: Why Japan is Still on Track to Overtake the United States by the Year 2000* (Houghton Mifflin, 1995).
5   Koh, *op. cit.*, pp. 87, 91–92, 97, 140–41; Wolferen, *op. cit.*, p. 111.
6   Chalmers Johnson, *MITI and the Japanese Miracle* (Stanford University Press, 1982); James C. Abegglen and George Stalk, Jr, *Kaisha: The Japanese Corporation* (Basic Books, 1985).
7   Wolferen, *op. cit.*, pp. 115, 118–19.
8   Koh, *op. cit.*, pp. 238–39; Bernard Eccleston, *State and Society in Post-War Japan* (Polity Press, 1989), pp. 113–14.
9   Koh, *op. cit.*, pp. 242–43.
10  *Ibid.*, pp. 242–43.
11  *Ibid.*, pp. 228–29; Chalmers Johnson, 'Tanaka Kakuei, Structural Corruption, and the Advent of Machine Politics in Japan', *Journal of Japanese Studies*, vol. 12, 1986, p. 1.
12  Cf. Laura Hein, *Fuelling Growth: The Energy Revolution and Economic Policy in Postwar Japan*, (Harvard, 1990); Takatoshi Ito, *The Japanese Economy* (MIT Press, 1992).
13  Cf. Laura Hein, 'What do Economists dream about? – Doubling Income to Build Community', unpublished paper at Conference of Association of Asian Studies, Los Angeles, 27 March 1993.

14  Alan Sked, *Britain's Decline* (Blackwell, 1987), p. 30.
15  OECD, *Historical Statistics, 1960–87*, p. 44, Table 3.1 (the years averaged are 1960–68; 1968–73; 1973–79, 1979–87).
16  Chalmers Johnson, *MITI*, p. 71.
17  Eccleston, *op. cit.*, p. 94.
18  Cf. Edward A. Feigenbaum and Pamela McCorduck, *The Fifth Generation* (Addison-Wellesley, 1983); but see J. Marshall Unger, *The Fifth Generation Fallacy: Why Japan is betting its Future on Artificial Intelligence* (Oxford University Press, 1988).
19  Chalmers Johnson, *MITI*, pp. 242, 247.
20  J. P. Womack, Daniel T. Jones, and Daniel Roos, *The Machine that Changed the World* (Rawson Associates, 1990), Part 2.
21  Shintaro Ishihara, *The Japan that Can Say No* (Simon & Schuster, 1989).
22  Womack *et al.*, *The Machine that Changed the World*, p. 195.
23  OECD, *Economic Surveys: Japan* (Paris, 1989), Basic Statistics.
24  OECD, *Japan*, pp. 96–97.
25  OECD, *Economic Survey: UK, 1994*, Basic Statistics. By 1991 Japan had a per capita GDP of $27,005 but at current PPRs of only $18,957, compared with USA $22,204 (exchange rate and PPP), Germany $19,687, France $18,152, Italy $16,866, and Britain $15,608.
26  World Bank, *World Development Report, 1989*, Table 30.
27  *Japan Statistical Yearbook, 1985*, p. 109; Eccleston, *op. cit.*, p. 165.
28  *Newsweek*, 15 January 1990.
29  Misiko Hane, *Peasants, Rebels, and Outcasts: The Underside of Modern Japan* (Pantheon, 1982), esp. pp. 138–71, 236–45.
30  Cf. Norma J. Chalmers, *Industrial Relations in Japan: The Peripheral Sector* (Routledge, 1989).
31  Eccleston, *op. cit.*, p. 205, from Management Coordination Agency, Foreign Press Centre, 1986.
32  *New York Times*, 9 October 1994.
33  In *Kumamoto Nichinichi Shimbun* newspaper, quoted in Edward P. Hoyt, *The New Japanese* (Robert Hall, 1991), p. 21.
34  Wolferen, *op. cit.*, pp. 133–35.
35  *Ibid.*, pp. 118, 136–37.
36  *Independent*, 22 July 1993.
37  Wolferen, *op. cit.*, pp. 100–7.
38  Bill Emmott, *The Sun also Sets: Why Japan will not be Number One* (Simon & Schuster, 1989).
39  Michael Young, *The Rise of The Meritocracy* (Penguin, 1948).

## 8  TOWARDS A GLOBAL PROFESSIONAL SOCIETY

1  *Guardian*, 8 March 1995.
2  US Senate Committee on Banking, Housing, and Urban Affairs, 15 November 1979, p. 666.
3  *Statistical Abstract of United States, 1994* (US Dept of Commerce, 1994), p. 860.
4  OECD, *Economic Surveys: UK, 1994*: Basic Statistics.
5  UNCTAD, *World Investment Report, 1994*, pp. 215–16.
6  *Ibid.*, pp. 3–9.
7  *Statistical Abstract of US*, p. 871.
8  Robert B. Reich, *The Work of Nations* (Knopf, 1991), Chap. 10, 'The Global Web'.

9 *World Investment Report*, pp. 6–7; World Bank, *World Development Report, 1993*, Table 3.

10 *World Investment Report*, pp. 12, 17.

11 Edward Said, *Culture and Imperialism* (Vintage, 1993); Immanuel Wallerstein, *The Modern World System* (Academic Press, 1974); Eric R. Wolf, *Europe and the People without History* (University of California Press, 1982).

12 *World Investment Report*, Chapters 5 and 6.

13 J. M. Keynes, *The General Theory of Employment, Interest, and Money* (Macmillan, 1936).

14 Vilfredo Pareto, *The Rise and Fall of Elites* (Bedminster Press, 1968), p. 36.

15 Chalmers Johnson, 'Tanaka Kakuei, Structural Corruption, and the Advent of Machine Politics in Japan', *Journal of Japanese Studies*, vol. 12, 1986, pp. 1–28.

16 Ralf Dahrendorf, *Society and Democracy in Germany* (Weidenfeld & Nicolson, 1968).

17 *The Economist*, 11–17 March 1995, p. 160; OECD, *Economic Surveys, 1994*: Basic Statistics.

18 See *inter alia* F. A. von Hayek, *The Road to Serfdom* (Routledge & Kegan Paul, 1944), *The Constitution of Liberty* (Routledge & Kegan Paul, 1960), and *Law, Legislation and Liberty* (Routledge, 1982).

19 Cf. Lionel Robbins, *The Theory of Economic Policy in English Classical Political Economy* (Macmillan, 1952); Herbert Spencer, *The Man versus the State* (Williams and Norgate, 1884); Alexander Pope, *Essay on Man* (1733), Epistle 4, line 396; Bernard Mandeville, *The Fable of the Bees, or Private Vices Public Benefits* (1714).

20 Cf. Harold Perkin, *Origins of Modern English Society* (Routledge, 1969), pp. 52–55.

21 John Donne, *Devotions on Emergent Occasions*, 17 (1624).

22 Kevin Phillips, *The Politics of Rich and Poor* (HarperCollins, 1991).

23 *Social Trends, 24, 1994*, p. 76.

24 Derek Bok, *The Cost of Talent: How Executives and Professionals are Paid and How it Affects America* (Free Press, 1994).

25 *Guardian*, 6 January, 1 February 1995.

26 *New York Times*, 12 April 1992.

27 Alfred D. Chandler, *The Visible Hand: The Managerial Revolution in American Business* (Harvard University Press, 1977).

28 Charles Perrow, 'Markets, Hierarchy, and Hegemony', in Andrew Van der Ven and William F. Joyce, *Perspectives on Organization Design and Behavior* (Wiley, 1991).

29 Robert Heller, *The Naked Manager* (E. P. Dutton, 1985).

30 OECD, *Historical Statistics, 1960–87*, p. 44, Table 3.2.

31 Angus Maddison, *Dynamic Forces in Capitalist Development* (Oxford University Press, 1991), p. 49.

32 *Statistical Abstract of US*, p. 806; *Britain: A Handbook* (HMSO, 1994), p. 122.

33 *Social Trends 24, 1994*, p. 79.

34 Hayek, *A Tiger by the Tail* (Institute of Economic Affairs, 1972), p. 111.

35 *Guardian*, 18 February 1995.

36 Richard J. Franke, *A Business Man's View of Responsible Participation in Democracy*, Lecture at Sangamon State University, Springfield, Illinois, 13 April 1989 (John Nuveen & Co., 1989).

37 *World Development Report*, pp. 319, 321.

38 *Ibid.*, p. 323.

39 *Ibid.*, pp. 324–39.
40 *Ibid.*, pp. xxiv, 215–18, 225, 228.

## EPILOGUE: WHAT IS TO BE DONE?

1 Cf. Harold Perkin, 'The History of Social Forecasting', in Christopher Freeman *et al.*, *Progress and Problems in Social Forecasting* (SSRC, 1974).
2 John Stuart Mill, *Principles of Economics* (1848, Longman, 1904 edn), p. 123.
3 Lester Thurow, *Head to Head: The Coming Economic Battle among Japan, Europe and America* (Morrow, 1992); Robert B. Reich, *The Work of Nations* (Knopf, 1991); Will Hutton, *The State We're In* (Jonathan Cape, 1995).
4 David Marquand, *The Unprincipled Society* (Jonathan Cape, 1988).
5 John Gray, 'Hollowing out the Core', *Guardian*, 8 March 1995.
6 George Soros, *The Alchemy of Finance: Reading the Mind of the Market* (Wiley, 1994); Felix Rohatyn, *The Twenty-Year Century: Essays on Economics and Public Finance* (Random House, 1983).
7 Hutton, *op. cit.*, pp. 21–22; Robert B. Reich, *The Next American Frontier* (Times Books, 1984).
8 Cf. Chapter 7, above.
9 Gray, *Guardian*, 8 March 1995.
10 UNCTAD, *World Development Report, 1994*, p.278

# SELECT BIBLIOGRAPHY

Abegglen, James C. and Stalk, George, Jr. (1985) *Kaisha: The Japanese Corporation* (Basic Books).

Aberbach, Joel D. *et al.* (1981) *Bureaucrats and Politicians in Western Democracies* (Harvard University Press).

Abrams, Mark, Gerard, David, and Timms, Noel (eds) (1985) *Values and Social Change in Britain* (Macmillan).

Aganbegyan, Abel (1988) *The Challenge: Economics of Perestroika* (Hutchinson).

Albrow, Martin (1970) *Bureaucracy* (Macmillan).

Almond, G. A. and Verba, S. (1963) *The Civic Culture: Attitudes and Democracy in Five Nations* (Princeton University Press).

Ambler, John S. (ed.) (1991) *The French Welfare State* (New York University Press).

Anderson, Annelise and Bark, Dennis L. (1987) *Thinking about America: The US in the 1990s* (Stanford University Press).

Ardagh, John (1982) *France in the 1980s* (Secker & Warburg).

—— (1987) *Germany and the Germans* (Hamish Hamilton).

Armstrong, John A. (1973) *The European Administrative Elite* (Princeton University Press).

—— (1986) *Ideology, Politics and Government in the Soviet Union* (University Press of America).

Aso, Makoto and Amano, Ikuo (1972/1975) *Education and Japanese Modernization* (Japanese Ministry of Foreign Affairs; London: Japanese Embassy) .

Auletta, Ken (1986) *Greed and Glory on Wall Street* (Random House).

Bacon, Jeremy and Brown, James K. (1977) *The Board of Directors: Perspectives and Practices in Nine Countries* (New York: Conference Board).

Balfour, Michael (1982) *West Germany: A Contemporary History* (Croom Helm).

Bark, Dennis L. and Gress, David R. (1993) *A History of West Germany, 1945–63* and *1963–88* (Blackwell, 2 Vols).

Beauchamp, Edward (ed) (1989) *Windows on Japanese Education* (Greenwood Press).

Bell, Daniel (1973) *The Coming of Post-Industrial Society* (Penguin).

Bergahn, Volker R. (1987) *Modern Germany: Society, Economy and Politics in the 20th Century* (Cambridge University Press).

Berghahn, Volker R. and Karsten, Detlev (1987) *Industrial Relations in West Germany* (Berg).

Blackaby, Frank (ed) (1979) *Deindustrialization* (Heinemann).

Bledstein, Burton J. (1976) *The Culture of Professionalism* (Norton).

Böhme, Helmut (1978) *An Introduction to the Social and Economic History of Germany: Politics and Economic Change in the 19th and 20th Centuries* (Blackwell).

234

Bok, Derek (1994) *The Cost of Talent: How Executives are Paid and How it Affects America* (Free Press).

Boltansky, L. (1983) *Les Cadres: La formation d'un groupe social* (Editions de Minuit).

Boudon, Raymond (1973) *L'Inégalité des chances* (Colin).

Bourdieu, Pierre (1989) *La Noblesse d'état: Grandes écoles et esprit de corps* (Editions de Minuit).

Bourdieu, Raymond and Passeron, J.-C. (1964) *Les Héritiers: Les Etudiants et la Culture* (Editions de Minuit).

—— (1970) *La Reproduction* (Editions de Minuit).

Brint, Steven (1994) *In an Age of Experts: The Changing Role of Professionals in Politics and Public Life* (Princeton University Press).

Brittan, Samuel (1988) *A Restatement of Economic Liberalism* (Macmillan).

Browning, Alison (1984) *L'Europe et les intellectuels* (Gallimard, for the Centre de la Culture).

Bulmer, Simon and Paterson, William (1987) *The Federal Republic of Germany and the European Community* (Allen & Unwin).

Burks, Ardath W. (1984) *Japan: A Post-Industrial Society* (Westview Press).

Burnham, James (1941) *The Managerial Revolution* (Day and Co.).

Butler, Sir Robin (1992) *The New System of Public Management* (Frank Stacey Memorial Lecture, Conference of Joint Universities Council, September).

Cadbury, Sir Adrian (1992) *Code of Best Practice* (Committee Report on Corporate Governance).

Cerny, Philip and Schain, Martin A. (eds) (1985) *Socialism, the State and Public Policy in France* (Pinter; Methuen).

Chalmers, Malcolm (1985) *Paying for Defence: Military Spending and Economic Decline* (Pluto Press).

Chalmers, Norma J. (1989) *Industrial Relations in Japan: The Peripheral Sector* (Routledge).

Champy, James (1995) *Re-engineering Management* (HarperBusiness).

Chandler, Alfred D., Jr. (1977) *The Visible Hand: The Managerial Revolution in American Business* (Harvard University Press).

—— (1990) *Scale and Scope: The Dynamics of Industrial Capitalism* (Harvard University Press).

Chapman, William (1991) *Inventing Japan: The Making of a New Civilization* (Prentice-Hall).

Charkham, Jonathan (1994) *Keeping Good Company: A Study of Corporate Governance in Five Countries* (Clarendon Press).

Childe, V. Gordon (1983) *Man Makes Himself* (New American Library).

Childs, David (1988) *The GDR: Moscow's German Ally* (Unwin Hyman).

Childs, David and Johnson, J. (1978) *West Germany: Politics and Society* (Croom Helm).

Childs, David, Baylis, Thomas A., and Rueschmeyer, Marion (eds) (1989) *East Germany in Comparative Perspective* (Routledge).

Clarke, Peter (1991) *A Question of Leadership: Gladstone to Thatcher* (Hamish Hamilton).

Cockett, Richard (1993) *Thinking the Unthinkable: Think-Tanks and the Economic Counter-Revolution* (HarperCollins).

Cocks, Geoffrey and Jarausch, Konrad H. (eds) (1990) *German Professions, 1800–1950* (Oxford University Press).

Conquest, Robert (1968) *The Great Terror* (Macmillan).

—— (1986) *Harvest of Sorrow* (Oxford University Press).

—— (1986) *The Last Empire: Nationality and the Soviet Future* (Hoover Institute Press).

Corbett, James (1994) *Through French Windows: An Introduction to France in the Nineties* (Michigan University Press).

Crafts, Nicholas F. R. (1985) *British Economic Growth during the Industrial Revolution* (Clarendon Press).

Cronin, James E. (1979) *Industrial Conflict in Modern Britain* (Croom Helm).

—— (1983) *Labour and Society in Britain, 1918–79* (Schocken).

—— (1991) *The Politics of State Expansion: War, State and Society in Twentieth-Century Britain* (Routledge).

Crouch, Colin and Dore, Ronald (eds) (1990) *Corporatism and Accountability: Organized Interests in British Public Life* (Clarendon Press).

Crystal, Graef (1991) *In Search of Excess* (Norton).

*Current Digest of Soviet Press*, various dates.

Dahrendorf, Ralf (1968) *Society and Democracy in Germany* (Weidenfeld & Nicolson).

—— (1982) *On Britain* (BBC).

—— (1990) *Modern Social Conflict* (University of California Press).

—— (Chairman) (1995) *Commission on Wealth Creation and Social Cohesion: Report* (Liberal Democratic Party).

Dale, Peter N. (1990) *The Myth of Japanese Uniqueness* (Routledge).

Dennis, Mike (1988) *German Democratic Republic: Politics, Economics, and Society* (Pinter).

De Vos, George A. (1973) *Socialization for Achievement: Essays on the Cultural Psychology of the Japanese* (University of California Press).

Dilnot, Andrew, and Walker, Ian (eds) (1989) *The Economics of Social Security* (Oxford University Press).

Djilas, Milovan (1957) *The New Class* (Praeger).

*Données Sociales, 1990* (1990) (Paris: Institut de la Statistique et des Etudes Economiques).

Dore, Ronald (1973) *British Factory – Japanese Factory* (Allen & Unwin).

—— (1980) *Flexible Rigidities: Industrial Policy and Structural Adjustment in the Japanese Economy, 1970–80* (London University: Athlone Press).

—— (1987) *Taking Japan Seriously: A Confucian Perspective on Leading Economic Issues* (Stanford University Press).

Druus, Peter (ed.) (1989) *The Cambridge History of Japan*, Vol 6: *The Twentieth Century* (Cambridge University Press).

Duchen, Claire (1986) *Feminism in France from May '68 to Mitterand* (Routledge).

Dunlop, John (1983) *The Faces of Contemporary Russian Nationalism* (Princeton University Press).

Dupeux, Georges (1972) *French Society, 1789–1970* (Methuen).

Dyer, Colin (1978) *Population and Society in Twentieth-Century France* (Hodder & Stoughton).

Dymytryshyn, Basil (1984) *USSR: A Concise History* (Scribner).

Eccleston, Bernard (1989) *State and Society in Post-War Japan* (Polity Press).

Edwards, G. E. (1985) *GDR Society and Social Institutions: Facts and Figures* (Macmillan).

Edwards, Jeremy and Fischer, Klaus (1994) *Banks, Finance and Investment in Germany* (Cambridge University Press).

Eddy, Arthur J. (1912) *The New Competition* (Appleton).

Eltis, Walter and Sinclair, Peter (eds) (1988) *Keynes and Economic Policy* (Macmillan).

Emmott, Bill (1989) *The Sun also Sets: Why Japan will not be Number One* (Simon & Schuster).

Estrin, Saul and Holmes, Peter (1983) *French Planning in Theory and Practice* (Allen & Unwin).

Evans, Richard J. (1989) *In Hitler's Shadow: West German Historians and the Attempt to Escape from the Nazi Past* (Taurus).

Ewing, Keith (1991) *The Employment Act, 1990* (Institute of Employment Rights).

Ewing, K. D. and Gearty, C. A. (1990) *Freedom under Thatcher: Civil Liberties in Modern Britain* (Oxford University Press).

Feigenbaum, Edward A. and McCorduck, Pamela (1983) *The Fifth Generation: Artificial Intelligence and Japan's Computer Challenge to the World* (Addison-Wellesley).

Fingleton, Eammon (1995) *Blindside: Why Japan is Still on Track to Overtake the United States by the Year 2000* (Houghton Mifflin).

Fitzpatrick, Sheila (1993) *The Cultural Front: Power and Culture in Revolutionary Russia* (Cornell University Press).

Flora, Peter and Heidenheimer, A. J. (eds) (1981) *The Development of Welfare States in Europe and America* (Transaction Books).

Flora, Peter and Alber, Jens (eds) (1983/1987) *State, Economy and Society in Europe, 1815–1975*, 2 Vols (Campus Verlag and Macmillan).

Floud, Roderick and McCloskey, Donald (eds) (1994) *The Economic History of Britain since 1700*, Vol 3, *1939–92* (Cambridge University Press).

Fox, Alan (1974) *Beyond Contract: Work, Power, and Trust Relations* (Faber).

Franke, Richard J. (1989) *A Business Man's View of Responsible Participation in Democracy* (John Nuveen and Co.).

Freeman, Christopher, Jahoda, Marie, and Miles, Ian (eds) (1974) *Progress and Problems in Social Forecasting* (Social Science Research Council).

Friedaman, David (1988) *The Misunderstood Miracle: Industrial Development and Political Change in Japan* (Cornell University Press).

Fukutake, Tadashi (1983) *The Japanese Social Structure: Its Evolution in the Modern Century* (University of Tokyo Press).

Fulbrook, Mary (1991) *The Divided Society: A History of Germany, 1918–90* (Oxford University Press).

Fullbrook, Kate and Fullbrook, Edward (1994) *Simone de Beauvoir and Jean-Paul Sartre: The Remaking of a 20th-Century Legend* (Basic Books).

Gaffney, John (ed.) (1988) *France and Modernisation* (Avebury).

Galambos, Louis and Pratt, Joseph (1988) *The Rise of the Corporate Commonwealth* (Basic Books).

Galbraith, John K. (1986) *The New Industrial State* (Mentor).

—— (1992) *The Culture of Contentment* (Houghton Mifflin).

Garon, Sheldon (1987) *The State and Labor in Modern Japan* (California University Press).

Gerschenkron, Alexander (1962) *Economic Backwardness in Historical Perspective* (Harvard University Press).

Gilmour, Ian (1992) *Dancing with Dogma: Britain under Thatcherism* (Simon & Schuster).

Girard, Alain (1961) *Le Réussite sociale en France* (PUF).

—— (1974) *'Population' et l'enseignement* (PUF).

Girvan, Norman (1976) *Corporate Imperialism: Conflict and Expropriation: Transnational Corporations and Economic Nationalism in the Third World* (Monthly Review Press).

Goldman, Marshall I. (1983) *USSR in Crisis: The Failure of an Economic System* (Norton).

Goldthorpe, John H., Llewellyn, Catriona, and Payne, Clive (1980) *Social Mobility and Class Structure in Britain* (Clarendon Press).

Gorbachev, Mikhail (1988) *At the Summit* (Richardson, Steirman and Black).

—— (1988) *Perestroika: New Thinking for Our Country and the World* (Fontana/Collins).

Gouldner, Alvin (1979) *The Future of the Intellectuals and the New Class* (Macmillan).

Granick, David (1972) *Managerial Comparisons of Four Developed Countries: France, Britain, United States, and Russia* (MIT Press).

Gray, John (1993) *Beyond the New Right: Markets, Government and the Common Environment* (Routledge).

—— (1993) *Post-Liberalism: Studies in Political Thought* (Routledge).

Green, James R. (1980) *The World of the Worker: Labor in 20th-Century America* (Hill and Wang).

Green, Mark and Pinsky, Mark (eds) (1990) *America's Transition: Blueprints for the 1990s* (University Press of America).

Greenbury, Sir Richard (1995) *Report of the Committee on Executive Pay* (Confederation of British Industry).

Grey, Frances de Plessix (1990) *Soviet Women: Walking the Tightrope* (Doubleday).

Grignon, C. and Passeron, J.-C. (1970) *Innovation in Higher Education: French Experience before 1968* (OECD).

Guha, Ashok (1981) *An Evolutionary View of Economic Growth* (Clarendon Press).

Gustafson, Thane (1981) *Reform in Soviet Politics: Lessons of Recent Policies on Land and Water* (Cambridge University Press).

Halsey, A. H. (1978) *Change in British Society* (Oxford University Press).

——, Heath, A. F., and Ridge, J. M. (1980) *Origins and Destinations: Family, Class, and Education in Modern Britain* (Clarendon Press).

Hammer, Michael and Champy, James (1993) *Reengineering the Corporation* (HarperBusiness).

Hane, Misiko (1982) *Peasants, Rebels, and Outcasts: The Underside of Modern Japan* (Pantheon).

Hannah, Leslie (1976) *The Rise of the Corporate Economy* (Methuen).

—— (ed.) (1982) *From the Family Enterprise to the Professional Manager* (8th International Economic History Congress, Budapest).

—— and Kay, J. A. (1977) *Concentration in British Industry* (Macmillan).

Harding, Neil (ed.) (1984) *The State in Socialist Society* (Macmillan).

Harrison, Bennett and Bluestone, Harry (1988) *The Great U-Turn: Corporate Restructuring and the Polarization of America* (Basic Books).

Hayek, Friedrich A. von (1944) *The Road to Serfdom* (Routledge & Kegan Paul).

—— (1948) *Individualism and Economic Order* (University of Chicago Press).

—— (1972) *A Tiger by the Tail* (Institute of Economic Affairs).

—— (1973, 1977, 1979) *Law, Legislation and Liberty* (University of Chicago Press, 3 Vols).

—— (1988) *The Fatal Conceit: The Intellectual Error of Socialism* (Routledge).

Hayes, Peter J. (1987) *Industry and Ideology: I. G. Farben in the Nazi Era* (Cambridge University Press).

Hein, Laura (1990) *Fuelling Growth: The Energy Revolution and Economic Policy in Post-war Japan* (Harvard University Press).

Heitzer, Heinz (1981) *GDR: An Historical Outline* [Official GDR History] (Verlag Zeit in Bild).

Heller, Robert (1994) *The Naked Manager for the Nineties* (E. P. Dutton).

Hendry, Joy (1987) *Understanding Japanese Society* (Routledge).

Hendy, John (1990) *The Conservative Employment Laws* (Institute of Employment Rights).

Hennessy, Peter (1989) *Whitehall* (Secker & Warburg).

Hills, John (ed.) (1991) *The State of Welfare: The Welfare State in Britain since 1974* (Clarendon Press).

—— et al. (1995) *Inquiry into Income and Wealth* (Joseph Rowntree Trust).

Hobsbawm, Eric (1994) *The Age of Extremes: A History of the World, 1914–91* (Pantheon).

Hosking, Geoffrey (1986) *A History of the Soviet Union* (Fontana).

—— (1990) *The Awakening of the Soviet Union* (Heinemann).

Hough, Jerry F. (1969) *The Soviet Prefects* (Harvard University Press).

—— and Fainsod, Merle (1979) *How the Soviet Union is Governed* (Harvard University Press).

Howorth, Jolyon and Ross, George (eds) (1987) *Contemporary France: A Review of Interdisciplinary Studies* (Pinter).

Hoyt, Edward P. (1991) *The New Japanese* (Robert Hall).

Huebner, Emil and Rolfs, H. H. (eds) (1990) *Jahrbuch der Bundesrepublik Deutschland, 1990–91* (Beck/DTV).

Hughes, Jonathan R. T. (1970) *Industrialization and Economic Growth* (McGraw-Hill).

Hunter, Janet (ed.) (1993) *Japanese Women Working* (Routledge).

Hutton, Will (1995) *The State We're In* (Jonathan Cape).

Illich, Ivan, Zola, Irving. K., McKnight, John, Caplan, Jonathan, and Shaiken, Harley (1977) *The Disabling Professions* (Marion Boyars).

Ichiro, Nakayama (1975) *Industrialization and Labor–Management Relations in Japan* (Japan Institute of Labour).

Imai, Kenichi and Komiya, Ryutaro (eds) (1994) *Business Enterprise in Japan: Views of Leading Economists* (MIT Press).

Ishihara, Shintaro (1991) *The Japan that Can Say No* (Simon & Schuster).

Ito, Takatoshi (1992) *The Japanese Economy* (MIT Press).

Jallade, Jean-Pierre (ed.) (1988) *The Crisis of Distribution in European Welfare States* (Trentham Books).

—— (1990) *Les Premiers années d'enseignement supérieur dans la perspective de 1993* (Institut Européen d'Education et de Politique Sociale).

James, Harold (1990) *A German Identity, 1700–1990* (Weidenfeld & Nicolson).

Janowitz, Morris (1958) 'Social Stratification and Mobility in West Germany', *American Journal of Sociology*, vol. 64, July.

Japan: Ministry of Foreign Affairs (1977) *Labor relations in Japan* (Tokyo).

Johnson, Haynes (1992) *Sleepwalking through History: America in the Reagan Years* (Anchor Books).

Johnson, Chalmers (1982) *MITI and the Japanese Miracle* (Stanford University Press).

—— (1995) *Japan: Who Governs? The Rise of the Developmental State* (Norton).

Johnson, Paul (ed.) (1994) *Twentieth-Century Britain: Economic, Social and Cultural Change* (Longman).

Johnson, Terence J. (1972) *Professions and Power* (Macmillan).

Jones, Geoffrey (1993) *British Multinational Banking* (Oxford University Press).

Kaelble, Hartmut (1985) *Social Mobility in the 19th and 20th Centuries* (St. Martin's Press).

Kagalitskii, Boris (1988) *The Thinking Reed: Intellectuals and the Soviet State, 1917 to the Present* (Verso).

Kahn, Herman (1970) *The Emerging Japanese Superstate* (Prentice-Hall).

—— and Pepper, Thomas (1979) *The Japanese Challenge* (Crowell).

Katzenstein, Peter J. (1987) *Policy and Politics in West Germany: The Growth of a Semi-Sovereign State* (Temple University Press).

—— (ed.) (1989) *Industry and Politics in West Germany: Toward a Third Republic* (Cornell University Press).

—— (1991) 'The Taming of German Power: Unification 1989–90', unpublished paper delivered at Northwestern University, 20 April.

Kavanagh, Dennis (1987) *Thatcherism and British Politics* (Oxford University Press).

—— and Jones, Bill (1991) *British Politics Today* (Manchester University Press).

Kelley, Donald R. (ed.) (1980) *Soviet Politics in the Brezhnev Era* (Praeger).

Kennedy, Paul (1987) *The Rise and Fall of the Great Powers* (Random House).

—— (1993) *Preparing for the 21st Century* (Random House).

Kerblay, Basile (1983) *Modern Soviet Society* (Methuen).

Kesler, Jean-Francois (1985) *L'ENA, la Société, l'Etat* (Berger-Levrault).

Kester, W. Carl (1991) *Japanese Takeovers: The Global Contest for Corporate Control* (Harvard Business School Press).

Kimball, Bruce (1992) *The 'True Professional Ideal' in America* (Blackwell).

Kinzley, W, Dean (1991) *Industrial Harmony in Japan: The Invention of Tradition* (Routledge).

Kobayashi, Tetsuya (1976) *Society, Schools and Progress in Japan* (Pergamon).

Koh, B. C. (1989) *Japan's Administrative Elite* (University of California Press).

Kolinsky, Eva (1989) *Women in West Germany* (Berg).

Kosciusko-Morizet, Jaques-A. (1983) *La Mafia polytechnicienne* (Editions du Seuil).

Krejci, Jaroslav (1976) *Social Structure in Divided Germany* (Croom Helm).

Krisch, Henry (1984) *The German Democratic Republic: The Search for Identity* (Westview Press).

Lam, Alice (1992) *Women and Japanese Management* (Routledge).

Lane, David (1976) *The Socialist Industrial State: Towards a Political Sociology of State Socialism* (Allen & Unwin).

—— (1982) *The End of Social Inequality? Class, Status and Power under State Socialism* (Allen & Unwin).

—— (1985) *Soviet Economy and Society* (Blackwell).

—— (ed.) (1988) *Elites and Political Power in the USSR* (Cambridge University Press).

Laqueur, Walter (1985) *Germany Today: A Personal Report* (Weidenfeld & Nicolson).

Larson, Magali S. (1977) *The Rise of Professionalism: A Sociological Analysis* (University of California Press).

Lash, Scott and Urry, John (1987) *The End of Organized Capitalism* (Polity Press).

Lawrence, Peter (1980) *Managers and Management in West Germany* (Croom Helm).

Leaman, Jeremy (1988) *The Political Economy of West Germany* (Macmillan).

Lee, C. H. (1986) *The British Economy since 1700* (Cambridge University Press).

Lees, Andrew (1989) 'Social Reform, Social Policy and Social Welfare in Modern Germany', *Journal of Social History*, vol. 32, Fall.

Lesourne, Jacques and Lecomte, Bernard (1991) *After Communism: From the Atlantic to the Urals* (Harwood Academic).

Leuchtenburg, William E. (1983) *A Troubled Feast: American Society since 1945* (Little, Brown).

Lewin, Moshe (1985) *The Making of the Soviet System* (Methuen).

—— (1988) *The Gorbachev Phenomenon* (University of California Press).

—— (1995) *Russia–USSR–Russia: The Drive and Drift of a Superstate* (New Press).

Lewis, Jane (ed.) (1993) *Women and Social Policies in Europe* (Edward Elgar).

Ligachev, Yegor (1993) *Inside Gorbachev's Kremlin: The Memoirs of Yegor Ligachev* (Pantheon).

Locke, Robert (1989) *Management and Higher Education since 1940: The Influence of America and Japan on West Germany, Great Britain, and France* (Cambridge University Press).

Lovenduski, J. (1986) *Women and European Politics: Contemporary Feminism and Public Policy* (Harvester).

Ludz, Peter C. (1972) *The Changing Party Elite in East Germany* (MIT Press).

Lukacs, John (1993) *The End of the Twentieth Century* (Ticknor and Fields).

Luttwak, Edward N. (1993) *The Endangered American Dream* (Simon & Schuster).

McAuley, Martin (ed.) (1987) *The Soviet Union under Gorbachev* (Macmillan).

Maddison, Angus (1991) *Dynamic Forces in Capitalist Development* (Oxford University Press).

Madgwick, P. J., Steeds, D., and William, L. J. (1982) *Britain since 1945* (Hutchinson).

Malia, Martin (1994) *The Soviet Tragedy: A History of Socialism in Russia, 1917–91* (Free Press).

Manser, W. A. P. (1971) *Britain in Balance: The Myth of Failure* (Penguin).

Marceau, Jane (1977) *Class and Status in France: Economic Change and Social Immobility, 1945–75* (Oxford University Press).

—— (1989) *A Family Business? The Making of an International Business Elite* (Cambridge University Press).

Marquand, David (1988) *The Unprincipled Society* (Jonathan Cape).

—— (1991) *The Progressive Dilemma: From Lloyd George to Kinnock* (Heinemann).

Marquand, Judith (1989) *Autonomy and Change: The Sources of Economic Growth* (Harvester).

Marsh, David (1992) *The New Politics of British Trade Unionism: Union Power and the Legacy of Thatcherism* (Cornell University: ILR Press).

Marshall, T. H. (1950) *Citizenship and Social Class* (Cambridge University Press).

Marwick, Arthur (ed.) (1986) *Class in the 20th Century* (St Martin's Press).

Mathias, Peter and Pollard, Sidney (eds) (1989) *The Cambridge Economic History of Europe*, Vol. 7, *The Industrial Economies* (Cambridge University Press).

Matthews, Mervyn (1972) *Class and Society in Soviet Russia* (Allen Lane).

—— (1978) *Privilege in the Soviet Union* (Allen & Unwin).

—— (ed.) (1989) *Party, State and Citizen in the Soviet Union: A Collection of Documents* (Sharpe).

Medvedev, Roy (1986) *Gorbachev* (Norton).

—— (1989) *Let History Judge* (Columbia University Press).

Merkl, Peter H. (ed.) (1989) *The Federal Republic at Forty* (Cambridge University Press).

Mermet, Gerard (1993) *Francoscopie: Qui sont les Français?* (Larousse).

Metzger, Walter P. (1987) 'A Spectre is Haunting American Scholars: The Spectre of Professionalism', *Educational Researcher*, August–September.

Middlemas, Keith (1991) *Power, Competition and the State*, Vol. 3, *The End of the Post-War Era: Britain since 1974* (Macmillan).

Mokyr, Joel (1985) *The Economics of the Industrial Revolution* (Rowman and Allenheld).

—— (1990) *The Lever of Riches: Technological Creativity and Economic Progress* (Oxford University Press).

—— (ed.) (1993) *The British Industrial Revolution: An Economic Perspective* (Westview Press).

Monks, Robert A. G. and Minow, Nell (1991) *Power and Accountability* (HarperCollins).

Moreton, Edwina (1987) *Germany between East and West* (Cambridge University Press and Royal Institute of International Affairs).

Morgan, Kenneth O. (1990) *The People's Peace: British History, 1945–90* (Oxford University Press).

Morris, Jonathan (ed.) (1991) *Japan and the Global Economy* (Routledge).

Mosca, Gaetano (1939) *The Ruling Class* (McGraw-Hill).

Murakami, Yasusuki and Patrick, Hugh T. (1988) (gen. eds) *The Political Economy of Japan*, 3 Vols (Stanford University Press).

Nakane, Chie (1973) *Japanese Society* (Penguin).

Nau, Henry R. (1990) *The Myth of America's Decline* (Oxford University Press).

Newby, Howard *et al* (eds) (1985) *Restructuring Capital: Recession and Reorganization in Industrial Society* (Macmillan).

Nolan, Lord (1995) *Standards in Public Life: First Report of the Committee* (HMSO, Cm 2850-I).

Nye, Joseph S. (1990) *Bound to Lead: The Changing Nature of American Power* (Basic Books).

O'Brien, Patrick (1978) *Economic Growth in Britain and France, 1780–1914* (Allen & Unwin.

OECD *Economic Surveys: various countries* (OECD, various dates).

OECD (1989) *Historical Statistics, 1960–87* (OECD).

OECD *Labour Force Statistics* (1994) (OECD).

OECD (1981) *The Welfare State in Crisis* (OECD).

Oliver, Nick and Wilkinson, Barry (1988) *The Japanization of British Industry* (Blackwell).

Ormerod, Paul (1994) *The Death of Economics* (Faber).

Paxman, Jeremy (1991) *Friends in High Places: Who Runs Britain?* (Penguin).

Pareto, Vilfredo (1968) *The Rise and Fall of Elites* (Bedminster Press).

Paterson, William and Smith, Gordon (eds) (1981) *The West German Model: Perspectives on a Stable State* (Frank Cass).

Perkin, Harold (1969) *The Origins of Modern English Society, 1780–1880* (Routledge).

—— (1989) *The Rise of Professional Society: England since 1880* (Routledge).

Phillips, Kevin (1991) *The Politics of Rich and Poor* (HarperCollins).

—— (1993) *Boiling Point: Democrats, Republicans, and the Decline of Middle-Class Prosperity* (Random House).

Pollard, Sidney (1982) *The Wasting of the British Economy* (Croom Helm).

Porter, Michael (1990) *The Competitive Advantage of Nations* (Free Press).

Potichnyj, Peter J. (ed.) (1988) *The Soviet Union: Party and Society* (Cambridge University Press).

Prais, S. J. (1976) *The Evolution of Giant Firms, 1909–70* (Cambridge University Press).

Prins, Gwyn, (ed.) (1990) *Spring in Winter: The 1989 Revolutions* (Manchester University Press).

Pryor, Frederick L. (1980) *Public Expenditure in Communist and Capitalist Nations* (R. D. Unwin).

Putnam, Robert D. (1976) *The Comparative Study of Elites* (Prentice-Hall).

Reich, Robert B. (1984) *The Next American Frontier* (Times Books).

—— (1991) *The Work of Nations* (Knopf).

Reischauer, Edwin O. (1980) *The Japanese* (Tuttle and Co.).

Reisner, Marc (1987) *Cadillac Desert: The American West and its Disappearing Water* (Penguin).

Remnick, David (1994) *Lenin's Tomb* (Vintage).

Riddell, Peter (1991) *The Thatcher Era and its Legacy* (Blackwell).

Rigby, T. H. and Harasymiw, Bohdan, (eds) (1983) *Leadership Selection and Patron–Client Relations in the Soviet Union and Yugoslavia* (Allen & Unwin).

Ringer, Fritz K. (1979) *Education and Society in Modern Europe* (Indiana University Press).

Rohatyn, Felix (1983) *The Twenty-Year Century: Essays on Economics and Public Finance* (Random House).

Rose, Richard (1985) *Public Employment in Western Nations* (Cambridge University Press).

Routh, Guy (1980) *Occupation and Pay in Great Britain, 1906–79* (Cambridge University Press).

—— (1987) *Occupations of the People of Great Britain, 1801- 1981* (Macmillan).

Rubinstein, W. D. (1993) *Capitalism, Culture and Decline in Britain* (Routledge).

Rutter, Angie (1986) 'Elites, Estate and Strata: Class in West Germany since 1945', in Arthur Marwick (ed.) *Class in the 20th Century* (St Martin's Press).

Sampson, Anthony (1992) *The Essential Anatomy of Britain: Democracy in Crisis* (Hodder & Stoughton).

Sanderson, Michael (1987) *Educational Opportunity and Social Change in England* (Faber).

Said, Edward (1993) *Culture and Imperialism* (Vintage).

Savage, Stephen (1990) *Public Policy under Thatcher* (St Martin's Press).

Sawyer, Malcolm (1976) *Income Distribution in OECD Countries* (OECD).

Schindler, Peter (1983) *Datenbuch zur Geschichte des Deutschen Bundestages 1949 bis 1982* (Deutschen Bundestages Referat Offentlichkeitsarbeit).

Schumpeter, Joseph A. (1950) *Capitalism, Socialism and Democracy* (Harper & Row).

Scott, John (1982) *The Upper Class: Property and Privilege in Britain* (Macmillan).

—— and Griff, Catherine (1984) *Directors of Industry: The British Corporate Network, 1904–76* (Blackwell).

Scase, Richard and Goffee, Robert (1990) *Reluctant Managers: Their Work and Lifestyles* (Unwin Hyman).

Shaffer, Harry (1981) *Women in the Two Germanies* (Pergamon).

Shand, Alexander H. (1989) *Free Market Morality: The Political Economy of the Austrian School* (Routledge).

Shishkin, Sergei (1994) 'The Russian Ruling Elite Redividing Property among Themselves', Lecture to Woodrow Wilson Center, Princeton University, 25 October.

Silberman, Bernard S. (1993) *Cages of Reason: The Rise of the Rational State in France, Japan, the United States, and Great Britain* (Chicago University Press).

Simirenko, Alexander (1982) *Professionalization of Soviet Society* (Transaction Books).

Simon, Brian (1991) *Education and the Social Order, 1940–90* (Lawrence and Wishart).

Sked, Alan (1987) *Britain's Decline* (Blackwell).

—— and Cook, Chris (1979) *Post-War Britain* (Penguin).

Smith, Gordon, Paterson, William, and Merkl, Peter J., (eds) (1989) *Developments in West German Politics* (Macmillan).

Smith, Hedrick (1990) *The New Russians* (Random House).

Smith, Keith (1984) *The British Economic Crisis: Its Past and Future* (Penguin).

Solomon, Susan, (ed) (1983) *Pluralism in the Soviet Union* (Macmillan).

Solzhenitsyn, Aleksandr I. (1974) *The Gulag Archipelago, 1918–56* (Harper & Row).

*Social Trends* (HMSO, various dates).

Soros, George (1994) *The Alchemy of Finance: Reading the Mind of the Market* (Wiley).

Stanworth, Philip and Giddens, Anthony, (eds) (1974) *Elites and Power in British Society* (Cambridge University Press).

Stark, Thomas (1992) *Income and Wealth in the 1980s* (Fabian Society).

*Statistical Abstract of the United States, 1994* (1994) (US Department of Commerce).

Steven, Roy (1983) *Classes in Contemporary Japan* (Cambridge University Press).

Stewart, James B. (1991) *Den of Thieves* (Simon & Schuster).

Stokman, Frans N., Ziegler, Rolf and Scott, John (1985) *Networks of Corporate Power: A Comparative Analysis of Ten Countries* (Polity Press).

Stopford, John M. and Turner, Louis (1985) *Britain and the Multinationals* (Wiley).

—— and Susan Strange with John S. Henley (1991) *Rival States, Rival Firms: Competition for World Market Share* (Cambridge University Press).

Strange, Susan (1984) *The Casino Society* (Blackwell).

Suleiman, Ezra N. (1974) *Politics, Power and Bureaucracy in France: The Administrative Elite* (Princeton University Press).

—— (1978) *Elites in French Society* (Princeton University Press).

Tawney, R. H. (1920) *The Acquisitive Society* (Harcourt, Brace, and Howe).

—— (1931) *Equality* (Allen & Unwin).

Taylor, Lewis (ed.) (1983) *The Public Sector: Measurements and Explanations of its Size and Growth* (Sage).

Taylor, Russell (1993) *Going for Broke: How Banking Mismanagement in the Eighties Lost Thousands of Billions of Pounds* (Simon & Schuster).

Teichler, Ulrich (1986) *Higher Education in the Federal Republic of Germany* (Graduate School of City University of New York).

—— (1988) *Changing Patterns of the Higher Education System* (Kingsley).

—— (1989) 'The First Years of Study and the Role Played by *Fachhochschulen* in the FDR', Report presented to the European Institute of Education and Social Policy, July.

—— and Sanyal, Bikas S. (1982) *Higher Education and the Labour Market in the Federal Republic of Germany* (UNESCO).

—— Hartung, Dirk, and Nuthan, Reinhard (1980) *Higher Education and the Needs of Society: A Study for the International Labour Organization* (National Foundation for Educational Research).

Thane, Pat (1982) *The Foundations of the Welfare State* (Longman).

Thatcher, Margaret (1993) *The Downing Street Years* (HarperCollins).

Thompson, Grahame (1990) *The Political Economy of the New Right* (Pinter).

Thurow, Lester (1992) *Head to Head: The Coming Economic Battle Among Japan, Europe, and America* (Morrow).

Titmuss, Richard (1960) *The Irresponsible Society* (Fabian Society).

Torstendahl, Rolf (1991) *Bureaucratization in Northwestern Europe, 1880–1985* (Routledge).

Turner, Henry A. (1987) *The Two Germanies since 1945* (Yale University Press).

UNCTAD (1994) *World Investment Report, 1994* (United Nations).

Unger, J. Marshall (1988) *The Fifth Generation Fallacy: Why Japan is Betting its Future on Artificial Intelligence* (Oxford University Press).

Vaksberg, Arkady (1991) *The Soviet Mafia* (St Martin's Press).

Van der Wee, Herman (1978) *Prosperity and Upheaval: The World Economy, 1945–80* (California University Press).

Van Wolferen, Karel (1990) *The Enigma of Japanese Power* (Vintage).

Vaughan, Michelina, Kolinsky, M., and Sherrif, P. (1980) *Social Change in France* (Clarendon Press).

Vogel, Ezra F. (1979) *Japan as Number One* (Harvard University Press).

Walker, Martin (1986) *The Waking Giant: Gorbachev's Russia* (Pantheon).

Wallach, H. G. Peter and Francisco, Ronald A. (1992) *United Germany: The Past, Politics, and Prospects* (Greenwood Press).

Wallerstein, Immanuel (1974) *The Modern World System* (Academic Press).

Watson, Diane (1988) *Managers of Discontent: Trade Union Officers and Industrial Relations Managers* (Routledge).

Weber, Max (1978) *Economy and Society* (University of California Press).

Wiener, Martin (1982) *English Culture and the Decline of the Industrial Spirit* (Cambridge University Press).

Wilensky, Harold L. (1976) *The 'New Corporatism', Centralization, and the Welfare State* (Sage).

Wilkinson, Endymion (1991) *Japan versus the West: Image and Reality* (Penguin).

Wolf, Eric R. (1982) *Europe and the People without History* (University of California Press).

Womack, J. P., Jones, Daniel T., and Roos, Daniel (1990) *The Machine that Changed the World* (Rawson Associates).

World Bank *World Development Reports*, various dates.

Wright, Vincent (1983) *The Government and Politics of France* (Holmes and Meier).

Voslensky, M. (1984) *Nomenklatura: Anatomy of the Soviet Ruling Class* (Bodley Head).

Yeltsin, Boris (1990) *Against the Grain* (Jonathan Cape).

Yergin, Daniel (1991) *The Prize: The Epic Quest for Oil, Money, and Power* (Simon & Schuster).

Young, Michael (1948) *The Rise of the Meritocracy* (Penguin).

Zaslavskaya, Tatyana (1984) 'The Novosibirsk Report' reprinted with a Comment by Philip Hanson, in *Survey*, vol. 7, no. 1, Spring, pp. 88–108.

Zaslavskaya, Tatyana (1990) *The Second Socialist Revolution* (Tauris).

Zinoviev, Alexander (1984) *The Reality of Communism* (Gollancz).

Zunz, Olivier (1992) *Making America Corporate, 1870–1920* (Chicago University Press).

# INDEX

Acton, Lord xv
Aganbegyan, Abel 129
agriculture: in Industrial Revolution 4,
  6; in Neolithic Revolution 2; swing
  to services from 9, 10t, 178–9
Alford, Bernard 64
Aliev, Geidar 138–9
Althusser, Louis 82
*amakudari* 25–6, 153
Andropov, Yuri 129, 135, 136
Azerbaijan: corruption in 138–9

Bank of Credit and Commerce
  International 75
Barings Bank 75, 116, 214
Barnard, Chester 22, 30
Bauer, Michel 92, 93
Bodyul, Ivan 139
Boone Pickens, T. 153, 159, 164–5
Boulin, Robert 86
Bretton Woods system 195
Brezhnev, Leonid 126, 131, 136, 138,
  140; exploitation under 128, 130, 134;
  involvement in corruption 24; and
  Medunov 135
Britain xiii–xiv, 21, 49–76, 154, 186, 212,
  216; backlash against executive
  greed 72–3, 193; class conflict within
  20, 51, 53, 61–2, 63, 65, 179, 181; class
  politics 21, 51, 65; company
  ownership 44, 194–5, 199, 206;
  concentration of business in giant
  corporations 56–7; contrast in
  economic growth with other
  countries 195–6; criminal justice
  system 75; decline in power of local
  government 69–70; disillusionment

with free-market ideology 72, 209;
  economic decline xiii, 51–2, 46, 58–9,
  62, 75–6; effect of free-market
  ideology 74–5, 196, 209; emphasis on
  short-term profitability 214;
  executive pay 68–9, 72–3, 73–4, 193;
  fraud 75; and global economy 56–7;
  higher education 53, 56, 70, 180, 183;
  increase of power of state under
  Thatcher 66–7; industrial relations
  38, 53, 64–5, 67–8, 179; and Industrial
  Revolution 49–51, 62–3; inequality in
  income distribution 72, 73–4, 178,
  192, 196, 209; Japanese factories in
  64; post-war growth of government
  54–5; post-war prosperity 51, 58;
  privatizations 68–9; [reasons for
  economic decline 21, 56, 59–65, 75–6:
  cultural 61–2; economic 59–60; social
  62–5]; recruitment of elite 11, 53;
  rejection of Social Charter 68; rise of
  professionals xiii, 52; rivalry
  between public and private sectors
  xiii, 21, 52–3, 55; and Social Chapter
  122, 197; 'structural corruption' 186;
  swing from agriculture and industry
  to services 52, 178; and TNCs 19, 57;
  traditions of Victorian social
  thought 70–1; undermining of
  democracy by electoral system 65–6;
  ways of saving professional
  society in 211; welfare state 55–6,
  70; women's emancipation 53–4;
  and works councils 197–8
Brown, Ron 33
Bryce, Lord 29
Bush, George 33

Cadbury Committee 72
Cahill, Sir John 73–4
Cairncross, Sir Alex 59–60, 62, 64
Canterbury, Archbishop of 71
CBI (Confederation of British Industry) 73, 193
CEOs (Chief Executive Officers) 18; German codetermination and 42; need for reform of pay 213; payment of in Britain 72, 193; payment of in United States 41–2, 193
Champy, James 41
Chandler, Alfred D. 29, 43, 45, 72, 160, 194
Chief Executives see CEOs
Child Support Agency 70
Chirac, President Jacques 81
Chrysler 32, 38, 44
Churbanov, Yuri 137
CIA 170–1, 182
citizenship 16–17, 112, 215 see also welfare state
class: conflict in Britain 20, 51, 53, 61–2, 63, 65, 179, 181; in France 179–80; in Germany 105–7, 179–80; replacement of by professional hierarchy 9–11, 105, 179–80; in Soviet Union 180
Clinton, President Bill 23, 33
codes of conduct 210; differences between Anglo-American and others 199–200; and TNCs 198–200
codetermination 42, 94, 117–18, 122, 190, 206
Cold War 40, 100, 103, 171, 209
Commonwealth of Independent States 143 see also Soviet Union
communism 126, 127
companies 18 see also corporations
Conservative party 52, 65, 66
Cooklin, Laurence 73
corporate neo-feudalism 177, 185; aspects of 44–5; fragmentation of property under Anglo-American 43; growth of 45; in France 94; in Japan 158, 159, 164–5; in United States 23, 42–7, 48
corporations 6, 10, 206; concentration of business in declining numbers of 18–19, 183–4; power of 27; see also individual countries; TNCs
corruption 186, 189–90, 215; in Britain 186; in France 96–7, 190; in Japan 150, 155, 168, 170–4, 186, 189; in Soviet Union 24, 41, 126, 134–43; in United States 22, 186
Cresson, Edith 91
Crystal, Graef S. 41, 42

Dahrendorf, Ralfgg 63, 190
Danic, Dominique 92
de Beauvoir, Simone 90–1
de Gaulle, President 58, 82, 85
Delors, Jacques 86
Djilas, Milovan 131
Doi, Tukako 168
Donne, John 192

East Germany 100–22, 178, 180; collapse in 1989 103; corporations in 114–15; dealing with legacy of past 102; dominance of state 109–10; effect of reunification 112; exploitation by ruling elites compared to West Germany 119–22; higher education 106, 112, 113–14; industrial relations 114–15; post war economic recovery 103; as a professional society 104; and public expenditure 15; reasons for failure 119; recruitment of elite 11, 22, 106, 114; and Soviet Union 103; success of 100; swing from agriculture and industry to services 9, 105; welfare state 111–12; women's emancipation 108–9, 181
economy: consequences of over-exploitation on 188–9; see also global economy
Eddy, Arthur J. 29
Edmonds, John 197
education see higher education
E.I. Du Pont de Nemours 43–4
elderly: symptom of potential economic decline of Japan 174–5
elites see professional elites
Emmanuelli, Henri 96–7
Emmott, Bill 174
Esman, Milton J. 149
European Community 48–9, 118; and Social Charter 67, 68
European Union 198, 206, 210, 217; and Works Council Directive 118, 122, 212
executive pay see salaries, executive

Falklands War 60
Fifth Company Law Directive 94,
118
Ford 38
Ford, Henry 40
Fowler, Sir Norman 69
Fox, Alan 63
France 20, 21, 77–99; benefits of
meritocracy 98–9; central role of
state 84, 87–8; and class 179–80;
company structure 94–5;
corporations' recruitment from state
bureaucracy 92–3; corruption 96–7,
190; economic policy 86–7, 88;
executive pay and privileges 89–90;
and global economy 93–4;
government involvement in
industry 87–8, 92–3; growth of state
84–5; higher education 77, 78–9,
80–1, 83–4, 183; importance of
networking 81, 88, 93; inequality in
income distribution 90, 97–8;
opposition to meritocracy 82–3;
over-regulation of society by state
95–6; people's relationship with state
95–6; practice of *pantouflages* 72, 79–
80, 90, 92, 97, 154, 190; race relations
98; recruitment of elite 11, 22, 77, 81,
84, 92, 93; similarities to Japan 81–2;
social costs of meritocracy 98; state
control of meritocracy 78–81, 84;
swing from agriculture and industry
to services 87, 88–90; welfare state
85–6; women's emancipation 87,
90–1, 181
free market xiii, 47, 71–2;
contradictions of theory 187–90, 192;
contrast with regulated capitalism in
economic growth 195–6; effects of
196, 200–1; effect on Soviet Union
145–6; growing disillusionment with
198–9, 209–10; and income
inequality 192–5; and Social Chapter
197–8; supporters of 210–11; theory
of individualism 190–2; see also
Britain; United States
FRG *see* West Germany

Gaipov, Rais 137
Galbraith, John Kenneth 36, 74
GDR *see* East Germany
General Motors 44

Germany 19, 100–22, 178; and class
105–7, 179–80; and codetermination
42, 94, 117–18, 122, 190, 206;
company law 115–16, 205–6;
comparison of elites between East
and West 119–22; and global
economy 118; higher education 107,
112–13; history 100–1; industrial
relations 116–18; industry 114;
nationalism 112; respect of state 101,
115; reunification 110, 112, 117, 190;
role of banks 116; social market
model of professional society 121–2,
205–6, 207; welfare state 110–11; *see
also* East Germany; West Germany
Gerschenkron, Alexander 50
global economy 19–20, 45, 177, 184;
domination by TNCs xvi, 19, 184,
186; managing of 216–17; *see also*
individual countries
Goldman Sachs 33
Gorbachev, Mikhail 41, 103, 127;
ousting of 143; and *perestroika* 18,
129, 141–2; reasons for failure 24
Gordon, L.A. 127
government: growth of 14–16, 181–2;
*see also* individual countries
*grandes écoles* 22, 77, 78, 79, 80–1, 82,
83–4, 88, 91, 92, 93
*grands corps* 22, 77, 80, 82, 84, 88, 92
Gray, John 210, 216
Great Depression 58
Greenbury Committee 73, 193

Halpern, Sir Ralph 73
Hayek, Friedrich von 190–1, 192, 196
Heller, Robert 194–5
hierarchy, professional: replacement of
class by 9–11, 105, 179–80
higher education 11–12, 183; in Britain
53, 56, 70, 180, 183; expansion of
17–18; in France 77, 78–9, 80–1, 83–4,
183; in Germany 105–6, 107, 112–13;
in Japan 150–1, 183; in Soviet Union
183; in United States 183; and
women 13, 14t, 180–1
Hitachi 158
Hitler, Adolf 101, 110, 114
Hobsbawm, Eric v
Honecker, Erich 109
Honecker, Margot 109
Hosokawa, Morihiro 172

Iacocca, Lee 42, 44, 183
imperialism 186
income, distribution of 178, 203–5; in
    Britain 72, 73–4, 178, 192, 196, 209;
    effects of inequality of on society 35–
    6; in France 90, 97–8; in Japan 167–8;
    in Soviet Union 131; in United States
    34–5, 36, 192, 209; widening Anglo–
    American inequality 192–5; *see also*
    salaries, executive
individualism: origins of Anglo–
    American 190–2; and Victorians 71
industrial relations: Anglo–American
    attack on trades unions 38, 179; in
    Britain 38, 53, 64–5, 67–8, 179; in
    Germany 114–15, 116–18 (*see also*
    codetermination); in Japan 65, 147,
    164, 197; in United States 38, 40;
    works councils 68, 95, 117, 118–19,
    197–8
Industrial Revolution xi, 3–5, 9; and
    Britain 49–51, 62–3; effect of 50–1
Insull, Samuel 43
International Labour Organization
    (ILO) 67

Jallade, Jean-Pierre 85
Japan 15, 20, 25–6, 147–76, 215–16;
    ageing of population 26, 174–5;
    business culture 197, 199; company
    ownership 158, 164; corporate neo-
    feudalism 158, 159, 164–5;
    corruption 150, 155, 168, 170–4, 186,
    189; costs of economic success 167;
    culture of group loyalty 161–2, 207–
    8; difference between appearance
    and reality 148, 176; discrimination
    against ethnic minorities 169, 174;
    division between workers of small
    and large companies 169, 174; early
    opposition to elites 148–9; economy
    46, 166; flaws in system seen by
    Westerners 208; and global economy
    19, 165–6; goal of long-term
    profitability 39, 157; growing
    disenchantment with ideology of
    elite 174; higher education 150–1,
    183; income distribution 167–8;
    individualism and collectivism 161–
    2, 207; industrial relations 65, 147,
    164, 197; interconnection between
    public and private sectors 25, 160,
    162–3; and *keiretsu* 18, 25, 26, 149,
    152, 158–9, 164; 'lean production'
    system 163–4; managed capitalism
    160; means for survival 175;
    migration of retired bureaucrats into
    politics 154–5; 'money politics'
    170–4, 186, 189; movement of retired
    bureaucrats to private and public
    corporations (*amakudari*) 25–6, 153–4,
    156; networking 25, 81, 88, 152, 159;
    paternalism 148–9, 180, 189; post-
    war 'economic miracle' 156–7, 163,
    216; property incomes 169–70;
    quality of life 166–7; recruitment of
    elite 11, 25, 147, 150–1; role of
    bureaucracy 149–56; similarities to
    France 81–2; structure of
    corporations 18, 157–9, 164; success
    of 26, 59, 147, 148, 150, 159, 175,
    190–1, 208; success of elite in selling
    ideology to society 148, 150, 155,
    159–60, 164, 176; 'three sacred
    treasures' 148, 157–8, 164, 208;
    training by TNCs 200; use of *yakuza*
    by politicians 173–4; and *wa* 147, 207;
    welfare state 208, 216; women's
    emancipation 168–9, 174, 180–1
Jean-Pierre, Judge Thierry 96
Johnson, Chalmers xvi, 189

Kabashima, Ikuo 171
Kaelble, Hartmut 108
Kanemaru, Shin 172–3
Karimov, Abduvakhid 136–7
Karpinsky, Len 132
Kazakhstan 130, 137–80
*keiretsu* 18, 25, 26, 149, 152, 158–9, 164
Khrushchev, Nikita 126, 128
Kidd, Benjamin 71
Kiichiro, Sato 160
Komorovsky, V.V. 127
Krejci, Jaroslav 120
Kunaev, Dinmukhamed 137, 138

Labour Party 52–3, 65, 66
Lamont, Norman 69
Landes, David 88
Laroque, Pierre 86
law, company 44, 205–6; need for
    reform 212
LDP (Liberal Democratic Party)
    (Japan) 149, 150, 151; domination by

bureaucracy 154–5; and 'money politics' 170–4, 189
'lean production' system 6, 163–4
Lenin, Vladimir 123
Levi Strauss, Claude 200
Lewin, Moshe 125
Liberal Democratic Party (Japan) see LDP
Ligachev, Ygor 136, 137
living standards 8–9, 178 see also income, distribution of
Lockheed 32, 172, 186, 189
Longuet, Gérard 97
Lukacs, John 25

Maastricht Treaty: Social Chapter 68, 122, 197, 206; and works councils 95, 118–19, 197–8
MacArthur, Douglas 170, 171
McCloskey, Donald 59
McCrickard, Don 73
Macmillan, Harold 58
Madison, James 28
mafia (Soviet Union) 7, 134–9, 142, 144–5
Major, John 68, 193, 212
managers 10, 18, 86 see also CEOs; salaries, executive
Mandeville, Bernard 34
Mario, Dr Ernset 73
Marquand, David 210
Marshall, Alfred 70
Marx, Karl xvi, 3; and 'the contradictions of capitalism' 23–4, 35, 127, 187
Marxism 119
Masakichi, Funayama 154
Matthews, Mervyn 133
Medunov, Sergei 135, 136
meritocracy 11–13, 18, 180 see also individual countries; recruitment
Method II (French company law) 94
Mill, John Stuart 203–4
MITI (Ministry of International Trade and Industry) (Japan) 152, 156, 163, 197
Mitsubishi 18, 158
Mitsui Corporation 149
Mitterrand, François 81, 84, 96
Miyazawa, Kiichi 172, 173
Mokyr, Joel 50
Moldavia 139

Monks, Robert A.G. 41, 42
Morgan, J.P. 43
Morgan, Kenneth 66
Morita, Akio 39, 164, 214
Mosca, Gaetano 131, 144
Müller-Armack, Alfred 111
multinational corporations see TNCs

Naidenov, Viktor 135
Napoleon 77, 78
Nazarbaev, Nursultan 137, 138
Nazism 100, 102, 117
Neolithic Revolution xi--xii, 2–3
NHS (National Health Service) 69
Nolan Committee 72, 193
nomenklatura 23, 125, 126, 140, 189; after 1989 collapse 24, 144; and corruption 41; exploitation by 24, 128, 129–31, 141, 145; and perestroika 141–2; privileges of 24, 131–3
Nora, Simon 82–3

oil crises (1970s) 46, 59, 83, 103, 156
Owada, Masako 168

pantouflages 72, 79–80, 90, 92, 97, 154, 190
Pareto, Vilfredo 189
Parker, Sir Peter 73
Pearson, Karl 71
Pelat, Roger-Patrice 96
perestroika 18, 24, 143; and nomenklatura 141–2; reasons for 128–31
Perkins, C.E. 31
Perrow, Charles 30–1, 194
Peugot–Citroën 57
Phillips, Kevin 35, 42
Pigou, A.C. 70
political contributions 214–15
politicians: social origins of 12
Pollard, Sidney 51
private sector: rivalry with public sector 10–11, 21
professional elites 6–7, 119; abuse of power 175–6; consequences of over-exploitation by xiv, 188–9; dangers of xiv, 2; dominant professions 7; exploitation by 1–2, 146, 186, 187, 203; greed 188; see also individual countries
professional society 25, 71; benefits of xv, 1, 178, 202, 203, 217–18;

continental European version 205–7; dangers from domination of xv, 1–2, 202–3; diversity among 177–84; East Asian version 207–8; globalization of 184–6; growth of power in Industrial Revolution 5; main ideological struggle 11; major trends 8–20; persuasion as feature of 150; purpose 187; reasons for dominance of 1, 7; rise of xiii; ways of saving Anglo–American 209–17; *see also* individual countries

profitability: Anglo-American attitude towards 38–9, 40, 214; Japanese attitude towards 39, 157; need for long-term 213–14

public employment: growth in 15

public expenditure: growth of 14t, 15, 16t

public sector: rivalry between private and 10–11, 52

quangos 69, 72

Questiaux, Nicole 91

Rashidov, Sharaf 136

Reagan, Ronald, President 32, 40

Reaganomics 11, 17, 192

Recruit scandal 171, 172, 189

Reich, Robert B. 35, 38, 39, 184, 212

recruitment: of elite 11–12, 180; in Britain 11, 53; in France 11, 22, 77, 81, 84, 92, 93; in Germany 11, 22, 105–6, 107–8, 113–14; in Japan 11, 25, 147, 150–1; in Soviet Union 11, 23, 125–6, 180; in United States 180

rewards: need for national structure of 215–16; *see also* income, distribution of

Rockefeller, John D. 29

Ross, Steven J.41

Royal Dutch/Shell 199, 200

Rubinstein, W.D. 61

Sahashi, Shigeru 163

salaries, executive: backlash against greed in Britain and United States 72–3, 193; in Britain 68–9, 72–3, 73–4, 193; in France 89–90; need for equality 212–13; in United States 41–2, 193

Sartre, Jean-Paul 82, 90–1

Schmidt, Chancellor Helmut 63

Schumpeter, Joseph 30

Scott Inquiry 75

Second World War 51, 58, 205

service industry 6, 10, 18; swing from agriculture and industry to 9, 10t, 178–9: in Britain 52, 178; in France 87, 88–90; in Germany 9, 104–5; in Soviet Union 9, 124–5, 178; in United States 9, 37–8

shareholders: need for better incentives for 213–14

Shcholokov, Nikolai 135, 136

Simirenko, Alexander 23, 127

Smith, Adam xii, 28, 194, 216

Smith, Hedrick 135

Sochi mafia 135–6

Social Chapter 68, 122, 197, 206

Social Charter 67, 68

Solzhenitsyn, Aleksandr 142

Soviet Union 7, 15, 22, 23–5, 40–1, 99, 115, 123–46, 160, 204; analysis of occupational structure 127; black economy 20, 139–40; and class 180; collapse of 18, 20, 143–4, 189, 204; [corruption 24, 41, 126, 134–43: Azerbaijan 138–9; Kazakhstan 137–8; Moldavia 139; Sochi resort 135–6; Uzbekistan 136–7]; and East Germany 103; elite privileges 131–3; exploitation by ruling elites 23–4, 128, 129–31, 141, 145; failure of professionalism 178; and free-market system 145–6; higher education 183; inequality in income distribution 131; legacy of Tsarist regime 23, 123; and mafia 7, 134–9, 142, 144–5; nationalist struggles 143–4; and *nomenklatura* see *nomenklatura*; number of millionaires 139; *perestroika* 18, 24, 128–31, 141–2, 143; problems with meritocracy 126–7; reasons for downfall 127–8, 140, 141–2, 145; recruitment of elite 11, 23, 125–6, 180; Stalinist terror 128; swing from agriculture and industry to services 9, 124–5, 178; welfare system 133; women's emancipation 181

Spencer, Herbert 71

Stalin, Joseph 128, 130, 134

Standard Oil 33

state *see* government

Supple, Barry 59

Tanaka, Kakuei 172
Tapie, Bernard 97
Tawney, R.H. 71, 85
'Team 100' 33
Tebbit, Lord 69
Thatcher, Margaret 40, 54, 55, 60, 64, 66–8, 70, 74
Thatcherism 11, 17, 66–9, 70, 71, 192
Third Reich 102
TNCs (transnational corporations) 118, 177, 200, 217; benefits of 186; and codes of conduct xvi, 198–200; domination of xvi, 19, 184, 186; power of 185–6; provision of training 200; and European Union Works Council Directive 197
Todai (University of Tokyo) 150, 151
Tolstaya, Tatyana 128
Townsend, Bryan 69
Toynbee, Arnold 103
Toyota 199
trades unions: Anglo–American attack on 38, 179; in Britain 53, 64, 67–8; in Germany 115, 117
transnational corporations see TNCs

Ulbricht, Walter 15
United Nations: *World Development Report* (1994) 198–9, 200
United States 7, 11, 19, 20, 22–3, 28–48, 179, 212; backlash against executive greed 193; business involvement with election campaigns 33; CIA and Japan's LDP 170–1; company ownership 43–4, 194–5, 199; contrast in economic growth with other countries 195–6; [corporate neo-feudalism 23, 42–7, 48: aspects 44–5; effects of 45–6; history 43–4]; corporations 29–31, 36, 40, 41, 44, 45, 48, 210; corruption 22, 186; cost of mass production 30–1; decline in manufacturing 37, 46; economic decline 23, 46; effect of free-market ideology 196, 209; elite's responsibility for decline 47; emphasis on short-term profitability 39, 40; executive greed 24, 34, 41–2, 48; executive salaries 41–2, 193; export of jobs overseas 37–40, 41, 45,

47; and global economy 38; growing disillusionment with free-market ideology 198–9, 209; growth of government involvement 15, 32, 181–2; higher education 183; industrial relations 38, 40; inequality of income distribution 34–5, 36, 192, 209; interchange of personnel between government and business 23, 32–3, 126, 154; number of millionaires 139; public expenditure 32; recruitment of elite 180; reforms in executive pay 42; relationship between government and business 22–3, 31–3; swing from agriculture and industry to services 9, 37–8; threat of decline 40–2; ways of saving professional society in 211; and welfare 182–3; women's emancipation 181
universities see higher education
Uno, Sosuke, Prime Minister 169
Uzbekistan 130; corruption 136

Vaksberg, Arkady 24, 134, 135, 139
van Ruymbeke, Judge Renaud 96, 97
van Wolferen, Karel 150, 171–2

Walker, Lord 69
Wallace, Edward 69
wealth, distribution of see income, distribution of
welfare state 16–17, 110, 182–3, 206–7, 215–16; in Britain 55–6, 70; in France 85–6; in Germany 110–12; in Japan 208, 216; in Soviet Union 133; in United States 182–3
West Germany 20, 21, 100–22, 190; 'co-operative managerial capitalism' 115–16; dealing with legacy of past 102–3; economy 46; exploitation by ruling elites compared with East Germany 119–22; higher education 105–6, 107–8, 113, 183; industrial relations 106; post-war recovery 103; as a professional society 104; recruitment of elites 11, 22, 105, 107–8, 113; role of state 110; social market model of professionalism 121–2; success 100; swing from agriculture and industry to services 104–5; welfare state 110–11;

women's emancipation 108–9,
181
Wiebe, Robert 30
Wiener, Martin 61
women 13–14, 180–1; in Britain 53–4; in
France 87, 90–1, 181; in Germany
108–9, 181; and higher education 14,
14t, 180–1; in Japan 168–9, 174,
180–1; in Soviet Union 181; in
United States 181
work: Robert Reich's categories of 38
working class: decline in 179; lack of
business leaders from 12
works councils 68; in Germany 117;

and Maastricht Treaty 95, 118–19,
197–8
*World Investment Report* (United
Nations) 198–9, 200
World Trade Organization 217

*yakuza* 173–4
Yeltsin, Boris 24, 142, 143
Young of Graffham, Lord 69, 193
Young, Michael (Lord) 175

Zaslavskaya, Tatyana 24, 128–31, 134,
141
Zunz, Olivier 29